INSIDE THE FRENCH FOREIGN LEGION

ADVENTURES WITH THE WORLD'S MOST FAMOUS FIGHTING FORCE

N. J. VALLDEJULI

STACKPOLE
BOOKS

Essex, Connecticut
Blue Ridge Summit, Pennsylvania

STACKPOLE
BOOKS

An imprint of Globe Pequot, the trade division of
The Rowman & Littlefield Publishing Group, Inc.
4501 Forbes Blvd., Ste. 200
Lanham, MD 20706
www.rowman.com

Distributed by NATIONAL BOOK NETWORK

British Library Cataloguing in Publication Information available

Library of Congress Cataloging-in-Publication Data

978-0-8117-7240-2 (cloth)
978-0-8117-7241-9 (ebook)

Printed in India

For my father
Douglas K. Valldejuli
(1927–2007)
A Culver man, a Princeton man, a man's man

"I Have a Rendezvous with Death"

I have a rendezvous with Death At some disputed barricade,
When Spring comes back with rustling shade And apple-blossoms fill
the air—
I have a rendezvous with Death
When Spring brings back blue days and fair.

It may be he shall take my hand And lead me into his dark land
And close my eyes and quench my breath—It may be I shall pass him
still,
I have a rendezvous with Death
On some scarred slope of battered hill, When Spring comes round again
this year And the first meadow-flowers appear.

God knows 'twere better to be deep Pillowed in silk and scented
down, Where Love throbs out in blissful sleep, Pulse nigh to pulse, and
breath to breath, Where hushed awakenings are dear . . . But I've a
rendezvous with Death
At midnight in some flaming town, When Spring trips north again
this year, And I to my pledged word am true,
I shall not fail that rendezvous.

Alan Seeger American poet
French Foreign Legion
Killed in Action—1916

Contents

CONTENTS

Foreword

The French Foreign Legion is a unique and enduring institution among the military organizations of the world. Since its formation by imperial decree in 1831, the Legion has attained an image and renown far in excess of its numerical strength and global presence. Its steadfast performance in numerous military actions around the world has earned it the praise and respect of both military professionals and the general public, alike. The Legion has seen service in a wide range of conflicts of varying scale: from colonial actions and occupations to world wars; from special operations and hostage rescue missions to repeated deployments to present-day theaters of war in conjunction with international military partners. The Legion's professional reputation—overlaid with the gloss of service in exotic, far-off lands—has attracted both professionals and romantics to its ranks throughout its history.

My first knowledge of the Foreign Legion came at an early age. My late father was a professional soldier, and soldiers were frequent guests and visitors in our home. Most of these men were World War II veterans, and some had met and worked with legionnaires in the North African Campaign and in England prior to the Normandy Invasion and the subsequent campaign across France and into Germany. But as a child, I understood very little of these things.

The spiritual home of the French Foreign Legion has always been North Africa, for it was there that the legend was formed. After World War II, the Legion resumed its traditional role in manning the colonial garrisons of French Africa, and it was at that time that I became more aware of the Legion. In the late 1950s, there was a popular television program in America entitled "Captain Gallant of the Foreign Legion" starring the actor and former Olympic swimming champion, Buster Crabbe. My friends and I would faithfully watch this show together every Saturday morning. It was quite an interesting program, filmed on location in the Legion outposts of North Africa, and many of the small-bit parts in the series were played by the legionnaires assigned there.

My interest in the Foreign Legion increased as I grew older, and I often contemplated joining the Legion myself once I had completed high school. Life, however, can take some unexpected turns. By the time I had entered high school, the war in Vietnam was raging, and it appeared certain that the conflict was going to play a large role in my future and that of many of my classmates . . . and so it did. After high school, I entered the U.S. military and was soon in Vietnam, along with many thousands of others of my generation and age group. Interestingly, I went to the country with some knowledge of it and its history as my interest in the Legion had led me to study the previous French campaigns in Indochina. Thus, I went to Vietnam with few illusions as to what the war would be like and what I could expect to encounter there.

After the war, I elected to remain in the military and make it my career. But my interest in the Legion never waned. Most of my overseas service was spent in the Asia-Pacific region, but in 1985 I received a posting to the Southern Region Headquarters of NATO in Naples, Italy. The French military contingent there kindly assisted me in arranging a visit to the Legion for the 1988 Camerone celebration at Legion Headquarters in Aubagne, in the south of France.

My visit to Legion Headquarters permitted me my first opportunity to view the Legion up close. I was impressed by what I observed during my visit. The discipline and professionalism of the organization was quite evident in all that I saw and experienced during my stay. I had the opportunity not only to meet and converse with many legionnaires but also to form friendships that continue to this day. The strength of any military organization lies in the morale and dedication of its members. The Legion is a one-of-a-kind army in this regard as it recruits men from diverse backgrounds from around the globe (though accepting only 900 men from the nearly 9,000 who apply each year) and melds them into a cohesive, smoothly functioning combat unit. The reasons men join the French Foreign Legion are as varied as the legionnaires themselves. Nick Valldejuli has made an important contribution to the literature of the Legion by exploring this critical but often overlooked aspect of Legion recruitment and individual motivation. More than any other book on the Legion, this fascinating and engaging collection of stories will take the reader to the places and introduce the men who make the Legion an army unlike any in the world.

Thomas R. Cannon MAJ., U.S. Army Special Forces (Ret.)

Acknowledgments

Among the many colorful recollections and telling comments from those interviewed comes this to-the-point observation on Legion service from fifteen-year veteran *Sergent-Chef* Stanislav Gazdík: "You can't do it alone." Those interviewed represent a small part of the greater French Foreign Legion story, but each tale told here sheds light on an institution often shrouded in secrecy and rife with rumor. I thank all who contributed for their time, honesty, and courage.

Elementary school teacher and poet, Michael Maloney, led me to fellow Legion author David Hanna. Though we've never met, David pushed me to tell my Legion story and those of others; he stayed with me until the end, and I am forever grateful for his guidance, advice, and patience in seeing me through the grind of writing and publishing. One of the most eager and enthusiastic legionnaires I interviewed was Andrew Robeson. Andy and I have been friends ever since slogging through *instruction* together in 1986. We sat on horses and inside tanks at the *REC* and kept in contact after my discharge. Having served nineteen years, *Sergent-Chef* Robeson proved an insightful and informed source. At the same time, he was well-placed to understand the intricacies of this, sometimes, arcane army and help make this story more accessible to the average reader. Friends Tony and Kendra DePrato were my U.S./Canadian go-to couple when logistical (especially technical) support was needed. Andrew Hamilton and Francophile brother, David, were early and fervent fans, who offered encouragement in many ways. Two Czech friends, Michal Zeman and Martin Veverka, assisted me in securing interviews with Moravians, Stanislav Gazdík, and Filip Timbaris, respectively.

Literary agent Andrew Lownie of London and David Reisch military historian of Stackpole Books deserve special mention. Unlike others, both saw the story-telling value in this off-beat book on an obscure topic. I also wish to thank the Stackpole Books staff—chief editor Elaine McGarraugh in Maryland, assistant marketing manager Jason Rossi, and my liaison throughout the process, Chicago-based Stephanie Otto, who showed great patience and kindness to this new author.

Others who aided me were thirty-year IB English teacher Richard G. Coburn. His critical review of an early manuscript helped me focus. Another bit of early editing came from Culver summer friend, MIT undergrad, and Latin scholar, Scarlett E. Koller. As charming and attentive to detail as I could wish, she removed more than a few inconsistencies and hard-to-read passages, making the *malus* now *bonum*. And, finally, the man of the hour(s), Ralph W. Schusler Jr. of Rye, New York. A former news reporter and translator in the United States and Latin America, this versatile wordsmith has taught English to high school and college students at home and abroad for many years. Quite simply, his editing and proofreading are masterful. Ralph has made this book—an intimidating project for most to correct—more concise and readable. *Merci mille fois, mon pôte!*

Needless to say, a book of this scope has also required much research and material. Due to their sheer volume, many sources—news articles, reports, and people—will go unnamed; I do, however, wish to thank *Adjudant-Chef* Liben and his équipe in the *Musée de la Légion étrangère* and *Képi blanc* media services in Aubagne, France. Colonel Habourdin of the *Fédéracion des Sociétés d'Anciens de la Légion Étrangère* in Paris has also proven very helpful and supportive of this project. Many hours were spent back home reading and talking to staff in such places as the Pritzger Military Museum and Library in Chicago. Several books I found laid out the complexities of Legion history, especially its post-World War II colonial trauma: Bernard B. Fall, *Hell in a Very Small Place: The Siege of Dien Bien Phu* (Philadelphia: J.B. Lippincott, 1967); Howard R. Simpson, *Dien Bien Phu—The Epic Battle America Forgot* (Washington: Brassey's Inc., 1977); Simon Murray, *Legionnaire* (New York: Times Books, 1978); and Douglas Porch, *The French Foreign Legion: A Complete History of the Famous Fighting Force* (New York: HarperCollins, 1991). In fact, leaving the *1RE foyer* one evening in 1988, an English-speaking *sergent* escorting a visitor approached and introduced me to fellow American and French military historian, Douglas Porch. We shook hands, exchanged a few words, and parted. In 1988, I suppose we both got hooked on the stories within this inspiring, legendary army.

The French Foreign Legion—
A Brief History

"La Légion Étrangère—Une Exception Française"—so proclaimed a recent Bir-Hakeim-themed Camerone poster. In fact, the Legion has always been a unique army in the service of France: an army that for some is grand and glorious and for others mysterious and mistrusted. The French Foreign Legion was established on March 9, 1831, by royal decree of King Louis-Philippe to campaign in France's new African possession, Algeria. Formed from a mix of foreign refugees, adventurers, and political malcontents it soon quelled any Arab dissent to French colonial rule. This new army found a home and sanctuary in France's newest colony, where it remained in the small northwestern outpost of Sidi-bel-Abbès until forced to leave in 1962.

From the 1830s to the 1850s the Legion marched, trained, and waited for something more than the small skirmishes it fought in North Africa and Spain. Not until a world power conflict in Crimea (1854–1855) did the Legion see fierce combat. Italy (1859) and Mexico (1863–1867) also tested Legion battle skills. Indeed, the Mexican town of Camerone, near Puebla, was where the Legion most valiantly showed the world its disciplined and tenacious *esprit de corps*, living true to its credo *"honneur et fidé-lité"* (honor and loyalty). Returning to France in time to battle Prussian Junkers (1870), the Legion joined *l'Armée de la Loire* and quickly became a haven for Alsace-Lorraine refugees who refused to fight in the German army. The Legion, while "foreign," was at this time largely francophone. The late 1800s saw the Legion leading the charge in the colonial conquest of Indochina, Dahomey (Benin), Sudan (Mali), Madagascar, and Grand Sud Oranais (southern Algeria).

World War I again brought the Legion home to fight German aggression. Thousands of foreigners (including hundreds of idealistic Americans, among them pioneer black aviator Eugene Bullard and Ivy League poet Alan Seeger and lyricist Cole Porter) joined the Legion to fight for France. Some were quickly reassigned to regular French army units, but others were to serve in the celebrated *Régiment de Marche de la Légion étrangère*. Lazare Ponticelli, an Italian living in France, had joined the Legion in August 1914 and was the oldest Legion veteran at the time of his death in 2008, as well as the last French *"poilu"* of the Great War. Between the world wars, the Legion reached its peak strength of 48,900 men, comprising fourteen regiments. However, the traumatic events of the 1940 Nazi invasion and French capitulation soon thereafter scattered or compromised Legion combat units. General Charles de Gaulle, leader of Free French forces in London, could count on only one loyal Legion group—the famed *13ème DBLE* (13th Foreign Legion Half-Brigade). The *13ème DBLE* fought from 1940–1945 for French honor and pride with great achievement and distinction in North Africa, France, Norway, and Germany. Post World War II colonial battles in Indochina and Algeria took a heavy toll on the (very) Foreign Legion. (During the Indochina campaign, 40 percent of the legionnaires serving were German-speaking.) Diên Biên Phu, an isolated and surrounded French redoubt along the northern Vietnamese and Laotian border, was to be the twentieth century's last great battle and a juggernaut that ended French colonial rule in Asia. More than 10,000 legionnaires who served in Indochina never saw France again.

In April 1961 (close to the always emotional and symbolic April 30th commemoration of Camerone), several Legion units in Algeria were involved in a failed putsch against President de Gaulle's Fifth Republic following its concessions to Algerian nationalists. Nearly 2,000 legionnaires had fallen for France while defending the colony that was the Legion's birthplace. However, by July 1962, the bitter eight-year war in Algeria was lost for France. Many presumed that the Foreign Legion would also be lost to history. Former World War II Legion officer, Pierre

Messmer, de Gaulle's Defense Minister, no doubt played a crucial role in securing the Legion's unique role within the French Army. In 1962 (some units in 1968), the Legion left North Africa to regroup on the island of Corsica; territories; and, later, in mainland France.

A smaller and leaner Foreign Legion once again served as France's elite strike force, active in combat and support operations from the late 1960s to the mid-1980s. Chad, Loyada (on the Djibouti-Somalia border), Zaire (Democratic Republic of Congo), and Lebanon all saw the men of the white *képi* and green beret act on behalf of French geopolitical interests. The Legion in the early 1990s was just under 8,000 men and ready for action. Spearheading the French commitment in the Gulf War (1990–1991), the *1er REC* (First Foreign Cavalry Regiment) was one of the first units to cross into Iraq at the start of Operation Desert Storm's ground war. The 1990s and early 2000s also saw legionnaires engaged in military or peacekeeping and humanitarian activity in the Balkans, several African countries, Cambodia, Haiti, Iraq, and Afghanistan—as they had since 1831, all in the service of France, with 36,000 having honored their five-year contract with their lives.

Introduction

Daring to be Different

"Then, the most desperately wounded clung to life after a glass of schnapps and a promise; today, a simple cold can flatten a healthy man for several days. Then, we were certainly not supermen, but men in the most real and complete sense."

—FROM *LE SOLDAT OUBLIÉ* (*THE FORGOTTEN SOLDIER*) BY GUY SAJER—A FRENCH-GERMAN VOLUNTEER WHO FOUGHT ON THE EASTERN FRONT DURING WORLD WAR II. SAJER WAS A *WEHRMACHT* VETERAN, BUT HIS THOUGHTS RESONATE WITH ANY MAN WHO HAS SERVED IN THE LEGION.

Without a glance in my direction, the old man said quietly, "I've lost three wars."

It was May 2000, and I was in a French Foreign Legion veterans' hall in Marseille. The well-dressed old man was sitting next to me. He was too pale and too tall to be a local. His skin was transparent and his eyes watery, but clear. I knew he must have come to celebrate Camerone—the Legion's inspiring annual military commemoration—with the "mother regiment" in Aubagne, just outside Marseille. Other men were in the hall, but this one seemed to be on his own. I stopped reading the Legion magazine *Képi blanc* and listened to his story.

He told me of his service in the *Wehrmacht* on the Eastern Front in World War II—Warsaw, Minsk, Smolensk, and almost Moscow. Unemployed and hungry, he joined the Legion in Strasbourg in 1946 and arrived in Indochina via Madagascar in 1949. After two tours with the *1er*

Régiment étranger de cavalerie (*1ᵉʳ REC*/1st Foreign Cavalry Regiment) in the delta region around Saigon, he returned to North Africa, where only a few years later, he fought and lost for a third time in Algeria. The veteran ended his story as abruptly as he had begun.

I nodded but had no idea what to say. He was still motionless as I brought over two bottles of Kronenbourg. I offered a Camerone toast, but he left his beer on the table. Staring ahead, he said coolly, in German-accented French, "We're still here."

Indeed, from its founding in another era through to the twenty-first century, *La Légion étrangère* lives on in both story and deed.

* * *

Wanting to join the French Foreign Legion is not a natural impulse. Near the main Legion recruiting station of Fort de Nogent in Paris is a café. Let's call it the Last Chance Café. It's so close to the fort that the barman usually just shrugs and throws a thumb in the direction of the recruiting post when asked its whereabouts by nervous newcomers. One day in September 1986, I stopped in this nondescript place around 11 a.m. I decided against a beer and had a Coke. I looked at the man behind the bar and wondered if he was happy in his little café. I wondered if he had ever thought of joining the Legion. I also wondered how many others like me he had seen here. How many had talked themselves out of joining the Foreign Legion right here in his establishment? Perhaps at my very table? I couldn't tell. He had the look of a fellow who had seen it all, and to him it was just another day.

* * *

Leaving my last bits and pieces of doubt at the café, I made my way uphill to the fort, certain it was *not* going to be just another day.

* * *

Few books are fair to legionnaires; they portray them as either madmen on the run or lovesick lunatics. I was neither. Most legionnaires are ordinary men who dare to be different or are dissatisfied with what life has offered them. Many see their own military forces as neither unique nor challenging enough.

In today's lax, self-serving society, the Legion still expects its soldiers to obey without hesitation and complete all tasks assigned, regardless of difficulty or duration. Some people see the Legion as an anachronism and those who join as somehow out of step. Contented men do not volunteer for the kind of service and commitment the Foreign Legion demands; it takes the restless and roving and instills within them a deep military ethos of sentiment and sacrifice. Surrounded by its two centuries of tradition and prestige, the new recruit is generally no match for the "Big L." In the Legion, he loses part of himself yet gains a special, inspired confidence. The bravado and swagger so common to many legionnaires is, to a certain degree, encouraged by superiors. It is a given that many a new legionnaire is an alien in an army that lives in the shadow of the Republic. Since its formation by royal decree of King Louis-Philippe in 1831, the Legion has been both respected and feared by the French. (A measure of the Legion's importance to French culture that, up until 1977, the 1939 movie *Beau Geste* was banned due to a scene depicting a Legion mutiny.)

But who are these legionnaires? They come from Australia and Germany, China and Poland, also Brazil, Britain, Senegal, and dozens of other nations around the world . . . including, as in my case, the United States. All arrive in France to enlist in the world's most renowned fighting force. Some legionnaires have a higher IQ than cadets at West Point, Sandhurst, or Saint Cyr, while others can mark only an "X" for their signature. Some legionnaires think nothing of a night debauching twelve-year-old Djiboutian girls, while others will spend much of their monthly pay calling home to girlfriends who no longer care. A legionnaire is a complex and volatile character who lives under extreme conditions in a demanding environment. Only a legionnaire can truly understand another legionnaire and the Legion mystique. I hope, however, to give the reader special insight into this special army and the men who fill its ranks.

In this book, I let average men (and two future Legion wives) talk about themselves and their Legion experiences. The stories range from the 1960s to the early 2000s. The interviews are animated by an openness and candor that is as striking as it is rare in the often over-sentimentalized and stereotypical material presented in the media on the French Foreign Legion. All but three whom I interviewed were friends I had met while serving in the Legion. I tried to arrange interviews with active or former legionnaires living in Paris or Marseille whom I had met on the street or through contacts, but I found it impossible. I soon realized these fellow soldiers were as wary of me as they are of the many journalists who report on the Legion and distort the commentary. I've changed nothing from the recorded interviews, keeping all nuances of speech, dialect, and grammar. Fourteen interviews were conducted in English (plus two in French) with the following nationalities represented: American, Czech, Danish, Dutch, English, Irish, and Swedish. Global economic uncertainties, as well as online recruiting in thirteen languages, have pulled in more candidates than ever. As of 2023, foreigners make up 85 percent of legionnaires and NCOs within a total Legion force of 9,000 men. Indeed, men from Slavic countries now make up almost 35 percent of the Legion, with Asians (mostly Chinese) at 10 percent. Latin Americans also have made the journey to France in greater numbers and stand at about 6 percent. Men from the United States seldom enlist in the Legion. However, I have interviewed three Americans for this book and, like many of the others I spoke to, they are proud of their service and insisted I use their real names and carefully document actual events.

There is little exaggeration in this book. When writing on the Legion, one doesn't need to add color or drama—enough is already provided. Any legionnaire, regardless of intelligence, sensitivity, or even length of service, will see, feel, or do things he will remember forever: Jan Van Heek from the Netherlands can still picture sitting in the back of an open *VLRA* truck watching the evening Chadian sky turn from dark blue to incandescent white because of the day's searing heat; Englishman Andy Robeson recalls the unique pleasure of having French civilians buy him drinks after the Bastille Day parade in Paris; Czech Stanislav Gazdík can never forget the death of a close friend in the indiscriminate killing zone of

Sarajevo's infamous "sniper alley"; Chicagoan Dan Mazowski remembers how far away from home he felt as he watched *The Blues Brothers* at *Quartier* Forget in French Guiana; Denmark's Kurt Poulsen still savors his impromptu dinner of roast dog and snake with the mountain people of Marquis in French Polynesia; and Anna Carmody, from Ireland, laughs as she recounts her first experience with a weapon—a machine gun—in a Paris shooting range, as her future husband and other startled legionnaires ducked for cover.

At times, the stories and characters presented here seem beyond belief. Yet this book is not about upholding or promoting a certain image of the Legion. I hope to show the reader how an 18-to-40-year-old man might leave all that is familiar and expected and choose to live as a legionnaire. There is much to be said for an organization that seems not to change yet does evolve and adapt. The Legion's relevance today, however, may lie not so much in its military prowess as its continuing ability to give one the chance to start afresh and live life as a new person; it offers the ordinary man a passage to another time and place that proves irresistible to both doers and dreamers.

1

Through the Gate

"Goodbye to all my friends at home
Goodbye to people I've trusted
I've got to go out and make my way
I might get rich you know I might get busted
But my heart keeps calling me backwards As I get on the 707
Flyin' high I got tears in my eyes You know you got to go through hell
Before you get to heaven"

"Jet Airliner"
The Steve Miller Band

Before mustering the courage to join, or at least whittling down the reasons not to, Step One for foreigners is the trip to France. Most potential candidates then make their way to one of the Foreign Legion's ten recruiting stations or forts located in major cities across the nation.

For the benefit of the French population, the Legion also makes itself available via a specially equipped eight-wheel, thirty-six-ton Saab "national recruiting vehicle," which, with colorful graphics and a website link (www.legion-etrangere.com) on its sides, often accompanies the Legion's *Musique Principale* (since renamed *La Musique de la Légion étrangère*) on tours to towns and villages. After concerts, French youths roused by the martial music or awed by the slow marching converge on the eager recruiters.

However, most newcomers, regardless of nationality, join in the cities. Many British enlist in Lille or Boulogne; Germans make cross-border day trips into Strasbourg or Metz. The majority of foreigners, and all American legionnaires I know, join in either Paris or Marseille. The Legion forts there are solid and impressive. Standing outside the gates of Marseille's Fort St. Nicolas, built by King Louis XIV in the seventeenth century, you can feel its history. Together with the Crusader citadel St. Jean across the harbor, it guards the Vieux Port. The massive, weathered stone walls of Fort St. Nicolas rise a good sixteen feet, and to the right of the main gate, a simple placard reads: *LEGION ETRANGERE Recrutement—Ouvert Jour et Nuit.*

The next move is yours.

In that life-changing moment in 1986 when I stood before a similar sign outside Fort de Nogent in Paris, I remembered only hours earlier fidgeting in my aisle seat on the plane as I practiced my awkward and accented mantra, *"Je veux m'engager dans la Légion étrangère"*—"I want to join the Foreign Legion."

A perplexed but intrigued French businessman on that same United Airlines flight from Chicago to Paris had helped me with my pronunciation. But no amount of coaching could make my voice sound confident or self-assured. Still, my French seatmate on that flight was a pleasant introduction to France. René was forty-seven and from the southwest of France but had lived many years in Paris. He was a salesman of some kind and spoke passable English and good Spanish (language skills not typical of many French, I would soon learn).

René had been in an artillery unit in Algeria in the late 1950s and talked at length about the overpowering noise of his six-month tour. René's brief stint in Algeria with the big guns must have been traumatic because when I decided against an artillery experience he seemed quite pleased. He'd had little to do with the Legion but knew they had fought tenaciously in North Africa and were almost disbanded for political reasons. René took care not to ask me why I wanted to join the Legion and even offered directions and a well-used Paris *métro* and train map. As we neared the French coast, we both fell silent.

Upon landing, René looked at me, and my lone carry-on bag. "Good lucks and good courage," he said, trying to smile. (That I might need more luck than courage would often prove true in the rough and tumble randomness of the Legion's first few weeks.) I thanked him for everything and tried to smile back. I was nervous as hell.

My little black-and-red canvas gym bag marked "Hackley Athletic Association" seemed too preppy and soft as I stood before the massive oak-and-iron front gate of the Legion's Fort de Nogent. I hesitated and tried to calm myself by imagining that fellow Hackley graduate Alan Seeger, the young World War I poet, must have felt the same conflicting emotions when he joined the Legion in 1914. However, I also remembered that neither his Hackley nor Harvard education did much to stop the bullets that tore through his body at the Battle of the Somme. Though I might see a brief skirmish, I was sure I would not see war, or at least not war on the scale of Seeger's carnage. Still, I paused.

* * *

A long road had brought me here. I'd grown up with my grandfather's tales of his World War I exploits as an officer in an all-Puerto Rican volunteer unit and my father's stories of his U.S. Army experience among Ivy Leaguers, urban toughs, and rednecks in the immediate aftermath of World War II. But my father also told me of men who'd left family and friends to join a special kind of army that served France in far-away places. Often, the stories involved sun, sand, and cut-throat desert Arabs. Our neighbor, Mr. Ohlson, who had fought in the Norwegian Resistance in World War II and seen the Legion in action there, was highly impressed by how fiercely they had attacked an entrenched enemy. The Legion also came to me through a book in my Catholic grammar school library (I forget the title, but it had a shiny cover and showed Legion cavalry on a desert charge—just as my father had described in his stories) and a documentary narrated by *Mission Impossible* actor Peter Graves. I still recall the scene from Legion basic training in which legionnaires were lying on the ground in the path of an advancing tank. The men didn't move until the treads of the tank were inches from their hands—at which point they quickly rolled to safety. So far, every story and every image of these men was daring, gallant, and heroic. In the halls of my high school's English

3

department was a plaque honoring Alan Seeger, who wrote "I Have a Rendezvous with Death" shortly before being killed in action in 1916.

After college graduation, I held several nondescript sales jobs and taught Spanish at Culver Military Academy in Indiana. There, among Culver's fortress-like buildings, surrounded by young cadets and veteran military personnel, I found Simon Murray's book *Legionnaire* by my bed. Murray's story of his 1960–1965 Legion tour harkens back to the tales from P. C. Wren's *Beau Geste*. It seemed I needed only to buy a one-way ticket to Paris to finally be part of this saga. Abandoning my applications to federal law enforcement agencies and the U.S. Foreign Service, I bought that ticket. Only one friend who drove me to the airport knew of my plan. I didn't tell my father (my mother had died a few years earlier), whose bedtime stories from my childhood had started it all. I wasn't ready for the reality to meet the fantasy—I was sure that would come soon enough.

And here I was at Fort de Nogent, finally, ready and knocking on the gate. Nothing happened. I knocked again but still drew no attention. I then realized I had to pound with my fist, but even that barely made a sound. Suddenly, a small metal slat on the gate jerked open, and I saw my first legionnaire. In fact, I saw only part of this legionnaire's face—one darting blue eye and one half-chewed ear. The sentry listened to my garbled French and, without a word, closed the peephole. He made no move to open the door. Shortly, he got the response he needed as I banged loudly on the door and shouted my French in as deep a voice as I could. That was the sign the sentry required. The gate opened, and I walked in.

* * *

The sentry was solidly built and scarred. His mangled ear surely hadn't been acquired on a pilgrimage to Lourdes. "Weapons? Drugs? He asked me sharply in English. "No, sir." I answered. He searched me thoroughly and took my passport, which I wouldn't see again for two years.

I waited in the guardhouse next to the gate, along with other new arrivals, many of whom would be my comrades during the next four months of selection and training; some would remain lifelong friends. Right then they were utter strangers with whom I shared nothing more than the know-how of penetrating that gate.

The sentry moved four of us—an Englishman, an Asian, a German, and me—from the guardhouse to the encampment's main barrack. After a casual exchange with an older and fatter soldier who looked Indian or Pakistani, we new boys were led up several flights of stairs and escorted along a narrow hallway to an office on the right that held clacking typewriters and noisy fans. I was given to a soldier who spoke no English and questioned me in Spanish. My name, age, nationality, and then my parents' names and nationality were noted and slowly typed on my *fiche* (file). I was then directed across the hall to my new home.

Awaiting me were endless hours of international cigarette smoke and French-dubbed American action shows like *Baretta*, *Starsky et Hutch*, and *MacGyver*. That was the future; right now, sitting in white plastic chairs lined up along the wall were another thirty or so Legion hopefuls. Their bored eyes focused on me as I entered the *salle d'attente* (waiting room) and sat down quickly without speaking. The first to speak to me was English. "So where are you from, mate?"

"I'm American."

"You'll get over it," he snapped. His name, I learned, was Liam Turlane and he hailed from Rochdale, near Manchester. He asked the forbidden question, "So why'd you join, Yank?"

I knew I had to get a laugh from this tough crowd. "Well," I said slowly, "I wanted to join the Black Watch, but I didn't like their skirt color." All those who understood laughed, and I passed my first Legion test among the "lads."

I happened to sit next to another, soon-to-be, basic training friend, Phil Fairfield from Sheffield, England. Phil was a sturdy, pale-faced northerner and the son of a policeman. We got along well together and began to discuss movies ("pictures" for Phil)—recent and classic. I mentioned one of my favorites—*Zulu*. Fairfield knew it of course, smiled and said, "Yes, that's the way I like to see the English." I asked, "Weren't those Welsh soldiers at Rorke's Drift?" Without a moment's hesitation, Fairfield responded, "Welsh soldiers, English officers."

Normally a candidate is not long at the recruiting post—three to six days on average. The time spent at the fort, however, is a good introduction to what awaits the new legionnaire: endless cleaning, polishing, sweeping, mopping, and kitchen work. Today much more focus is placed on gaging a candidate's physical fitness (including swimming ability). How many push-ups and pull-ups you complete and the results of an eight-minute shuttle run help personnel determine who continues in the selection process and who is returned to the streets.

Most non-French speakers are in a daze. It's trying on the nerves to handle, all at once, the incoming barrage of French quirks such as handshakes every few minutes, strangers cadging cigarettes, light breakfasts, and so on. All is new but not necessarily welcome or understood. I remember a rather odd-looking shower at Fort de Nogent. Having put my feet in the indicated positions, I pulled the dangling rope. All that got wet were my feet. The hole in the middle of this "shower" was not an open drain, but a passage for waste. In my jet-lagged, unaware American condition, I had actually walked into a French toilet, not a shower stall (French pride insists we call this bathroom facility a "Turkish toilet").

After showers and measurements of height and weight, along with tests of vision and blood pressure, the first rejections are made. The obvious drug addicts and alcoholics are discovered and dismissed. Worn, ill-fitting, green sweat suits are issued to those who remain. A candidate's civilian clothes are "stored," but, in fact, as he moves closer to basic training, his old life's clothing ends up in a Legion secondhand shop. I never saw mine again, but friends swear they saw their shirts being worn by veteran legionnaires.

As evening drew near on my first day in the Foreign Legion, it was time for my first dinner. We lined up without much fuss. No attempt was made to march us, and we simply followed a *caporal-chef* to the mess hall, where tables had been set for four people, with pitchers of water and wine on plastic red and white tablecloths. One of us was to get the food, and we then would serve ourselves. I sat with Phil Fairfield from England, Jan Van Heek, a tall towhead from the Netherlands, and a skinny Moroccan who spoke no English. We joked about drinking wine with our meal on Day One and playfully argued over who was more qualified to test the vintage. Soon, however, we were brought back to our new world. The Moroccan, thirsty and excluded from our conversation, picked up the wine pitcher and took a long sloppy swig from its spout. For a moment, my new friends and I sat silent—then, we burst out laughing. If Legion tap water would have to accompany our first dinner in Paris, *c'est la vie*.

A few hours later that first night, as we prepared our bunks, jetlag hit me with full force.

I don't remember falling asleep, but I cannot forget waking up.

Reveille was a blinking blur of shouts, whistles, and buzzing corridor lights. It was still dark outside as we were roused from our bunks. Drowsily, the ten or twelve in my room made our beds and put on our baggy green sweatsuits. In the midst of this commotion, I heard something both strange and ironic; in a clear, strong voice, someone was singing Queen's "I Want to Break Free." I approached the singer, a black recruit, and asked, "Already? We just got here." He shook his head; he didn't speak English. His name was Adelbert, and he was from Senegal. Like many with whom I awoke that first Legion morning, Adelbert stayed with me for the next four months. He was one of the kindest and friendliest men I met in the Legion. Others in the room marveled at his shiny, pitch-black skin, free of any body hair. A few of the French recruits even touched his baby-soft skin in awe and simply dubbed him "Black." Who could know that Adelbert would end his career as the senior NCO administrator in the very office at Aubagne many of us were hoping to pass through unscathed. Adelbert retired from the *BPLE* (now *DRHLE)* in 2017 as an *adjudant-chef*, but, for now, he was just one of the many questioning whether he would last until the next day.

We mustered in the cold, moonlit courtyard and stood quietly in rows of two. For the first time since my arrival, everyone and everything was motionless. Not for long. An Indian *caporal-chef* with a handlebar moustache barked a greeting and led us on a brisk run around the inside grounds of the fort. While running I saw my breath and that of the others in the moonlight. Unseen that morning were our hopes and dreams. Indeed, some of us did not last too much longer inside those stone-gray walls. A German who had passed through the gate just before me was dismissed after a cursory physical. The medic, who spoke German, asked if the new recruit "liked to drink." The German nodded his head and smiled slightly, as did the medic. After a check of his eyesight and blood pressure, he was returned to the streets of Paris. In due course, however, I would learn how much of the Legion's hardness includes hard drinking.

In between the mind-numbing television and nervous chatter that occupied our time those first few days at the fort was also some classic Legion *corvée* (chores). We quickly learned French verbs like *balayer* (to sweep) and nouns like *serpillère* (floor cloth) and the eternal Legion-German *putzen* (to clean). My first *corvée* was in the kitchen. Another recruit and I had washed the evening's dishes and placed them on the rack to dry. An Algerian who later shared my room in Castelnaudary (basic training camp) insisted on drying the plates and stacking them in the cupboard. Two tattered, filthy rags were spread over the radiator by the cupboards. They had been used by an earlier *corvée* team to mop the floor of the mess hall and left on the radiator to dry. Kharadji, the Algerian, began drying the cleaned dishes with this nasty, damp rag. I pointed to the floor and the mop in the corner, but the earnest Arab knew best and continued to whistle as he dried the dishes by himself. Kharadji's sour tone and constant shrugging of shoulders showed he thought my European partner and I were loafers. I was learning that French, and in particular, Legion, standards of hygiene were unlike any I had seen in the United States.

Another *corvée* involved a ten-man detail assigned to remove an enormous safe from the third floor of the main barrack to ground level. As a boy, I had watched many old movies with my father, including his favorite vintage comedies starring Stan Laurel and Oliver Hardy. I couldn't believe how much we laughed at these old-time black and white films. *Swiss Miss* was yet another Hal Roach showcase for Laurel and Hardy to attempt serious business with hilarious results. In one absurd scene, the Alpine-clad duo tried to move a piano across a rickety rope bridge spanning an enormous gorge.

My *corvée* detail was set to do something similar. The safe was so large and so old that one could imagine the fort had been built around it. We took turns opening and closing the heavy door—the only thing that any of us could move, and then, only if we used both hands. The plan was to push this several-hundred-pound object from the hallway to the window and then lower it by winch to the bed of a waiting truck, which would then carry the safe to Les Invalides for burial (or so we joked). In any event, we needed to move this overweight veteran out of Legion territory.

After much energetic and noisy collaboration, all we'd achieved was to master the art of cursing in one another's languages. Eventually, after several futile, however creative, attempts, we decided to use floor polish to ease it along. The safe slid quite well, but so did we. Finally, the ten recruits, moving like novice ice skaters, slid the massive relic to the wooden ramp leading to the windowsill. However, it proved too steep and more creativity was needed. A *caporal-chef* suggested using the straps and canvas of the nearby winch to push and drag the safe up the ramp. With great effort and coordination, we assured the safe a precarious balance on the window frame. Meanwhile, an acrobatic legionnaire first class from the detail below (who had been yelling at us throughout) took hold of one of the ropes and climbed, hand over hand, to our floor. He then straddled the winch and gave more instructions that few of us understood. Somehow, safe and soldier were lowered, swinging, to the ground, the legionnaire singing the whole time. Truly a Legion *corvée* with panache, and yet another early, dramatic display of the life awaiting me.

I celebrated my twenty-sixth birthday in Fort de Nogent. Feeling alone but content, I walked the corridors that September 8th morning, singing "Happy Birthday (to me)." It was only my fourth day, and I had a long way to go, but it was a start. Those of us who had been selected would be leaving the next day for further processing at the Legion's headquarters in Aubagne.

Before departing, we were required to have our heads shaved. Today this does not happen until the candidate passes more tests and is selected for the detachment to Castelnaudary. We sat in the *salle d'attente* staring at the lone chair placed in the middle of the room. The chair seemed ominous—almost like a guillotine. A *caporal-chef* plugged in his razor, tested it twice in mid-air like a weapon, and cheerily called the first recruit to the chair. It was fascinating to see this one small and ordinary machine have the same impact on so many different personalities. Missing only among the grim humor and sense of dread was a wicker basket for our

9

falling locks. Soon all heads looked alike. Each recruit's hand would glide back and forth over his freshly-buzzed scalp and a smile would appear. He would then shake his head in disbelief, mumble some expletive, and quickly retreat to his seat to behold the exact same reaction in the next victim.

I had never had my head shaved and felt a sense of finality in this birthday haircut. Indeed, a new year in my life was beginning. I had been stripped of my hair as an outward declaration of my very personal decision to start anew. Clearly the idea was to shed the recruit's past as well as his hair.

Our green sweatsuits were now traded for green military fatigues and oversized *Chasseurs Alpins* berets. Through haircuts and uniforms, the Legion was edging us closer to the world of soldiering. When the time came, our detachment of sixteen was taken by French army bus through Paris to the Gare de Lyon, where we boarded a train south to Marseille; from there, it was a short trip to Aubagne, where we would begin the next stage of our induction along with other recruits who had enlisted at the various Legion recruitment centers around France. I will always remember first seeing the Eiffel Tower while seated in that Legion transport taking us from the fort to the train station.

Little did I know that my friends and I were soon to discover another French icon.

* * *

My entry into the *Légion étrangère* was typical in some ways, but the roads leading to that portal are as many and varied as the men who tread them.

* * *

Born in rural Cornwall but raised in the eastern town of Ipswich, Englishman Simon Atherton first became aware of the Legion in his midteens. A BBC documentary he had seen on television was very dramatic, highlighting the plight of a British deserter who, as Atherton remembered, "had to emigrate to the United States because Legion hit squads were after him." It sounded exciting to the young Atherton, who had left school at sixteen and was working as a butcher in Norwich. At age nineteen, he acted on his dream. "I went into the train station at St. Charles in Marseille," he recalls, "and went to the police station that was there and just said in English, 'Where's the French Foreign Legion?'" They gave him directions and told him to get the *métro*. "'Get off at Vieux Port and walk up towards the fort.' So that's what I did. I only thought . . . outside that fuck-off gate . . . I hope they take me. Just hope they take me." They did and Simon Atherton went on to serve fifteen years in the Legion, including several at a Legion recruiting post.

* * *

The neighborhood in Chicago known as Ukrainian Village (nicknamed "the Island") is an enclave within the city. Buttressed by traditional Eastern Orthodox churches and strict schools where the study of Ukrainian history and language is required, the surrounded and outnumbered Ukrainians have been able to hold the ever-encroaching Mexican and black populations at bay. Living in this neighborhood as the son of a second-generation Polish father and a first-generation Mexican mother, Daniel Mazowski always had to prove himself since the locals see cultural differences and things non-Ukrainian as threats to their stability. That his family was tolerated within the Island was no doubt due to Mr. Mazowski's position as a Cook County deputy sheriff. After one semester of college at Loyola University, the bookish, nineteen-year-old Daniel considered joining the U.S. Marine Corps, but then had an even bolder idea.

"I called the French consulate in Chicago, and they sent me a list of recruiting offices in France. I felt good about leaving home. My mother thought I was going to get killed and die and thought she'd never see me again. My friends didn't know how to take it; it was just so totally out of their league. They didn't understand. They never will. To them it was *Beau Geste*." Mazowski's reasons went deeper than a lust for excitement: "Really I was pissed off with everybody and everything. I didn't like the way people in the U.S. acted. I hated the materialism. Like I said, I wanted to learn another language. I wanted to travel. And I wanted to be in the military." And, like so many other Legion recruits, "I wanted to do something very different."

Joining angry is not uncommon. Per-Inge Persson, a hardy, broad-shouldered Swede, also felt unsettled in life. After graduating from the Plönninge Forestry College, he worked as a lumberjack foreman for two years. In Sweden, military service is required for all able-bodied males. Having happily served a twelve-month tour in the army, Persson signed for an additional twenty-four months. But he was angered when the authorities refused to let him serve with U.N. forces in Lebanon, due to a drunk driving incident four years earlier. "I was so mad," he recalls. "They started giving me so much shit about this drinking thing. I had only five or six months before this would be cleared from my record. It was really stupid." After completing his service, he left Sweden and joined the Legion at age twenty-seven.

* * *

Most who set off for France to join the Foreign Legion do not tell family or friends for fear of ridicule or discouragement. Arriving at the gate of any Legion fort, hopeful recruits often receive the same message. Still, a tall, strong, and resolute twenty-one-year-old, Craig Donlon, left the high unemployment of Carlisle, England, in 1983 to "have a go at the *képi.*"

"I said (to parents) that I was going to join the army and they naturally thought the British Army. The silly thing is we'd been in the Army Cadet Course. I mean, you start about twelve-years-old or even younger, you know . . . you get to about seventeen . . . usually they take you in the army straight away as a junior soldier. But the British Army's pretty limited where they go or what they do . . . manouvres in Germany or stationed in Northern Ireland. You know, I wanted something more than this."

* * *

As Donlon entered the fort at Lille, France, he happened to meet an English-speaking regular army NCO at the security post. The sergeant, however, was as nervous and discouraging as Donlon's friends and family might have been had they known which army was his objective. "No. Oh, no. You better have a good think about what you are going to do. Go home. It's still not too late. This is the Foreign Legion." And Donlon recalls, "So this, like, spurred me on. As if to say, yeah, this is what it's all about. This is what I want."

* * *

Kurt Poulsen of Copenhagen joined in 1987, aged nineteen. The eldest son of a bank president father and schoolteacher mother, he lived comfortably with his parents in the suburbs. As if to spite his family's social standing, Kurt began to date their Turkish maid, Isa, which resulted in his father's throwing him out. He and Isa tried to live together, but prejudice from all sides forbade it. Isa's family also found it scandalous that she was dating a foreigner. The couple was unwelcome at both families' homes and on the street had to contend with the xenophobic and fanatic "greenjackets," part of the right-wing skinhead scene and extremely violent to non-Viking types. Seeking refuge, the couple squatted in that Danish anomaly called Christiania. Located on prime Copenhagen real estate, Christiania had been home to the Royal Artillery Regiment, but now its walled perimeter keeps out most any semblance of Danish order. The abandoned military base was taken over by local hippies in 1971 and proclaimed a "freetown" within Copenhagen by its new anti-establishment residents. Rules are few, and all are welcome. Isa and Kurt were able to be together openly without worry of comment or confrontation.

A week in their new Bohemian neighborhood would have included a stroll along Christiania's main crossroad Pusher Street. At this junction, the young couple might have listened to a bongo and tambourine jam session or sampled the homegrown marijuana and organic hash brownies at one of the many open-air stalls selling light snacks and assorted paraphernalia. The Christiania honeymoon ended rather quickly, however. Within two weeks, Isa was snatched by her father and sent back to Turkey. Shortly afterward, Poulsen left Copenhagen for Paris.

"I still remember the taxi ride from the airport to Fort de Nogent ... 275 francs, and that was in '87. At the fort, the driver just shook his head and pointed to the gate. Everyone knows about the Legion in my country. They think it's criminals and stuff like that ... tough guys that's coming. But they also know of some good people like Prince Aage of the royal family ... in it for twenty-five years." (Aage was the first cousin of Christian X, heroic King of Denmark during World War II.)

"Mírnej vztek s mírnou hlavou, Duši často měni v alkohol, Tam v Karviné, v Karviné"

"Hollow anger with a hollow head, Often turns the soul into alcohol, There in Karviná, in Karviná"

"Karviná"
The Yo-Yo Band

In Czechoslovakia in the late 1980s, the city of Karviná and the surrounding region, near the Polish border, were a grim Communist-era landscape of coal mines and steel mills with clusters of drab workers' hubs—a typical Eastern European industrial zone where young people dreamed of a different future but too often lacked the will to change their dreary, unfulfilled lives. Stanislav Gazdík was a miner's son and grew up in Orlová, a pupose-built mining town near Karviná. Gazdík recalls: "Well, one day I said to my father, 'I want to work like a miner.' He went into the bathroom and filled the tub with water. He called me. I said, 'Yes, are you going to wash, or what?' He said, 'No, son, look: you are going to choose your profession. If you choose miner, I will drown you right now.' He was very serious. OK, understood. So, sure, I decided to do something else."

Gazdík comments on the path that led him to a soldier's life: "At high school in Orlová, military recruiters came by. I thought ... fuck it ... the uniform—I liked it a lot. They talked about school for helicopter pilots. I signed up for helicopter school and was accepted, but at that year they didn't have enough applicants and didn't open a new class." Gazdík chose a civilian construction job. He earned good money climbing high beams of fifty or 100 meters "like a monkey," but it wasn't steady employment, and he again turned to the army.

* * *

In 1989, Czechoslovakia was one of the many Soviet-bloc countries to experience political, social, and economic upheaval. In Poland, after decades of Soviet-enforced terror and deprivation, Lech Wałęsa's once banned *Solidarność* party overwhelmingly won the vote in the country's first (partially) free elections since 1939. Drama unfolded in Lithuania, Latvia, and Estonia as two million citizens protested Soviet occupation by joining hands across their Baltic states and then whispering the word "freedom" to one another. To the cheers of long separated friends and relatives, Hungary dismantled the barbed-wire fences, minefields, and guard towers that lined its border with Austria. Trabants and Wartburgs, packed with families and their meager possessions on "summer vacation," sputtered to West German embassies in neighboring countries. By the hundreds, the "happy socialists" piled out of their circus cars and asked for asylum. A few months later, massive demonstrations outside churches in Leipzig and Dresden (with the rallying cry *"Wir sind das Volk"* or "We are the people") brought party leaders in Communist East Germany to the realization that the Berlin Wall and its ideology could no longer separate Germans. Eastern Europe was in tumult. As a Czechoslovak soldier, Stanislav Gazdík, a stern and determined twenty-one-year-old, watched his country's "Velvet Revolution" unfold.

"I was in an NCO school in Prešov in 1989. I remember I was in Prague on November 17, 1989. We had a leave and . . . I was on leave visiting my girlfriend . . . just passing through, really. I was in uniform . . . red beret on my head. Before going (to Prague) I spoke to my mother by phone. She said, 'Son, you haven't seen the TV this week? People in your uniform are beating the students.' I didn't know anything. I didn't look at TV or newspapers. Well, I came to Prague by train and had a look. But fuck it . . . what's going on? Then a man said to me, 'Hey, shitface, what are you doing? Fucking Red Berets!' After, I walked to the train station's toilets, and . . . another man followed closely behind me. I turned and said,

'What do you want?' He said, 'Yeah, asshole, it's you guys that are beating the crowds!' I said, 'Who? Who is beating people?'—I didn't know anything. I was on leave . . . in Prague to see my girlfriend. So, I said, 'What's happening?' The man said, 'It's the revolution!' Revolution? Fuck! I put my red beret in my pocket and left the station. By early 1991, I left the Czechoslovak Army, and in March I went to Strasbourg (France) to join the Legion."

Sergent-Chef Gazdík would return to the Czech Republic fifteen years later as a highly decorated and accomplished Legion veteran.

* * *

Within days of Gary Lineker's sixth and final goal for England at the 1986 World Cup in Mexico City, Ian Griffiths left for the Netherlands. A fervent supporter of English football and especially Manchester City, he'd decided to couple his love of football with a little continental adventure and hoped to win a spot as a midfielder in one of the junior clubs of a Dutch first division team. Griffiths, who would soon charm French girls with his Johnny Hallyday-rocker looks, was born to working-class parents in Radcliffe, near Manchester, in 1968. Good at math and science, he grew bored with school and left at seventeen. Estranged from his family, he drifted south to London where he took a well-paying factory job with assistance from a kindly Presbyterian minister, who also offered the young Mancunian free accommodation at the church. "Yeah, the Reverend put me up in a church. He sorted me out. You know, he sorted me out there that year . . . and, like, from there I got a job. I mean, I saw things stabilizing but, like, it was just a dead end, you know, dead end. Go to work at the factory, do your overtime. I was earning a lot of money for that age, but I wanted to get out of there. I wanted out. I went to Holland to play football and see a little of Europe."

* * *

After a month of intensive training with PSV Eindhoven's under-21 team, Griffiths was told by the coach in strange Dutch-Mancunian talk that he was "definitely maybe a good player" but would not fit in with this team. Thanking the coach for his time, Griffiths went in search of the sun and the possibility of playing with less demanding teams in France or Spain. The tourist information desk at Gare St. Charles in Marseille provided him with a city map on which the only English was a recruitment advertisement for the French Foreign Legion. With resources and patience dwindling, Griffiths approached the massive walls of Fort St. Nicolas. "I knew what I was doing. I wanted to join. I asked some questions. The *sentinelle* (sentry) had said to me you go to, like, Aubagne. And I said, 'What, you don't go to Africa no more?' And he was, like, . . . his face was . . . are you sure you want to join, like, Beau-Peep? So that's when I learned there was no ferry to Africa leaving that weekend."

* * *

Walking past the laughing *sentinelle*, Griffiths entered a small room where an *adjudant-chef* and a *caporal-chef* stared at him. No English was spoken—only sign language and grunts. Griffiths was sent to a courtyard where he met several others, some in baggy green sweatsuits, milling about, talking and smoking. After the evening meal, he and a Frenchman from Nice went atop the ramparts of the seventeenth-century fort, lit up a joint of Dutch skunk that Griffiths managed to sneak past the guards, and watched the civilians and lights of Marseille one last time.

Sunday saw a brief medical check-up, a signing of some kind of contract, and new clothes for the new boys. Sundays at Legion bases usually allow a sleep-in with a coffee and croissant breakfast (optional) and a large midday meal with only cold food served in the evening. Griffiths was the only English speaker among the fourteen or fifteen hopefuls at the fort, but with all those Europeans and a free Sunday afternoon, it was not long before the football fanatic organized a game among the various nationalities. Griffiths approached the *adjudant-chef* for a soccer ball.

"He was Italian, but he seemed to understand me. '*Inghilterra, Inghilterra*,' he kept saying . . . making a fist . . . and I said, '*Italia*' so we got a ball. This was a year after Brussels where it went off between Liverpool and Juventus. But it wasn't just Liverpool fans . . . a lot of British Army there, you know, that are based in Germany. How many were killed? Thirty-nine or something. Thirty-eight Italians and one Belgian—dead."

Twenty-five years earlier another English teenager had also presented himself to Legion personnel on a Saturday afternoon. However, France, in 1960, was mired in the fifth year of its bitter and bloody colonial war in Algeria. Simon Murray would serve France for five years in the parachute regiment and record his time in combat in the classic *Legionnaire*—a book many join with in their back pocket today. I interviewed this legendary man in London when he was eighty years old. A storyteller par excellence, Murray, who nearly crushed my hand when greeting me, remains a bundle of energy and enthusiastic supporter of all things Foreign Legion.

Only sixteen years after the end of German-occupied Paris, Murray, a small, posh-speaking Brit with a disarming smile, met a German *sergent* at Fort de Nogent. As Murray recalls, "He kept saying, '*Was?*' '*Warum?*' then said in English, 'Yeah, yeah, you English think it's all camels and bloody stuff . . . running around the desert. It isn't. It's modern weapons and it's very tough and if I was you I'd go away and think about it.' So I came back the next day. I spent the night in Paris. The next day was a Sunday and I came back. Met the same sergeant and was shown upstairs to a room with about forty guys. I was in a three-piece suit, with a double-breasted waistcoat."

A laughing Murray adds, "Everybody looked tough and dressed completely differently from me. It was an important day, but a day for wearing blue jeans. I missed that one. But I was one of the seven they took out of that batch of forty or so."

* * *

Like many a future legionnaire, Michael "Tex" McCue from Amarillo tried to do what his family and community expected. But neither the Jesuit professors at his college in Houston nor his pediatrician father was impressed with his first semester "D" average. Tex decided to go to Europe and worked his way through eight countries. Upon his return to Texas nearly two years later, everything seemed very strange. "I had gotten to the point when I didn't feel at home in my hometown. I felt like an outsider."

Against the wishes of his parents, Tex McCue returned to Europe. For almost a year, he resumed his itinerant lifestyle. One day, however, at age twenty-five, the tall, lean American came to Fort St. Nicolas in Marseille. "I was frightened . . . as frightened as I've ever been in my life when I came in through the gate. As I approached, there was a couple of German guys on the street outside. Kind of *clochards* (bums). They said to me, 'Are you going in? You going to join the Legion?' I said, 'Yeah, I am.' Basically, their story was that they'd been there for a couple of days, but they really didn't feel they were fit enough to join, or they hadn't worked up their balls to walk through the gate yet. And they were absolutely skint. And one of them said, 'Well, if you're joining you know you won't need your gear any more then, will you?' And I said, 'No, I won't.' And they said, basically said, 'Could we have your sleeping bag?' And I said, 'Yeah' . . . I gave them my sleeping bag and that was like the seal. Now I'm committed. No turning back. Absolutely none."

McCue went through the gate "like a dumb fool" and encountered the *sentinelle*. "He's standing there staring straight ahead. No smile on his face or anything. And I say, 'Hi, where do I go now?' in a mix of French and English, I guess. He looked at me like I was a worm that had just crawled out from under a rock . . . you know, kind of nodded his head in a general direction. I didn't bother asking any more questions."

McCue found an *adjudant* who spoke some English and sat him down and said, "You're American . . . you want to join the Legion?" McCue said yes, he did. "Well, you're American . . . why do you want to do this? You have a good life in America. Why do you want to come to join the Legion? It's not what you're expecting it to be." McCue repeated that he wanted to join, so the *adjudant* said, "Well, listen, I tell you what. Go back in town. Get a hotel. Stay another night in town. Have yourself a bite to eat. Go have a drink. Think about it. If you still want to do it, come back tomorrow.' A somber McCue told him, "There's no point. I've got no money. I couldn't get a hotel. I'm skint. I haven't eaten in two days."

When McCue handed over his passport, "my hands were shaking like leaves in the wind . . . I remember looking at my hands thinking, 'Pull yourself together. Get it together . . . you're making a right fool of me. Get it together.' And I kept expecting the *adjudant* to laugh, or say something . . . but he didn't acknowledge it at all. I'm sure he's seen that many other guys in the same state. He took the passport. Filled it out, and then, after all that, he says, 'Are you hungry?' I hadn't eaten in two days, so I was bloody starving. They had already had the evening meal, but they had some cold stuff they pulled out. And I ate until I couldn't eat any more. And then that was it. I was in. On the road."

* * *

"Reality is for people who can't cope with drugs," said Andrew Robeson's key chain. A recruiting officer in Lille wasn't amused and threw it out the window. Key chain aside, Robeson was a promising candidate. He was twenty-one, athletic, a French-speaker, and recently a student at the Polytechnic of Wales. As with many Brits in the Legion, Robeson had been unable to enter Her Majesty's Forces due to a minor run-in with the police.

When asked why he joined in 1986, Robeson, also a Genesis/Pink Floyd-loving music fan and bon vivant, laughs and replies, "That's the impossible question." He continues, "I needed an adventure holiday. I fancied the idea of working in Europe for a while . . . of getting away from the boring British climate and the boring British rat race. And there was always something that intrigued me about life in the army. Something that turned me on . . . something I wanted to know. My father had served in the army in Burma during the war, and I'd always enjoyed his stories. Lots of good stories from out there, and I respected him for that. And I respected guys I knew who were in the forces. Well, not so much respect . . . jealousy, in a way, more than respect. I wanted to experience forces' (military) lifestyle and I wanted to travel a bit. I was just gone (age) twenty-one and driven by a need to gain some life experience before moving on. So, yes, I was a kind of "tourist," which is popular Legion parlance for those hooligans of Brits who came over in waves during the 1980s.

* * *

After many overseas tours, marriage and two children, Andy retired from the Legion in 2005. He ended his career as a *sergent-chef* (staff sergeant) at 4th *RE* in Castelnaudary.

* * *

Upon passing through Legion gates, the volunteer is searched for drugs or weapons and must surrender his passport or other identification. After being led to a large room filled with other candidates, he waits until called. Soon, he is questioned about his background and reasons for joining. Many of the recruiters speak English or German, but choose not to, and will make the non-French-speaking applicant struggle to communicate. Often the applicant is asked to write a paragraph or two on why he wants to join. If the senior man on duty finds him satisfactory, the applicant is directed to the showers. He must then pick out a faded green sweatsuit, which will serve as his first uniform until he is ready to be sent to Legion headquarters at Aubagne. At some point, between the first interview and the shower, he will sign his five-year contract. (Since the late 1990s, the candidate has been offered a flier in various languages outlining basic Legion requirements and possible career paths.)

* * *

Most of today's European and North American armies have well-established, non-discriminatory policies toward those they recruit. In fact, a force such as the U.S. Army often includes a disproportionately high number of members of minority groups—especially in certain units. The Legion, however, has long been a white man's army and intends to remain so. Years of socialist governments in Paris have not changed how the Legion pursues recruitment or deals with the limited number of non-whites it allows to wear the *képi blanc*. Non-whites must prove their worth to the Legion more than white legionnaires. During the Camerone 2019 festivities at Aubagne, I saw more black legionnaires than in my day, yet many of these Africans were with company and regimental cross-country teams that represented the Legion in national and world competitions.

21

* * *

Regardless of origin, Asians in the Legion, are called *"chinois"* or *"chintok"*—"Chinese" or "chink"—and are seen by the European legionnaires as comical little yellow men who neither drink, fight, nor whore very much and always seem to be uncomfortable with a knife and fork. Many work in the mess hall, barber shop, or laundry. Tough, reliable, and generally known as followers, Asians are a good foil to the often loud, carousing, and independently minded English and German legionnaires. Many Asians have distinguished themselves in combat roles, however. Notable are the number of *chinois* in the cavalry regiment as tank gunners and pilots. Usually small and slight, they are a perfect match for the none-too-roomy *AMX-10 RC* tanks of the Legion's cavalry. In addition to practical reasons, many choose the *Régiment étranger de cavalerie* for the sake of tradition, knowing that throughout the 1946–1954 war in Indochina the *REC* was prominent in many bloody campaigns, signing on a good number of locals to help wage that jungle war. After the French defeat, a number of Asian legionnaires continued to serve or left for the *métropole*, where they found homes in the established Chinese or Vietnamese quarters of Paris and Marseille. Their sons and grandsons have served the Legion well.

Blacks are rare in the Legion. Almost all hail from France's former African colonies, speak good French, and accept the fact they are in a white man's army. Racism is strong in the Legion, though generally not malicious. African legionnaires are often addressed as "Negro," "Chocky" (a popular French chocolate drink), or simply "Black." The use of "nigger" is not uncommon. I remember walking along the *REC* parade ground and hearing a young lieutenant yell across to a Malagasy legionnaire, "Hey, nigger there, come here on the double!" More than 150 nationalities are represented in the Foreign Legion. Jokes are made about everyone's origins, but overt racism is severely reprimanded.

Nevertheless, an openly racist, long-serving Legion *PM* (military police) crossed my path in my final year of service. The name "Ludwig Klein," given by the Legion to this German giant from Bremerhaven, was indeed ironic. Massive and menacing, Klein was the proud son of an unrepentant Nazi, who had been a sergeant in the notorious World

War II *Einsatzkommandos*. Operating mostly in Eastern Europe to exe-
cute Jews and Communist party cadre, these special task forces served as
mobile killing units of the SS.

Klein had no love of non-Teutonic people (we spoke German) and
was amazed that he had tolerated "a race like the French" for so long. He
had contempt for black legionnaires and told me of a practical joke he had
once played on a black *PM*.

"The drums of the *Musique Principale* ... hour after hour practicing
... I thought I was back in the jungles of Bangui. So, finally, I woke up
the one black M&M they slipped into our company and told him he had
an urgent telephone call. He goes to the phone, but no answer. So I open
the window and shout at him, 'Nigger, can't you hear your family calling?
It's long distance from Africa.'"

* * *

Not all whites mock black legionnaires. Although I knew him for
only one week, I don't think I can ever forget "*Blanche Neige*" ("Snow
White"). He was a slightly bent over black legionnaire who seemed to
hobble, not walk, and was so nicknamed for the white hair on his bald-
ing head. *Blanche Neige* was probably only in his forties but looked years
older—something like a combination of Methusulah and Uncle Remus.
He was a *caporal-chef* with fifteen years' service and at the Legion headquarters in Aubagne for his final week of Legion duty. "Hotel" *CAPLE*
is the barracks at Aubagne that houses all those passing through the
regiment. Some legionnaires are going overseas, some are heading to
other regiments in the *métropole*, and some are returning from extended
leave. The happiest legionnaires who pass through this transient barrack every year, however, are those at the end of their Legion contracts.
Blanche Neige was at the end of something—that's for sure. One could
see the Legion had been hard on him, yet he had made it and was having the last laugh.

During his final week, which involved the usual barrage of paperwork, medical check-ups, and last-ditch meetings with high-ranking
officers attempting to sign the legionnaire on for still another hitch, all

anyone at the camp remembers of *Blanche Neige* was his insane, high-pitched laugh, which ended in a spasm of wheezing and coughing. He so changed the mood at the *CAPLE* that week that even the company captain addressed him as *Caporal-Chef Blanche Neige*. He seemed to be outwardly showing the wear and tear, physically and mentally, the Legion exacts on its soldiers after fifteen years of service. *Blanche Neige* soon became a Legion Everyman. Regardless of rank or time spent in the Legion, we all wanted to slap this guy on the back and wish him well.

I had little to do with him but found myself also caught up in *Blanche Neige*-mania. I remember seeing him after midday ranks shuffling along the administrative corridor of the *CAPLE* and asking him how things were going. As he was apt to do that last week, he didn't so much answer as just flap his arms and cackle. Every time I saw *Blanche Neige*, he was repeating this motion. As a black legionnaire in the early 1970s, he had to have been harassed in an awful way. In my many months in Aubagne, I never saw another black *caporal-chef* with fifteen years' service. *Blanche Neige* had defied the odds and pressed on—something the Legion values and respects more than anything.

Jews in the Legion have a limited but colorful history. Jewish enlistment came during, between, and just after the trauma of World Wars I and II. Since the infamous Dreyfus affair of the 1890s, the French military's anti-Semitism was no secret. Still, in 1914 and 1915, hundreds of French Jewish volunteers flocked to recruiting posts to fight the invading Hun. As with those Jewish recruits fleeing Hitler's Germany twenty years later, these men were somewhat older, more urban and middle class, and often university graduates. Because of their background, the new Jewish legionnaires were suspected of being "*intellectuels de gauche*" (smart-asses) by many enlisted men—and some anti-Semitic officers. The slur, "*intellectuel de gauche*," is still used in today's Legion as a barrack retort to anyone expressing himself too eloquently on anything other than a football match or right-wing politics.

The German occupation of France during World War II was a problem for any Jew in the French military. Germany's racial policies in collaborationist Vichy French territory meant that Jewish legionnaires had to be discharged and then imprisoned. In the French colonies of North Africa, Legion Jews were forced to work in labor camps established by the Vichy government. At least 1,500 Jewish legionnaires were made to toil alongside other enemies of Germany in building the Trans-Sahara Railway. Built under brutal conditions and fully supported by the Vichy regime, this Axis project led to the deaths of hundreds of Jewish legionnaires in North Africa.

While unlikely brothers-in-arms, the fallen soldiers of the *Wehrmacht* were also joined by Jews in Legion recruitment after 1945. Many central and eastern European Jews, with family dispersed or decimated and weary of moving from one Displaced Persons camp to another, joined the Foreign Legion. It's said that one Italian Jew joined the Legion in 1946 intending to find and kill his SS jailkeeper and torturer. Sent to Indochina, the Jew found his Nazi tormenter and, under the guise of battle, also found his revenge. Another Jewish legionnaire, David Shaltiel, was later to command Jewish forces in Jerusalem during the 1948 War of Independence. And Jewish officer (non-Legion) and future Israeli general Moshe Dayan lost his left eye after a 1943 battle with Legion-supported Vichy troops in Syria.

* * *

Jewish legionnaires, most of whom are Ashkenazi, must also endure and accept the taunts and prejudices of the Christian European majority. I found the French to have a particularly high disdain for Jews among their ranks, with Germans' anti-Semitism running a close second. I knew five Jews: one English, two French, and two Israelis. In fact, Israeli Sergeant Gideon "Hollywood" Lev (name changed) is the young legionnaire featured on the cover of John Robert Young's 1985 picture book, *The French Foreign Legion*. Like the other minorities in the Legion, Jews have to be extra tough.

* * *

Still, neither Asians, nor Africans, nor Jews can ever feel the animosity, distrust, and scorn that the Legion holds for Arabs in its ranks. That an

Arab could even make it to a combat regiment should be credit enough to his tenacity and spirit. Historically speaking, of course, one might argue: no Arabs, no Legion. The Foreign Legion was raised to fight in the Algerian *bled* (countryside). From its formation by King Louis Philippe in 1831 until the 1962 Evian Peace Accords under President de Gaulle, Algeria had been the Legion's home and sanctuary. France has still not fully come to terms with its traumatic 1954–1962 war in Algeria nor has it learned how to handle the growing Maghrebian population now living in the *métropole*.

This colonial scar has a major influence on public sentiment and French politics. Discussion and debate over Western socio-cultural values and Islam often fill the media. Many French mutter among themselves that recent violence in public schools and large city suburbs, along with general urban decay—including graffiti, crime, and the depressingly high national unemployment rate—is a result of too many Arabs living in too small a French space. Many of these same French also protest what they regard as the unfair social and economic benefits allocated to North African immigrants and their large, often very extended families. A political voice for many alienated and disheartened French is found in the far-right proclamations of the *Front national*, whose founder, Jean-Marie Le Pen (now retired in favor of his daughter Marine), is a veteran of the *Légion étrangère*.

Le Pen was an officer in a Legion paratrooper unit during the colonial wars in Indochina and Algeria. Like many Legion combat veterans of Algeria, Le Pen shows no remorse about the use of torture against the Arab enemies of France. He entered politics at a young age and developed a style and showmanship atypical among his peers. When active in the *Front national*, he would enter indoor political rallies under a spotlight and to the cadence of Verdi's impassioned "Slaves' Chorus" from *Nabucco*. He may spew rubbish during formal interviews ("the Holocaust is a minor detail of history"), but Le Pen is a confident, dynamic speaker in front of a crowd. Attending a rally in Marseille, I saw how easily he works the faithful into a frenzy. In keeping with the party's ultra-nationalistic pitch, soldiers in uniform and any legionnaires are freely admitted and made to feel most welcome at gatherings of the *Front national* (renamed

Rassemblement national in 2018 by Marine Le Pen, and, since 2022, led by the son of Italian immigrants, Jason Bardella). Usually the key speaker will ask all military personnel present to stand and receive the applause of the patriotic crowd.

Given the Legion's history and France's racial tension today, it is no wonder that Arabs are not a welcome group *chez Légion. Caporal-Chef* Simon Atherton (the former butcher from Norwich) became a Legion recruiter in the south of France in the 1990s; he described the standard operating procedure for minority recruitment: "For starters, it depends on their faces. It also depends what color they are—Arab or black. If they're Arab or black, they automatically get a test . . . an intelligence test because their intelligence is pretty low . . . but, if they pass the test, they get put in. About one out of one thousand passes. I've been here for five months now and not one has passed. They come for one reason only, and that is to become naturalized French. That's the only reason they come, and that's why we give them the test. We don't feel like helping them *se foutre de la gueule* (to cum on the face) of France."

* * *

One Arab youth who did ejaculate on France's phiz was Mohammed Merah. Perhaps a low-scoring intelligence test led to his rejection, but more likely it was Merah's surly attitude and many petty prior convictions that kept him from more than a few days' stay at a Legion recruiting post in the south of France. Less than two years later, in March 2012, Toulouse and France were shaken by the murders of three Jewish children, a rabbi, and three French *paras* (paratroopers) in the name of al-Qaeda and Legion-wannabe Merah's interpretation of Islam.

* * *

National and ethnic tension can surface among white, Christian Europeans, too. During the Balkan wars of the 1990s, a major brawl broke out between Croats and Serbs in my former *1er REC escadron.* All involved were discharged. Since the early 2000s, many Russians and Ukrainians have joined the Legion. If these groups come to blows *en service* because of the war in Ukraine, a similar fate will await.

* * *

Whatever his race, nationality, or background, once a recruit has made it past the gate and the initial screening and donned the green fatigues, he is channeled to Aubagne, near Marseille. This is home to the *1er Régiment étranger* (*1er RE*/First Foreign Regiment), headquarters of the Foreign Legion and site of its main selection center. That was where I arrived in September 1986, along with my fellow raw recruits from Paris.

2

Aubagne: Going *Rouge*

"Dear Mom,
Today I saw a guy eat an entire orange—peel and all. These are my
new friends."

—*ENGAGÉ VOLONTAIRE* MASALA

Late of Sidi-bel-Abbès, Algeria, the 1ᵉʳ RE *in Aubagne is now where*
those who pass initial screening at Legion posts and forts are sent for
further selection. If all goes well, the potential legionnaire is then sent
to Castelnaudary, near Toulouse, for basic training.

* * *

Quartier Viénot (the Aubagne Legion garrison, named for Colonel
Raphaël Viénot, a renowned commander of the *1ᵉʳ RE* who served with
distinction in the Crimean War) is home to the heart and soul of the
Legion, which comprises: the band (once named the *Musique Principale*,
it is smaller today and officially called *La Musique de la Légion étrangère*);
all administrative personnel and the top brass (including the one and only
general of the Foreign Legion); and the world-class Legion cross-country
team—*ATHLEG*. Also posted at *Quartier* Viénot during the early 2000s
was my first Legion officer, Victor Le Coeur Grandiose.

My lieutenant during *instruction* (basic training) in 1986, he was for several years the chief of staff in Aubagne and is now a three-star general at the divisional level. In 1986, Le Coeur was a twenty-five-year-old officer fresh out of Saint Cyr Military Academy, and my section was his first Legion command. Hailing from a military family, he was a fine junior officer—firm but fair—and, to his credit, our section had no deserters.

Quartier Viénot is also home to the *Monument aux Morts* (Memorial to the Dead). Built in 1931 at the Legion's old desert headquarters in Sidi-bel-Abbès, Algeria, it was transferred piece by sentimental piece to Aubagne when the Legion was forced out of North Africa. Here, too, is Legiondom's holy shrine, the Legion Museum (free to the public). Inside, down a flight of stairs, among a golden cross and numerous battle flags, is encased the wooden hand of Captain Jean Danjou. What Davy Crockett and the Alamo are to Americans, and Rorke's Drift is to the British, Captain Danjou and the Battle of Camerone are to the Legion. On April 30, 1863, Danjou, two lieutenants, and sixty-two legionnaires, having fortified themselves in a remote hacienda, withstood almost twelve hours of assault by a Mexican force of more than 2,000 infantry and cavalry. After the slaughter, the Mexican commander allowed the four surviving legionnaires to gather their sole remaining officer, a wounded lieutenant, and surrender with honor. *El Commandante* is said to have referred to the survivors as *"diablos"*—and a legend was born. The anniversary of the battle is the Legion's grandest holiday. Camerone observances at Aubagne have a solemn and almost religious overtone as the salvaged hand of the heroic Captain Danjou is paraded before the regiment, Legion veterans, and guests, and then returned to airtight security in the museum.

Into this atmosphere of mystical tradition, new recruits come for selection.

* * *

I arrived at Aubagne in September 1986, along with the rest of my batch from Fort de Nogent. Here, we underwent a process after which those of us judged suitable were formally accepted as fledgling legionnaires and proceed to the next stage.

* * *

A recruit is now called an *EV—Engagé Volontaire*. His time at Aubagne is always uncertain as he waits from one roll call to the next to be told whether he is to continue or go home. Friendships are formed quickly, and stories of home, jobs, and girlfriends are generously swapped. The *EV* camp is also an inviting place for many to strut and boast. While most are cautious or brooding in their new environment, others are all mouth. The number of 2 Para, SAS-qualified, Green Beret/*GSG*-9 cross-trained airborne SEAL team Ranger-tabbed medics with combat experience is impressive.

An *EV's* day begins at 05:00. A breakfast of chicory coffee with bread, butter, and jam is served in the mess hall at 05:30, followed by ranks at daybreak. The barrack housing the 300 or so *EVs*, built in 1986, is sturdy and modern. No other Legion barrack is like the *section EV*. Solar panels heat the water, and a library, with books in several languages, is available for recruits. No *EV*, of course, has time for a long hot shower or leisurely read in the library. While at Aubagne, he is too busy being tested, questioned, and herded from one *corvée* to the next.

At morning ranks, *EVs* are split into various groups for an assortment of tests and chores. The duty NCO, standing before men of more than forty or fifty nationalities, will give the foreigner his first test: cultural adaptation, calling each *EV's* name not as the *EV* knows it, but in something garbled and Gallic.

The intelligence test and complete physical given at Aubagne are two decisive exams for a prospective legionnaire. The former, which shows the recruit's *niveau général* (IQ), is given in several European languages and is a mix of basic math, science, history, and vocabulary. A far more elaborate IQ test is given to those who may work in the Legion's (small) IT departments. Also tested is one's *niveau culturel*, with questions on European art, music, and film (a self-contained army of 8,000–9,000 men needs all kinds of soldiers). The *niveau général* and *niveau culturel* scores are important in determining a legionnaire's career path as they will establish whether he is eligible for certain courses or ranks.

Perhaps the most mysterious, nerve wracking, and, certainly, most talked about part of an *EV's* stay at Aubagne is his meeting with "Gestapo"—the *Bureau de Securité de la Légion étrangère*—*BSLE* (now called *Division des Statistiques de la Légion étrangère*). The only bit of information this organization lets out to the *section EV* is that it works closely with the French security services in Paris and Interpol in Lyon. Its job is to interrogate each *EV* about his background. The following three legionnaires now share their first impressions of this dreaded office.

Legionnaire First Class Martin Walton left school and Hammersmith in west London at age fourteen. Before joining the Legion at age twenty, he'd held many menial jobs. Walton's sinewy forearms tell you he supports Arsenal, loves mum, and hates Pakis. He remembers his *BSLE* interview in 1989: "There was a little bloke with glasses . . . I think he was a Frenchman because he didn't speak English. I think I was more petrified than anything the way he was asking the questions . . . in butchered English, this guy, but I understood what he was saying. I wanted to get in that much I say, 'You want to keep my papers? I don't want to keep anything.' I just wanted to forget what I'd done before. I just wanted to get in that's what I wanted. And I thought if I don't get in here, I don't know what I am going to do. So I took me bankcards, snapped them up, and threw them in his bin. I was extremely nervous. I just wanted to get in."

* * *

Simon Atherton, who enlisted about two years before me, was only nineteen at the time: "They couldn't believe how old I was . . . thought I was a lot younger. I was in there *(BSLE)* for quite a while, yeah, and they went through all the same questions. Then they'd turn them over and ask you in a different order . . . stuff like that. I spoke to a Mexican who spoke good English. I think I was pretty calm, not real tense. I just thought it's no use going in nervous because then they'll think you're guilty straight away. I went in twice for three hours, but some guys went in three or four times, and for longer."

* * *

Chicagoan Dan Mazowski was interviewed by an English sergeant: "He really discouraged me . . . said Americans never make it, they last a month and, then, they leave." Eventually, Mazowski cracked and admitted he wanted to leave. "The sergeant went to the captain and told him my decision. And the captain said, 'No, give him another day to think about it.' So, I did think about it. And I thought I'd come all this way and all my plans were based on me getting into the Legion." He withdrew his request to leave. "They asked me everything: 'Why did you come here? Did you make somebody pregnant? Did you desert the American army? Is this your real name? Who's this in your wallet? Why are you lying to us? We know everything about you.'"

* * *

Compared with the rudimentary medical check-up on day one or two of his Legion experience, the *EV*'s Aubagne physical is fairly comprehensive, including many modern diagnostic tests with lab work or X-rays, as needed. However, unless the *EV*'s experience with the medical profession has been limited to witch doctors and *santeria* practitioners, he surely has to notice the low standards of hygiene, abusive orderlies, and lackluster doctors that are all part of his assembly-line physical examination.

* * *

"Is it safe?" That is what I was sure the Legion dentist was shouting at me as he counted my teeth with fingers still wet with saliva from the *EV* before me. Grateful, I left the angry dentist and followed the crowd to the next medical station. Sloppy fingers in one's yanked-open mouth are unpleasant enough, but standing bare-assed before a group of strangers is another, more awkward, discomfort. When this same inquisitive group of strangers is a seated, note-taking, Gauloise-smoking collection of French medical officers who then begin to prod and poke wherever they want, well . . . the situation becomes quite unsettling. However, it is all part of the timeless, calculated military rite of losing one's individuality.

33

In addition to taking note of a candidate's posture, balance, and coordination, the doctors are well versed in reading scars and ink. Even if hidden by clothing, some tattoos will disqualify an aspiring legionnaire almost immediately. I am sure doctors rejected British Royal Navy veteran Burt Buxton for his bizarre markings. As the ten or twelve of us hurriedly stripped to our underwear in a musty hallway outside the reviewing room, Burt's tattoo, among all others on display, stood out: A sweet-faced angel floating up his right leg. Starting at his right calf, the angel followed a fluid and wavy arrow outlined by clef notes to the inner right thigh. The cherub's now-smiling face flew straight to Burt's crotch, where it then reappeared on his upper left thigh as a grinning devil. Pitchfork in hand, the devil squirmed his way down to Burt's left calf and disappeared in a puff of expletive smoke.

The *EV's* physical exam is made more unnerving by loud and belligerent orderlies: Too slow with that urine sample? Boff! Not quiet enough in the waiting room? Clack! Dirty underwear? Slap! The medical care also seems very random and sloppy. I can't believe that in 1986, with the AIDS epidemic raging worldwide, I allowed myself to be the third international candidate to share a needle for an injection. After each shot, it was wiped with antiseptic, but one needle per three *EVs* was the cost-saving procedure at the time (now discontinued).

* * *

Dodgy needles and dodging punches aside, we all knew that something very different was occurring. We were in the process of rejecting everything that was familiar to us for God knows what. In his own way, each of us prepared for this strange new world and wondered how we would announce it to those we had left behind. I remember sitting in the *EV* compound with a Canadian named Tony Masala. We watched another *EV*, sitting alone, eat his Sunday evening meal. Sunday is a mellow day in the Legion, even for new boys. As *EVs*, we were given a *repas froid* (a cold boxed meal) and then allowed to eat and socialize in the yard behind the compound. Dessert that Sunday was an orange. The *EV* we were watching ate the orange whole. Mimicking a letter home Masala said out loud,

"Dear Mom, Today I saw a guy eat an entire orange—peel and all. These are my new friends." We laughed, but it was all part of the formula we were looking for. We wanted something different—something out of the ordinary. Scenes like this *EV* eating his orange whole fit well into the expectations of our strange new lifestyle. We needed moments like this to help purge ourselves of the conventional world. Our Legion journey was soon to begin, and we were ready for the orange eaters and whatever else was to follow.

* * *

Most of the chores assigned *EVs* are the routine drudgery common to any army: picking weeds, peeling potatoes, washing trucks, and cleaning toilets. But one unique duty gives a glimpse of the Old Legion and, for some, a legionnaire's future. Once a week, during grape picking season in August and September, a group of twenty-five or thirty *EVs* are taken by truck to Puyloubier, a Legion outpost near Aix-en-Provence. Since 1954 this small, picturesque town has been the site of the *Institution des Invalides de la Légion étrangère*. Puyloubier is the end of the line for many a colorful legionnaire, home to those veterans who, for physical or emotional reasons, cannot readjust to civilian life. Legion officials are quick to point out that veterans, if need be, are cared for until death. If the Legion is a strange and insular house, then Puyloubier is its drawing room. All the men are old: veterans of North Africa, Indochina, World War II, and (in the 1980s) even the campaigns between the World Wars. There is no talk of the future and little of the present. As American legionnaire Alan Seeger might have noted, the men, having never met their rendezvous with death, are still talking and arguing about that disputed barricade. Faded tattoos of blood type under the left arm reveal that many of those men drinking and playing cards in the *foyer* have served in other armies.

* * *

Legionnaire Persson, who visited Puyloubier three times as an *EV*, recalls some of the veterans. One of them "had lost everything, even his pride because he was into drinking a lot and he couldn't control himself. I was standing at *rassemblement* (ranks)—he had only stumps for legs—and he just wheeled by and threw up in front of us, almost on me." Persson encountered another veteran at Puyloubier who proudly wore his "medals" every day. "He was in Algeria and wounded. Had seven bullets in him. The whole chest was full of bullet holes. I counted and there was seven. And I thought, this is not real. But still that made me respect him in some way because I know to survive that...."

* * *

Puyloubier, the retreat, does contribute to the Legion of today. Its fertile 100-acre vineyard located on the southern slope of Cezanne's beloved mountain Sainte Victoire yields more than 250,000 bottles a year of *AOC*-Côte-de-Provence Legion reds, rosés, and whites. This Puyloubier wine can be found in the mess halls of every Legion regiment and many regular army camps. Since 2007, the Legion has had a special *cuvée*—*Esprit de Corps*—made with the best grapes from the best of the estate and now available to the general public. Also, no Legion *foyer* (PX) would be complete without the *képi* ashtrays, regimental crests, and ceramic soldiers made by the veterans at Puyloubier.

* * *

Legionnaire First Class Kurt Poulsen was a *PM* on duty at Puyloubier when American General H. Norman Schwarzkopf, Commander of U.S. and Coalition forces during the first Gulf War, visited the Legion home in 1991: "We sent all the TV and radio people away. Schwartzkopf came by from Aubagne to Puyloubier in helicopter. He had a good time with an old English bloke, walking arm in arm like that, singing and everything. He really said, 'I hope I soon can come back here.' He really loved Puyloubier. He bought six cases of Puyloubier wine. *Képi* on the head and all that." The late General Schwartzkopf was made an honorary *Légionnaire* at the end of the First Gulf War; he liked to tell how, upon receiving his *képi* from the Legion high command, he was also given a card with a telephone number and told that, were he ever in trouble, he should call the special number and the Legion would be there—any time, any place.

* * *

During his stay at Aubagne, an *EV* gets a feel for what is to come if he is selected to go to Castelnaudary. My recollections of physical abuse at that early stage remain vivid. Those in charge of the *EV* barrack had to let us know that they were in command of us at all times. But discipline was often inconsistent. Some *EVs* who fought or stole were beaten or given physical punishments by the corporals or corporal-chefs. Yet, other *EVs* charged with the same offense might simply be scolded or held back from the regular Thursday night fun of *cinema chinois* (Chinese movie night). Like most Legion regiments, the *1ᵉʳ RE* has a movie theater. Legion film buffs at Aubagne stuck to modern Asian classics like *Hong Kong Fists* and *Chinaman's Fury*. These silly films were well attended due mostly to our boredom and a desire to see people other than us get kicked and punched. A fair number of us also thought we might soon be learning similar martial arts.

Two *caporaux-chefs* during my time at Aubagne were very consistent with their discipline. Any English speakers during those years would certainly remember them—one Portuguese and one Vietnamese. I imagine both had joined soon after the 1974 and 1975 upheavals in their countries. They had an intense dislike of English speakers. Sometimes, before meals, we would gather behind the *EV* compound to talk or gossip. Regardless of nationality, many *EVs* spoke English. The Portuguese and Vietnamese *caporaux-chefs* were always suspicious of us, and, on one occasion, broke into our group swinging bamboo rods. I missed getting a good crack on the head only by inches, but several of my friends were hit hard on their backs and faces.

So that everybody could hate them equally, they later visited their wrath on the entire *section EV*. During an evening inspection, a *caporal* had found black hairs from someone's razor strewn over the sink in one of the common lavatories. We were called to *rassemblement* and told in no uncertain terms (even translated into English) that whoever made this mess had better step forward. No one moved. The order was repeated. The only movement was our looking around for the culprit to identify himself. Everyone seemed to be focused on a big Romanian fellow who was as fidgety as he was clean-shaven. Many of us remembered his having had a bushy black beard earlier in the day. When he vehemently denied the clippings on the sink were his, the *caporaux-chefs* made us all do push-ups. The *rassemblement* ground was more like a gravel pit, which made it extra grueling. The *caporaux-chefs* went through our ranks and anyone slowing down was either kicked in his stomach or hit with the big bamboo rods these little men always seemed to carry. This went on for at least thirty minutes before the beardless Romanian cracked and confessed. That night he got a beating from the irate *caporaux-chefs* and, then, Round Two from the sore *EVs*.

When *EVs* are deemed ready to transfer to basic training, it is called "going *rouge*." During morning ranks, without ceremony, our names were called and we were given a bright red band to wear over the right shoulder of our faded green fatigues. Phil Fairfield tells me that he can never forget the expression on my face the morning they called out "Valldejuli,"—a mix of emotions, but mostly shock. It was now all real . . . real for me, real for Fairfield, and real for many of the others who had joined on that same September day in Paris only a few weeks earlier.

Those of us who had gone *rouge* were still housed in the *EV* barrack but in our own wing on the ground floor. We had already done what many could not: last two to three weeks at Aubagne without failing a Legion test or interview.

It was a special moment for all of us. Chris Montrell, a fellow American in his mid-thirties, was a tiny but strongly built, devout Christian from Kansas, who went *rouge* a week before me. No one was too sure of his story—caught distributing Bibles in Albania, Europe's only Muslim nation—but he was popular with the Brits for his folksy talk and generosity in the *foyer*, which opened every other night to the aspiring legionnaires. A muscle-bound Brazilian behind the bar kept order and served *EVs* only candy and colas and sometimes a lemon-beer called Panaché. However, most *EVs* had no money. Many in our group would latch on to those who had arrived with cash and could debit their money from an account the

Legion had established for them. Padre Montrell would buy the Mars bars and Panaché if the audience could handle a bit of the Good Word. On the night he went *rouge*, he drawled, "Yeah, man, they laid a *rouge* tab on me, so the Lord and I are going to witness at the Castle."

The *rouge* boys ruled the *EV* barrack. On our last night at Aubagne, we watched music videos and tried to avoid thinking of the next day's trip to Castelnaudary, where basic training would begin. What we saw on television helped distract us. The video that transfixed us was French singer Mylène Farmer's "Libertine." Even if some of us were unsure of what libertine meant, the pictures helped clarify things and excited everyone. The French *EV*s bounced along and sang the refrain, "*Je suis libertine*" as we watched an eighteenth-century dinner party degenerate into an orgy. All of us were lost in this display of food and flesh when suddenly we heard laughter from the back of the room. We turned and saw a small, very tanned man in a bright green sweatsuit, but no one recognized him. The stranger shook his head and said, "*C'est fini . . . alles kaput.*" He left the room, and we went back to the videos.

Standing in front of our bus to the train station the next morning was none other than the mystery man from the night before. No longer smirking, his face was now grim and serious; he was to be one of our three drill sergeants for the next four months.

Boarding the bus, I felt both happy and nervous, as if my adventure was officially starting. As our bus pulled away, I saw an incoming bus full of new arrivals, and wondered what their stories were, and how many of them would make it through the selection process we had just passed.

* * *

To mark the serious and emotional divide between their past lives and their new ones as legionnaires, recruits, shortly before leaving for Castelnaudary, are ushered over to the hallowed Legion Museum.

* * *

Those recruits in my section stepping into a museum for the first time displayed a strained and almost absurd somberness. A few walked among displays as they imagined one did in these places—hands behind the back and head nodding in silent approval at every exhibit passed. Ashes and body parts lay surrounded by lists of dead from worldwide campaigns. The museum's colors and lighting were subdued, and one remained equally restrained during the tour. (A new, more modern museum was opened on Camerone Day, April 30, 2013.)

At some point, the recruits are led into the main hall where the story of Legion demi-god Danjou and his heroic last stand at Camerone is read to them in French. Few understand a word of what is said, but everyone is hushed and respectful. Then there is a talk by a high-ranking Legion officer, who speaks in passable English and German, as well as French, so that most can now understand. The officer talks of loyalty and dedication, of honor and service. He looks each recruit sternly in the eye and rails against desertion. We cannot desert. We will not desert. He inquires about the nationalities represented and admonishes foreign recruits with a few choice words in their own, respective tongues. Sadly, while most everyone is impressed or intimidated, the odds are that very few gathered in the hall of martyrs that day will sacrifice much to the Legion; indeed, many will not even finish their five-year contract, and the veteran officer knows this.

Engagés volontaires come and go on any Friday at Aubagne. Many new friends are processed, and many others are never seen again. The duty sergeant, however, will call out forty or fifty very special names—those, by virtue of the Legion's unique selection process (about one in nine candidates succeeds), deemed fit to wear the *rouge* band and become *Légionnaires*. The next stop is Castelnaudary.

3

Castelnaudary—*Instruction*

"Why can't they march like normal soldiers?"

—*Légionnaire première classe* Van Heek

Forced to leave its desert home in 1962, the Legion relocated its basic training regiment *(4ème Régiment étranger)* to Bonifacio on the sunbaked, isolated southern tip of the French island of Corsica. The island's steep and inhospitable mountains replaced the wide expanse of desert and offered new challenges for Legion recruits on long marches. Birthplace of Napoleon and an integral part of France, the island has, nevertheless, always been home to deep-rooted nationalist spirits. By the mid-1970s, the atmosphere was becoming more anti-French and very anti-Legion. The murder of a local shepherd at the hands of two Legion deserters did not calm matters, and the ministry of defense looked, once again, to relocate the Legion. But Corsica has never been a peaceful Mediterranean island. This clan-dominated, mafia-infested land of reluctant French citizens is (proportionally per violent acts and murder) the most dangerous region in Europe—in other words, a perfect Legion training ground. Still, Paris decided to move the regiment to the mainland, where a permanent training camp had never been allowed. *Quartier* La Passet, an old, abandoned regular army camp, was taken over by the Legion with much national fanfare in November 1976. This new training regiment was in Castelnaudary, a sleepy market town and self-proclaimed "capital of cassoulet" along the Canal du Midi, thirty-six miles southeast of Toulouse.

The Legion soon outgrew the La Passet *quartier* in town and constructed its own camp on seventeen acres of farmland about one mile from the limited distractions of downtown Castelnaudary. *Quartier* Danjou, where I did my basic training, was opened in 1986. With neat cream-colored stucco walls and Spanish-tiled roofs, the three-story-high barracks—graced by well-tended geraniums and bougainvillea and, since 1995, an Olympic-sized swimming pool—resemble an upscale Florida retirement complex. Castelnaudary hosted three basic training companies, each with four sections of forty-five to fifty men (now smaller at thirty to forty). A section will have one officer with usually three NCOs and three or four corporals. Castel also houses one NCO training company, one specialist training company, and one logistical and support company.

* * *

Yet, behind its tranquil façade, lives the Legion a recruit loves to hate.

* * *

Regardless of the army, few recruits forget basic training. No Legion recruit, including those with prior military service, can forget *instruction*. It is four months unlike anything he has experienced. Legion basic training is everyone's own personal hell—either physical or mental. A legionnaire is to do quickly and completely anything asked of him. It's all action-reaction, and nerves are frazzled in many ways. During *instruction*, one sees it all: degradation, humiliation, violence, sadism, as well as unparalleled moments of collective and individual stamina that become the basis of intense and lasting camaraderie.

* * *

On Day One, a recruit will meet the men who are to instruct him for the next four months. Legionnaire First Class Poulsen recalls the opening act of his Legion drama at the Castelnaudary train station: "We came out of the train and a big Swiss guy . . . a big one—lots of muscles—a tough guy as well . . . he opened his gob and got a smack in the head. He got one hard that's for sure. I think he tried to be funny or something. That's the first one . . . *instruction* started like that."

Upon arrival at *Quartier* Danjou, the new boys then saw an unusual sight outside their barrack. "We stood outside Third Company . . . our company. And there was guys (Valldejuli's section) that was nearly finished *instruction*. We saw them, and they was pumping (push-ups) with *képis* on the head and *tenue de sortie* (dress 'A' uniform) in the rain outside on the street. Some of the guys got a kick in the stomach and all that." Into only thirty minutes of Day One, Poulsen surmises, "but when you have never seen something like that you're a bit shocked in the beginning. Fucking hell, man, you've got to be careful here."

* * *

Brigadier-Chef Donlon remembers the winter's day in 1983 when his group arrived at *Quartier* La Passet: "It was in January . . . very cold, miserable place, very old, more like a prison. It was raining at the time. We knew it would be shit anyway, because I mean *instruction* . . . it's got to be that way. You know, everybody realizes we're in for shit. Four months of shit. And it starts from Day One until the last day, you just know this, so you don't build your hopes up too high."

After a brief ride from the train station to La Passet, Donlon and the others remained seated and silent. Nobody wanted to make a move. "And then there's this— '*Debarquez!*' (Get out!)—and it starts. You haven't got time to think about it. You just get on with it." Jumping from the back of the truck with duffel bags in hand, wearing "this stupid *tenue de sortie* with the floppy big beret." Donlon and recruits follow orders. "They then make you run up and down stairs a few times with all those sacks and shit. You got one corporal, like, standing at the bottom of the stairs and one, like, at the top of the stairs. The one at the bottom is shouting he wants everybody upstairs quick now and you get to the top and the other corporal's saying, 'I want everybody downstairs now.' By about five times, you soon realize you've just got to know when to switch off."

* * *

After the requisite yelling and screaming (but no rain) of Legionnaire Persson's first day, he remembers thinking it hadn't gone too badly. The corporals seemed helpful; every non-francophone had been assigned a *binôme* (French-speaking partner), and all had been fed well. It was in the late evening, just before lights out, that Persson and friends first met their drill sergeant: "We had an ironing board in one of the rooms and we started to iron some of our clothes. And the sergeant comes in with his uniform and wants that to get ironed, and he's in a bad mood. The first thing he does is kick the ironing board across the room with the iron and everything on the floor. And he throws his uniform on the floor and shouts and screams like hell and storms out again. Some corporal had to explain exactly what he wanted—that someone had to iron his uniform tonight. That's about it. After seeing him, we were dead scared of the sergeants."

* * *

In a section of fifty men there may be more than twenty nationalities represented. Imperative to becoming a useful legionnaire is the ability to understand, speak, and, eventually, read and write French. Learning French names for rifle parts and other equipment, in addition to the numerous Legion rituals and traditions, can be overwhelming. While slap-happy instructors often help motivate newcomers to speak French, the Legion also assigns a French-speaking *binôme* ("buddy") to every non-francophone. In principle, this system should work well. *Sergent-Chef* Robeson: "I thought the *binôme* system was a good idea terribly executed. The foreigners had to learn French in some way and there wasn't much time given to French lessons. Unfortunately, the contact between the foreigners and the French was bad. The French became a disliked nationality. No one wanted to know them, especially the English."

The French who join the Legion are a mixed group, but they usually share a sense of superiority over foreigners. Even the dumbest and lowest-class Frenchman feels he can lord it over the non-French speaking in his section. Tensions can run high in the intensity of *instruction*. Robeson, though half-French, admits "everyone was frustrated with the physical and mental side of what we were getting all the time, so getting on with a French guy wasn't easy. We were putting up with French bullshit all day and night. Now, when we were free, we had to put up with our French bullshit partner who was feeding us more of this French crap. On our free time we wanted to get away from anything that was French."

Robeson continues: "And the French were just basic assholes ... it wasn't just *mauvais esprit* (negative attitude) on our part. They just wanted to get out of everything ... do as little as they possibly could. And it was impossible to get along with someone with that mentality when you were prepared to do quite a bit. Most French are just not made for being soldiers. They just weren't into it at all. And though some of the foreigners weren't into it, either, as a general rule, they wanted to give it a go. The whole mentality of life in *instruction* just didn't help to be able to get on with these French assholes."

* * *

In recent years fewer francophones have joined, so foreign recruits are being paired in threes (*trinômes)*: one native French-speaker with two non-French-speakers.

* * *

In my section, there was a tall Londoner named Jirrells. The Englishman was assigned a local who appeared more gnome than *binôme*. Nodane was a squat, crinkly-faced Frenchman who had the habit of seldom smiling except at another's misfortune. All day, Nodane would curse under his breath at Jirrells and the other *putain d'anglais* (fucking English). One October morning, encamped at the foot of the Pyrenees, we awoke to a thunderstorm and torrential rain. Since it was 04:30, we hoped we could stay in our tents until *réveille* at 05:30. No such luck. Whistles blew. Sergeants screamed. We damned it all. The entire camp had to be dismantled in this pre-dawn storm. Rain gear and pocket flashlights were of little use as we quickly pulled down and packed our two-man tents. Amid the darkness and confusion, we could easily distinguish two voices shouting at each other—those of Jirrells and Nodane. In as much as they could understand each other, they were arguing over clothing. It seemed (as we later saw in the light) that Nodane, the Small, was wearing the fatigue pants of Jirrells, the Tall. Despite the oversized fit, Nodane was not about to give up the pants on this cold wet morning, leaving Jirrells to run around on the French-Spanish border in his olive-green Legion underwear.

* * *

Although told to pack the *képi* along with the rest of his issued clothes at Aubagne, the recruit does not have the right to wear the distinctive head gear until he completes the *Képi* March. Marching is an integral part of Legion training and continues at the regimental level.

* * *

A recruit must be able to force-march for hours—in all conditions, with a full pack, web belt, and weapon. A basic pack will hold a sleeping bag, canteen (always full), mess kit and stove, complete change of clothes, toiletries, personal belongings, and two-man tent—all weighing about forty pounds. Additional survival and first aid gear for certain field exercises or "special marches" such as the Raid March or deep jungle missions in French Guiana, can make this backpack weigh seventy-five pounds or more. A web belt adds extra weight, and, of course, no soldier is complete without his weapon. Legionnaires carry a standard-issue, French-made "bullpup-style" 5.56mm *FAMAS* (now HK-416) assault rifle with a twenty-five to thirty-round magazine—weighing about ten pounds, fully loaded. Since the mid-1990s, Legion command and medical personnel have become increasingly concerned about back problems among soldiers caused by their often too heavy, ill-fitting packs. Much effort has been made to lighten the load, as well as provide better webbing and boots to increase legionnaires' agility and speed.

* * *

The *Képi* March is the first major trek a recruit makes after a month's training. He is called a *Légionnaire* upon completion of the thirty- or forty-mile two-day hike. Normally at the end of the *Képi* March, a special nighttime Nuremberg Rally-like ceremony is held, at which the *képi* and regimental insignia are officially presented.

For many, the *Képi* March is difficult simply because it is the first long march. No amount of Legion physical training can fully prepare the new soldier for the cramps, blisters, loose bowels, dehydration, and complete exhaustion he will suffer during this ordeal, which comes only three weeks after arrival at Castel. However, the "graduation march," or Raid March, is usually the most memorable to a legionnaire. Coming in the last two weeks of *instruction*, this challenge is the culmination of everything military learned so far. Recruits march, rappel, fire a variety of weapons, navigate with Zodiac rafts, and return to camp bruised and bloodied, but thankful that the end of basic training is only days away.

Like many a legionnaire, Martin Walton will never forget his Raid March: "That was the worst fucking march I'd ever done in my life. We did four days. On our Raid March, we had four deserters, including a corporal. Then there was me, an Italian, another Englishman, and a Portuguese. We weren't doing very well on the march—this is the third day—and we started to stagger a bit. And the sergeant, a massive Taipot (Tahitian) threw a few punches left, right, and center. I took a good three of them. What he decided to do was chain us all up. So he chained us up, and that was it. We were chained extremely close together and you could hardly walk."

* * *

Whether portrayed by Jean-Paul Belmondo or Jean-Claude Van Damme, Gary Cooper, or Gene Hackman, a legionnaire's life on film and in print has been rife with brutality. While Hollywood may have hung up its *képi*, the lurid accounts (usually from deserters) appearing in today's tabloid newspapers and magazines detailing violence and physical abuse still make good copy, and further the Legion's outlaw image.

* * *

It is with some hesitation that I present additional stories. Yet tales of Legion cruelty continue to make headlines.

* * *

In September 2015, a trial began in a Paris criminal court over the 2008 death of a twenty-five-year-old Slovak legionnaire—Joszef Tvarusko—during an intense, four-day, anti-terrorist exercise in the scorching deserts of Djibouti. The events leading to the Slovak's death are an eerily familiar story to anyone who has undergone Legion training. A legionnaire learns quickly that he may curse and grumble quietly in his new world, but he must never make an official complaint regarding conditions or activities. Unfortunately, the elite Legion *para* Tvarusko made the mistake of informing superiors of his sore knee on the second day of the exercise. The attention was swift: After his canteen was emptied into the sand at his feet, he was kicked and punched, later denied the unit's brief respites, and, finally, made to finish the day's training by running up a nearby hill. An autopsy revealed he had died of a heart attack caused by sunstroke and physical activity beyond his capacity and not from dehydration or the *patates* (punches) he had most certainly received.

The civilian judge and jury decided Tvarusko's immediate superiors were guilty of creating an atmosphere of "extreme and unusual harshness and abuse, which, involuntarily, led to death." A lieutenant (French), sergeant (Chilean), and corporal (Mexican) were given suspended prison sentences of two to four years.

* * *

The Legion has always been, and continues to be, a tough, aggressive army. I watched my company captain at *1er REC* become so enraged at a malingering legionnaire on a field exercise that the helmeted officer headbutted the sloppy soldier for not wearing the proper cover. In an environment like the Legion, with such a mix of men and backgrounds, violence is almost a given. Though now changing, an organized level of violence and cruelty seems to be tolerated, if not promoted. As if the transformation to legionnaire from civilian is not traumatic enough, the newest members are often subject to mental and, sometimes, physical abuse that can leave permanent damage. Usually under the guise of discipline, a recruit will feel or see violence every day at Castelnaudary.

Similar to late night "hall meetings" a plebe might find at a U.S. military academy, the Legion's evening *appel* (roll call) is a time for those in charge, either the duty sergeant or corporal, to pick on those who were especially slow, weak, or troublesome that day. Legionnaire Persson remembers how "you could expect some real terrible beatings . . . really criminal things happened." His section of new boys always dreaded the evening *appel* of the cruel and often unhinged *Caporal* Lex: "There was a German in our group. He was quite thick, even in German. Just didn't get it very quick. French no way. Once, Lex was drunk, and he was pissed with everybody. There was something wrong with this German guy. And Lex took a big fucking needle . . . it was maybe three or four inches long . . . and walked up to this German and put it right through his cheek and kept moving it around. The German guy was crying actually and blood coming out. We didn't know what to do."

Many lined up at attention in the hall that night knew *Caporal* Lex was dangerous and carried a gun in his pocket. Persson had seen the gun several times and believed "he could easily have shot us on the spot." As Lex twisted the needle, the German continued to sob. The *caporal* said to the recruit, "This is nothing. Nothing for a legionnaire." Lex then "put the needle in his own cheek just the same way and just laughed. That's how rough that guy was."

* * *

Often a recruit sees even more brutality when he is away from camp. Sergeants—and even more so the frazzled corporals who live almost like the recruits, grow weary of conditions in the field. Motivating a company of legionnaires the way a commanding officer might unrealistically demand also takes its toll on many corporals. However, corporals know that, often without any recrimination against the offender, a legionnaire can be harassed more intensely in the isolation of a field encampment than in the company barrack. Tex McCue's section gathered for lunch in an outdoor mess tent and watched their corporals degrade and abuse a fellow recruit: "I expected the Legion to be brutal, but this shocked even me. It was a French kid . . . a street kid . . . that the corporals took a dislike to. He was very stupid. Basically illiterate. Couldn't read or write. He was also ugly. He had heavy acne on his face. He's also one of these guys who has the look of a whipped dog about him, and the corporals just took an intense dislike to him."

Wine is served at all Legion meals, though recruits' amounts are limited. On this occasion, the corporals had drunk their fill. "We used to hate it when they got drunk because it would bring out the sadistic in them. Well, they called your man up . . . your little French guy . . . and said for him to come to the front. He got up and started walking. They said, *'Non, tu est un chien. Tu vas bien ici sur quatre patte.'* ('No, you're a dog. You need to come here on all fours.') They made him crawl through that mud under the tables. It's humiliating for a start, right. So you're sitting there trying to eat while this is going on. He's crawling past you under the table, you know. Then he got up there. They stood him at attention. They started abusing him. I mean, I didn't know the full repertoire of the French cuss words yet, but I heard all of them. They just abused him."

But the abuse was more than verbal. "Finally what happened was . . . one of the corporals grabbed him by the arms. Another one put his hands over the guy's mouth covering his mouth so he couldn't shout out or scream. And the third one just started hitting him in the belly. The one who was hitting him in the belly carried on solidly, just striking him in the gut for a good five minutes—until his arms got too tired to hit hard anymore and then they traded places. He held the guy's arms, and the other one came forward and started on him and it went on for a good ten minutes. It was appalling. I remember after watching that episode I thought if they ever . . . ever tried to do anything like that on me they were going to have to put me down. I'm just going to take as many of them down with me as I can. I don't care what happens. I'll not go through that shit."

* * *

Sometimes violence in the Legion, especially during *instruction*, is used to send a message. Rules and logic that apply in the civilian world, and in many of today's armies, have little bearing on the Legion. No matter how difficult and intense basic training may be, a new soldier must not waiver in his desire to become a *Légionnaire*. Those in charge are quick to point out a slacker or malcontent and will often isolate and harass him until he breaks down or deserts. Legionnaires are constantly reminded of Article One in the Honor Code: "*Tu es un volontaire servant la France avec honneur et fidélité.*" ("You are a volunteer serving France with honor and loyalty.") There is no tolerance for a legionnaire who attempts to lie or cheat his way out of a duty.

Caporal Lewis explains an especially cruel act of Legion justice meted out during *instruction* against one determined no longer to be part of the team: "The Turk was called in one day. We were out at Bel-Air (a Legion training 'farm') and we had a situation where this French guy said his knee was hurting, and that's why he couldn't make the march, and I'm sure *mon adjudant* (the commanding officer) would understand. Well, we had *mon adjudant* there, and he called in the Turk. The *adjudant* called for Mahmoud the Turk because of his skills as a masseur. Mahmoud had given massages to the officer and others on many long marches and was popular with the men. The *adjudant* also had reason to believe the French recruit was faking his injury.

Lewis continues, "The Frenchman was asked if he would mind if the Turk massaged his knee a little bit to determine where the problem was. The Frenchman gave his absolute permission." Lewis and Irish friend Maloney were on the scene, and, through a translator, the Turk tells the officer that there is a bit of minor stress in both knees, probably not unlike everyone elses's knees at that point, and that "all the ligaments were there, that everything was attached, everything was fine … that the guy was basically faking. The *adjudant* then said, 'OK, I want you to make it so that he can't march because I'm going to excuse him from the march.' So the Turk, through the translator again … and I don't know how much was lost in the translation … got the word to do this."

Mahmoud had Lewis and Maloney hold the shoulders of the hurt legionnaire in a way that would cause pain only if he tried to move. "So the Turk was walking around him and checking us and moving our hands and stuff like that. The Turk went back to the Frenchman's leg and proceeded to turn his foot all the way around. Just grabbed him at the knee, but his foot went all the way around. All the way around … just one-two-three … like rubber bands popping. Just completely dislocated it. And the way that he did it was that he had to stop halfway to move a bone out of its way to finish it. He knew exactly what he was doing. This guy was messed up for life. They put him in a little *Mehari* (Jeep-like buggy vehicle) and took him back to camp, I suppose. I never saw him again."

For a recruit, violence may also be self-inflicted. The intensity and pressure of basic training can be too much for those who are weak in some way. *Caporal* Mazowski recalls an attempted suicide at *Quartier* La Passet: "Castleton (the corporal) made a guy slit his wrists. I mean, he pushed him to do it. It was a German guy, Bielerfeld. He was busting Bielerfeld's nuts twenty-six hours a day. I remember Bielerfeld went off to the bathroom and our room was maybe five meters from the bathroom, and he came back. Bielerfeld came back into the room and just stood in the middle of the room with his hands dripping. There was blood everywhere."

* * *

Most of the physical training (PT) at Castel is geared toward making the new legionnaire fit for marching. Of course, PT will include a healthy amount of pull-ups, push-ups, sit-ups, and rope climbing, but long runs in *tenue de combat* (boots and fatigues) as well as the even more unwelcome 8,000 *TAP* (8,000-meter full-gear run), are also prominent features of *instruction*.

* * *

Unlike how airmobile units are trained in the United States, the Legion (as well as French parachute regiments) needs to know their men are capable of running to a helicopter landing zone from a good distance. The 8,000 *TAP* run is done to simulate this kind of battlefield evacuation. A recruit's *sac-à-dos* (backpack) is stuffed with his tent, sleeping bag, full canteen, and a change of clothes. He is to run the four and a half miles in less than one hour (under forty minutes for top marks). This grueling ordeal is hard on the body but even harder on the mind.

The Legion demands tenacity and confidence from soldiers; a *sac-à-dos* run is the perfect test. Logic says that, if a soldier can complete this challenge in the specified time, he is as fit mentally as he is physically. *Brigadier-Chef* Donlon agrees that "If you're going to train guys you've got to give them shit so they know what to expect sometimes and don't get psyched out." The 8,000 TAP can be run anywhere and often is. But, for many legionnaires, their running along the otherwise pleasant Canal du Midi during *instruction* is what leaves traumatic memories. Donlon describes this infernal run: "You've got to push yourself past a certain point when you're doing one of these *sac-à-dos* on the canal. I mean, it's so mind blowing because everything is the same—the trees along one side—and the canal is just straight. You do a half turn and then all the way back again. I mean, there's cases where you've just got to switch your mind off, and that's it."

Exhaustion and accomplishment are often the immediate sensations 8,000 *TAP* runners feel. Other effects do linger. As I prepared for a shower at the barrack after my first run, bunkmates noticed my blood-streaked t-shirt. The ill-fitting *sac-à-dos* had swung back and forth enough to cause large skin abrasions along my lower spine and back. I carefully took my shower, but from the shouts and curses in the other stalls I knew many had stripped quickly and jumped into the showers without noticing their wounds. A legionnaire normally runs the *sac-à-dos* at least three times during instruction and at least once a year thereafter as part of compulsory annual physical tests *(COVAPI)*. As one might expect, the 8,000 *TAP* run features prominently during commando, airborne, and NCO training programs. No surprise, then, this test is run by men of the *2ème REP's* super-elite *GCP* unit in Corsica at least once a week, with times expected to be under forty minutes.

* * *

Another timed event in the Legion's myriad of physical tests at Castel is the *PC*—*parcours du combatant*. It begins innocently enough with an obstacle called the *échelle de corde* (15-foot high rope ladder) and ends with a zig-zagging climb-out-of-this-one tank trap known as *les tranchées successives*. Among the twenty obstacles on this short but intense course is every sort of running, jumping, dodging, climbing, crawling, and balancing feat imaginable. While techniques in negotiating the obstacles usually go untaught, instructors do offer encouragement à *la Légion*. At La Passet, *Caporal* Lewis watched a Polish friend struggling with Obstacle Ten—*la table irlandaise* (the Irish table)—which required a coordinated grab and swing motion: "I saw a *caporal* just—Bam!—and hit Datka on the back with something like a baseball bat as he was swinging his body . . . trying to get the momentum . . . to get over the table and get to the next obstacle. I'm surprised he didn't have permanent damage."

Legionnaire Persson, a veteran of the Swedish Army, found the lack of instruction on how to run this unique obstacle course shocking: "We were fifty in our section, but, after the first day on the *PC*, we were forty. Ten broke legs or ankles. You know how they did it? Sergeants put us through some really hard stuff without being proper trained, so a lot of accidents happened in our section. We were probably the most wounded section at Castel. Even our sergeant got jail for that—because of stupidity. No demonstration. No warming up. No stretching. Just jump and go."

* * *

As with the 8,000 *TAP,* a *PC* is also found at the new legionnaire's regiment and can hold some surprises. Ours involved the seventeenth obstacle and man's best friend: an attack dog from the next-door *Gendarmerie's*

(French paramilitary national police force's) K-9 unit, brought in to give us more "confidence." *La fosse* (the pit) is a submerged gravel bed enclosed by concrete walls seven feet high. The legionnaire is to jump into the gravel pit, run the three or four strides to the opposite wall, lift himself out with whatever upper body strength and leg power he has left, attack the next three obstacles, and time out. On our day of unwelcome visitors, the fully padded *Gendarme* keeper waited in the pit along the near wall with his yapping Cerberus. The trick for us that day was to exit this hellish obstacle without teeth marks on our bodies. The *Gendarme* was told he could only release his companion when the legionnaire had touched the far wall. We had just one chance to make it up the wall and out of the Pit before the German shepherd was upon us. My close canine encounter came when I slipped back down the wall after my initial weak jump. I'd heard the *Gendarme* yell—*"Allez!"* (Go!)—and knew his beast was fast approaching biting range. With a surge of adrenaline, I scurried up and over the wall. The dog snapped at my leg but got only a mouthful of rubber—leaving deep teeth marks on the heel of my right boot.

* * *

Another non-Castel element added to the *PC* in Orange was fire. A relatively easy *PC* obstacle involves jumping from one small, raised stump to the next. The stumps, though, have little surface area on which to land and are spaced at various distances and heights. On one occasion, our section leader doused these small landings with gasoline, making us hop from fire to fire. Those who fell or proved too slow had to wash out their mouth with the gasoline.

* * *

After the marching, running, singing, shooting, grenade throwing, rocket launching, and sport (not to mention the long hours of guard duty and cleaning), a legionnaire is more than ready in spirit and body to move to his new regiment.

* * *

The tests a legionnaire undergoes, plus the opinions of his sergeants and corporals on his overall progress and attitude during *instruction*, yield a final score. A high score enables the legionnaire to request, and, most likely, receive appointment to the regiment he wishes. Those with low scores have to be content with whatever regiment the command decides. Troublesome and disliked legionnaires have been known to be sent to French Guiana. Those in command at the training regiment hope a two-year stint in the jungle will straighten out an undisciplined legionnaire, or at least make his deserting close to impossible.

* * *

The most requested regiment at the end of instruction is the *2ème Régiment étranger de parachutistes* (*2ème REP*/Second Foreign Parachute Regiment). The *REP* has an international reputation as one of the toughest airborne units in the world. Its men can fast-pace march for miles and, once airborne, exit the plane more quickly than any other parachute regiment. The *REP* is considered France's premier strike force. In addition to the extra training, overseas tours, and jump pay, a Legion *para* earns higher wages than other *métropole*-based legionnaires. Money aside, *REP*-men agree that nothing compares to a mid-summer's jump into Calvi Bay and swimming ashore only to have to fight through a beachhead of well-oiled, thong-bottomed, topless Scandinavian girls on holiday.

Perhaps the least requested posting at the end of four months at Castel is the *1er REC*. Formerly based in Orange, but since 2014 located near Aubagne in Carpiagne, this cavalry regiment is very old-school. The *REC* suffers from the same "better-than-you" mentality as the *REP*, only, instead of proudly showing off his silver wings, a newcomer must be content with shining his silver buttons, washing his *housse* (special *REC*-only *képi* top cover), learning cavalry names for once-familiar ranks, and, in general, understanding and accepting the *REC*'s unique code of conduct. An aristocratic officer corps and enduring, ball-breaking, *REC*-only traditions make the regiment unpopular with many legionnaires. After the no-nonsense discipline of Castel, most newcomers are unwilling to go to a regiment regarded by other Legion regiments as *traumatisée* (traumatized). But while our *REP* friends may be the number-one choice for new legionnaires and bikini-clad tourists, there is still something timeless and thrilling about a Foreign Legion cavalry formation leaving camp on maneuvers as the locals gather in the streets to wave and shout *"Vive la Légion!"* to the passing jeep, *VAB*, and tank crews.

4

The French Foreign Legion Overseas and in Europe

—Djibouti
—Mayotte
—Tahiti
—French Guiana
—Chad
—Central Africa and Other Posts
—The Balkans: Sarajevo, Srebrenica, and Mitrovica
—Afghanistan and Mali

"Vous autres Légionnaires, vous-êtes soldats pour mourir, et je vous envoi où l'on meurt." "You Legionnaires are soldiers marked for death, and I am sending you where you can die."

—High-Commissioner in Indochina and Far East Commander-in-Chief *Général* Jean de Lattre de Tassigny reminding troops in 1951 French Indochina of *Général de brigade* Oscar de Négrier's words to their Legion brothers in the same colony in the 1880s. This quote is familiar to legionnaires today and is posted at many company headquarters.

DJIBOUTI

*"They asked for four ringleaders . . . and they got the Wrecking Crew
plus one. And all volunteered."*

—*CAPORAL-CHEF* ATHERTON

The Legion comprises eleven regiments or corps formations: six in the
métropole, one overseas (French Guiana), and a detachment in Mayotte.
Also on the French mainland are the basic training regiment, admin-
istrative/staff regiment, and a corps of recruiters spread throughout
the country. As of 2023, the Legion had nearly 9,000 men, representing 11 percent of the French military. Prior colonial commitments had
demanded a much larger force. At the height of the war in Indochina,
the Legion numbered 36,000; later, 25,000 men served in Algeria. Every
Legion regiment has bled for the glory of France or Empire, but some
more than others.

The *13ème DBLE* was formed in March 1940 in France and waged
continuous combat until 1962. From 1962 to 2011, the *13ème* regiment
was based on the strategic Horn of Africa in Djibouti engaging in combat as well as humanitarian support missions in Eritrea, Somalia, Yemen,
Rwanda, Côte d'Ivoire, and Indonesia. The *13ème*, once known as *la Phalange magnifique* (the magnificent phalanx), downsized considerably after
leaving Africa. For a time, the unit, comprising merely 50-60 men, was
stationed at the U.S. Navy's 5th Fleet port. The detachment in Abu Dhabi
operated more as a training and supply base for French forces in the Middle East. However, the French Army was not about to let this storied unit
wither. Plans were made to move the *DBLE* to France and greatly aug-
ment its strength. In 2016, the *Demi Brigade* relocated to a former regular
army base (*camp militaire du Larzac*) north of Montpellier and has, since,
grown to 1,300 men. While some regular army formations have been
downsized or disbanded, Paris is eager to have a crack mechanized infantry unit (similar to its *2ème REI* in Nîmes) at the ready to project French
power.

* * *

All this confidence in *la Phalange magnifique* seems a far cry from the events of June 1940, when it became embroiled in the complexities of France's political and emotional trauma.

* * *

The German invasion of the Third Republic left French civilians and military personnel bitterly divided over which government to support. Some French collaborated with and fought for the Nazi-sponsored Vichy regime of aging war hero *Maréchal* Pétain while others heeded the call of resistance from London by Free French leader Charles de Gaulle. Much like the nation, the Legion split and fought itself—most tragically in Syria. The Gaullist Cross of Lorraine worn on the uniform of today's *DBLE*-men attests to the unit's loyalty to De Gaulle and the Free French forces during World War II. Legendary battles in Norway and North Africa—at Narvik and Bir Hakeim, respectively—showed the mettle of the *DBLE* and rallied loyal Frenchmen everywhere. It still resonates. At Camerone 2012 in Aubagne, a ninety-two-year-old veteran of the *13ème DBLE* and its many World War II campaigns was chosen to carry the hand of Captain Danjou and, so, honor all Legion dead.

However, the post-war colonial morass of Indochina was where the *DBLE* was to attempt national salvation with the most tragic of consequences, as 750 legionnaires of the *13ème DBLE* held fast to firebase *Béatrice* in that valley of death and defiance called Diên Biên Phu. After eight hours of concentrated and unrelenting artillery fire from captured 105mm cannons (guns French intelligence had claimed impossible for the Viet Minh to transport to the battle site), *Béatrice* fell. Only 200 legionnaires—their commanders having been killed—managed to escape to other forts. Another casualty of this first combat was the senior French artillery officer at Diên Biên Phu, a World War I veteran officer and trench-warfare expert who had approved the highly inaccurate reports sent to Hanoi and Paris detailing the enemy's firepower. Less than 48 hours after the opening barrage on *Béatrice*, the one-armed French artillery colonel pulled a grenade pin with his teeth and blew his chest apart. It was the spring of 1954, and France was soon to lose its empire in Indochina, though not without the enemy feeling the fury of the French Foreign Legion. Veteran U.S. Foreign Service officer and on-the-spot correspondent during the Franco-Vietminh war, Howard R. Simpson, pays homage to the grit of the men defending *Béatrice* in his landmark book *Dien Bien Phu: The Epic Battle America Forgot.* His comments on the unrelenting Vietminh assault include this accurate appraisal: "The deafening, deadly bombardment, the determined successive enemy attacks, and the lack of a friendly counterattack or the arrival of reinforcements would have already broken the will of a lesser unit. But this was the Legion. A unique mix of discipline, professionalism, tradition, and camaraderie kept the majority of survivors—including many of the wounded—at their posts." Still, vastly outnumbered and skillfully outplayed, French forces surrendered to the Vietminh after fifty-seven days of epic battle and siege. The losses of *13ème DBLE* and other Legion (especially paratrooper) units at Diên Biên Phu pushed the final tally of Legion killed in Indochina between 1946 and 1954 to more than 10,000.

Following the French withdrawal from Indochina in July 1954, the *13ème DBLE* and other foreign regiments regrouped in Algeria, unaware of the Legion's next all-consuming drama. Even during France's 1954–1962 colonial "action" in Algeria (not officially recognized as a war until 1999), French war-dead and POWs from Indochina continued to arrive in the *métropole*. In fact, during *instruction* at Castelnaudary in 1986, I was chosen to be part of a burial detail for a Spanish legionnaire whose remains had been returned to France from Vietnam. Two family members had come from Spain to attend, and the simple, but solemn, ceremony affected us all.

After the French loss of Algeria in 1962, the *13ème DBLE* was the only Legion regiment permanently stationed in Africa. Formerly the French territory of Afars and Issas, the Republic of Djibouti was proclaimed in 1977. Located at the strategic southern mouth of the Red Sea, with important port facilities and listening stations, the region was to France what nearby Aden (now part of Yemen) was to Great Britain. Indeed, the Bab al Mandab (Gate of Grief) strait that separates Djibouti and Yemen, just eighteen miles wide at spots, is one of the world's major oil-supply choke points. Though independent, Djibouti asked France to stay on and provide military assistance and training (many believe France would not have granted independence otherwise). Until 2011, the *13ème DBLE* protected Djibouti with one combat company, one engineering company, one ordinance company, and one reconnaissance squadron. On standby during the first Gulf War, its twin regiment in the *métropole—1er REC*—was instead sent to Saudi Arabia. Before departing the region, the region, the *DBLE* had been put on alert many times over border infractions with both warlord-ravaged Somalia and strife-ridden Eritrea.

Djibouti hosts the only permanent U.S. military base on the African continent. Since 2002, thousands of American troops, including hundreds of Special Operations forces, have moved to forward operating posts throughout the country. Camp Lemonnier, a former Legion garrison, is a 550-acre American base and center for launching drones, training Somali commandos, and keeping elite units at the ready. The mission of these specialized U.S. and local troops is to gather intelligence and pursue terrorists in the region. Somalia, a hub of active al-Shabab cells, and Yemen, site of the October 2000 attack on the destroyer U.S.S. *Cole* and ancestral home of former al-Qaeda chief Osama bin Laden, have both been countries targeted by the United States. French and U.S. forces are a welcome presence in this tough neighborhood. Indeed, in 2014, Djibouti's foreign minister openly applauded the use of drone strikes and commando raids on his neighbors.

After his two-year assignment in Djibouti in 2003, *Sergent-Chef* Robeson recalls his teammates in the war on terror: "Yeah, we welcomed the Yanks. Special Ops . . . around 2,000 of them. U.S. Marines and regular army crew—many women among them, too. They steadily increased their numbers over the time I was there. The locals couldn't believe there were so many of them. Lots of cash and lots of gear. Most were there for only two-month stints, like it was just some transit and acclimatization base camp."

Though a mere two miles down a dirt road from each other, the two armies had little contact. Legionnaires found the Americans aloof and discipline lax. "There's a lot of local weed in Djibouti, and we got word they abused it. Yeah, one of their lot got sent home after blowing pot smoke into a cop's face." Of course, maybe some Americans had enough sense to avoid any more time in the blast furnace heat of Djibouti. *Caporal* McCue from Amarillo, Texas: "When I first got in country . . . within a matter of five minutes . . . my clothes were wringing wet. I was drenched with sweat. I had also drinken a bottle of whiskey and a bottle of vodka on the plane ride over, but it all came out pretty quickly once we stepped off the plane. I found out Djibouti City—the capital—shut down in the middle part of the day. So did our camp. During the *sieste*, the temperatures used to get up close to 130°F a lot of times. The only people out working were the *taulards* (prisoners) and that included some guys who got caught smoking the local stuff."

* * *

While no longer a permanent base, Djibouti still hosts units that will rotate through when needed. A legionnaire's day runs from 06:00 to 13:00 and from 15:30 to 17:30. A midday regimental *sieste* is required because extreme temperatures make physical labor impractical, and nearly impossible, between 13:00 and 15:30.

* * *

In the past, a legionnaire was expected to complete two years in country. Even on a long permission, he was not allowed to leave and was restricted to certain areas. Only legionnaires who were "rectified"—had proven they were who they said they were—and had at least twelve months' service were allowed to leave the country, and then only to France.

As might be expected given the temperament of many legionnaires and the limited social life in Djibouti City, trouble happens. A legionnaire in town will meet only mindless young African girls and mouthy young French soldiers, and both are often Legion targets. It's not uncommon for a legionnaire with full pockets, equally full balls, and a week or more of permission to pay twenty-five dollars for a Djiboutian whore to cook, clean, and perform most any deviant sexual act. The girls are often no older than seventeen and sometimes as young as ten. Neo-colonialism or neo-slavery, neither the legionnaire nor girl give it much thought.

Legionnaire First Class Griffiths of the *REP* describes "just another Saturday night" in Djibouti City with several paratrooper friends. Indeed, this group of young legionnaires found that even without bucks they could still get a bang: "Me, Ashton Wilson, "Cowboy" Andy, Skip Jack and "Scouse" Dominguez. You know, Scouse, he was just mad about explosives. He just loved it. You'd go in his locker, you know, and he'd have, like, pounds of fucking TNT, detonators, and everything."

Usually *REP*-men have plenty of money to spend in town and are made welcome wherever they land. Oddly, Griffiths and friends had no cash but hoped for credit at their regular haunts. Cash is the language of love, however. "We took these *nayas* (local girls) back to their place—about five of us and four *nayas*. So, like we're all in the bed pissing about and they say, 'Money, money, you pay, you pay.' And we said, 'No, we don't have any.' And they said, 'No fuck-fuck, no money.' So we got a bit pissed off and smacked them around a little bit, and, as we was leaving—I mean I didn't know—Scouse Dominguez had this homemade fucking grenade he'd done. So, as we was leaving and that, he pulled the pin and threw the grenade. We ran off back to camp leaving them that fucking big explosion."

The next morning, the guilty legionnaires were apprehended by Legion *PM*s. All quickly confessed, though no remorse was shown. Griffiths remembers: "A *naya*, like, she got burn marks on her fucking ass and some things in the room got burned, but that was mainly it. One of them claimed she got shrapnel on the backs of her legs. But she was a *pute* (whore) anyway, so it really didn't matter." Local police wanted the matter hushed up. The Legion obliged and gave the Guy Fawkes Five ten days in *taule*.

* * *

Even when not on leave, a legionnaire's day in Djibouti seemed to belong to a time long past. *Caporal* McCue describes some typical interaction with locals on the base: "In all the French camps, the Legion and all the rest of them, you had boys that washed the clothes. You could wash your own clothes if you wanted to, but for a pittance you could pay a guy to come once a week and pick up your clothes and wash them for you. It was just so much easier and nearly everybody used to have them do it. The regulars would have boys cleaning clothes for them, too, and they'd also have some women clean. They didn't have that in the Legion. The only women on base were the ones who worked in the *bordel militaire* (military brothel, also called *pouffe*). No women cleaned clothes. I think they tried it one time and you had some problems with rape and such arising. It just didn't work."

Unique to Legion bases overseas was the *bordel militaire*. Never officially sanctioned, it existed and was popular with legionnaires, even as a social center. McCue on how it worked: "The girls used to have biweekly check-ups, and any time they went off to town—when they returned, they got a check-up. They were all kept pretty clean. There was an *infirmier* (medic) there outside of the rooms and, before you went back with one of the women, he'd have a look at your old fellow—make sure it wasn't weeping, or no running sores or anything on it, you know. I never heard of anyone catching anything from the *pouffe*. It was pretty well controlled." And he adds wistfully, "But the best talent you didn't see in the *pouffe*."

* * *

When a good legionnaire isn't whoring, he's usually drinking and later fighting. For a legionnaire to be returned to France *disciplinaire* (in irons) because of one particular fight is rare, but then, the "Wrecking Crew" was a gang of three unique characters.

* * *

All three were in the same *13ème DBLE* company based in the isolated Legion cavalry outpost of Oueah, nicknamed "the Rock," some twenty miles from anything. An international mix, the Crew was led by Legionnaire Jamieson, who came from a former slave-merchant family in Charleston, South Carolina; Legionnaire Powers, from the rough

Handsworth neighborhood in Birmingham; and Legionnaire McHenry, from the grim Shankill Road area of Belfast. Jamieson had been in Africa several times before as a weapons specialist with the U.S. Army's 10th Special Forces group. A massive fellow, who looked a bit like a redneck Fred Flintstone, he joined the Legion at age thirty. Powers was almost as tall as Jamieson but not nearly as bulky. A veteran of Britain's 2nd Parachute Regiment, Powers, with his pockmarked face, always seemed to be smirking. Lesser in size, but not in force, was the Northern Irishman McHenry. One wrong look at little McHenry, especially after a night of plenty of pints, and you'd see plenty of trouble. Jamieson, the oldest and most commanding, was the one who usually decided the Crew's evening entertainment plans.

* * *

Djibouti is a busy military post and holds a variety of elite French units. While there is rivalry between Legion regiments, any legionnaire will support another if he is threatened. An inter-army brawl that started with a bar fight between an English legionnaire from Bristol and two Tahitians eventually received notice in left-wing French newspapers and led to courts-martial and the dishonorable discharges of the Wrecking Crew.

C/CH Atherton was on the scene: "Ward, the Bristol guy in *REP*, was in Arta, kind of near this outpost in Oueah. In Arta, the French built a social center open to all." (If a desolate place serving alcohol to men from a variety of rigid and highly competitive military units doesn't sound like trouble—read no further.) Atherton continues: "Ward was a bit drunk and two *taipots* (Tahitians) from 5 *RIAOM*—it's got a lot of *taipots*—got hold of his *képi* and poured beer into it and then Ward went into a fight. He smashed a bottle into one of them's faces, yeah, and the other *taipot* just rammed into him. Just beat him up, like, because he's only small."

Within a few days the story of an English *REP*-man abused by Tahitians in Arta had gotten back to the *DBLE* based in Oueah. After a Saturday afternoon of drinking in the *foyer* on base, British legionnaires decided to go to Arta and start a "Polynesian punch-up." The British legionnaires knew the culprits would be found in a 5 *RIAOM* uniform.

Unable to find any Tahitians, the Brits spotted a group of *Commando Marines* and launched an attack "since a Frenchman's a Frenchman." After a fight that left marines with broken limbs and one with a severe concussion (and eventual coma), the legionnaires carried on drinking and smashed up several bars. The mob sobered up slightly only when "around fifteen minutes after the fight, a GMC (truck) and a van pulled up and, just like, the whole detachment of *Commando Marines* got out with pick-axe handles and the rest of the stuff. The Legion were surrounded, yeah, by about thirty-five to forty guys."

Moments before a new street battle erupted, an armed intervention group (*PQ)* appeared from the 5 *RIAOM*, soon followed by the *adjudant de compagnie* of the legionnaires. The Legion NCO made it clear to the *PQ* leader "to take his boys back into the camp or the Brits would take the guns off them and use them on the *Commando Marines*." So the *adjudant* calls the *PQ* from *REP* and has the Brits escorted in two trucks back to their camp in Oueah. At this point Legion boys at the *REP* base in Arta went "over the wall looking for *Commando Marines* but couldn't find any and were rounded up by their officers and made to *marche canard* (squat-walk) back to camp."

* * *

The next morning Atherton's captain was "almost crying on the parade ground, saying the Brits are wankers and with nothing better to do since the Falklands . . . and he hopes that next time we go out for a fight some of us get killed—that way, it might stop us. He was just whining on the parade ground for about half an hour thinking about his stripes coming and going up in flames." At the end of the officer's tirade, legionnaires had to be held accountable. "They asked for four ringleaders . . . and they got the Wreaking Crew plus one. And all volunteered."

* * *

Another spontaneous act of fighting to salvage Legion honor was instigated by an officer who usually maintains the peace. Atherton recounts:

"We had trouble with the British Royal Marines. A French guy got beaten up by a couple of Royal Marines, so our *SM* (officer from the security department), yeah, he come into the *foyer* where all the Brits hang around, and he said, 'I'll give you fifteen minutes to get out in town. They'll be no *PMs* out in town tonight.' And he goes, 'By the way, a French legionnaire got beaten up, so I hope you'll keep the honor of the Legion up. If I find any Brit in the camp in the next fifteen minutes, he'll be going to jail with a big head.' So that was just like . . . go out and fight."

* * *

Not every legionnaire sent back to France in irons is charged with extreme counts of drunk and disorderly conduct. One soldier appeared before a Legion tribunal in Aubagne and was dishonorably discharged for: "emitting fecal matter in a hotel (Djibouti Hilton) swimming pool" and "in the area of a coffee machine by his barrack" (which I almost stepped in). Patrick "Logs" Logan was a twisted, young London-Irish boy who treated his bowel movements like calling cards, but soon found himself out of the Legion business.

Another legionnaire, Pablo Herrera (name changed), was also returned to France, but in a body bag. While on guard duty, he put his *FAMAS* on full automatic and then put it to his head. Seven bullets tore through his brain, but he was still alive and talking when they took him to the hospital. I had done *instruction* with Herrera and found him to be very strange. There was only one other Spaniard in the section, Martinez-Goy, yet the two never spoke. Martinez-Goy bunked across from me at Castel and was a real go-getter. In fact, by year seventeen of Legion service—much of it in the parachute regiment—he'd risen to the rank of *adjudant-chef* and would command a section of recruits at Castel before retiring in 2004. He was the opposite of Herrera, who was both a comical and pathetic character.

At our first medical exam at *Quartier* La Passet, we laughed at Herrera's oversized and baggy boxer shorts that came to his knees. A bungler, he was also our section's bugler. Given his dark complexion, skinny body, foppish behavior, and ability to torment us with only his instrument, we

English-speaking legionnaires (and later even the NCOs) began to call Herrera "Gunga Din." All of this went through my mind one night at Aubagne when a Welsh corporal recently back from Djibouti pulled bits of bone and dried scalp from his vest pocket and, with a broad smile, told me of the death of Gunga Din.

* * *

The Legion loves to run regardless of the climate or terrain, and the blast-furnace weather of Djibouti does not stop them. Le Grand Bara is a *wadi*—an Arab term for any dried-up expanse. Le Grand Bara is world famous for its awe-inspiring size and dramatic scenery, though most legionnaires would rather forget the place.

Every December the *DBLE* organizes an annual cross-desert run open to all comers. Quite a few regular army soldiers, *Gendarmes*, military wives and girlfriends, tourists, and locals take part in the "fun run." This early morning race covers more than nine miles of straight, flat, arid desert, and every legionnaire available in Djibouti at the time must complete it. The event is held twice on consecutive days so no one on duty can dodge it. From *C/CH* Atherton: "The morale is zero, yeah. You can see the end even before you start, so, you know, all your morale is gone when you get there. We always get Djiboutians in now and again, yeah, because their main man (Ahmed Salleh), who did the marathon in the Olympic Games for Djibouti, is there. He did the Grand Bara in forty-five minutes. That's 15k of desert in forty-five minutes. But the blacks always win it . . . always."

Others I spoke to about Le Grand Bara race noted that, at the starting line, the runner thinks he sees the finish line, but it's actually only a truck, offering refreshments at the halfway mark. Runners comment on how demoralizing it is to have reached only the mid-point and still have the haze from the heat make it impossible to clearly see the finish line on the horizon.

* * *

A disheveled legionnaire, empty canteen in hand, staggering across desert sands is one image some may have of the French Foreign Legion. The story would have him the lone survivor of an Arab or Tuareg attack on his patrol, or perhaps he'd had his fill of sun, sandbags, and sergeants back at Fort Zinderneuf and was deserting.

In reality, few legionnaires desert from posts overseas; finding a way out of a country is difficult and costly. Still, it happens.

* * *

CPL McCue tells how Northern Irishman Terry Quinn, who eventually was to complete fifteen years of Legion service, once tried to quit: "He went overland. Overland in Djibouti. He got down almost to the Somali border. He was heading south. He was going to go through Somalia to Kenya, where he knew people. There was an English guy with him. Well, down there in that rocky desert near Somalia—they had made a distance of about 100K—the English guy went down with heat stroke."

Quinn wanted to continue the trek but knew his friend might die without medical attention. Turning around, the two came to a village they had bypassed. Quinn managed to get in contact with the Legion and transport was sent to retrieve them. The English legionnaire was taken to the hospital, and Quinn spent a couple of nights under watch in the infirmary due to his less critical condition.

Captain Leinfellner, a Legion legend, saw to it that, once Quinn's condition improved slightly, he was sent to prison. "They took him out to a tree that's by the *PM*s there where they used to have a punching bag and so forth. They took him out there and basically hung him from that tree by handcuffs . . . the handcuffs so that they straddled the tree . . . just about high enough so that he hung. Anyway, they left him hanging there for a day and a night and another day. He was underneath the tree, so there was a degree of shade, but it was still pretty damn hot. During that course of the time when he was hanging there, whenever one of the more vicious *PM*s would go by or anything, they'd give him a quick dig or, you know, if they had a *matraque* (police baton) handy . . . just whack him in the gut with that . . . amusement. But he stuck it out. He didn't start crying, and never broke with it."

* * *

Another Djiboutian desertion concerns a lovesick Frenchman only recently arrived in country. Had his well-intentioned girlfriend not telephoned, maybe the two would have married, as planned. LFC Griffiths explains: "There's this French guy, and his girlfriend was in France, and he was really pissed off. He finished his *instruction* and just went into the 3rd Company, which was like real *gateaux-gateaux* (numbskulls). He had *permission* (leave) and managed to catch a boat to Kenya. There's a lot of rumors going around Djibouti that there's an ex-legionnaire, you know, living in Djibouti, that can arrange you safe passage on a boat for about 4,000 francs. I can't say for certain, but these were the rumors. So this guy, when he got to Kenya, sent a telegram to his girlfriend and asked her to send him some money so he could fly over."

Unfortunately for our Romeo . . . "What the girlfriend did is ring the embassy in Kenya, which just happened to have an ex-colonel of the 2 *REP*. So she said, not knowing, yeah, 'I've got a boyfriend. He's in the Legion in Djibouti and I've just got a telegram. He's in Kenya, and I think he's in trouble.'" The former Legion officer calmed the girlfriend and assured her he would take care of the matter. When the deserter came to the embassy to report his passport stolen, he was directed to the colonel's office where "he was told about how his girlfriend rang up and then given a big morale boosting speech about not deserting . . . facing the music. And the next day two *PMs* came over in a Transall (military air transport) and, like, took him away, and he got forty-days jail."

MAYOTTE

"Mayotte, for me, was just a dirty tropical island. I don't know. You get the impression they're dirty, but I'm sure they're clean by their standards."

—*LÉGIONNAIRE PREMIÈRE CLASSE* WALTON

Similar in appearance to Tahiti, Mayotte differs most notably in its standard of living. Whereas Tahiti is a final destination for fun-in-the-sun American, Australian, and French tourists, Mayotte is merely a stopover for French military units. The small, volcanic island belongs to the Comores Archipelago, which was discovered by the French in the nineteenth century and has always been valued for its strategic location in the Indian Ocean. Mayotte lies 185 nautical miles due northwest of Madagascar and in the middle of the all-important shipping lanes of the Mozambique Channel. Supertankers and aircraft carriers too large for the Suez Canal must pass between the African mainland and Madagascar and within range of the French military on Mayotte. In the mid-1970s, France let the four islands that form the Archipelago vote on whether to remain French. Three of the Comores quickly opted for independence, but Mayotte, even after a second vote, stunned France by declaring its wish to remain French territory. Nevertheless, a 2009 referendum, in which 95 percent of those on the loyal island voted to replace their French *TOM (Territoire Outre-Mer)* status with a *DOM (Departement Outre-Mer),* made the *DOM* designation effective in 2011, and Mayotte one of France's five overseas departments.

Many living in France are not too clear on *DOM/TOM* meanings. *TOM,* or Overseas Territory, and *DOM,* or Overseas Department, are distinctions the French Foreign Office has made regarding overseas possessions since the term "colony" fell out of favor. A *DOM* has representation in the French National Assembly and is generally a richer and more integral part of France than a *TOM.* For example, Reunion Island and Guiana are *DOMs. DOM* status awards better social welfare benefits to inhabitants and the right to vote in French local and national elections.

The attraction of living in Mayotte is not lost on many in the region. Making it to the island can be the first step toward passage to France and the European Union. As such, the once sleepy island has become a site of clandestine immigration and conflict with French law enforcement. In 2018, an Ecuadoran *sergent* from the *13ème DBLE* was killed in an operation against a gang of human smugglers. France continues to be vigilant and, of course, will use the Legion as needed.

* * *

Mayotte's population of 260,000 is a mix of nationalities, mostly African. The island of Reunion, to the east of Madagascar, is the richer cousin, home to wealthy French mainlanders and playground to Club Med vacationers. Late model Porsches and Ferraris zip along the island's modern highways. Comoro, a nearby island, was the scene of no fewer than four coups or attempted coups by ex-French Marine and old-school African mercenary, "Colonel" Bob Denard. The Legion has no regiment on Mayotte but billets a permanent detachment of 282 men. Various mainland regiments will send units for a four-month tour on the island, in addition to rotating detachments of regular armed forces and *Gendarmerie*. Unlike Tahiti and Guiana, which contribute to, and directly affect, France's foreign policy, Mayotte is one of a handful of scattered and neglected French possessions. Electricity and telecommunications were fully established on the island only during the 1990s.

* * *

While in *1er REC*, *B/CH* Donlon did a four-month tour on Mayotte: "Well, I mean let's face it . . . they're about fifty years behind what's going on here. When I was there (1985) they didn't have television, telephones, you know, practically nothing . . . apart from that, they live in mud huts. From what I saw, the French do nothing for them. Basically, the French are there to have a base. They do nothing for the locals."

LFC Walton, *6ème Régiment étranger de génie* (*6ème REG*/Sixth Foreign Engineering Regiment—since 1999 called *1er REG*), on his first impressions of Mayotte and the locals in 1990: "Strange . . . very different and black. All black and extremely dirty, I thought. I had the impression . . . dirty place. I never experienced anything like it. Still living in mud houses, quite a lot of them, yeah. Mayotte for me was just a dirty tropical island. I don't know. You get the impression they're dirty, but I'm sure they're clean by their standards."

* * *

However, not all legionnaires see Mayotte as a filthy and unpleasant island. Most see the assignment as the only truly cushy overseas post, with world-class fishing and SCUBA diving opportunities available at very low cost. In 1990, LFC Van Heek volunteered for an eighteen-month tour. He fell in love with the island and, later, married one of its women. After service with the *REP* and several tours in Africa, Van Heek notes, "Mayotte was regarded upon by almost any legionnaire as being holidays. It was holidays. Imagine a coral island being sixty kilometers long, twenty to twenty-five kilometers large, surrounded by the biggest closed barrier reef in the world which is a circle the diameter of 220 kilometers. Under a climate where it is never cold . . . with no strain from any wanton neighbors . . . just being a very tranquil piece of France overseas."

Van Heek on work and play on the island: "You almost have the feeling not to be a soldier. You do your work from 06:00, working without a break, until 13:00, and, then, you're ready . . . finished. But then you have an obliged *sieste* until 15:30, and, after that, you can go out the gate. But you are supposed to be there at 05:00 the next morning for *appel*, which means you get up at half past four. In the rainy season, with its 98 percent relative heat, weather between 9 a.m. and 5 p.m. is not supportable. And I was judged very lucky because I worked in the radio transmission center with conditioned air because we had a computer-steered apparatus. We had one maneuver one week a year, right, and when there were maneuvers on Madagascar, Comores, or Reunion, they had to look for volunteers among the ninety of us."

Van Heek adds: "And in Mayotte, the AIDS contamination percent-age under the female *sou-sou* (prostitute) population is known to be not over 3%, which compared to Central Africa 80% of the whores under Bangui and Bouar, is quite good."

In fact, duty was so casual that Van Heek and a friend were able to rent a house in town. "I found a mate, an English mate, and we got a house. For the Legion this is incredible stuff. It was simple—a concrete floor, concrete walls, windows without glass … simply iron bars, a roof of corrugated iron, two doors—and that was our house. There was water and a telephone and a huge garden with some banana trees. And this was our house, where we should pay 2,200 *francs* per month, which was very expensive for Mayotte standards."

* * *

Whereas many legionnaires were grateful to be on the island, Van Heek tells of one co-worker from Scotland who was not at all happy with his situation. Granger, a former British Royal Marine based at *2ème REI* in the *métropole*, had requested transfer to Djibouti for its famed commando course. Instead, he was sent to the radio transmission center in Mayotte. Bored and unchallenged, he plotted his escape from paradise.

"So, at a certain moment when he had his balls full, there were volun-teers being asked for Reunion and he volunteered. He took all his money from the bank. Stuffed his personal belongings he couldn't take with him and sent them by civil transport back to Scotland, which all can be done. I mean, Mayotte is so relaxed nobody takes care of a legionnaire sending about fifty kilos to Scotland. As soon as they arrived at the airport, he fucked off. Took a plane back to France and from France took a plane to Scotland. He didn't have any problems and wrote me back as soon as he was in Scotland. My captain was very surprised that somebody wanted to desert from Mayotte because it's holidays here. Yes, that's the first deser-tion from Mayotte, I'm sure."

TAHITI

"Lots of radiation around. We were tested all the time."

—*LÉGIONNAIRE PREMIÈRE CLASSE* POULSEN

French Polynesia . . . where Melville, Stevenson, Gaugin, Renoir, Picasso, and a host of other authors and artists found solitude and inspiration. Where careless breezes still caress the skin and multicolored sunsets dazzle the eyes. Where soothing emerald-blue waters entice lazy Club Med vacationers. Where hula girls in the evening *loai* bare their firm bronze breasts, and the flaccid voice of Don Ho has never droned. All this and fresh baguettes.

Truly paradise, this French territory comprises a large expanse of ocean and islands, nearly twice the size of the neighboring American territory. Annexed in the 1800s as a classic colonial land grab, the island has since hosted a military force ready to defend this faraway bit of France. Until the late 1990s, the *5ème Régiment étranger* (5*ème* *RE*/5th Foreign Regiment) was France's primary armed contingent in the region. The *5ème RE* mission has varied over the years, as have French reasons for remaining on the islands.

A French nuclear force independent of NATO was begun by President de Gaulle in 1958, and some 200 nuclear tests, including forty atmospheric explosions, took place on several islands in French Polynesia off and on until 1996. Nuclear tests were moved underground or underwater until President Chirac stopped any form of nuclear testing in 1997. Earlier, however, Chirac had restarted underground testing in 1995 only to retreat soon after in the face of world condemnation (protests or not, the Gaullist Chirac did complete the five tests he said would be carried out). As of today, France has not renewed its nuclear arms testing program in Polynesia. Before being disbanded, the *5ème RE* had guarded the controversial test sites, but it later continued with construction projects (building an "emergency" airfield on a remote island) and providing island security as needed. Today, however, the Legion stations only a token force of soldiers on the islands, mostly administrative types attached to the *1er RE.*

* * *

In the past, most local legionnaires visited the capital, Papeete, on leave every third month, as normally they were sequestered on remote islands during their service. A two-year tour in French Polynesia would take the legionnaire to some of the most scenic and undisturbed islands left in the world. Mururoa, however, is not one of them.

The circular island, with a 35-miles perimeter, is solid volcanic and carbonate rock and has a population (almost entirely male) of only 2,000. Due to radiation, women and children were evacuated in the 1970s. France has deemed the island safe only for some natives, highly compensated civil servants, and her most expendable soldiers. LFC Poulsen remembers: "Mururoa was a pretty shit island." Not one to mince words, he adds, "Man, I fucking hate that place. I'll never go back there again. It's flat. Flat like a table. There's nothing. No women, no kids. Have a wank, you know what I mean, or fuck a transvestite, you know." As Poulsen ages, he may want to take advantage of Denmark's quality health care. "We worked with concrete, blocking the holes made by nuclear explosions with concrete, and also built an airport. Lots of radiation around. We were tested all the time."

FRENCH GUIANA

"He was sitting next to me on the plane. He looked like Jimmy Sommerville ... a skinny guy ... red-blond hair ... and he was just looking down. And the look in his eyes, I remember. And he was just repeating, 'I'm going to die there.'"

—*CAPORAL* MAZOWSKI

In what army but the Legion could a young man join to get away from it all and be sent to *Quartier* Forget in the jungles of South America? At the end of the war in Algeria, the *3ème Régiment étranger d'infanterie* (*3ème REI*/3rd Foreign Infantry Regiment) was based in Madagascar, mostly in the strategic northern inlet of Diego Suarez. The *3ème REI* now calls

Quartier Forget in Kourou, French Guiana, home. Today, France entrusts this most decorated Legion regiment (formed in 1920) to guard her last colonial outpost on the mainland of the Americas. More important than symbolic, however, is France's much-touted Ariane space project. The site in Guiana offers France and the European Union the only reliable alternative to NASA for launching their various spacecraft—Ariane, Soyouz, and Vega. (As political winds blow, Kazakhstan and China are possible European alternatives.) France's small space program had been in southern Algeria, but the victorious *FLN* could not be persuaded by de Gaulle to let the scientists and technicians stay. Lured to her former penal colony by its isolation, proximity to the equator (hence less gravitational pull on rockets), and relatively calm native population, France sent the *3ème REI* to the jungle country in 1973. Guiana remains, however, in a Second World state.

In the early 1970s, France tried to homestead off much of the jungle land to mainland French but had few takers. Guiana remains largely underdeveloped and unknown to French people, apart from those two extremes—rocket scientists and legionnaires. Not eager to lose any of its considerable high-tech investment to an independence movement, France has made sure that this South American department is fully dependent upon her for even such items as sugar and coffee—both of which could easily be produced in Guiana at less cost. (French Guiana, however, is the world's leading exporter of orchids.)

* * *

While many legionnaires have no desire to do a tour in Guiana, and some are sent there on disciplinary grounds, others do volunteer. Even then, many eventually have misgivings about their Rambo-itis. *Caporal* Mazowski recalls arriving from Paris: "As we flew into Cayenne airport, I remember seeing this big river . . . just like you can see in the movies . . . like a snake, a giant snake just winding through the forest. And a French guy who was with me, who was sent to Guiana—I volunteered—he was sitting next to me on the plane . . . he looked like Jimmy Sommerville . . . a skinny guy . . . red-blond hair . . . and he was just looking down. And the look in his eyes, I remember. And he was just repeating, 'I'm going to die there.'"

The reluctant jungle soldier had been in Mazowski's section during *instruction* at La Passet. Mazowski remembers the day the unlucky Frenchman, disliked and marked by those in command, learned of his new assignment. "You know at Castel when you go in the room with the colonels and everyone? And they tell you where you're going to go? Well, he was in front of me. I was outside the door, and I could just hear, *'3ème REI?'* and then, *'Non, mon Colonel, non. Pas le 3ème REI...non!'* And he threw the door open, and tears were coming down his eyes and he runs out. And I just looked at him like, 'What's going on?'"

Unlike his French *instruction* mate, the American Mazowski was to complete his two-year tour in Guiana. He explains why he chose the *3ème REI* over other regiments: "I volunteered and they couldn't understand why. I wanted to go there because of the jungle . . . because of Vietnam. I couldn't understand how guys cracked up, so I wanted to see what it was like."

* * *

At one time, Guiana was so popular with Anglo-Nordic—especially, German legionnaires—that the regiment was known as the *3ème REIch*. Even today, the regiment's song, "Anne-Marie" is sung in German. Legion high command, however, has greatly restricted the number of Northern Europeans in Guiana, ostensibly due to their propensity to contract blood and skin diseases far more readily than their Southern European, Asian, and African counterparts. The actual reason fewer legionnaires of certain nationalities came to Guiana in the late 1980s was not medical, but rather the fallout from a 1985 incident involving a drunk and, later, dead English legionnaire.

* * *

Though no longer mandatory, altering a legionnaire's name and identity upon joining is still possible. If the recruit wants this anonymity, the

Legion will usually switch the month and day of the birth date and take away one or two years from the year of birth. Country of birth will often change, as will the names and birth dates of parents. Finally, the prospective legionnaire, himself, will be given (at the sometimes imaginative discretion of the recruiting station's NCO on duty) a new name. When one Castel detachment of thirteen new boys arrived at the *REC*, the roll call had the following four surnames: Castro, Paul, Fidel, and McCartney. It was no surprise, then, that Johnny Carson should turn up in the jungles of Guiana. Mazowski, who came to Guiana in late 1985, tells how the former Tonight Show's Legion namesake caused a *bordel* that was featured in the international press. "From what I heard, there was an English guy named Johnny Carson and he'd gotten into a fight with some black guys in front of the Tropicana disco. Tropicana was one of the few discos we were allowed to go to. OK, Johnny Carson is fighting with some blacks. They beat him up. He's unconscious, and they leave him on the beach, and the tide comes in. It drowns him."

Carson's death would be avenged. One evening, a few weeks later, an unusually large number of English-speaking legionnaires left camp. All were in uniform, but wearing boots, not shoes, and many were carrying *sac para* (tough, lightweight, medium-sized green hold-alls—the Louis Vuitton of Legion luggage) with *matraques* (night sticks/clubs). The plan was to visit the Vieux Bourg—the old part of Kourou—where the night clubs and bars are located. At some point, "they were all sitting in a bar ... everyone was enjoying themselves ... and then somebody got up and pulled out a *matraque* and just started to destroy the place. And then all the *matraques* came out. They just started from one end of the street to the other. Just destroyed everything. Cars, people, shops, everything."

Outnumbered, the *PMs* simply stood by. Even by Legion standards, the mood was too violent and intense. "These were, maybe, 200 guys. I mean it was everybody. Kind of like a way to get their aggressions out. Mostly Brits, Germans, and Vikings (Scandinavians), definitely."

* * *

Essential to the kind of organized riot the Johnny Carson affair inspired is a solid and loyal infrastructure of certain nationalities. In no regiment except the *REP* was the *mafia anglais* (English mafia) so strong as in *3ème REI*. The core of the mafia is the English who preside over the rest of the UK legionnaires, as well as the assorted colonial shock troops mustered from North America, Australia, New Zealand, and South Africa. Also welcome to the mafia for their size and spirit are Scandinavians and Dutch. Germans usually stick to the *Deutsch*-speaking side of the *foyer* but are also welcomed in limited numbers.

Tradition dictates that once an English-speaker arrives at his new regiment he must "pass" the mafia. Part of the test will be drinking with this ex-pat gang of hooligans and holding his own. If the new boy doesn't pass, he will not be accepted (or protected) by any English-speaker. He then not only will have to work with the French but also socialize with them, too. Understandably, most anglophones try to pass even if, as in Guiana, it means doing the outrageous.

CPL Mazowski describes "*stage* (course) drains": "If you could imagine a gutter which was from one end about two and a half feet deep by one and a half feet wide, and it was thirty-five feet long. And it got smaller at the end, so it was maybe six inches deep—it became like a wedge shape. And a guy would start at the deep end and he would crawl in the drains. There was like a grille over it . . . a grille you could take off to brush the drains. He would crawl through this drain while members of the English mafia would stand there and piss on him, puke on him, shit on him—not necessarily in that order—but by the time he came out he'd be covered in piss, puke, and shit and a full-fledged member of the English mafia."

* * *

The *mafia anglais* is not solely a brainless booze-and-bash club, however. Per-Inge Persson from Sweden describes what the mafia meant to him as a new legionnaire at the *1er REC* in Orange: "People tell you all the time, 'That guy's OK, he's English.'" Even if he's not English. English-speaker, that's the important thing. So, they stick together. So you know exactly who you can trust and who you can talk to. I thought this was good with the mafia system because you know where you stood. You know exactly where to go if you had problems."

The system works well, but in terms of unit cohesion, drawbacks exist. "You never had much contact with the French. I had very few French friends. I had some, yeah. I should say there was two or three . . . the majority were English-speaking or German."

* * *

Both Kourou and Cayenne are along Guiana's mangrove and mosquito-covered coast. When not stationed as guards at the Ariane launch site, units of the *3ème REI* move to the interior for jungle patrols and training. All legionnaires in a combat company must complete the tortuous *mission profonde*, a forty-day, full-gear trek in the jungle involving land and river navigation. Forty days with virtually no resupply or contact, other than radio, with hikes from one interior base camp to another is a one-of-a-kind test of endurance and perseverance. Every member of the patrol must be mentally and physically ready to face this march. In recent years, however, these deep jungle missions have been halved to twenty-day treks, largely due to increased activity at the space center. In fact, since 2003, all but a small contingent of the regiment is mobilized to serve their primary function, to guard the vast perimeter surrounding the Ariane launch site *(Opération Titan)*.

Apart from jungle training, these Legion treks contribute to other French surveillance operations along a Brazilian border area rife with illegal immigrants, especially clandestine gold miners. In 2019, media reported more than 7,000 gold prospectors operating in some 400 sites scattered across the French-owned jungle. The illegal profit is staggering. Nearly ten tons of gold, worth half a billion dollars, is extracted annually from Guiana. The miners are armed and violent, with firefights between them and Legion or *Gendarme* units becoming more and more common. Begun in 2008, France's *Opérations Anaconda* and *Harpie* have sought to thwart illegal border activity, though not without casualties. In 2012, two French Marines *(9ème RIMa)* and one *Gendarme* were killed in action while several police and legionnaires were wounded by these gold-seeking raiders.

* * *

The *parcours du combatant (PC)* in Guiana has been adapted to the jungle terrain and consists of obstacles a patrol might have to overcome, with most everyone in knee-deep mud. Teamwork is essential, and officers carefully note the legionnaires' responses to fatigue and stress. At no other Legion regiment is the *PC* so often run as at the *3ème REI*. The *PC* and several other jungle training facilities are located at the *CEFE (centre d'entraînement en forêt équatoriale* or Equatorial Forest Training Center). U.S. Navy SEAL teams and Marine Recon units visit the *CEFE* periodically and leave with lifetime memories of, and great respect for, Foreign Legion training. CPL Mazowski shakes his head and recalls the ordeal: "The hardest thing was the new assault course that they have in Guiana. It's seven obstacles and it took us one hour to do seven obstacles with a ten-kilo sack on, full of rocks. Never . . . never in my entire life have I been so physically fucked. You know, when you use your arms so much that you can't grip anymore—just tremble."

The *PC* can wear a man down on many levels. "It was up and down walls, and you're covered in mud with a ten-kilo sack on, having to go over slippery logs, and at the end of it, you have to run up a hill over a big tree—and the tree is six-foot round or so—and you have to climb over that. I mean, never have I ever experienced that feeling of where life didn't really matter anymore. I would have been happy if someone were to have killed me right there. Total exhaustion—physically . . . spiritually."

Years later, the grueling obstacle course remains vivid for Mazowski. "And the other guys' faces, I mean, it was incredible. Never in my entire life will I forget it. There was so much frustration because your mind wanted to do these things, but your body wouldn't work. You know, you felt like, really, just breaking down and crying because there was nothing you could do about it."

* * *

When not hacking through the bush with his *coupe-coupe* (machete), a legionnaire might enjoy plowing through a different kind of bush at the regimental *pouffe*. Since 1975, the *BMC (Bordel Militaire de Campagne)* has been phased out on the mainland of France—but it still exists (unofficially) in her overseas territories. Most of the whores who work in the Legion's brothel in Guiana are Brazilian or Colombian. The *pouffe* is popular enough with legionnaires that the girls have arranged their own "layaway" plan. CPL Mazowski explains: "At the *pouffe* there was credit for 1,000 *francs* for legionnaires and 1,500 *francs* for corporals. And a screw, one screw, that means if you pop your nuts once . . . that was 100 *francs*. Even on credit, they took it directly from your pay."

Legion brothels house some of the cheapest and basest forms of entertainment, setting loose a wide range of emotion and behavior. Some staid house regulars approach everything in a matter-of-fact way, while others revel in an atmosphere they find more carnival than carnal. For sure, a *pouffe* night can be "magical": Drinks might appear on a bill, yet not have been served; the pretty girl you paid for can disappear and reappear as her mother; and, for the right price, a young girl can lose her virginity several times in one night. Nevertheless, regardless of deceitful or lackluster girls, stale perfume, and moist sheets, alcohol animates everyone. In fact, no one knows what craziness might happen next. Each nationality will find its own corner and drink the girls pretty in a race against sobriety and a sex-less evening.

Often more enjoyable for the girls, however, is watching the spontaneous combustion of legionnaires at leisure. While a rapid turnover of paying customers is preferred by the house madam, many of the girls take more pleasure in socializing with the cast of alcohol-sodden Legion characters assembled. Though seldom understanding the slang (unless sexual) or accents of legionnaires, the girls seem to enjoy the noise and nonsense of their foreign military clientele. Bawdy drinking songs and silly games, as well as dancing skills, are amusingly noted by these amateur brothel anthropologists.

Not exclusive to a Legion love shack, and seen wherever frivolity, exhibitionism, and a newspaper come together, is the "Dance of the Flaming Asshole" (also dubbed the "Dance of the Zulu Warrior"). Without question, one's innocence and inhibition are memorably abandoned when dancing for a cheering crowd with pants at the ankle and a hastily rolled newspaper stuffed in the anus. This already madcap dance quite naturally picks up the tempo once the legionnaire's swinging newspaper-tail is lit on fire. For many a discriminating audience, this particular Legion light show, however entertaining, is over too soon. *Pas de problème,* a solution was found in a brothel in French Guiana.

Told to me by a *PM* who was there, the following story has been dubbed "The Candle Scandal":

Many Legion moons ago, the English mafia assembled in fine form one Saturday evening in a popular Kourou *pouffe.* The sex and samba already in the air that night were soon to mix with Anglo-Saxon absurdity. A half-naked and half-crocked line of English legionnaires sang and swayed to an infectious Brazilian beat. The girls clapped and cheered as one particularly nimble Anglo undressed and scampered on all fours among patrons on the busy dance floor.

Tired of having his rear end slapped by fellow drunken legionnaires, the Englishman decided on something that would continue to draw himself attention, yet safe-keep his kiester. The imaginative Brit inserted a candle in his ring piece and had a friend light the wick. Not a flaming newspaper, but a long slow burning candle now had everyone's attention. Unfortunately, Legion *PMs* had already been called to the brothel by the no-nonsense madam afraid of a real fire. A path was cleared and everything stopped as the stolid, sober *PMs* strode toward the oblivious ass-shaking fire dancer. An English *PM* bellowed, "That's enough of that, then" and brusquely yanked out the candle. The *PM* just as deftly turned the candle around and jammed the still lit end into the legionnaire's wax-speckled bottom.

My *PM* friend told me the English were easy to apprehend that night, offering little resistance due to the drink and laughter surrounding the dance. This story and its moral were passed along from regiment to regiment like one of Aesop's fables. It seemed true what the officer corps had long warned: Legionnaires on leave should not burn the candle at both ends.

* * *

On a longer *permission,* a legionnaire might spend a holiday on Devil's Island. Closed since 1946, the infamous penal colony is now home to a small museum and several bungalow-style motels. Others will choose cheap "hotels" run by Chinese in Kourou or Cayenne as a base to forage for food, drink, and women. The hotel operators are wary of renting to legionnaires, but the local market doesn't give them many options. Prices are raised and expectations lowered when legionnaires check in. Mazowski describes this typical scene of legionnaires on *permission:* "My second *PLD* (*permission de longue durée*) was with Stratton and Redding. We rented a hotel room for three and we bought some *taft* (local sugar cane rum). And we bought these Danishes to eat, but, after drinking a while, put them on the floor to walk on like land mines."

With the rum finished, they opened bottles of beer. It was agreed not to wreck the room—to drink the beers and then go into town. "I finished my bottle of beer. Then I threw the bottle in the bathroom, and that's when it started. After we finished the bottles we started throwing them around and eventually there was broken bottles everywhere." Before passing out around 9 p.m., Mazowski had fallen onto a floor littered with broken glass and cut himself in several places. His friends were also drunk but put their comrade in a safe position so he wouldn't choke on his vomit. The two legionnaires then went into town for more alcohol and amusement.

The American who came to Guiana to experience a bit of Vietnam felt many sensations that drunken evening: "We had been burning incense and playing the soundtrack to *Apocalypse Now* because we used to call Cayenne "Saigon," and they said when they came back and they opened the door . . . the smell of stale beer, of sweat, and blood. And for that, which was tradition in Guiana, the first one to pass out got one eyebrow shaved off. So off it went. I got some really weird looks when we went back to ranks."

* * *

The normal desire of legionnaires with any bit of ambition is to become a corporal. Those who wear the *galons* (stripes) of a *caporal* in the Legion have truly entered the Legion family. The rank enables a soldier to have a sense of command and authority; he, now, is no longer a follower but a leader. And everyone in the Legion knows what it takes to become a corporal. The rank is not awarded automatically owing to length of service or conduct (as is now true with LFC). A legionnaire must be well regarded before his superiors will even think of sending him on the demanding corporal's course, the *CME (Certificat Militaire Elementaire)*.

A Legion *CME*, which is a two-month endurance run, tests the physical, mental, and emotional strength of those in training, and those in charge are looking for those who stumble. A variety of demands are placed on the candidates during their two-month ordeal, such as using more advanced military weapons and tactics, developing teamwork and leadership skills, and providing medical care in the field, even rules from the Geneva Convention are to be mastered. The instruction is more rigorous than basic training because the men involved are now acclimated to French and Legion expectations. A *CME* can happen in any country where the Legion is permanently based and under any climate or conditions. One of the most difficult courses takes place in the jungles of French Guiana. Here American Daniel Mazowski underwent a 36-hour trial—repeated in some form in the Legion *CME* worldwide and designed to subject candidates to maximum levels of stress and fatigue.

Adding to the misery of training in suffocating heat among poisonous snakes and spiders, with blood-sucking bats swooping over piranha- and parasite-infested rivers, were two other creatures, the pair of sergeants in charge of Mazowski's section. These NCOs were "probably the two most hated men in Guiana: SGT Roudil, an ex-boxer from Marseille, and SGT Kalavich, the flathead (Yugoslav) . . . ball-breakers like you've never seen."

* * *

Mazowski's training started at daybreak and was filled with non-stop activity until the generator was turned off at 11 p.m. At 10:45 one night, Kalavich formed the cadre of thirty or so on the parade square and announced, "Boys, tonight is *La Nuit des Longs Couteaux* ('The Night of the Long Knives'). In fifteen minutes the lights go out. At one o'clock in the morning we're going to have an inspection of the rooms. I want them clean. *Nickel!* (Spotless!) Everything correct. Inspection of the rooms is to be on the *place d'armes* (parade field). I want everything taken out of the rooms and put on the parade square to the centimeter. I will come out, and I will measure everything. Then I'm going to go in the rooms and they'd better be scrubbed clean. *Nickel!* Everything has to be clean. When the lights go out you can start."

At 11 p.m., the section was dismissed, and Mazowski and his English bunkmates got to work. Lockers were emptied and beds taken apart. Two from his room moved everything downstairs and began setting up the floor plan on the parade field—measuring everything in detail—with pocket flashlights. Two others remained to clean the candlelit room with the little equipment available. The team moved fast—"we had the *pêche*"—and was in the lead. Soon, 1 a.m. arrived, and all were standing at attention in their clean, empty rooms. Kalavich made the inspection and then reported, "Boys, the rooms look fine, but the parade square looks kind of dirty. At 3 a.m. we'll have a review of the parade square. All the lockers and beds have to be back in the rooms."

The parade square was large "maybe 50 meters by 30 meters wide." The wanna-be corporals had to use their World War II vintage shovels to uproot weeds and find rakes to smooth the dirt. "Luckily it wasn't raining out because if it was raining we'd still have to do it in the rain." Finally, it's time for the 3 a.m. parade square inspection. SGT Kalavich sarcastically commented, "Parade square looks fine, but you know you got those brooms dirty when you put the beds and lockers back in. I'm going to have a review of the rooms, and it had better be clean.'"

Mazowski spoke for all the tormented corporals-in-training: "I'm like, 'God damn!' And by this time, you are physically and mentally fucked. I'd never seen guys stand up and sleep and clean at the same time. There were some twenty-five of us, and there were two that really cracked . . . one guy was from the music section, a German, and another guy was from the *bureau major* (company office). He was French."

By 4:30 a.m., everything was again arranged on the parade square. While waiting for Kalavich's room inspection, Mazowski and bunkmate made the mistake of sitting on their beds.

Spotted by Kalavich, who "had been sneaking around the whole night . . . very quiet . . . always sneaking around and watching," the two were immediately punished. Kalavich made them run to the sand pit—about 100 meters—and fill their back packs with sand. Mazowski remembers, "And, for the whole time, we had to wear this back-pack while we were picking up the lockers, beds, the works. The *caporal du jour* (a fellow trainee who was the immediate supervisor of the cleaning and moving process) was even in more trouble. He was wearing two sacks full of sand. One on the front and one on the back because Kalavich used to love to bust this guy's nuts."

At daylight, "The Night of the Long Knives" à la French Guiana came to an end. The section continued with shooting, running, and classroom lessons "but the ones who had to have the sacks of sand . . . we wore those till 11 o'clock that night. We did everything with them on." The extra-oufitted Mazowski remembers sitting on a metal stool, not allowed to slouch and "when everything was quiet, when we were studying, you could just hear slow, strained wheezing because the weight pulled your shoulders down and pulled your chest back. So you just concentrated on breathing. And just, like, looking at each other and looking at your watch and the time's going backwards."

* * *

Sergeants Roudil and Kalavich did their best to break the section over the next two months, but only two left—due to injuries. Daniel Mazowski graduated fourth out of twenty-three candidates.

* * *

Love it or hate it, the Legion instills a strong and lasting camaraderie within its ranks. This might take on the raucous kind of brotherhood that is the *mafia anglais* or may appear, as the officer corps hopes, at the company and platoon level, as in this example of a permanent display of support for a well-liked platoon member who had gotten himself into serious trouble.

Willy Gee is typical of the many British in the Legion. An extreme Scottish nationalist, he had served in Northern Ireland with the Royal Fusiliers. As a reminder of God and country, the red-headed Gee had tattooed on his back the Red Hand of Ulster with a small Union Jack and St. Andrew's cross on either side. A good soldier, he was also a good drinker. SGT Roudil was the duty sergeant the day Legionnaire Gee was missing from ranks. A punctual and zealous NCO, he ran to the barracks to fetch him.

CPL Mazowski was there: "You heard some screaming and yelling and then Roudil comes down the stairs carrying Gee over his shoulder." Gee had polished off a bottle of whiskey and was comatose. Mazowski and others in ranks raised a cheer for the *steif*-man (drunk) legionnaire. Gee was taken to the infirmary, and "they were sticking needles in his scrotum to try to wake him up—in typical Legion fashion. They finally sent him to the hospital. They woke him up. Got him out of a slight coma and they put him in jail—in typical Legion fashion."

Demoted in rank and dejected in spirit, Willy eventually turned himself around. He stopped drinking. He ran and lifted weights. He ironed his clothes daily—even ironing his paper money.

The platoon was so impressed with this *pêche* "that quite a few of the guys got tattoos on their left shoulders written 'Red Willy' . . . kind of in memory or solidarity with the guy."

* * *

Spring break for American college students is an annual ritual that celebrates youth and excess from the beaches and bars of Cancun, Mexico, and South Padre Island, Texas, to the fleshpots of Florida. Aware of the spring migrations south, many airlines have charter flights or special rates to entice students to fly with them, often directly to their fun-in-the-sun destination. Cynthia Lott's spring break trip took some unusual turns, however. The flight to visit her boyfriend proves that love can triumph over stale peanuts and jetlag. Cynthia flew from Sacramento, California, to San Francisco to Chicago to Newark, New Jersey, to Miami to San Juan, Puerto Rico, to Martinique, to Guadeloupe, and, finally, eighteen hours after her start in California, to Cayenne, French Guiana, and the waiting arms of her *beau Légionnaire*, Robert "Cool Hand" Lewis.

Cynthia and Robert started dating as high school students in Yuba City, California. They stayed in touch during his *sejour* in the Netherlands and after his enlistment in France. She was sure he would quit the Legion within a year and return to California. However, determined to stay, the closest CPL Lewis got to northern California was the northern coast of French Guiana. While on her two week "spring break," Cynthia met three drunk English legionnaires, two Japanese samurai, and one French Rat.

* * *

French Guiana was the first poor country that Cynthia had ever visited, and her impressions are still vivid: "Taxi drivers drive through blind inter- sections forty miles per hour with one hand on the Bible, one hand on the wheel. I was ready to get out of the taxis, but really the only way to get around was with taxis."

So, maybe, relaxing over a coffee and croissant breakfast at a local café without worrying about taxis or other possible calamity might calm her nerves. But as Cynthia observed, "At a café there was a woman who had a gold penis around her neck and I was trying to figure out what the hell that was all about. It turned out to be it's to ward off the evil eye." Cyn- thia the college student got an education. "Yeah, it was just like the Wild, Wild, West. It was real Third World. It's like time just moved very slowly there. I've traveled to Europe and throughout the United States, so it was kind of an eye-opening experience."

It was difficult finding a room for Cynthia near the Legion base because the East Indian and Chinese proprietors of the several small hotels in the area were wary of any girl with a Legion connection. Only a few weeks earlier, a Legion-run prostitution ring had been broken up in one hotel and the manager, though unaware of any illegal activity, had to pay a substantial fine. After a careful screening of Rob and her, Cynthia was allowed a room for a limited time. She soon absorbed more of the local scene.

* * *

Since it was her spring break, Lewis took Cynthia to the best spot in town—the beaches of Devil's Island. On one of the three islands that make up the former penal colony, a woman from Toulon opened a small hotel (using the guards' quarters as bungalows) and welcomes the few tourists who visit Guiana. It was on these infamous islands ten miles off the coast of Guiana, nicknamed "The Green Hell" and "The Dry Guillotine," that Cynthia met many of Rob's friends. "We stayed on St. Joseph (island). There was no escaping the Legion in French Guiana. It wasn't like France where you can just go to any of the Mediterranean, like, resort towns. Especially, you know, camping on the island where, at five or six o'clock in the morning, the Legion ran by singing and shouting out."

Having a pretty, white girl visiting him made CPL Lewis a very popular man. Cool Hand (so named because he bucked authority) was soon introducing the shy Cynthia to all his eager friends. Cynthia first met a number of English legionnaires "with accents I could hardly understand" at a gathering in town. "Jack Gaston had to leave England because he was a car thief, and things were getting too hot for him—that's why he joined the Legion. I also met Redding, Castleton, and Madison, and they were all very drunk. Redding started going on and off about his girlfriend. He had his arm on my shoulder and started getting real touchy-feely and he knocked over his beer and that kind of pretty well called attention to what was going on. Then Castleton took his shirt off and started touching his nipples and making crazy sounds, and Madison started yelling over and over, 'Oh, what might have been, fair lady'—kind of laughing at me. It was awkward because Robert was right there. I don't know. I was in kind of a funny situation."

* * *

Cynthia, who was studying psychology in college, tried to find reasons to explain her encounters. But sometimes it was obvious. "Most of the British people I saw there were just total alcoholics—lots of rum, lots of beer. The month before one of Rob's English friends I met had fought an anteater . . . the ones with claws. He was drunk and thought it was a man."

* * *

At least two other legionnaires she met on that trip, while odd and speaking stilted English, were sober. Rob's friends, Naoto and Shintaro, were Japanese and usually kept to themselves. They liked Rob because he was American and artistic. Both claimed their families came from the warrior class and found the Japanese Defense Force "very without action and history." The two had prepared a gift (Rob was unaware) to welcome Cynthia and help her "be with her long far-away man now here and full." Cynthia opened the small carefully wrapped box and found highly crafted origami figures—one color male, one color female—in a variety of sexual positions.

In her two weeks in Guiana, Cynthia had met very few civilians. One of the locals she did encounter was a Frenchman named Rat, who claimed the government had forced him to leave for political reasons. He worked in the capital, Cayenne, as a tattoo artist. Tattoos are common among legionnaires, and Cynthia often found herself surrounded by drawings of Union Jacks, bulldogs, and a variety of Legionalia. Some unusual tattoos she saw ran from the rebellious, to the religious, to the racy "FUCK OFF" on a Belgian's upper back, a Calvary scene of Christ on the cross covering an Italian's entire back, and a sausage-shaped penis with the word "Tiens, violà du boudin" on a Yugoslav's muscular, veiny forearm. In fact, tattoos are so much a part of Legion tradition that the museum at Aubagne, in 2014, featured a seven-month photo exhibit titled *"La Légion dans la peau"* *("The Legion on the Skin").*

Still unsure why this happened, Cynthia describes a visit to Rat's parlor: "Apparently Robert did some Legion drawings that Rat used for tattoos. He's always liked art. So, yeah, I kind of got caught up in it all. You see, when I was getting the tattoo from Rat I was watching a Nazi concentration camp movie. Michael York was in it. I could relate to the pain. I got a black cat on my upper left thigh."

* * *

Cynthia's visit ended in Cayenne with a gathering of Rob and several friends over a feast of alligator and shark at a Chinese restaurant. Unfortunately, upon returning from her unique spring break vacation, she fell ill with 104°F temperature and all the symptoms of salmonella poisoning. Oh, *l'amour*.

CHAD

> *"Chad was everything I wanted it to be. It was my personal conquest. It was my wall. I had to get over it. It taught me a lot of things. Things like camaraderie. I've never felt camaraderie like that outside it . . . no, never."*
>
> —*LÉGIONNAIRE PREMIÈRE CLASSE* FAIRFIELD

For a country with a name that seems best suited for crossword puzzles, Westchester County golf instructors, or election ballots, Chad has seen its share of world headlines. Formerly part of the condominium known as French West Africa, Chad, in 1960, became an independent country, within the French *Communauté* (a loose alliance of francophone nations). As had many other African states, Chad, upon the abrupt departure of European law and order, broke out into tribal warfare, pitting the mostly Arab-backed Islamist North against the more Christian-Animist South. France sent in the Legion only when civil war seemed unavoidable in 1969 and 1971.

Further complicating the region's turmoil was the 1969 overthrow of pro-West King Idris I of Libya, Chad's neighbor to the north. The so-called "Green Revolution" in Libya was led by a young, charismatic, self-proclaimed Arab visionary named Muammar el-Qaddafi, a twenty-seven-year-old army captain. In the name of Arab nationalism, anti-colonialism, and anti-Zionism, the new leader quickly and dramatically expelled the remaining British and American military forces. To bolster his image among anti-West Arabs as well as his nation's treasury, Qaddafi also nationalized most Western-owned oil operations. Neighboring Egypt, still rebuilding its morale and armed forces after the crushing Israeli victory in the 1967 Six-Day War, supported Qaddafi with as much bombastic rhetoric as possible. Indeed, from the time he took power in Libya, Qaddafi sought to fill the political and emotional vacuum left by the 1970 death of Egypt's Gamal Abdel Nasser.

Nasser's heady ideas of Pan-Arabism and expansion suited the ambitious young Captain Qaddafi. As if to spite any remaining Western influence on the African continent, the Libyan leader challenged the standing Organization of African Unity's (OAU) agreement on African borders. For the sake of stability and cohesion, the OAU has maintained the old colonial borders set out at the Berlin Conference in 1884–1885 for today's new African nations. Qaddafi, however, always challenged the OAU position and contested the Libyan border with several neighbors—most aggressively with Chad. The Legion was again called to that theater in 1983. *Opération Manta* saw the *1er REC* and *2ème REP* drawing a political line in the sand—a demarcation established at the 16th parallel. If Libyan troops crossed it, France would retaliate militarily. Faced with French Mirage F-1 jets and sun-tapped, trigger-happy legionnaires, Qaddafi soon retreated to a more verbal offensive. For the rotating Legion detachments in Chad, it was mostly sandbag and wait. Along with sandbags, Legion symbolism is ever-present in Chad. The Legion more than wants to make its presence and whereabouts known to Libyan forces, as well as the local population.

* * *

Sergent-Chef Robeson describes his first St. George's Day (April 23, in honor of the patron saint of the cavalry) and Camerone Day, both celebrated in Chad with the *1er REC*: "For St. George's Day we did a parade at midnight, lit by flares, and it was all quite impressive. We had all the civilian population coming from Moussoro who were sitting down in the sand watching us do our parade, and, where we marched by, we had a lot of guys lining the road, and they looked smart. The Chadians definitely took notice."

95

After another impressive evening parade in commemoration of Camerone one week later, again lit by flares, the locals offered a spectacle of their own.

"The Chadians laid on a horse race. The Chadian horses are a bit tatty, but they're quite proud of them. So, after the parade, they did that and ran this sort of Chadian Grand National. It was impressive, you know. We were still lined up watching this race go by . . . it was a there and back again race . . . and, then they came round with the horses in back of us, sort of shaking our hands and saluting us, and everyone was feeling good."

Robeson was a new legionnaire and soon to experience the first of his nineteen April 30th ceremonies. He still feels this "was the most impressive Camerone I've done." After the parade and horse race, "We went back to camp and had a massive *pot* (feast). They managed to get a load of ice together, fresh champagne, fresh beer, loads of food, smoked salmon, and lobster. I don't know how they organized it, but we had everything. It was an incredible meal—just tons of this food and drink, and we had a very good time."

To further buoy the spirits of legionnaires touring in Chad, a *foyer*, unlike any seen in the *métropole*, was built by the *1er REC*. "*Pouffes* are now, or have been since maybe the mid-70s, illegal . . . don't exist," Robeson continued. "Unofficially, they're still all over the place: Djibouti, Chad, Guiana, Tahiti . . . all over the place for Legion regiments. Totally unofficial. Absolutely illegal. In Chad . . . the commanding colonel of the detachment obviously was there to make sure discipline was respected at all levels, so the *pouffe* we constructed. We made out it was a *foyer*. We were instructed if ever anyone asked where we were going, we were going to the *foyer*. There was never any mention of the *pouffe*."

* * *

Robeson and other new boys were assigned the task of building the brothel. It went up in record time and had six small rooms, a large bar area, and a place for the medic and his table of tonics and elixirs. There were no doors, but the rooms were built maze-like so no one could see in. Once a week, every platoon from each of the Legion units rotating there—

2ème REI and *1er REC*—would travel by truck to visit the *"foyer."* Local currency was used to buy the cheap beer and foul-smelling girls. Supposedly, the girls had been inspected by military doctors and all legionnaires were given condoms and an alcohol-prep by the medic on hand. AIDS had infected many in that part of Africa, and "some guys were interested in blow jobs, but the girls there wouldn't have it. Some religious bullshit. These girls were against it. It was improper. I'm sure most guys didn't enjoy it that much because the girls were so very ugly. I, myself, went once and found it so boring . . . I didn't bother wasting another 3,500 *CFA* for that lot."

The real fun wasn't in the back rooms, but in the bar area.

"It was magic," Robeson said. "I've never known anything like it. There was no music, just laughter and shouting and drinking and throwing of women around. They got some bad abuse over there. That was a crazy atmosphere. There were all ranks in there except officers; they had their own day. So, all NCOs and other ranks mixed up and everyone just got on. It was an insane atmosphere. It was that that people went back to. That's why I went back. I didn't go back to get my end away. Just the excitement and the whole atmosphere would turn people on more than the girls. The girls themselves, I mean, Christ, they were a right turn off."

* * *

Just as the smell of cheaply scented whores reminds *S/CH* Robeson of his off-duty leisure hours in Chad, so another pungent smell greeted Legionnaire First Class Philip Fairfield upon arrival. For *REP*-man Fairfield, with only eight months of service, his most trying experience was the five and a half months he spent in the Chadian desert. Fairfield recalls his first few days: "Khalaheet . . . 16th parallel. We arrived there at nighttime—pitch black. The smell was very, very noticeable. I'd never smelled anything like it."

After a good meal served by the happy-to-be-relieved French *paras*, and a bit of sleep, Fairburn was given guard duty from 04:00–06:00. In the morning light he discovered the cause of the pervasive stench. "I wouldn't say bodies because that's probably the wrong word to use . . .

skeletons . . . corpses . . . some kind of battle I presume. I have no idea, you know, I couldn't speak French very well. There was still hair on the guys so, you know what I mean, it couldn't have been too long. Funny thing was . . . no boots. They stripped them. If they've got boots on, the boots went. Whereas the trousers . . . vest . . . left. Like I say, there were guys in the sand . . . and shells."

The officers told the men to get used to the sights and smells. "We were told you mustn't veer off the path. You mustn't touch these bodies or try to bury them or whatever in case anything was wired. So, we never did. That's the hardest thing mentally for me."

* * *

Despite being an airborne unit, Fairfield and the others were usually deployed around the country by truck. It was not only the dead that stank. Miles before entering a village, those in the trucks could smell it. Usually, these convoys of white men in white hats riding in from the desert would be met in such places with great curiosity. As in any Third World country, hawkers and gawkers crowd around foreigners hoping to sell or steal. In these brief stops, Fairfield saw the extremes of French behavior toward the native population. Acts of kindness could just as often be coupled with acts of cruelty. Fairfield reports on such incidents: "As we pulled up toward this stinking village, this black woman came running out. Tits bouncing, you know, I mean obviously dressed how they dress, like, but with a child in her arms. I mean the child was, like, three and a half foot long, you know what I mean? You wouldn't have known the age of this kid. I mean the head was massive. The belly was massive. But the arms were skeletal. Really, really horrible. She came screaming up, like, not in French but in her language . . . whatever it was. We realized obviously the kid was dying. And this French corporal, a good guy, actually, got down, opened his kit, took out a needle of *vitamines* and injected the kid, like. That to me, that were nice. That was a nice gesture."

* * *

I know of another medic in the same country, who, a few years earlier, had not been so caring. *BRG* Grubenz was a German *REC*-man in my *escadron* in Orange with whom I got along fairly well. He collected stamps and would always come to my room to see if I had received any letters from home. He'd served with the Legion in Lebanon, Central Africa, and Chad and loved showing photos of dead and mangled bodies. Grubenz's favorite snapshot (which I've seen elsewhere) is of a charred, severed head placed on a destroyed tank to which legionnaires added a cigarette in the mouth and a green beret on the head. I'm sure if the Legion *foyer* had sold calendars with pictures of these grisly photos Grubenz would have bought several as gifts for friends and family. When not defiling the dead, he was mocking the living. While on a desert run in Chad, similar to Fairfield's convoy, Grubenz administered care to an elderly woman by taping an aspirin to her head. Other times he would have children yell *Arbeit macht frei!* before giving them sugar cubes with drops of antiseptic.

* * *

Fairfield also offers a darker view of the Legion's "hearts and minds" campaign in Chad. "You know in the ration packs that we had? You know you got those tablets to dry everything up? We used to give the blacks the tablets, which were poisonous, to eat. Not to children so much, but to youngish kids. Nasty, really. But, I mean, sometimes we'd used to drive along, and, sometimes, bricks would fly into the wagon. I hated those people. I mean I hated them."

Most soldiers in European or American armies never adapt well to tours of duty in impoverished countries. The extremes in standard of living and hygiene are shocking and often provoke a range of emotions. "In a way, it was silly, really. In one way, it was pure disgust in the way they were living . . . in which, for me was out of order. I'd have shot the lot of them . . . and I mean that. At that particular time, if you'd have given me a nuclear bomb I'd have blasted them. For me they were just a waste of space. Worthless people. Horrible, horrible people who hadn't got a clue."

As with many English-speakers abroad and out of the range of television, Fairfield and friends would listen to radio broadcasts for the latest in news and sports. While based at Abeche, Fairfield heard from BBC World Service that, in celebration of the twentieth anniversary of Libya's Green Revolution, Qaddafi, on a certain day that week, would bomb Chad in a show of strength. Fairfield laughs as he remembers, "We were sat there, like, at the front line thinking what a knobhead. And it was, like, two or three weeks after that, over they came. Bombed the fuck out of us. There were only three jets—Russian MIGs—but more bombed N'djamena (the capital) at the same time."

Fairfield later learned from his sergeants that two jets had been shot down around the capital by an American rocket defense system and, ironically, "one of the guys that was found was American—who was flying the jet. No kidding. A mercenary. Absolutely true. He was dead, but at Khalaheet, they've got two Americans there held prisoner. The only reason they kept them alive was because they were Americans. At the time, I thought, just blow the bastards away. I mean, fighting for Qaddafi . . . Christ."

Of Phil Fairfield's three and a half years of service, almost six months were spent in Chad. On that one tour, only three months after basic training, and seven months after leaving Sheffield, Fairfield confronted much of the harsh reality of today's French Foreign Legion. Here Fairfield answers the question, "Did you find what you were looking for in the Legion?" He grins and replies, "What was I looking for? Well . . . yes . . . adventure . . . adrenaline. I mean, Christ, that is the wildest drug ever. I mean that to me . . . jumping out of planes, being bombed, seeing death, smelling death, being around death. Christ . . . guard duty two (hours) on two off, two on two off twenty-four hours a day, like, five and a half months. I mean we had about two days off in that. Two days off! We were wild people. We were well gone, like. Everybody . . . everybody was absolutely out of it. I mean, you were on a different kind of plane."

Isolation and a state of constant alert led to some strange sensations. "The slightest noise . . . nobody ever woke you up by shaking you. You touched the feet. Nobody would ever shake you. You'd smack them. You just touched the foot. I had my boots on for twenty-one days out in Chad. Twenty-one days I never took my boots off. I mean my skin had grown over my socks. It was bad out there. I mean, bad . . . in a bad way."

Years later he muses, "I don't know . . . Chad was everything I wanted it to be. It was my personal conquest. It was my wall. I had to get over it. It taught me a lot of things. Things like camaraderie. I've never felt camaraderie like that outside it . . . no, never."

CENTRAL AFRICA AND OTHER POSTS

"There was a discussion going on for a few minutes, and then this corporal-chef took out his automatic pistol, armed it, and shot the guy in the head."

—*LÉGIONNAIRE PREMIÈRE CLASSE* VAN HEEK

The longer you serve in the Legion the longer your own sense of right and wrong is tested. Crucial to being a good soldier is the ability to follow orders and not ask too many questions. Any combat veteran can tell of the indiscriminate killing and needless destruction in the name of objective. For a legionnaire in the field, a conscience can, sometimes, hinder operations. Legionnaire First Class Van Heek relates an event that happened in the Central African Republic but came to the attention of the French Minister of Defense and, even, President.

Slow to begin his story, Van Heek eventually let it all out: "I didn't tell this until now. The unit was split in half. One half stayed in the combat base, the other half being sent into a big game reserve in the north of the country looking for poachers. We had to go after them and take the maximum of them back to Bangui (the capital) for an eventual show trial."

Once in the field, the *REP* captain was more direct: Shoot to kill. Adreneline-pumped soldiers, locked and loaded weapons, and an innate sense of superiority over the local population is an explosive mix. Knowing the poachers were close, the eager legionnaires were told to spread out and be ready. "So, everybody walking in the terrain with sharp rounds engaged in his *FAMAS* . . . with sharp hand grenades. At a certain moment, somewhere, somebody opens fire. Everybody hears it's a *FAMAS* shooting, and nothing shoots back. It's only *FAMASs* shooting."

* * *

A cease fire was called, and the unit regrouped. It seems men were spotted and shot at, but no return fire meant something was strange. Van Heek explains how "some guys under the command of an old corporal-chef, a German, had been so excited by this corporal-chef of seeing blood, of seeing action that they opened fire upon the first Central African black guys they saw. These guys turned out to be simple peasants coming back from their fields. One managed to escape . . . probably not wounded. The other one was very badly wounded."

Among the forty men gathered around the man bleeding from his groin area and neck was the company medic. He applied bandages and did what he could. The captain wasn't on the scene, but two sergeants and the seventeen-year veteran *caporal-chef* were there to take charge. What came next for Van Heek is something he still can't reconcile. "There was a discussion going on for a few minutes, and then this corporal-chef took out his automatic pistol, armed it, and shot the guy in the head. Mentally, the hardest thing I've had to do is standing there and not withholding this corporal-chef from shooting this guy. We were all there—about half a company—but it was him at that moment. It was simply this corporal-chef leading. He was old and supposed to be experienced. And such a guy is supposed to do the right thing."

Not long after burying the African, orders came from Bangui to return to the capital immediately. It seems one of those shot at was "not so much of a peasant as we thought and made it to a post office. Every post office is still equipped with telegraph equipment, and a telegraph to Bangui takes about four minutes. It must have been him. And he said, 'They've shot my friend, or my brother, or my father,' or whoever it was. It did get back to Paris and we were pulled back to France within a few days. The whole unit of 2 *REP*—even the combat base that stayed behind."

* * *

As if the captain and unit didn't have enough worries, one last act of Africa-be-damned occurred. "We went back to France, not before having set fire to a school, and everybody paid. This fire to the school was set by an English legionnaire standing guard. We had each to pay before leaving this place, which is called Rudresse, a beautiful place; I believe it was 400 *francs*. So, we were about 100, so these people had 40,000 *francs* which in Central Africa is enough to build three schools. He burned it. I don't know . . . probably *plein les couilles* ("full balls") . . . and drunk. This, to a typical English legionnaire, is enough for setting fire to a school overseas."

* * *

The results of the bush murder: "So, this captain and corporal-chef were finally put on trial in Paris. I believe the captain served two years in military prison, but the corporal-chef went back with the same group, the same section, same regiment. The captain took all the responsibility."

* * *

And, now, the heartwarming Legion story of the little schoolhouse on the African hill that burned to the ground—as told by someone who saw the first flame. LFC Fairfield on the schoolhouse fire: "We were all stood there. There was me, Jeffrey Stokes, Haverty, an Irish kid, another English bloke . . . I've forgotten his name . . . Cowboy Andy, he was there, yeah. Anyway, what happened was we were basically stood there and Stokes like, who didn't smoke, picked a lighter up off the table because obviously some of us did and . . . I mean, it wasn't a school . . . just a thatched roof open hut—that's all it was, you know what I mean? But, that was their schoolhouse. And he lit the lighter . . . put it underneath the straw and it went—whoosh (up in flames). So we ran off rather quickly. And that was it, like. It had gone."

And was Stokes caught? "We're all English together, so nobody'd think of grassing up on him. To me, like, what he did was bloody stupid.

Legionnaires thought only of day after day, basically. You thought of tomorrow. I hope I'm home tomorrow. That's about it."

* * *

Whatever the current political party in power, a robust French foreign policy, especially in Africa, seems to be expected. Most francophone nations are African, and French influence in those regions is both emotional and economic. French presidents do not want Gallic interests in Africa eclipsed by "*les Anglo-Saxons*."

* * *

French muscle has often been flexed in post-colonial Africa, and *Opération Leopard* in May 1978 was a classic example of French élan. Offering troops from the *2ème REP* in place of the initial force of Belgian *para-commandos*—recalled at the last minute—French President Valéry Giscard d'Estaing sought to rescue hundreds of European mining personnel and their families from the savagery of advancing African rebels. The Legion was ready for the fight in Kolwezi, Zaire (now Democratic Republic of the Congo—DRC), but French aircraft were not available. Relying on American C-141 Starlifters (with U.S. pilots and army jumpmasters from the 82nd Airborne) meant, in some ways, compromising the French operation. A mix of frequency ranges for radio transmission, as well as a different kind of rigging and static line for the 650 Legion *paras*, caused great anxiety in Paris, as well as among the soldiers involved in the hastily planned operation. In the ensuing battle, the Legion lost five men (first KIA was an English legionnaire), with twenty-five wounded, and killed an estimated 250 rebels. The number of bodies scattered about the mining town was gruesome: 200 black civilians and more than 200 whites, many defiled and mutilated. Still, *Leopard* was a successful and stirring foreign policy action for French forces. Even more than usual, the Legion drew the loudest applause and cheers at the Bastille Day parade in Paris that summer.

* * *

The role of the French military in 1990s Rwanda, however, is a long way from the heady days of Zaire in 1978. Since gaining independence from Belgium in 1962, Rwanda has had intermittent tribal warfare, but nothing like the carnage that occurred in 1994.

* * *

Under the guise of a humanitarian mission *(Opération Turquoise)*, Legion and regular army units were sent to Rwanda in June 1994. However, by the time the French military (officially) arrived in Rwanda nearly 800,000 Tutsi had been slaughtered by Hutu military and civilian death squads called *Interahamwe*. Some 2,500 French troops offered assistance, but rumors and informal reports circulating in France indicated something dark and murky. In 1994 and 1998, Africa specialist Patrick de Saint-Exupéry of *Le Figaro* wrote several articles that confirmed the stories and documented French involvement in the genocide committed in Rwanda. *Le Figaro* reported that French forces took an active but secret part in fighting rebel Tutsi infiltration of Rwanda from 1992 on, operating at front-line level with the full authorization of President François Mitterrand. In effect, the French military was present during the 1994 genocide and failed to intervene. In addition, French forces allegedly helped the Hutu hatchet men, *Interahamwe*, and officials responsible for the massacre escape to neighboring francophone countries.

Great bitterness besets the French Army today because of the role it was ordered to play in the Rwandan genocide, *Le Figaro* reporter de Saint-Exupéry writes, quoting an internal army document that speaks of soldiers who "cracked, not because of the corpses and violence and hunting down of victims . . . but because of a sense of guilt" (de Saint-Exupéry, Patrick. *"France-Rwanda: Une Génocide sans Importance." Le Figaro*, 12–15 January 1998). I cannot imagine this was a Legion document simply because Legion officers know their men feel guilty about very little in terms of military action. De Saint Exupéry, however, did not shy away from further controversy. He wrote a book in 2004, *L'inavouable—La*

105

France au Rwanda that named prominent French military men and politicians (many listed on the book's cover) as directly culpable for the tragic events in 1994 Rwanda. De Saint-Exupéry was charged with slander and brought to court shortly after publication. However, a few months later, the charges were dropped and de Saint-Exupéry soon wrote another book on the same issue.

* * *

As I read newspaper reports, sections from his books, and court transcripts regarding Rwanda, I also recall in great detail the stories I heard from Legion veterans of *Opération Leopard.* An oft repeated anecdote about legionnaires handling the chaotic flux of small firefights and ambushes that characterized the Kolwezi operation was "If it was black, and moved, you shot it." With such crude "pull-the-trigger-on-that-nigger" sentiment common in Legion barracks, one might wonder why France offers the Legion's services to any United Nations peacekeeping operations. However, legionnaires do wear the U.N. patch on their fatigues, and, while some dislike replacing their hard-earned green berets with baby blue helmets, many are proud to serve. In addition, all welcome the extra pay U.N. service earns them. *Et bien sûr,* France sees any international activity as good activity and military engagement as proof that it is still a major power.

At least for the world press, French officers will maintain that the Legion is well suited for peacekeeping in places like the former Yugoslavia because of the number of legionnaires who speak or understand Serbo-Croatian. Of course, a polyglot Yugoslav legionnaire can also have no problem killing another because of linguistic or religious differences. Most certainly, Milorad Luković, nicknamed *"Legija" (Légionnaire)* for his earlier service in the Legion, helped organize the 2003 assassination of Serbian Prime Minister Zoran Djindjić. More recently, Ante Gotovina has been in Foreign Legion, Balkan, and world news. In 2011, after an international manhunt, this former *REP caporal-chef*—veteran of the Battle of Kolwezi and, later, Croatian general—was sentenced by an international tribunal in The Hague to twenty-four years in prison for ordering

106

the "ethnic cleansing" of Krajina (a region of Croatia where Serbs had lived for generations) in August 1995. Gotovina and another Croatian general were convicted of allowing their troops to burn, stab, and shoot Serbs in order to reclaim Krajina for Croatia (Operation Storm). However, in late 2012 by a 3–2 verdict, a U.N. appeals court in The Hague overturned Gotovina's earlier conviction, and he returned to his homeland and a hero's welcome. How pleased this would have made a Serb named "Petar Kara," who joined the Legion in 1867 is anyone's guess. Due to his royal lineage, Legionnaire Kara was made a *Sous-Lieutenant.* He later became Peter I, King of Serbia.

Notable Yugoslav legionnaires aside, the urban destruction caused by the conflicts of the 1990s made the Balkans a perfect job site for the highly mobile and experienced construction units of the Legion's *6ème REG* (now *2ème REG*), as well as snipers and Special Forces from the *REI* and *REP.*

* * *

A few other hot spots the Legion visited in the 1990s and early 2000s were Cambodia, Tahiti, Republic of Congo, Côte d'Ivoire (Ivory Coast), Haiti, Afghanistan, Mali, and several large cities in France.

* * *

In Cambodia, formerly part of French Indochina, the Legion and other foreign armies were asked to help keep the Communist Khmer Rouge at bay during national elections monitored by United Nations personnel. The Khmer Rouge killed Bulgarian, Japanese, and Chinese peacekeepers, but avoided attacking the one army in which those three nationalities might have been in the same platoon—the French Foreign Legion. The main job of the Legion units sent to Cambodia in 1992 was to train the Cambodians in clearing the estimated one million land mines sown in a quarter century of warfare. French commanders are proud to note that the Cambodians, indifferent to most U.N. troops, mobbed Legion units, touching the French flag on their sleeves.

* * *

Le bleu, blanc, et rouge was not so welcome in the summer of 1995 on the French Polynesian island of Tahiti. Nuclear testing at Mururoa (begun by de Gaulle and halted years later by the Gaullist Chirac) led Tahitian separatists to violently protest in the streets of the capital, Papeete, only to be quelled by legionnaires from the *5ème REG.* That same year, in a very unusual display of Legion force in the *métropole*, patrols of heavily armed legionnaires escorted regular police and *Gendarmes* in the Paris *métro* and other sites; elsewhere, Legion muscle helped local forces respond to the wave of Algerian-based *GIA (Groupe Islamique Armée)* terrorist attacks that left eight dead and over 100 injured. Former *GIA* member, Mokhtar Bel Mokhtar, would harass France and the West again in the eastern Algerian desert in 2013.

* * *

Bel Mokhtar is believed to have organized the assault and mass hostage-taking at an international gas refinery plant in eastern Algeria, close to the Libyan border. The attack left many dead and missing Europeans, Americans, and Japanese and was claimed to be in response to Algeria's allowing France to use its air space to move men (including Legion units) and equipment to northern Mali in that former French colony's fight against al-Qaeda–sponsored militants.

* * *

In March 2013, a series of coordinated French-Chadian ground and air attacks in Mali killed Bel Mokhtar, the Chadian government claimed. Unconvinced, the United States, a few months later, announced a $5 million reward for information on his whereabouts. A U.S. drone strike was believed to have killed the elusive Bel Mokhtar in Libya in June 2015; however, the "Uncatchable" (or his henchmen) again surfaced in Mali's capital in November. A well-planned jihadist assault and hostage drama unfolded inside the Radisson Blu hotel in Bamako, leaving five U.N. workers and more than twenty others dead.

* * *

The conflict that brought the Legion to Brazzaville, Republic of Congo (a former Belgian colony), in 1999 was typical of the strife that has torn African nations apart since the end of European colonialism. In place of scheduled free elections, a civil war broke out in 1997. The war pitted not tribes but whole countrywide ethnic groups against one another in a vicious struggle for power. U.N. estimates put the death toll at 10,000– 20,000 within the first five months of fighting, with more than 250,000 Congolese eventually fleeing into the forests along the border regions. France sent units of the *2ème REP* to the troubled capital, Brazzaville, in 1999 to escort French citizens and thousands of other foreign nationals to the airport for evacuation. By the time Legion *paras* landed in Brazzaville, the city had been divided into three bloody parts, each under the control of drugged and dangerous soldiers representing rival militias.

Crazed gangs of soldiers with names like "Mamba," "Zulu," "Ninja," and "Cobra" fought neighborhood by neighborhood, killing, raping, and torturing members of whichever "wrong" ethnic group they found. Eventually, non-Africans became targets. Legion *paras* brought some order to the chaos of Brazzaville and saw to the successful evacuation of more than 5,200 civilians from fifty-two countries. Among those escaping the Mamba madness, courtesy of the *2ème REP,* was the grateful U.S. Ambassador and some 120 fellow citizens.

* * *

The Legion was sent to the former French colony of Côte d'Ivoire for not so much humanitarian or peacekeeping reasons as regime stabilization and the rescue of foreign nationals (including many American students, teachers, and missionaries). Côte d'Ivoire is the world's leading cocoa producer, a major West African port, and a regional economic powerhouse.

In September 2002, a bloody failed coup attempt against "President-for-life" Laurent Gbagbo led to an insurgent army taking over much of the north of the country. The embattled but unseated President Gbagbo needed French soldiers and tanks to block a rebel advance on the capital (he would face the same problems ten years later). President Chirac saw to it that Legion and other elite combat units were quickly sent to Côte d'Ivoire in order to avoid yet another African country slipping into civil war. *Caporal* Filip Timbaris, a muscular, Krav Maga instructor from the Czech Republic, and future five-year combat veteran, was new to the Legion when his *REI* company was sent to Côte d'Ivoire in 2003. He still sees this mission—a white man put in the middle of a vicious West African tribal war—as his most difficult: "Yeah, I mean I was new so getting a lot of shit, but also the things I saw—machetes and long knives, lots of blood on the streets, women raped, arms and legs cut off, babies burned alive in roadside fires. Damn, it was a hell of an intro to Africa."

While a successful mission for France, there was much anger and frustration in Legion ranks. "It's this black against black thing. Who understands that shit? Bingo Bongo vs. Mingo Mongo or whatever the fuck they were called. But they both attacked us, also. AKs and even RPGs they shot at us. We were there to defend civilian villagers, you see, Ivorian villages. But when the rebels attacked, sometimes destroying three or four villages in our region, we had to give chase and attack them. Legionnaires are like that. Peacekeeping and guarding is shit. Can't stay and watch from the base when the rebels attack. It's not like that for us."

* * *

As the situation in the West African nation eventually calmed and world stock markets saw cocoa prices return to normal, Chirac and France won international praise . . . and the Foreign Legion waited for its next posting.

* * *

Only two years later, the Legion heard the call of duty from another former colony—the poorest nation in the Western Hemisphere—Haiti.

Then called Saint-Domingue, the Caribbean nation was the rich, verdant prize of the French Empire until 1798, when a young patriot, Toussaint L'Ouverture, inspired by the ideals of the Enlightenment and French Revolution, led a Spartacus-like slave rebellion that drove European planters and Napoleon's troops off the island. Since the glory days of independence, however, foreign military intervention, corrupt governments (often allied with drug cartels), and countless natural disasters have pushed Haiti to the brink of non-existence.

In 2004, France joined the soldiers and police of other nations and sent 200 legionnaires to help patrol and secure Haiti's capital, Port-au-Prince, and the northern port of Gonaïves, the country's second largest city. A rebellion against former Cité Soleil slum-priest-turned-president Jean-Bertrand Aristide had left Haiti once again in a chaotic and lawless state. French, Brazilian, Chilean, Canadian, and U.S. forces were on the ground to make sure a bad situation did not get worse after Aristide's hasty departure to South Africa in February 2004. Sadly, while the operation was truly a peacekeeping mission, it did cost the life of one legionnaire.

* * *

Perhaps the best-known Legion foray after the first Gulf War was Operation Restore Hope in hapless and hungry Somalia. (Legion activity—especially *REP/GCP, REC,* and *REG*—would be much less publicized in the 2013 Mali *Opération Serval*.) In some ways, Somalia proved to be the Legion's finest hour in this new peacekeeping role, yet the mission was not without problems, as the world witnessed the no-nonsense approach legionnaires took to soldiering.

Journalists in the Somali capital of Mogadishu in the 1990s reported how U.S. Marines landed in-country smiling, waving, and handing out candy and cookies. French Legionnaires took a different approach to the local population. Television crews showed the world a Legion checkpoint, where swarming crowds interfered with operations. Several legionnaires waded into the crowd swinging rifle butts, and yelling obscenities in various European languages, in order to drive the Somalis back. Nine

111

hundred legionnaires served in Somalia, and establishing order, not distributing Oreos, was their objective. Just days after arriving from Legion bases in Djibouti, legionnaires at a downtown checkpoint opened fire on a fast-moving truck filled with locals. Several civilians were killed. An investigation showed that the truck's brakes had failed, so the vehicle could not possibly have stopped. *Rien à branler* (Who gives a toss.) was the collective Legion sentiment.

Legionnaire First Class Griffiths, on tour with the *REP* in Djibouti, had friends involved in the roadblock shooting: "A group from the 3rd company of 2 *REP* had shot them. What happened was, there was a fucking pick-up truck coming down the road with a bunch of niggers in the back and everything. No brakes. Couldn't stop. So, you got 3rd company just arrived in Somalia set up all these, like, fucking checkpoints and everything and like visible everywhere, to everyone. Two guards stood there, *chef de section* (platoon commander) just behind them, or whatever. And this pick-up truck, like, going fast and, like, not stopping. So, like, normal reaction is to, like, blow it away, yeah, and they did."

* * *

Griffiths maintains that, before so much U.N. interference, the original American-French part of Restore Hope had been a success. "At the beginning, Restore Hope was, like, American and French and, like, they made their own rules, and it was working. You know, they cleared off all these mines. Supplies going here, there, and everywhere. They cleared out different sections of Somalia around Mogadishu (Somalia's capital) or whatever and, you know, it was working OK. We had it all sewn up."

He also blames the image of weakness the U.N. projected to the Somali warlords for causing even more misery and conflict. "How can you keep peace when you got cunts shooting at you and you can't open fire? It's not how it works there." Griffiths also faults the U.N. for forcing the Legion into an unsuitable role. "Because of their reputation as, like, *marche ou crève* (march or die), you know, this peacekeeping is ruining the reputation. The peacekeeping roles is like, ruining the reputation of hard-fighting men and the nothing-gets-in-our-way reputation. We are expendable. If you get killed, so what. Now, it's kind of like, dig in and wear them down with propaganda. Wear them down with attrition. It's just not the Legion. I mean, like, Operation Restore Hope . . . fuck me, how about restore ammo!"

THE BALKANS: SARAJEVO, SRBRENICA, AND MITROVICA (KOSOVO)

"What was it like? I'll be damned—how many times I jumped into the VAB *and closed the door only to hear the ping of bullets hit the metal. The metal or my head—yeah, how many seconds did I have?"*

—SERGENT-CHEF GAZDÍK

Sarajevo

Until the Russian invasion of Ukraine in 2022, the Balkan Wars of the 1990s had been the worst fighting in Europe since 1945. A volatile mix of religion, ethnicity, nationalism, and history was to ensure that any armed conflict in the former Yugoslavia would be savage and bitter. More than twenty years later, the International Court of Justice in The Hague (Netherlands) is still hearing cases of "ethnic cleansing" and other crimes committed in the Balkans from 1991 to 1996. Outside intervention, especially NATO airstrikes against Serb targets, eventually helped end the war but did not resolve all the territorial disputes or deep-rooted regional prejudices among various groups.

A disparate assortment of international post-war Balkan mission teams soon arrived in the war-torn region, each with its own agenda. American service groups, such as the Peace Corps and Church of the Brethren, were soon joined by several U.N. agencies, as well as NATO forces. The latter two worked side by side, especially in such places as Sarajevo and Srbrenica, to monitor the situation and prevent further ethnic bloodshed. NATO armies were later assigned to Kosovo (once part of Serbia) to maintain order and separate rival factions—mostly the vocal Serb minority from the majority ethnic Albanian Kosovars.

* * *

113

Sergent-Chef Gazdík, from the Czech Republic, a young legionnaire with less than two years' service, was part of a *2ème REP* company stationed in Sarajevo in 1992. Under a statute from the United Nations, the Legion was to keep watch over several flashpoints within the divided city, especially the Serb-controlled airport area. "They said the Albanians (Bosnian Muslims) should stay on their side—in their area. Our job was to allow people, any people, to cross the tarmac from one side to another, north to south. Day and night, we watched the tarmac and maintained security. The U.N. Blue Helmets were also at the airport, but it was us in charge of the tarmac." Gazdík, now smirking, adds, "Kind of like that other dream job in Lebanon in 1982, where the Legion provided cover for (Yasser) Arafat when the PLO left the airport in Beirut."

* * *

The U.N. mandate in Sarajevo was clear: Allow unhindered passage of all people and support free and open commerce in the greatly damaged city. Gazdík shakes his head and recalls Sarajevo's deadly reality. "What was it like? I'll be damned—how many times I jumped into the *VAB* (armored personnel carrier) and closed the door only to hear the ping of bullets hit the metal. The metal or my head—yeah, how many seconds did I have? There was shooting all the time. Snipers everywhere, like during a war. We'd move out on the tarmac in *VABs* . . . letting people take cover or giving help—rescue—if we could."

Gazdík, the multi-Slavic-speaker, was a welcome addition to Legion ranks in the Balkans. He comments on his interpreting duties and two "VIPs" he met: "For us, it was good with the language. The Czech Republic was well looked at there. For this reason, I could pass among Serbs, Croats, Albanians—not true for English or Americans." Even though young in service and having extra duty, *corvée*, and other demands, Gazdík boasted such singular language skills that his superiors asked him to be an interpreter. He boldly defended himself in front of his officers: "I said," and this took balls, "And when do I sleep?"

But Gazdík's linguistic talents could not be wasted. "They came after me again, and, within two weeks, I was a translator at the general's bureau.

I stood right next to (Radovan) Karadžić and (Ratko) Mladić and others as a translator. All this work was official and special, but, still, I had all my other duties. It was hard for me. I was new to the Legion. Lots of duties now, plus translating for these big men—plus the bullets."

Srebrenica

Srebrenica, July 1995: After a tense standoff with Bosnian Serb forces, outnumbered Dutch peacekeepers in a United Nations compound in the town of Potočari surrendered or withdrew. No shots were fired, and Serb forces were allowed to pass through the Potočari checkpoints and continue on to nearby Srebrenica (also in Bosnia/Herzegovina). Mindful of the intense religious and ethnic hatred in the region, the U.N. Security Council in 1993 had designated Potočari and Srebrenica as a "safe area" for the minority Muslim population. However, Bosnian Serbs (Orthodox Christian) had already planned Operation *Krivaja 95*—the "removal" or dispersal of all Bosnian Muslims in eastern Bosnia/Herzegovina. (Islam was brought to the Balkans by the invading Ottoman Turks in the 1500s.) With no international opposition in sight, the Serb Army, along with several police units from Sarajevo, began *Krivaja 95* in earnest. Exact figures are not available, but more than 7,000 Bosnian Muslim men and boys are believed to have been killed, often after beatings or torture. Hundreds of Muslim women and girls were taken to a school gymnasium. Here they were separated by age and physical characteristics and used as sexual playthings for off-duty Serb forces.

Until the 2022 Russian barbarity in Ukraine, what happened in and around Srebrenica were the worst atrocities on European soil since World War II. The Bosnian Serb with the authority and power to intervene—Radovan Karadžić—did not. Labeled a war criminal by most of the world, Karadžić, the self-proclaimed poet-warrior (and trained psychiatrist), who once served as commander-in-chief of Bosnian Serb forces, eluded authorities until captured near Belgrade, Serbia, in 2008. Imprisoned in the Netherlands and ordered to stand trial before the International Court of Justice in The Hague, he was sentenced in 2016 to forty years in prison for the crimes of genocide ("intent and participation") against Bosnian Muslims. As Bosnian Serb president, Karadžić had authorized General

Mladić to "purify" Srbrenica. In 2019, a U.N.-mandated court increased Karadzić's sentence to life in prison.

* * *

Gazdík and Legion Special Forces arrived in Srebrenica in August 1995, one month after the slaughter. The situation was tense and the danger of more attacks or counter-attacks very real. Western powers put their best military units in the mix to root out the agitators, many of whom were agents of foreign governments. Without flair, and with some hesitation, Gazdík adds: "Srbrenica was all fucked up. Lots of shit happening, so we hit it hard. We were there six months with *CRAP (GCP)*. We were looking for terrorists. We were based in Mostar (city in Bosnia/Herzegovina on the Neretva River, and site of fierce fighting between Serbs and Croats) but operated all over that area. It was an international operation with the SAS (Special Air Service, an elite British Army commando unit) and all that. We were looking for a terrorist training camp we knew existed. We learned this from prisoners . . . interrogating prisoners. A Muslim training camp existed. Yeah, we also learned they were Iranians operating the camp. Typical of that place. Everything was divided—ethnic or religious. We are Christian . . . you are Muslim . . . and then the politics, of course."

Mitrovica
S/CH Gazdík takes us to Mitrovica, Kosovo, in 1999. Interestingly, he comments more on personal matters and the tension within his small Special Forces unit than the much larger external conflict and danger he and his men faced daily. As Gazdík notes: "For me, mentally and technically, the most difficult mission was our time in Mitrovica. At the start it was the *CRAP/GCP* that was to take this mission because of all the past problems between the locals (Serbs and Kosovars). We were to work with international police and security details already there—some special units that were like anti-riot police—units that had men up front with shields and batons and behind them men who would be ready to grab the leaders of the demonstrations and all that . . . getting information and so on."

Gazdík and a Greek, Lavdas, were the two sergeants in charge of a team of eight legionnaires. Lavdas was a radio operator, as well as a specialist in computers and video surveillance. Gazdík was in charge of the unit's fitness and tactics while Lavdas handled intelligence. The captain was quite satisfied, but the small group needed a *chef d'equipe* (platoon leader). Unfortunately, the team got an *adjudant-chef* who was of no use and caused the unit unnecessary problems. "I knew the name, that's all, and that he was German. And what I heard wasn't too good. Every time there was some action—like in Africa and elsewhere . . . he hid. Hid in the vehicle or somewhere and came out when it was over. 'Everything better? Everything good?' he'd say. Real bullshit guy, this German. So, he shows up in Kosovo." Gazdík complained to the captain after a week of conflict with the lazy and incompetent *adjudant-chef,* only to have him replaced by another type that sometimes shows up in a war zone—the medal chaser.

* * *

The new NCO was French and felt superior to Gazdík. He quickly tried to turn the men against the sergeant with subtle comments and insinuations as to which side the Slav really supported. All the while, Gazdík was training his men during the day and working undercover at night looking for weapons-traffickers and doing surveillance with SGT Lavdas.

Rank is respected in the Legion, but one can't hide behind it. Things between Gazdík and the French *adjudant-chef* soon came to a boiling point. "One time he actually said to me, 'Where were you on our last action in town? Were you hiding?' I said, 'Listen, you prick, take off your rank and we'll talk about it. You want that damn medal. I don't give a shit. I'm here for the mission. Everything you do is for a medal." This classic Legion tirade continued: "What good are you at these demonstrations? You don't understand Serb. If one of them said to you your mother has a hairy ass, would you know what he said? Would you say, 'Oh, can you say that in French?' What can you do at a demonstration, you fucking ballsack!' (apologies to Honoré.) This guy was an asshole who thought he was a warrior . . . but he didn't understand the terrain or people at all. That was the real problem."

S/CH Gazdík, the fifteen-year veteran, concludes his thoughts on his most challenging Legion assignment. "'I tried to focus the unit on the mission—peacekeeping. But the young ones were ready to fight, not keep the peace. I remember a young one, a Polish legionnaire, who said, 'Yeah, I want to make war.' I said to him, 'No, you're not here for war. You're here for the mission.' I said, 'It's not a restaurant. You don't come here and order from the menu what you want to do. On our *menu du jour* is—keep watch, protect, gather intelligence, give advice—that's it. That's the mission. You can't choose.'"

Yet, many of these Legion elite resisted the passive role and were vocal about it. It wasn't what they had signed up for, they complained. Gazdík, a sure and steady professional, had to juggle a range of personal problems and dangerous situations. As he told his captain, "Damn, I've got 'medal chaser' on my ass . . . a confused platoon . . . angry Serbs everywhere."

To make matters worse, "There was a *caporal-chef*, an Italian, who was doing lots of black market deals . . . even selling some of our stuff. A real fucker. One that many of us actually wanted to get shot in town. A very stressful time. A lot of little bullshit things like that. In addition, I had things happen back home. My wife wanted a separation—no reason given. So, I had problems at work, at home—all of this, but I managed. Still, it was really the toughest assignment."

AFGHANISTAN AND MALI

"France sent only legionnaires. You know, if legionnaires are killed, well, not so many French mothers and fathers cry."

—*Caporal* Timbaris

Men I've spoken to in the Special Operations community often quite willingly sign on for a third or fourth tour in a "hot zone." Among regular U.S. military units, the reaction to yet another dangerous deployment is mixed, at best. However, for all soldiers in the French Foreign Legion an assignment—the longer the better—to any area of conflict is seen as a true test of their Legion manhood and a very real way to connect with their combat-rich Legion patrimony. No legionnaire joins thinking of future college financial aid, health care benefits, or impressing a civilian employer. A man joins the Legion to fight. Upon learning of combat deployment, in no other army do deserters voluntarily return to their units. These AWOL soldiers only hope that, after their forty days in a Legion stockade, they will be sent directly to the war zone with their comrades.

* * *

In 2009, a massive deployment of the *2ème REI* spearheaded Task Force Dragon in the Surobi and South Tagab regions of Afghanistan. Joining the French in stabilizing and rebuilding this broken country (in addition to discreetly fighting the Taliban) were the *1er* and *2ème REG* (both combat engineering units), the *1er REC* (at times patrolling on horseback), and, of course, the *2ème REP*. Taliban prayers in the French sector are said to include special pleas to eternally damn the men who slow march in white hats and fast walk in green berets. Several recipients of medals from Legion General De Saint Chamas at Camerone 2012 were veterans of intense nighttime attacks by Taliban troops upon isolated Legion forts. Sadly, a few medals during recent Camerone ceremonies have been awarded posthumously.

CPL Timbaris' reaction to his new duty is typical of a legionnaire: "Yeah, we were glad. Glad because that's it. I mean, it's the mission that matters, that gives a reason to the whole thing. We also knew with Afghanistan that we'd see action and be there for eight months. Chad or Africa or like that is only four months, unless there's a real problem."

* * *

2ème REI had three companies based at an old Russian camp called Tora. They later exchanged positions with Legion cavalry *(1er REC)*, which, Timbaris notes, was "a damn good unit for this fight." His infantry company later moved locations "to another valley—that's all that fucking place is, mountains and valleys" and established Camp 42. Not far from the Pakistani border, the camp was "a small area with lots of sandbags and rocks, but we had to be there to protect this nothing place." The valley bordered a Taliban stronghold, and the bearded ones let the Legion know they were not welcome in the neighborhood. "Every night, they shot the *tchikon*. Do you know what the *tchikon* is? It's a rocket the Russians used and left there when they split. You hold the tripod and take a hammer and hit the rocket with the hammer. They really don't know where it will land—just the distance. It's done just to let you know they are out there and to unnerve you, that's it."

* * *

Timbaris spent six weeks at Camp 42. Every day, patrols took fire from the cliffs; then, silence reigned until the evening fireworks. The Taliban waited for this group of French to be worn down by the bombs, bullets, and boredom. Only three months earlier, they had killed forty-five regular army soldiers. To now sustain this war of attrition, "France sent only legionnaires.

You know, if legionnaires are killed, well, not so many French mothers and fathers cry."

* * *

My 8th grade English teacher had been a Marine Corps officer in Vietnam. He told my class of boys a wartime story of chance that I've never forgotten. While leading a patrol in familiar territory and over a well-worn path, he lost his seventh man, who was cut to shreds after triggering a land mine. My teacher and six others had set foot on the same small area, but survived.

* * *

If not for a last-minute phone call, CPL Timbaris and fellow legionnaires would have been killed in Kabul. "Damn—those IEDs (Improvised

Explosive Devices) play with your head. There was 100 or 150 kilos of explosives, you see. It made a hole in the road three meters deep. The armored vehicle, something like an APC, was moving along the road, and, then, it disappeared. It just wasn't there. Just the chassis was there. The rest was everywhere. The vehicle in front and behind it was completely busted up, but the guys in the middle vehicle—blown apart. The explosion, you see, blew their heads off and everything. I don't know—twelve dead Italian Army guys."

Timbaris and others learned later that they had originally been assigned to drive the deadly city street, but central command called moments before the convoy left and directed them to another route. "So, it was the Italians who got killed. That was in Kabul. Yeah, after that shit in Kabul, I'll take the mountains and valleys . . . and enemy you can see and shoot back at."

* * *

As noted, *Opération Serval* in Mali (2013–2014) was successful, yet the French military remains wary of any long-term commitment in Africa. Mali had been a rarity among the continent's fifty-six nations, a somewhat stable and democratic government. However, discontent within Malian forces over a lack of money and materiel in the fight against separatist Tuareg rebels in the north of the country eventually led to a more serious problem.

* * *

By 2012, the Tuareg rebels had their anti-government partners of convenience (Islamist extremists) take over their liberation struggle. In January 2013, French President Hollande ordered air strikes against Islamist militants and, soon, French ground troops landed in the former colony. In coordinated attacks with other allied African forces (mostly Chadian), French troops captured former Islamist strongholds, including the historic city of Timbuktu. While occupying the fabled, ancient city, the Islamist militants (allied with al-Qaeda) had banned music, watching sports on TV, drinking alcohol, and women in any garb but black sacks. In addition, several World Heritage sites in the once famous center of Islamic learning and tolerance were destroyed or damaged by the fanatically holier-than-thou Muslim invaders.

Legion paratroopers and cavalry have been an important part of French success in Mali. After February 2013, the Legion has focused on sweeps in the country's north, especially in the inhospitable al-Qaeda infested Amettetai Valley. Carrying more than 100 pounds of equipment in temperatures that rise to 125°F during the day and drop to nearly 30°F at night, legionnaires have found caches of weapons, explosives, and suicide belts in the caves that dot the Mars-like landscape. The search for Islamist militants in the desert has also yielded something very welcome for the French soldiers: fresh tomatoes and onions. Legionnaires pick through hastily abandoned jihadist gardens and gladly add the fresh food to their ration-pack meals.

* * *

Combat experience against an elusive enemy in the harsh terrain of Afghanistan helped acclimate legionnaires, mentally and physically, to the fight in northern Mali. Understood and accepted by all is that any combat operation (including routine patrols) produces casualties. *Opération Serval* and later engagement in that region had killed fifty-eight French soldiers as of 2023. One of the final Legion casualties in Mali, suffered under the first phase of operations in the Sahel, was a Serbian *major* from the *1er REG* with more than twenty-five years' service. During a 2014 Bastille Day parade, which also marked the official end of *Serval*, he was killed by a suicide car bomber. On his eighth *OPEX,* he was due to retire in a few months.

More counter-terrorist fighting pulled France back to the Sahel region of Africa in late 2014. *Opération Barkhane* deployed some 5,100 soldiers, including detachments from four Legion regiments participating in task forces Altor, Centurion, and Dragon. More legionnaires patrolling the dangerous corners of Mali, Niger, and Burkina Faso meant more deaths in the Legion family. In the spring of 2020, a Ukrainian *brigadier* was blown to bits when his tank was hit by an IED. Four days later, a French *légionnaire première classe*, also from *REC*, was shot in the head during an encounter with Islamist militants. While mourning the loss of two of its own, the Legion was actively hunting the one responsible, Abdelmalek Droukdel, an explosives expert and the fanatical leader of al-Qaeda in the Sahel. A Koran-quoting zealot and follower of the late Abu Musab al-Zarqawi, Droukdel believed in Providence. On Friday, June 5, 2020, *REP*-men from the *GCP*, supported by U.S. Black Hawk helicopters, made sure Droukdel praised Allah in person that particular Muslim holy day.

France has even brought the fight against Islamic extremism home in the form of *Opération Sentinelle*. All Legion units, even those just returned from overseas duty, partake in this program of national defense. Launched in 2015 by President Hollande in response to public outrage over the brazen attacks on a satirical newspaper office and popular music club in Paris, thousands of soldiers, including legionnaires, deployed to streets throughout France. The military was assigned to assist local security forces by patrolling cities and keeping watch over more than 700 "sensitive" sites, including selected government buildings, schools, cathedrals, synagogues, and transportation hubs. Yet another act of domestic terror shook France during a Bastille Day parade in Nice in 2016 and led to a full 10,000 French troops being assigned to *Sentinelle*.

How times have changed. During the April 1961 crisis between President de Gaulle and the military in Algeria, many Parisians were terrified Legion *paras* would visit the capital uninvited. Now, heavily armed patrols of legionnaires are a familiar and welcome sight to French civilians. Yes, times have changed but, for many French, the face of the real enemy remains familiar.

And, while vigilance against Islamic terrorism continues in the *métropole*, French enthusiasm for protracted struggle against extremists elsewhere has waned. In 2021, President Macron announced a "rethinking" of French military policy in the Sahel, especially in Mali. Political corruption and constant turmoil (coups in 2020 and 2021), Malian ties with the Wagner group, a brutal, state-backed-Russian mercenary force, and monetary concerns in Paris forced Macron to cease all military operations in the country by November 2022 and reduce activities in other parts of the Sahel. While thousands more French and Legion lives were lost in Indochina and Algeria, the 2014–2022 *Opération Barkhane* remains the longest and most costly French military operation since World War II.

France is eager to show its mettle and military commitment in Europe, as well. In 2017, 300 troops, including legionnaires from the *2ème REI*, joined British and Danish counterparts in Operation Lynx. This NATO exercise in Estonia is part of a show of solidarity (an "Enhanced Forward Presence" in diplomatic parlance) with the little Baltic nation, which seeks to avoid a Crimea-like land grab, or full invasion, from its not-so-friendly neighbor, Russia.

* * *

Whether in Africa or Europe, Afghanistan or Iraq, Paris or Marseille, the Legion continues to be in the vanguard of French military efforts in the twenty-first century. General Paul Rollet, "Father of the Legion," and a man who fastidiously promoted the traditions (and myths) of this special army in the 1920s and 1930s would today be proud that so many can see what a few good men from the world over can do.

5

Haircuts, Horses, and "Heroes"

"Only one thought went through the minds of all, from the sergeant of the guard to the lowest ranking legionnaire: Do not fail."

—LÉGIONNAIRE VALLDEJULI

Often, before any overseas adventure comes a two-year tour in the *métropole*. Either here or there, any man wearing a Legion uniform steps into another world. While computers, cell phones, ATMs, and other touches of modernity have appeared, soldiering in the Legion today still evokes a time long ago. I arrived at the *REC* in January 1987 with *instruction* mates Andy Robeson from England and Paolo Riva from Portugal. During the first week of our *REC* orientation, we were temporarily placed in the care of the *3ème escadron* (cavalry jargon for "company"). Even though the *REC* is a strict regiment, we felt quite free after almost four months of lockdown at Castel.

When the first evening in our new surroundings arrived, we were a bit on edge. Robeson and I warily asked the orientation *brigadier (REC caporal)*, a friendly English-speaking Norwegian named Sather, what we needed to do. Sather smiled, then laughed heartily. "You can do whatever you like," he told us. "The evening *soupe* (meal) is over." We decided to stay together in our room and begin re-adjusting our uniforms. We removed the gold *4ème RE* buttons from our dress coats and sewed on shiny new silver *REC* buttons. We also scrubbed our *képis* with *Savon de Marseille*

125

and refitted our headgear with the *REC*'s unique *képi* covering, called a *house* (tight-fitting white cloth stretched over top of *képi*). While a work-intensive evening, we could not have been happier since no one bothered us, and we could talk freely among ourselves, something that would not have been allowed at Castel.

Since we had an appointment with the *escadron*'s captain the next day, we decided to give each other haircuts. Riva had been our company barber at Castel so he cut and shaved Robeson's hair to the regulation length, then attended me. I had watched Riva glide the razor over Robeson's head; it seemed easy enough. I took it to Riva's bulbous head in a room that had no mirror and learned the perverse humor in giving a bad haircut when the one receiving can't see the unfolding disaster.

Riva was small, but had a big head and was aware of its comic value. During *instruction,* he would often have us laughing as he tapped his noggin with his knuckles and then made a strange hollow-like sound with his mouth. Riva would finish the routine with a quick shrug of his shoulders, turn around, and walk away in a Charlie Chaplin waddle. The *REC* haircut I was giving him was going terribly wrong. Robeson began to laugh, and I, too, started laughing so hard I had to halt the haircut. Riva dug into his Legion toilet kit for his mirror and looked at the uneven shave on his oddly shaped head. He cursed us for laughing, but, then, began to chuckle, as well. The next day in the captain's office, however, none of us felt too giddy.

* * *

On top of the many physical challenges given us that first week, came the traditional riding test. *REC* horses are used for ceremonial occasions and, as with any modern cavalry unit, serve only as romantic reminders of days past. Nevertheless, we were taken by *SM8* truck to the *REC* stables and riding hall, about two miles from camp. The instructor asked if we had ever ridden. While no cowboys, Robeson and I had been on horses, but Riva had never even been near a horse and was terrified. Still, all of us had to be tested. We mounted and began trotting, but even at this slow pace, Riva nearly fell out of the saddle. Eventually, after only an hour, the instructor had us galloping around the ring with our arms straight out from our sides. (All the while, *BRG* Sather had been practicing French mounts and fast-paced turns on his horse.) Though a purely *REC* drama, it was also a classic Legion lesson in taking on something new and overcoming one's fears.

As well as being a kind host to new boys in the *escadron*, Sather was an exceptional cavalryman, both on a horse and in a tank. After fifteen years of service, he left the Legion with the rank of *sergent-chef*, although he should have been made at least an *adjudant*. During his five consecutive years as tank commander in *1ᵉʳ REC*, Sather's *premier escadron* team was the one to beat. On all written tests, and every live fire exercise, his tank crew came in first. They also showed their expertise in Iraq during the First Gulf War in 1991, racking up many first shot direct hits on Soviet-built Iraqi tanks. After leaving the Legion, Sather returned to the Middle East and worked as a security consultant.

* * *

Your service counts for a lot in the Legion. A hierarchy of sorts is established so that even a lackluster legionnaire is given some respect after having served fifteen years or more. Sometimes, depending upon the old soldier in question, this "code" was difficult to accept, especially for new legionnaires still unable to put it in that particular Legion perspective. I remember two such long-standing veterans at the *REC* in the late 1980s. One was a German, who'd joined in 1957, the other, an Italian who had signed on in 1965.

The German worked at the gas station. However, whenever we pulled in to fuel our vehicles, I saw only an old man leaning back in his chair, scratching his face, and reading the newspaper. He would more or less acknowledge us and motion that we sign the proper books to record our vehicles. To those who were new to the Legion game, the German *brigadier-chef*, while *en service* (on duty), was breaking rules that were a legionnaire's fantasy. Primarily, he seemed oblivious to the NCOs and officers yelling orders around him; secondly, he was having others do his job; and, most brazenly of all, he was reading a newspaper from home.

The Italian was a swarthy and stubby little *brigadier-chef* who also seemed unconcerned with this Legion around him. He rode a bicycle to work. Everyone else at that regiment marched or ran around the *quartier* during working hours. Walking slowly while *en service* was enough reason for a legionnaire to be grabbed by an NCO for his own work detail. Thus, the unfortunate strolling soldier would have double the work. *B/CH* Torrefattori (whom we called "T-Fats") was the only man who worked in the regimental laundry. He was a logistical laundering genius, daily planning *Operazione Domani*. He opened more or less when he wanted and washed clothes not in the order received, but according to one's length of service and/or nationality. T-Fats was quirky, but, unlike the old German at the gas station, friendly if you appeared not to rush him. I quickly learned to accommodate him and always had my laundry done sooner than others.

The *brigadier-chef* was keen to tell young legionnaires that he had been in the Legion over twenty years—perhaps because none of these young ones would ever stop and ask, "Say, *B/CH* Torrefattori, you seem quite an interesting little fellow here surrounded by all these smelly socks and dirty underwear; tell me, how long have you been in the Legion?" Since it was never requested, the *brigadier-chef* would have to have you hear his unimpressive life story. The history of Don Torrefattori, however, would be rendered only if he felt a legionnaire was rushing him. No hurry, no story, but time, then, for a long friendly chat. Are you in a hurry? Well, now, how about a long chin-wag combined with a lecture on deference to *les anciens* (veterans) and a much longer wait for your clean clothes.

* * *

Another classic *REC*-man, albeit in another vein completely, was *Adjudant-Chef* (later *Major*) Reinecke. Many in the Legion thought his was the scowling and hardened face that inspired fellow *adjudant-chef* friend and senior *Képi blanc* artist Rudi Brabač to draw the 1980s recruiting posters. Found at train stations and *Gendarmeries*, the posters are often the first look a civilian has at a "typical" Legion face. Supposedly, Reinecke had been in the Hitler Youth and later involved in Werewolf (post-World War II fanatic Nazi resistance—more storied myth than reality) activities in the Russian sector of Berlin. All that mattered little. No one cared about Reinecke's past exploits when the legend himself was standing in front of their guard unit reviewing them for morning inspection. Only one thought went through the mind's of all, from the sergeant of the guard to the lowest ranking legionnaire: Do not fail.

Reinecke seemed to stare at the guards and their uniforms as if the men were toy soldiers that had fallen, and he was trying to reposition them using only his well-practiced glare. I remember one Reinecke review in which he felt a young Japanese guard had failed to present himself strongly enough. The soldier, Tanaka, had joined the Legion because he felt he had shamed his family by not passing the entrance exams to a university in Japan. He was small and soft spoken; Reinecke, we can say, was not and let out a tirade that went something like this: "What? Did I hear someone fart? Or was that rice soup bubbling? Why you fucking little chink, you call yourself a legionnaire? You call yourself a man? In Indochina, we used to kill puny dinks like you for laughs, but now they think they can be legionnaires, is that it? Sound off again and let them hear you in China!"

As terrifying as it was for all, it was also, in a very Legion way, quite funny. Interestingly, after that incident, Tanaka never had any problems with Reinecke. (Ironically for *Herr Major*, the *REC* is about 20 percent *"chinois"*: Chinese, Laotian, Vietnamese, and one proud Japanese.)

6

What Does It Take to Be a Legionnaire?

"It's a good place for those people who have nothing left to lose."

—*LÉGIONNAIRE* PERSSON

Those who adapt best to the Legion are able to accept the fact it is a multicultural, off-the-wall boys' club, which they had all but begged to join. Although the Legion has its share of big soldiers with rippling muscles, a sculpted physique is not what it takes to start the Legion adventure. All too often, the mental strain is more intense and onerous than the passing physical fatigue.

* * *

Upon accepting you, the Legion is being generous and constantly reminds you of your fateful choice. You may have been something somewhere, but, inside the Legion, you are nothing until you prove otherwise. By inner strength, guile, resilience, and a fair bit of leg and arm power, you must impress those around you—or look for a way home.

In the months before joining, you can do the sit-ups and push-ups. You can time your sprints and run long distances; you can even learn some French. But what it takes to be a legionnaire is sometimes getting through the small things. For some, the challenge will be overcoming those emotions that trigger the doubts and disillusion that fill the weary, lonely mind, especially in the early days.

* * *

I would hold it deep inside me every time we practiced marching during *instruction* and sang *"Adieu mon pays, adieu mon pays, jamais je ne t'oublierai"* from *"En Afrique."* I had learned enough French to feel the emotional pull of this verse; nor was it lost on the others. Fellow American CPL Mazowski presents early life in the Legion very clearly: "You have no friends. You don't speak the language. You're in a foreign country. Plus, you're subject to military lifestyle. So that's four things coming down on you, and you have to survive under that environment." He adds, "but it takes a special person. I'm not saying we're better than anybody else, but it takes a special mentality to get through that."

LFC Fairfield talks about "opting out . . . going for something that you've read about or seen on television . . . and you want to be that person. Once in the Legion, surrounded by it, you have to adapt to its unique demands and lifestyle. You're made a legionnaire. You don't have a choice. When they're in charge, your past is over. But to get there—it takes a lot of personal guts and heartache and pain."

C/CH Simon Murray also notes it's a very personal matter. "You've read about it or something like that, and you might think, 'Can I hack it with this lot? These are tough boys. Let me put myself through that. I want to fucking do it. And it's sort of a challenge to people, although you don't think of it like that. Still, [Murray smiles] if you've done it, you carry it for your entire life, don't you? It's, you know, part of your system."

Combat-veteran Murray remembers many challenges in the Legion. And, in his book, he offers insight into how one's mental and physical stamina can be tested and pushed almost to the breaking point: "We rose at 3 a.m. It has been raining for eight days and everything is drenched— our sleeping bags and our tents, inside and out. Our clothes are soaked through and through, and we shiver hard in the black wet mornings when we rise. It's not easy to be cheerful. There is no reason to be, anyway."

Murray finishes describing the scene and speaks for many legionnaires, past and present: "This is the moment when one needs morale; this is the time it pays to hold on to yourself, when everything is perfectly bloody and conditions are impossible, when one is an inch from letting go completely. Character comes through in moments like this, and those without fiber bend."

* * *

Street smarts is a valuable commodity in the Legion and one well worth bringing along when joining. "You've got to know when someone's fucking you about, or when he's not. If you come here and don't have brains, you're going to get shit on."

I was friendly enough with LFC Walton, but, as he adds, "If you don't have the intelligence to turn around and say, 'Don't fuck me about!' you won't make it. I ain't got any best friends here except me. I look on everyone here as an acquaintance. It's not a friend . . . it's nothing. I trust some of the guys, but I wouldn't call them friends, and, on the outside, I'd barely speak to some of them."

Taking stock of your new environment, one filled with unknown challenges and unfamiliar characters, is key to surviving more than a few months. The Legion, in many ways, is its own special army. *B/CH* Donlon: "You've got to put up with the nonsense. You've got to know when to switch on and off." CPL Lewis agrees: "You can't beat yourself up on a march that doesn't mean anything. If you risk it all because you're taking what a no-nothing sergeant is saying to you seriously, then you're going to strain yourself. If you hurt yourself, that's it. Sometimes, it ends well. Sometimes, it doesn't; more often than not, it doesn't."

The Legion is filled with all classes and stock of people. You will have to adjust to your new environment quickly or find it turning hostile. As Lewis warns, "You have to be able to accept everybody. You have to change your tolerances. If you go in there and one of your tolerances is, I can't stand human waste, OK, I can't stand shit: Then chances are that, in the first week, you're going to have fifteen different episodes with it. There's going to be the time the legionnaire just shits on your fruit cake from mom, you know, and on and on. So, that's not good to stick to restrictive ideas."

* * *

The first days and weeks in the Legion will be the most difficult. Family and friends—or, at least, some thoughts of what has been left behind—will be a constant pull. Legionnaire Persson advises: "It's a good place for those people who have nothing left to lose. Like if you have a nice girlfriend, I wouldn't go to the Legion because you're going to miss her and want to go back and probably will go back before five years is gone."

Some years later, Persson, who deserted within a year, reflects, "So, it's the final thing you should do, really. My options are out. I don't want to do anything else. I don't want to work there. I don't want to live there, and I have nowhere to go. If you enjoy your life most days and just go there for some excitement, it's not a good idea, that's for sure."

Future *caporal-chef* and author Simon Murray maintains that: "You have to be tough, but more so you've got to be pretty independent mentally . . . and this is an issue. If you're coming from a very tight-knit family background, you probably are going to get a bit miserable very soon after joining."

Another future Legion author and NCO, *sergent-chef* Gazdík, sees a pattern in those who join and what it takes to be a legionnaire: "I'll say, from my point of view, there are three categories, OK? First category is like me: I know what I want. I leave home. I don't care. I did it. No questions. It takes this kind of focus to be a good legionnaire."

Gazdík's next two types are probably the more common among the 150 nationalities that make up this unique army. "Second category: the guys who have a problem and they know the Legion offers a second chance. That means family problems . . . troubles in society . . . all that. But they come to the Legion to change their lives. And the third category is the ones who don't give a damn. They don't know. They'll try it . . . see what happens . . . an old sergeant or veteran who says, 'Maybe I'll like it and stay. Who knows? Maybe I'll stay a long time.' Or, he says, 'It's not for me' and deserts."

* * *

According to LFC Van Heek, most of those who join have a reckless spirit: "Stable guys think twice before they join the Legion. It takes a certain blindness to the long-term consequences of what you are doing." Yet, fellow *REP*-man Stanislav Gazdík was a very determined twenty-one-year-old with a bold plan. Without notifying family or friends, he bought a one-way train ticket from Prague to Strasbourg, France, and went directly to the recruiting station. Few who join are as sure and single-minded. After fifteen years of hard service, and now sitting in his comfortable living room in Prague, Gazdík—ever precise—comes back to the question of what it takes to be a legionnaire: "But what it takes? The process takes a hell of a lot of decisions . . . very personal ones. You've got to be focused and know what you want . . . to do well."

* * *

A high level of physical endurance is a must, but so is "a lot of patience and a sense of humor," says CPL Mazowski. "The Legion wants you to be confident and not afraid to do things. You'll get your nuts busted, but, then, you'll say after, 'Hey, I did that. Maybe I am a little stronger.' So then you go on to do something else, and it builds in so many ways."

* * *

At the same time, for a new legionnaire to succeed "he's going to have to learn to sacrifice things, to accept a lot of constraints and get on with it and force himself to make a go of it," states nineteen-year veteran *sergent-chef* Robeson. "I mean, there's bullshit in any army, and there's probably a whole lot more in the Foreign Legion than anywhere else, but it's, well, I . . . don't know . . . something you've just got to take. I've got no regrets for what I've done."

* * *

I agree with most of these comments and observations. Attitude and state of mind are crucial to lasting in the Legion, but, without a doubt, physical fitness is a must. Proving oneself a man, and a very tough one, is what has drawn recruits from all over the world into the ranks of the Foreign Legion. For all who join this elite brotherhood, it will be a test on many levels and unlike any endeavor they have experienced. Instilled among new legionnaires is a collective sense of *mission* to help the ones who have lost the *pêche*, but you, alone, must also have the will to continue the struggle.

Some maintain that one's fitness level must rate acceptable, or, perhaps, a bit above average for one to be selected for *instruction. S/CH* Robeson trained several sections of new recruits at Castelnaudary: "You have to be reasonably fit or prepared to get fit." Felllow Englishman *C/CH* Murray, who did his basic and airborne training in North Africa, feels, "the Legion thing—it's not a physical thing—you don't have to be 6'4" and so on. You have to be fit, but then you have to be fit to play rugger (rugby) on a school rugger field." For my part, any man wanting to be a legionnaire must understand that his body will be punished far more than his coaches or teammates would accept in any school athletic program or sports club. Most non-life-threatening injuries, including broken bones, will simply have to be mended as best as possible. A true legionnaire is then expected to carry on. I experienced this, as have many others.

Even highly trained military veterans of special units are stunned by the pace and rigor of Legion marches. In fact, these epic feats of endurance have more in common with those undertaken by Roman legionnaries of old than by those of most any infantry company of today. The Legion will trek over any terrain in any temperature or weather condition, with full gear, for periods of time that do not seem humanly possible. I can't remember how many times, since leaving France, I've played the numbers "13," "7," and "52" in state and national lotteries. I've come up just as unlucky (though less battered) with these combinations of numbers on my ticket as I did all those years ago on a legendary Legion jaunt along the French-Spanish border.

At 03:00, on a frigid morning in late November, we started a march that would see our company of fifty new recruits, led by Lieutenant Le

Cour Grandiose and his veteran team of sergeants and corporals, in constant motion—not one rest for food or drink—for 13 hours, 7 minutes, and 52 seconds. How am I so sure of this time? My good friend and protector, the built-like-a-bull Serb, Krković, was the man in front of me and served as our official timekeeper. No one was sure why Krković was so obsessed with recording every march; he said he'd done the same in the Yugoslav Army. Somehow, it seemed to give him pleasure to note the hourly passage of our agony and, given his size and enthusiasm for this project, no one challenged him. Nevertheless, for me and my friends, the Serb's running clock only added to the misery surrounding these endless marches.

Thirteen hours of continuous movement, with the last hour or so in snow up to our knees, left even the strongest of us slumping and staggering. I will never forget my Senegalese friend, the gentle Adelbert, on that torturous day. I was five or six men behind him and could see that he was struggling. I noticed, however, that Adelbert had had the clever idea of putting snow under his beret to keep cool. Not until our weaving line bunched up, and I saw his shaved black head more clearly, did I notice that the white mass under and around his cover wasn't snow, but foam. Due to the altitude, duration of the march, and exhaustion, his irregular core body temperature was producing a freakish, bubbling white foam atop his head.

* * *

In addition to being in top physical and mental condition, a legionnaire can't expect too much support or direction from his superiors, especially in the early part of his service. The Legion will scold, scorn, and often sour the new boy, who'll have to take it like a man if he's to become part of the team. You have to accept a lot in the Legion, whose members can't stomach excuses, complaints, or comparisons to other armies. This army is very clear on the matter: If you don't like us, catch the civvy express and get off at the stop called Whiney Manor. The Legion will not change for you, and the sooner that is understood, the better.

Yet the Legion is such an institution that even the malcontent leaving after three or four months will have felt moments of true camaraderie with men who, not long before had been perfect strangers. Furthermore, at some point, he will have reveled in the Legion's unique mix of past and present and understood that this feeling is also part of what it takes to be a legionnaire.

7

Song: *Chante ou Crève*

"It's dead appropriate for instruction *or a corporal's course because you're having your balls broken non-stop and you can identify with the sons-of-bitches."*

—CAPORAL McCue

Much as marching is vital to being a good legionnaire, so is singing. Aside from jody calls, group singing has all but disappeared in U.S. forces. Just as American soldiers no longer march with fixed bayonets or cummerbunds (special details excepted), nor do they sing. Cavalry units singing the "Gary Owen" are found only in John Ford westerns. It should come as no surprise that group singing is an important and continuing tradition in the Foreign Legion, whose soldiers sing for their supper and often at any other meal formation. Legion songs can be serious or sarcastic, melodramatic, or bawdy.

Songs are sung while marching and at special dinners. On the command of *Envoyez!*, the apéritif at regimental dinners will be knocked back and glasses slammed to the table in unison. Legionnaires remain standing and sing the traditional *"Le Boudin"*, in honor of the blood sausage that was a common dish for early legionnaires. *Boudin* also refers to the blanket roll legionnaires carried across their chest or back, as well as the rolled and crossed bed sheets a modern-day legionnaire must have on his bunk whenever it is to be inspected "battery-style." *"Le Boudin"* is one of the first songs a legionnaire learns, since neither its lyrics nor melody is overly long or complicated. In fact, the song is the Legion's anthem, sung or played at all gatherings before even *La Marseillaise*. (The French national anthem is played only at official Legion gatherings or when rendering honors to the national flag.)

Though most Belgians are comfortable singing in French and will belt out the beginnings of *"Le Boudin,"* few will even mouth the last line of the anthem. After singing that there is enough *saussage* for the Alsacians, Lorrains, and even Swiss, the Belgian legionnaires are to sing there is none left for them because they are *"des tireurs au cul"* (assfuckers). After the official version of *"Le Boudin"* is sung, many legionnaires will continue the same back door motif and tag on a raunchy final one-liner calling for a pretty boy to drop his pants or still another tasty one to be sodomized next to the tent of the regiment's chaplain. Three regiments—*1er REC, 2ème REI,* and *4ème RE*—actually have this vulgar refrain in their songbooks and expect their men to sing it heartily.

* * *

While it might not seem the most necessary or macho item to issue, the Legion sees to it all new legionnaires have a *carnet de chant* (song book) with them at all times. A legionnaire will practice singing almost as much as shooting while at Castelnaudary. Indeed, viewed by those in command, singing is part of the foreigners' French language acquisition training. Soldiers with good voices are singled out and complimented. Legionnaires, even those close to finishing their service, carry vivid memories of learning to sing.

Of course, especially during months of training, such moments are not always "warm" ones. Legionnaire First Class Poulsen remembers a field exercise during *instruction*: "The night before, we'd put up these big tents, but no flaps—some idiot left them back at Castel. So we had to sleep with the snow blowing in the sides ... at least 40cm of snow by morning. It was too fucking cold to sleep that first night and those bullshit French sleeping bags ... they were probably too cold for Tahiti.

I put my gloves on my feet. And by 05:00 *réveille* guys sleeping on the edges were covered with snow."

Following that frigid night came an exhausting day of running and shooting. The drill sergeant (mine, also), "Frenchie" Duprey, then decided to treat the boys to a cozy and dry evening of song inside the warm barrack. But, as Poulsen remembers, "Everyone was so fucking tired around 9 p.m. We were glad to be inside at night but couldn't concentrate on singing. Just too tired. Some of us, me included, began to nod off. Frenchie warned us there'd be trouble if he saw one more person sleeping. He did, and so the fucker opened the windows . . . all of them and shouted, 'Now, no more sleeping!'"

Poulsen and his fellow Danes are used to long, cold winters—and usually manage to sleep comfortably—but not in the French Frozen Legion. "The snow came in one side and out the other," he recalled. "No one got more than one or two hours of sleep that night—worse than the last night. It was too cold, and all our clothes got wet. I will never, ever, forget that in my life."

It should be noted, however, that, since the end of the First Gulf War and mandatory military service in France, the army has been allotted much better equipment. Lightweight sleeping bags with GORE-TEX shells, warmer socks, and better boots are now issued to all Legion units.

* * *

Though memories of learning to sing are often filled with stories of fatigue or discomfort, there comes a point when a legionnaire wants to sing because he knows how good it can sound and how proud he will feel. Legionnaire Persson on such singing during basic training: "I remember after the Raid March we walked into regiment (*4ème RE*), you know, with all the weapons and everything . . . *sac-à-dos* (backpacks), the flag in front, and yeah . . . really tough and slow. That was probably one of the best. We were singing our company song—*"Honneur, Fidélité"*—an old German song. That was something special because we could see that in the regiment everything stopped off and everybody was watching. That was beautiful. I heard people say afterwards who saw us marching that was one of the best things they've seen."

Most armies march at 120 steps per minute. The Legion has a distinctive slow-march of 88 steps, which takes time to master. Nearing the end of *instruction*, Persson's section had finally come together. The men held their heads straight and high and their bodies didn't wobble while marching. He reasons that "we got it really slow, with perfect pace and singing—because we had all the equipment and were really so fucked-up tired. So, we wanted to do this perfect, so we could just go and do what we had to . . . take the showers, the food, everything like that. You know what happened if you don't succeed; so, we said, let's do this perfect. Everyone was damn sure about that."

After the months of struggle and pain, mixed with moments of doubt about it all, Persson and the others felt like legionnaires. "And we felt tough as well after the March. We felt like soldiers . . . done something. I felt proud marching. It was feeling good. It was beautiful. I could hear the echo in the *quartier*."

* * *

Five-year veteran CPL McCue also notes how Legion *esprit de corps* will surface in song, especially during the intensity of *instruction* or training sessions for promotion. Years after leaving the Legion, he has a lingering memory of a song that is not found in the *carnet de chant*. The song, originally sung in German as *Die Moorsoldaten*, is from the time of Nazi concentration camps (although McCue notes its history in the *taule* of Guiana). "It's a Devil's Island song. If you've ever seen that movie *Papillon*, there's a scene in that movie where the guys walk by singing that song. And, of course, it's an ideal song for those slow 88 beats to the minute. It has a funeral air to it. It's dead appropriate for *instruction* or a corporal's course because you're having your balls broken non-stop and you can identify with the sons-of-bitches. And when that song goes off right, it is the best song I've ever heard the Legion march to."

The song is *"Le Chant des Marais"*—"Song of the Marshes"—and without hesitation McCue sings it for me:

"Far into the infinity extend the great marsh,
where not a bird sings in the trees, dried and withered,
Noise of chains and noise of arms, sentinelles day and night, Not a cry,
not a tear,
Death for him who tries to escape,
But one day in our life, the spring will flower again: Freedom, free-
dom dear, I want to say that you are mine."

During the last weeks of basic training at *quartier* La Passet, McCue's section would march and sing this melancholy song with "all the buildings'. . . all the barracks' windows open . . . and guys just hanging out the barracks watching. You'd see NCOs, as we would pass by, would come to *garde-à-vous* (standing at attention) in respect for us because we were doing the thing so well. The whole regiment would be watching." (For many years, however, the French military avoided the song or melody of *Le Chant des Marais* because its political prisoner authors had been communists.)

Interestingly, for McCue and many other *anciens* (veterans), bans on nearly all songs were lifted by the mid-1990s, including the works of French folk singer Jean-Pax Méfret, whose "Best of" double-CD compilation sold well in Legion *foyers*. Indeed, his rousing version of "Camerone" gives the listener a feel of what it is to be in the Foreign Legion.

* * *

For many, singing becomes an open and outward sign as to what kind of army they've chosen to serve. The idea that we do many things differently from other militaries is evident in the slow-step march, song lyrics, and dress. One of the most eye-catching parade uniforms is worn by Legion sappers or *les pioneers*. Most anyone watching a group of bearded men with shaved heads, leather aprons, and sharpened slowly march toward them would run, but this is the traditional look of *pioneers*. This quirky-looking unit usually leads the Legion contingent in the Champs-Elysee Bastille Day parade; every July 14th, the men of the Foreign Legion draw the loudest cheers from the spectators. Civilian or military, it's hard not to be awed by the Legion *en marche*. McCue still feels his "proudest moments were on parade, without a doubt. Especially if you were on parade in front of civilians or in front of regular army. The Legion does pull together well."

Children also find the cadence and chants hypnotic. During his corporal's course in Djibouti, McCue recalls two officers' children playing a game with the candidates as they marched, once again singing *Les Chant des Marais*. Robot-like legionnaires marching with head up and eyes forward, swinging left arm to web belt of the man in front, were objects of fascination for the boys. One would race to the front of the column and "stand there, stalk-still, with his arms tucked in, a little smile on his face, and, then, as we'd pass, he'd run around in front of us, so it could be done again. Of course, there's another one of the little children kind of marching along beside us. And it was surreal. Marching through there on a Friday when you should have off. The whole regiment watching you sing this funeral march song with these two little children. And those two little children playing their little game with us. Life meets Death . . . kind of that feeling."

* * *

Not all legionnaires learn to enjoy singing. Of the many nationalities represented in the Legion, the British seem to resent the chants the most. Aside from the French, Germans are the least antagonistic toward singing, perhaps because the Legion has incorporated many German songs, or at least German melodies. One kept by the Legion is a rousing World War II *Panzerlied* now sung with the same gravitas in French as *"Képi Blanc."* The French lyrics are equally inspiring, if not daunting, to the hundreds of non-francophones who have to master this graduation song during *instruction*. Other old-time songs learned later in one's Legion career such as *"Westerwald"* and *"Lili Marleen,"* are sung entirely in the original German, while an *instruction* favorite like *"Les Oies Sauvages"* ("The Wild Geese") is presented in French with only the final verse sung in German. Indeed, *"Les Oies Sauvages"* is a beautiful song, and will always remind me of what life in the Legion demands of its soldiers: total commitment.

143

While at *REC*, my platoon was on a six-day winter field exercise in the north of France. It was a cold and icy affair, with much marching and running, and small unit orienteering. Conditions (especially for new boys like me) were difficult, with lots of bullying and bullshit directed at those new to the regiment. After an early morning "march" over rocks covered with ice, during which whoever fell was laughed at and chided, and an afternoon run in full-gear with corporals purposely tripping new boys. By early evening, I felt I'd had enough. We had chow (and plenty of wine) in a barn that also served as our field barrack. After the meal, our platoon leader wanted to sing Legion songs. Not in the mood for this forced camaraderie after our abusive day, two other new boys and I snuck upstairs and went to bed. What a mistake. As the drunken strains of *"Les Oies Sauvages"* drifted upstairs, I heard our platoon leader curse the "deserters." Moments later a white smoke grenade was thrown into our room, and we reluctantly went downstairs and were made to sing *"Les Oies Sauvages."* Jokes were made about these "birds shot down from the clouds" and more wine was drunk by all.

* * *

Many British, however, find speaking any language other than English more than a mouthful and can't see the purpose in struggling to learn song lyrics that mean nothing to them. *Brigadier-Chef* Donlon notes how, for him, the tradition of singing is another example of the Legion's preoccupation with the past: "But you see, I mean, it's so easy to live off the backs of what these guys did before. It's so easy singing songs about Algeria. I mean, listen, I was born in '62. The end of the war in Algeria was '62. What the fuck do I want to sing songs about Algeria? I've never been there. I will never go there. Full stop. It doesn't mean anything."

Donlon agrees that British regiments have their traditions and ceremony but feels the Legion is far more stuck in the past. He feels a soldier in today's British Army is "more interested in his combat skills in the field than learning about fucking dates and songs. It seems, you know, unimportant."

* * *

Not all tunes heard in the Legion are found in the *carnet de chant.* The first month in the Legion (Aubagne), I encountered two singing characters who later would become good friends: Phil Fairfield from England and Danny Kastening (name changed) from the Netherlands. The three of us did *instruction* together, and Phil and Danny went on to the *REP.* While on his first official leave from Corsica to mainland France, Danny fell back in with his old drug crowd in Amsterdam and, only two days before he was to return to his regiment, died of a heroin overdose.

* * *

Danny was as colorful as he was confident. He had been an acrobat in a traveling circus in Holland and was one of the strongest and fittest in our group, in both long-distance running, representing our section on the regimental cross-country team and in rope climbing. He could climb up and down a fifteen-foot rope almost effortlessly and would often challenge our lieutenant to a contest—not of speed, but to see who could outlast the other in repeatedly climbing up and down. Danny won the contest every time. While the highly competitive officer was displeased at losing a match to a recruit, he found the idea of a new legionnaire daring to challenge him stimulating. Yet, this was Kastening's unorthodox style. Danny's manner showed itself especially when he walked. This Dutch legionnaire, with a perpetual smirk, cocky air, and mass of flexible muscles, didn't walk or march in a soldierly way at all but loped and bounced along with a gait that drove both sergeants and corporals crazy. He constantly reminded us what it was like to be a civilian again. Danny's charm lay in his ability to stay so relaxed and carefree in an environment that didn't at all promote that attitude, nor reward it.

* * *

His prowess on the rope was similar to that of a man in a story my father used to tell. While in a Veterans' Administration hospital in California

145

during the Korean War, he watched in awe as a fellow "disabled" veteran, paralyzed from the waist down, climbed a rope in the physical therapy room. The injured soldier and showman would then extend his body from the rope with one hand and light himself a cigarette with the other. Whether for my father and the other wounded or me and my section of battered recruits, such feats of strength and resilience by one of our own in the midst of our trials boosted morale tremendously.

I first met Danny in the kitchens of Aubagne. He was carrying a stack of dirty pots and pans while swaying back and forth singing the John Denver tune, "Annie's Song." I couldn't think of anything more out of place at that moment. Elsewhere in that hectic and noisy kitchen, the head chef was "singing" in his own special way. The rotund *caporal-chef,* an Iranian, seemed, to us, completely out of his mind. He'd put a cardboard box over his head with slots cut out for the eyes and mouth. He'd also attached a string to the semi-cut out mouth area that he would tug to make the mouth move up and down like a ventriloquist with his dummy. All the while he would shout *"Allez . . . Allez . . . Allez la-bas! La-bas allez!"* ("Go . . . Go . . . There! There, go!") over and over whenever he saw a new recruit slow down or not look busy enough. Nonetheless, Danny and his Annie were the only ones among us that chaotic day able to outmaneuver or maybe outdo, in absurdity, the singing Iranian.

* * *

Another recollection of a strange song in a strange place was back at the *EV* barrack in Aubagne. Danny and I, along with Phil Fairfield and other new friends from Paris, were now at the final stage of processing. We'd gone *"rouge."* The *rouge EVs* were on the bottom floor of the barrack and secluded from the other recruits. At certain times of the day during that final week at Aubagne only a few *rouge EVs* were on the floor, and life, at least for an hour or so, could be relatively quiet and, even, private. During one of these down times, I was sitting on my bed reading when I heard a voice at the other end of the corridor singing, clearly and loudly, Clint Eastwood's song from *Paint Your Wagon*—"I Talk to the Trees." Hearing that light Broadway melody (sung well, this time) made me smile.

However, I also thought of all I'd left behind and wondered where I was headed. It was nice to know that someone like Phil Fairfield would be with me on the journey.

During *instruction*, Fairfield also boosted the morale of all English speakers with campy renditions of Cliff Richard's "Summer Holiday" (usually sung at the beginning of a long march) and Erasure's "Oh, L'Amour." The latter tune was belted out in mock deference to the corporals and sergeants who disliked his singing in English. Our most memorable non-Legion song fest came at the end of *instruction*. The night before we were to depart for our combat regiments, we had a company dinner in town. Even though 3rd Company had not had one AWOL or even attempted desertion, we had been given only two four-hour leaves during our four months of basic training. I believe our final dinner together in Castelnaudary (which few companies had) was Lieutenant Le Coeur Grandiose's way of saying thank you to a section that had been strong and caused him no embarrassment in his first year of Legion command. The food was delicious. There was plenty of red meat and sauce and *beaucoup* wine. The atmosphere was convivial as corporals and sergeants no longer cared about the distance they had felt they needed to maintain during training.

At one point, Le Coeur called on *les anglais* (the English) to sing. I'm sure he had wanted to hear one of the many Legion marching songs that had been drilled into us, but, as we gathered in front of his table, we prepared something quite different. In a quick huddle our song leader, Fairfield, said, "Right, lads, who knows "Hotel California?" By the time we had gotten to the first word of the second line, we were joined by Dutch, Portuguese, and African legionnaires. All of us were happy to sing this song and celebrate the end of basic training in such a non-military way. We certainly were well aware of what we had just gone through, but we also wanted to show the lieutenant and others that we had not forgotten the civilian side of our lives.

* * *

Yet another incident of legionnaires gathered in non-Legion song occurred at the *"Hôtel" CAPLE*, the *1ᵉʳ RE* barrack housing legionnaires in transit and the personnel administering their paperwork. In the months before my discharge, I was based at the *1er RE* and worked in an administrative position in the *CAPLE*. The three floors above the administrative offices billeted the 8,000 or so who would call the *CAPLE* home for a few days or a few weeks every year. Time spent at the *CAPLE* was a limbo of sorts for most legionnaires. A good deal of guard duty and a variety of Legion *corvée* kept us busy, but this transient company could be a very social place, as well. Old friends were popping up all the time—friends you hadn't seen since *instruction*, friends you hadn't seen since your corporal's course, friends who'd transferred regiments, and, even, friends you were sure had deserted. Since much at the *CAPLE* was informal, a legionnaire, if possible, might arrange work details with pals. Regardless of whether they had spoken during the day, friends would meet that evening at the *foyer* after dinner.

On one such occasion, a Thursday, I left the *foyer* at closing time with quite a cast of characters: three legionnaires sent back *disciplinaire* from Djibouti (a.k.a. the Wrecking Crew), another *13ème DBLE* compatriot named Darby, who was also required to exit Djibouti (Darby, however, was returned to France so he could try another "*stage limonade*," a Legion detox program, his second in nine months); Hollingate; and Turlane, paratrooper friends of mine from *instruction*, fellow *REC*-men Alphie Dunn (ex-Australian Army officer), Gilchrist (soon-to-be barman at popular Legion haunt "Irish Tony's" in Paris); and smarmy, former used-car salesman, and all around quirky Canadian, Terry Myers. Myers was convinced that its new logo, which had the *képi* covering half of the seven-flamed grenade, was proof that the authorities in Paris were plotting to do away with the Legion. Also joining us that night was a jolly 6'8" Swedish giant we had nicknamed "Sven Jorga the Hurdy-Gurdy Man" (he seemed to like this). Sven's baby face had recently been scarred by a *PM* in a *pouffe* brawl in French Guiana. Several other English-speakers rounded out this colorful mob that weaved its way uphill from the *foyer* to the *CAPLE*.

The dozen or so legionnaires gathered in the room Dunn and I shared on the second floor. Except for two French, whom we kicked out without caring where they would sleep, the room was empty. With a case of *Vitamine K* (opened bottles, per *foyer* rules, of Kronenbourg beer), we settled down to a night of song and drink. Those gathered began to gulp the beer and run through assorted English drinking songs when little Darby, the drunk from Belfast, began to sing a tender tune about the Troubles back home. I expected ill feeling or, at least, some comments among the English, but none arose. All eyes watched Darby and listened in silence as he sang us a picture about a British soldier on his last day of duty and the young Irish boy he shoots. Before the melancholy of Darby's ballad ended, we were interrupted by the *caporal de semaine* (duty corporal of the week), "What was the problem? Why all the beer and singing?" Jamieson of Wrecking Crew fame rose to get in the corporal's face and said in drawled English, "Boy, go!" When the *caporal* continued speaking, Jamieson answered in a very deep voice, "Go now!" The corporal departed, and we went back to singing and drinking. He returned shortly, however, accompanied by the *sergent de semaine* (duty sergeant of the week). At this point, I was sure we would call it a night but Jamieson, the big American from South Carolina, again growled, and the intruding authority figures again went away.

The corporal and sergeant retreated only to get more back up, which I think even the none-too-sober Jamieson realized. After closing the door, he turned to face us and took off his *képi*, placing it over his heart, he said, "Gentlemen, stand." He then began to sing "Dixie," and the rest joined in as best they could. In about ten minutes, we were visited by the same corporal and sergeant, as well as the *officier de permanence* (duty officer), and two *PMs*. Jamieson was now much drunker than he had been at the first notice but was smart enough not to threaten this new force. Still, he tried to make a case for not ending the party, albeit he stopped as soon as he saw the officer put his hand on his sidearm.

I was sure the next day we'd all be punished; however only Jamieson was put in the local lock-up. A unique feature of the *Hôtel CAPLE*, the company jail was a dingy one-man cell with a low ceiling and little air located in the basement opposite the armory. Jamieson spent only a few hours scrunched up in the cell since he and the rest of the Wrecking Crew were scheduled to be dishonorably discharged that Friday, as scheduled. One repercussion that shocked me was what happened to *Brigadier* Gilchrist (Gilly) who, after completing seven years of service to France,

Inside the French Foreign Legion

was also returning to civilian life that day. The Anglo-hating Catalan *Adjudant-Chef* "Bull" Torrons, however, wanted to make an example of the previous night's activities and picked, of all the rowdies assembled, one of the calmest and sanest. Before the Legion, Gilly had served three years in the Royal Green Jackets. He was a good soldier, but one whom the Legion was pressuring out because of a drinking problem. Nevertheless, I found Gilly to be one of the most intelligent and witty legionnaires I'd met.

Brigadier Gilchrist didn't tame the Bull, however. A mere three hours before he was to become a civilian again, Gilchrist was publically humiliated by *Adjudant-Chef* Torrons, who confronted him in the busy *bureau de semaine* (duty office) that Friday afternoon, scolded him, and slapped him. Ironically, Gilly, on his last night in the Legion, had wanted to sing some Legion songs but was shouted down by the others.

* * *

Maybe Gilchrist just had bad luck. Until 1991, the Paris *métro* offered first and second-class (general) cars, with tickets issued accordingly. Anyone who has ridden the subway in Paris has seen people jump the turnstile or sneak through the doors to the platforms. *Métro* police are few and rarely stop passengers for their tickets. Our hapless friend, however, on leave in 1980s Paris, inadvertently boarded a first-class car with his general ticket and was subsequently "controlled" and fined by the *métro* police.

8

Germans and British in the Legion: *Was Ist Das*, Mate?

"Both groups come from soldierly nations with long histories of European and world military conflict."

—LÉGIONNAIRE VALLDEJULI

Above the clamor of the other 150 nationalities in the Legion (at least in the 1980s and 1990s) are the two that traditionally harbor the strongest dislike for the French: the Germans, and the British. These two boisterous and headstrong nationalities may give the French a hard time, but they have also served France well. Both groups come from soldierly nations with long histories of European and world military conflict. However, the air of superiority and accomplishment carried by German and British legionnaires is bound to collide with the same national pretentions of the French. Germans and British complain about the French, but the longer-serving ones will usually stop short of criticizing the Legion, often believing that foreigners such as they carry this army.

A soldier's dissatisfaction with Legion lifestyle can take many forms: anger, insolence, apathy, or simply a sudden unemotional departure. High desertion rates among German and British legionnaires over the years, however, also couple with a high fatality rate, particularly among Germans.

151

In fact, soldiers from Germany died in the service of France even before the Legion was founded. Until the late 1950s, German school children were taught that nearly half of Napoleon's *Grande Armée* was German (mostly from Alsace-Lorraine). The exploits and sacrifices of German legionnaires in Indochina and Algeria are legendary. For the Germans I have met, old or young, the Legion seems to fill a military and emotional post-World War II void. After the fall of the once mighty *Wehrmacht* in 1945, Germany was divided and occupied by Russian, British, French, and American forces. The country, once having one of the highest living standards in the world, lay in ruins, its people shamed and disgraced. Not until 1955—the same year Chancellor Konrad Adenauer bought the release of the last of Nazi Germany's military and civilian POWs held in Soviet labor camps (men Khrushchev described as "convicted war criminals")—did the Federal Republic of Germany reestablish an army, the *Bundeswehr*. Germans in the Legion, most of whom drink beer and talk politics on the far right side of the *foyer*, know their country's military history and are proud, yet find it difficult to display this emotion in the *Bundeswehr*.

Lost causes and discredited ideology still resound among German legionnaires. For many Germans in the Legion, a military career masks a nationalistic or even neo-Nazi fervor. I was in the *1ᵉʳ REC foyer* not long after Russian guards found their lone inmate, Rudolf Hess, hanged in his jail cell in Berlin's Spandau prison. Hess had been imprisoned often. As an early and eager National Socialist, he'd helped transcribe *Mein Kampf* while in prison with Hitler in Munich in 1924. In 1941, Hess was imprisoned by the British after a failed "peace mission" flight took him to Scotland. Finally, the Nuremberg tribunal sentenced Hitler's loyal but loony henchman to life in prison. By the early 1980s, all countries involved in Hess' 1946 sentencing, except the Soviet Union, agreed to his release from Spandau. The ninety-three-year-old Hess committed suicide in August 1987, more than forty years after his first futile attempt with a butter knife. While having beers with a table of Brits that week, I noticed several German legionnaires at another table raising their bottles of Kronenbourg and giving the Nazi salute. Later, I asked a fellow platoon member, who had been sitting among them, what had happened that night in the

152

foyer. The group had offered a final salute to Rudolf Hess, "our last Nazi," he stated.

* * *

In another Germanic Legion moment, I once shared an *SM8* truck and a bit of history with *BRG* Rolf Steiner. My young *REC* driver felt honored to have received this loaded name. Throughout the drive from Orange to Marseille, he proudly told me the story of Rolf Steiner, the famed ex-Legion *para* and 1960s African mercenary.

* * *

While German World War II veterans' groups tend to keep a low profile and often gather in secluded hideaways in Bavaria, former legionnaires are more open. Thousands of Germans served in the Legion after World War II, fighting and dying in French colonial hot spots in Asia and Africa. I have spoken to several German veterans from this post-war era, and all believe that their fight was against the same enemy that had divided their country and continent—international Communism. These proud Legion veterans point to a united Germany and a Communist-free Europe as vindication for whatever sins they may have committed in their jungle or desert Cold War campaigns. German Legion veteran associations or *amicales* are located in all major cities in Germany and their frequent and well-attended gatherings form an integral part of the continuing Legion brotherhood. Also, to honor the more than 220,000 Germans who have served since 1831, a Legion museum was erected in Schillingsfürst in 2015. On the grounds of a noble's castle in southern Germany, I found the museum compact but complete; it is now the only such museum outside of France.

* * *

The relationship between the French and their Anglo-Saxon cousins *outré Manche* (across the Channel) is a bit different. A handful of mostly upper-class British adventurers made their anonymous way to Sidi-bel-Abbès in the late 1800s, but it was not until P.C. Wren's *Beau Geste* and *Beau Sabreur* novels in the 1920s and adventure films of the 1930s that a greater cross section of the British public became aware of the Foreign Legion. Along with *képis* and camaraderie in the desert, Hollywood and Pinewood studios also showed impressionable and enthusiastic British boys the expanse and thrill of empire in films like *Gunga Din* and *The Four Feathers*. In addition, World War II was soon on hand to offer very real service to King and Country.

The number of Anglo-Saxon recruits in the Legion, though never near that of Germans, has corresponded with the decline of Empire and an overall less insular (Brexit aside), more open British approach to European trade and politics. As more and more colonies were granted independence by the Crown in the 1950s and 1960s, fewer troops were needed abroad. Many restless and adventurous Brits, in search of sun and something different from their country's shrunken worldwide military presence, now choose service in the Legion. While the kind of British young man who joins the Legion today has probably never heard of Rimbaud or Flaubert, he most likely will know about the stunning English victories over the French at Agincourt and Trafalgar, as well as the humiliating French capitulation to Hitler in 1940. That is, he may be a legionnaire serving *la France*, but he very much remains the proud son of Old Albion.

* * *

As noted, German and British legionnaires have long had high desertion rates from the Legion. Rumors swirled in the sands of 1920s Morocco that several German deserters had joined the forces of the charismatic Rif rebellion leader, Mohammed ben Abd el-Krim, who battled both the Spanish and French legions. Even more shamefully, during the eight-year war in Indochina, close to 1,400 German legionnaires deserted—with many giving their valuable technical and organizational skills to the Viet Minh. One notorious German deserter, a *sergent*, served his new cause well as a propaganda mouthpiece for the Vietnamese Communists. This

Legion traitor rose in the ranks of his former enemy to become a trusted confidant of Viet Minh master strategist and war-hero, General Vo Nguyen Giap. Indeed, by the early 1950s, several other German deserters had already been welcomed at Communist Party rallies in Moscow and East Berlin. In my Legion days, it seemed that two or three German or British legionnaires deserted per month, especially once posted to a regiment in the *métropole*.

* * *

Nevertheless, Germans and British can also provide highly capable soldiers whose skills and efficiency are needed at all levels. Indeed, whether from these two groups or others, diversity among personnel is one of the Legion's greatest strengths. In any situation, someone in the company or regiment will more likely have done whatever task it is that now needs to be completed.

* * *

My company captain at Castel in 1986, CPT Hans *"Mein Gott"* Geiger from Stuttgart, joined in 1965 and retired in 2002 as a lieutenant-colonel. *Capitaine* Geiger introduced me (and perhaps others) to the practice of "taking eyes" in ranks. Geiger would march in front of us during formation—make eye contact with each soldier, and bark, *"Les yeux . . . les yeux—toujours, les yeux!"* For those who might not understand our French-speaking German captain, he would sternly point his two fingers to his eyes as he looked directly at the new legionnaire. He let it be known that, when a Legion officer was reviewing his troops, all were to make eye contact until the officer passed beyond immediate sight (the opposite of American military procedure unless the command "stand at ease" is given). I liked Captain Geiger and, during our two official meetings—with my French lieutenant present—enjoyed speaking German with him since my French was too weak to carry any meaning. Though very distant, Captain Geiger was a role model for all foreign recruits in my section.

155

* * *

Unlike Germans, however, British legionnaires seldom stay long enough to rise in the ranks. I have never heard of a British legionnaire attaining officer rank or staying more than twenty-five years. However, one English legionnaire from Yorkshire with twenty years of service, who retired in 1985 as a *brigadier-chef* (nicknamed "Big Johnny"), was so popular at the *REP* and *REC* that he was accorded (unofficially) officer status among the enlisted men. Interestingly, Big Johnny's early years in the Legion may have coincided with those of another Englishman who was later to inspire hundreds of his countrymen to join.

* * *

Simon Murray joined the Legion in 1960 at age nineteen. He left Marseille aboard the S.S. *Sidi-bel-Abbès* with other recruits bound for the French colony of Algeria and its savage war for independence. The 1956 Suez Crisis had shown sixteen-year-old Murray and the world how the British lion's roar was no longer what it had been. By the late 1950s, military conscription was ending, and once famous British Army regiments and Royal Navy battle groups were being amalgamated or even disbanded. In fact, by 1960, the year Murray arrived in North Africa to join the Legion, British Prime Minister Harold MacMillan was speaking in Cape Town of "the winds of change" heralding a European colonial departure from that continent; 1960 also saw the film adaptation of John Osbourne's successful West End stage production of "The Entertainer." Featuring Lawrence Olivier as a worn-out vaudevillian still trouping on with his old song and dance to a changed audience, the play also mirrored the sense of uncertainty and despondency among the British over their reduced importance on the world stage. Murray, however, wasn't feeling sorry for himself. He left England for an intense mix of grueling Legion training, guerilla fighting, and gritty politics in French Algeria. He also found lots of Germans.

As among Hungarians or Czechoslovaks meeting Russians in the ranks after 1956 or 1968, or even Croatians side by side with Serbs in the

1990s, so emotions must have churned when London "Blitz Baby" Murray found himself surrounded by Heinrichs and Siegfrieds in 1960.

Still, the Legion is a leveler unlike any other army, and there is little time for continuing national squabbles or ethnic division within the ranks of its international body. Naturally, those from certain countries will seek others with the same language or similar culture, but the Legion could never be an effective fighting force if its men were busy settling old scores.

Every German or Austrian of a certain age (the ones giving Murray the orders) were former *Wehrmacht* soldiers, including combat veterans of elite German *Fallschirmjäger* (airborne), *Gebirgsjäger* (mountain), and *SS* units. While the Germans, who were Murray's age, also had memories of air raids and their aftermath, Murray, nevertheless, recalls the only war talk was in quick jokes or asides: "As the only Englishman, I felt very good . . . very good. There was a sort of respect for the Brits. You know, bloody Brits. They fucked us over in the war."

Even off-duty in an alcohol-soaked atmosphere, bitterness and recrimination never surfaced. "I remember standing on a table in the *foyer* pissed. All these Germans were there and they're yelling, 'Fuck you, Tommie.' [I'd then shout back] 'We've had you twice. We'll have you again—any time you want it, fuck you!' But they all clapped. No one was really angry. They didn't say, 'Right, fuck you.' In a way there was a kind of respect. I'm not the biggest guy in the book, but I was well treated in that sense."

* * *

While Murray was often the lone British legionnaire in his company or regiment in the 1960s, he later helped lead many others through the gate. His 1978 book, *Legionnaire*, lays down the Legion's living legend for a new generation of action-starved British youth. Somewhere between the pages of Murray's tumultuous five-year Legion memoir and the frenzy of John Bull jingoism surrounding the British victory over Argentina in the 1982 Falklands War, the Legion saw its ranks swell with British recruits.

* * *

Those British legionnaires who finish their contracts often maintain ties with their comrades or even the Legion itself. British Camerone celebrations in London were usually presided over by one of England's most colorful ex-legionnaires, Brigadier Anthony (Tony) Hunter-Choat. This remarkable man served five years in the *2ème REP* in Algeria in the late 1950s and early 1960s, then rose in the ranks of the British Army to retire as a brigadier. Much of Hunter-Choat's fast-track career in Her Majesty's forces was served with the famed 22 SAS regiment. Only another favorite among English legionnaires, right-wing politician Enoch "Rivers of Blood" Powell, was promoted so far so fast in the British Army. Brigadier Tony Hunter-Choat, who died shorly before Camerone 2012, was the general secretary of the Legion *amicale* in London and proud of the British contribution to the French Foreign Legion.

* * *

P.C. Wren may have immortalized the brothers Geste, but one sister—English ambulance and truck driver, Susan Travers, is one of only two women to have been awarded the title of honorary *Légionnaire* (fellow nurse Geneviève de Galard-Terraube "the Angel of Diên Biên Phu" being the other so honored). Travers, an English dilettante on the French Riviera during the 1930s, would prove herself a steely trooper under fire in 1940s North Africa. Fully understanding the danger, Travers volunteered to be the personal driver of Lieutenant-Colonel Dimitri Amilakvari. "Amilak" (as legionnaires called this popular officer) was the Russian aristocrat and Georgian prince who so gallantly led the *13ème DBLE* at Bir Hakeim and inspired Free French forces everywhere. Even in the throes of combat, Amilak would not replace his beloved *képi* with a helmet. Visitors to the Legion museum in Aubagne today can see the bloodied *képi* of the fallen prince and a slightly faded war-time photo of him with Englishwoman and honorary *Légionnaire*, Susan Travers.

* * *

Germans and British continue to serve in the Legion though their numbers have decreased in recent years. Still, Colombian and Chinese legionnaires will learn to sing *"Westerwald"* or *"Ich Hatt Einen Kameraden"* and Romanians and Brazilians will still marvel at the dexterity of already drunk English and Scottish legionnaires stumbling out of the *foyer* with cases of opened Kronenbourg bottles balanced on their shoulders.

9

Cultural Disorientation

"No one can understand why an American would join the Foreign Legion."

—*LÉGIONNAIRE* VALLDEJULI

It begins Day One at the recruiting fort and continues until the Friday you leave the Legion: cultural disorientation. No matter how long a foreigner stays in the Legion, some things simply never become habits. I could never get used to the constant morning ritual of shaking hands. French in the Legion simply have to press the flesh, and handshaking would occur while brushing teeth or shaving, dressing, or, even, showering. If my hands were occupied, I soon learned to offer my elbow or a pinky for a fellow legionnaire to grasp and shake.

There is little to prepare the average American for an extended stay in France. A head-chopping revolution, red wine with smelly cheese, sexy girls, and hard to pronounce words is about all an average American teenager knows about France. Regarding the language, American comedian Steve Martin probably said it best when he quipped, "the French . . . they have a different word for everything." And France, not to mention the Legion, is a place of extremes. A Gaullist would have us believe that, without France, the Occident would be devoid of any real culture or civilization. Yet, any tourist who watches Parisian men urinate between parked Citroëns in the middle of the day or sits through a *plat du jour* with an overly manicured poodle scurrying between tables knows that everyday France is, somehow, different from his high school textbook's description.

In addition, such modern conveniences as an efficient telephone system, central heating and air conditioning, supermarkets and malls, washers and dryers (not to mention exotic items like dental floss and deodorant) came to France twenty or thirty years after they appeared in the United States. Even given that the Legion is not a fair representation of French lifestyle, many Americans and non-Third World foreigners are shocked by its standards of hygiene, food preparation, dental and medical care, and overall lack of modernity. Indeed, we can assume that witty American songwriter Cole Porter, who enlisted in the Legion and served in a regular French artillery unit for a few months during World War I, received no inspiration for the song "It's De-lovely" from anything he observed during his brief induction.

* * *

Whether it be the pride of a young man who, at times, might rather be serving his own country, or, simply, long-standing cultural differences between similar peoples, most foreign legionnaires from Europe or North America have disparaging comments on the French or Legion culture they encounter. Carlisle, England, native *B/CH* Donlon, a fifteen-year veteran, never managed to acclimate to French or Legion habits: "I wouldn't say it's just Legion. It's French, in general. I mean, when you see these guys taking breakfast like pigs, dunking their croissants in the bowl, in the glass . . . it's like putting a sponge in, you know. I'm sure, you know, I could take your father or my father and sit him at a table with Frenchmen eating breakfast and, for sure, two minutes and following, he'd leave. He'd be disgusted."

In terms of hygiene among his fellow legionnaires, Donlon is more resigned. "All the dirty *slips* (underwear) in the *armoire* (locker) scenario, you know. Finding fucking *préservatifs* (condoms) and dildos in the toilet—we've got to put up with this."

* * *

161

Legion mess halls can offer some strange items for Anglo-American tastes. *C/CH* Atherton, another legionnaire in for the long haul, remembers his first meals at Aubagne: "The food was OK, yeah, just exotic things like sheep brains, hearts, tripe . . . stuff, you know, you get people to eat them in England but it's rare, yeah. Here we're having it as the main course meal which is just, like, yuck." And for many foreigners the portions were too small. "I remember always being hungry, always. The other Brits were always trying to get more to eat, too. The French were OK, though."

No Michelin stars for the Aubagne cuisine from LFC Walton, who learned that *pain* in French can also mean pain in English: "Disgusting food. I didn't know what half the things were. The thing I kept eating the most of was bread. Bread, bread, bread. That's all I could get on with. I was hungry all the time. I had things in front of me I wasn't going to try either. Bread all the time."

Of course, a steady diet of mostly baguettes led to problems for Walton. "I remember I was in Aubagne for what, three and a half weeks, and one night I'd eaten so much bread during the day that I had a pain from the front of my stomach to my back. I had that much pain it was hard to breath. But I didn't want to say anything to anybody because I thought they wouldn't take me."

* * *

Clear attempts are made to standardize hygiene, especially during basic training. Of course, personal hygiene varies from country to country and culture to culture. You'd think it normal, or at least more comfortable, to wear clean underwear, to wash your face and shave every morning, and to change socks daily, especially while on a march. In no way does the Legion expect every legionnaire from the six continents represented in its ranks to think in the same manner regarding personal grooming. As such, during *instruction*, the corporals and sergeants treat the recruits like children—only they go easy on the TLC aspect of parenting.

Legionnaire Persson, who served three years in the Swedish Army, tells of a common Legion ritual during his basic training, *inspection slip*.

"This underwear inspection was to see if you took care of your hygiene. This is quite insane. Never in the Swedish Army, that's for sure, and I'm sure it happens nowhere else. Maybe in some real terrible prison somewhere, but not in an army because you're supposed to take care of yourself."

These strange inspections could happen almost anywhere and at any time. "'The inspections were always by surprise. The first one was in the middle of a march ... out in the forest. They just commanded 'Pants down! *Inspection slip!*' And that's crazy because you're out in the forest and you couldn't expect something like that." Maybe Legion recruiting posters should continue to proclaim, "Change your life" but add, "and your underwear."

* * *

Many Northern European teens who join have not yet begun to shave. Legion rules dictate that, if one recruit shaves, everyone must, even if it means only going through the motions, as some Asians and very young ones do. I remember shaving at the Farm (an isolated training camp used during *instruction*) in November at an outside common trough with cold water, using my Legion-issued razor and pocket mirror. It was so cold I couldn't control my shaking hand and watched my blood and shaving cream mix in the trough with that of my fellow recruits. Hearing curses in various languages and looking at the cuts and scrapes on the faces next to me, strangely, almost made me laugh. However, we all knew there was nothing funny about dodging a morning shave.

* * *

Persson, the Swede, remembers what happened to a Scottish friend: "It happened twice that he didn't shave in the morning and this particular morning at the Farm there's a blizzard... minus 10 Celsius, ice, snow ... really, really cold. And this guy hadn't shaved for morning *appel (roll call)."*

Well aware of his previous reluctance to shave, the duty sergeant had been carefully watching the teenager since reveille. He ordered the unshaven recruit to the middle of the snow-covered parade field and told the boy to undress. "And after that the sergeant gets a rubber hose from the side and tells somebody to turn on the tap. The Scot was naked. So, the tap is on, and this goes on for about ten minutes . . . just spraying him with ice cold water."

Lessons are harsh in the Legion, and worth remembering. "And we had to watch. They made every one of us watch this punishment. We said, 'He's going to die.' . . . because at that cold . . . pneumonia or whatever. I thought it would never stop. That was quite terrible to watch because you could easily imagine how it feels. But he was a tough little guy, the Scotsman."

* * *

Legion rules or not, however, the French simply are a difficult group for the foreigner to please. Without question, *la langue française*, as spoken in France, is the most difficult cultural hurdle encountered (even for foreign francophones) followed closely by the long-standing suspicions of foreigners, in general.

* * *

After the fall of the Berlin Wall in 1989, the once closed or problematic border crossings to Western Europe became open and welcoming. Thousands from former Communist Eastern Europe flocked to cities in Germany, France, and other "golden countries." In 1991, Stanislav Gazdík arrived in Paris. After his many years of service, he had the right to apply for a French passport and settle in France. *S/CH* Gazdík chose to return to civilian life in the Czech Republic:

"I always had a problem with prejudice, and because of this problem, I left France. Always, I say that the French in their mentality . . . well . . . they carry themselves like the bourgeoisie. That means this class system—them against us—is very evident."

Shortly before his 2006 discharge at Aubagne, Gazdík almost came to blows with a haughty, anti-Slavic Legion officer. "He said, 'Yes, actually you people come here for food and to grab the money.' I said, 'Listen, asshole,' a man of two meters tall, I said, 'Take off your *galons* (stripes), and we can settle this like men, if you want it this way.' So, yes, I had a bit of history like this. The problem is that, yes, I left France because of this."

* * *

Most foreigners arrive at recruiting stations with only a few (if any) garbled words of French. After one year of service, those same non-French soldiers will have learned to speak the new language well enough to be understood by comrades. Those in the civilian world, however, might struggle to follow the legionnaire's meaning and, sometimes, even correct him or pretend not to understand. For a legionnaire who has spent several months or years on dangerous duty for France, this is not easy to process. Gazdík acknowledges he speaks accented French but feels, given the circumstances, it shouldn't matter. "I say, fuck it, yes, I have an accent, but I did something for your country. This is not my country. And I did more for your country than you did, or maybe even your parents, or others. This means you just can't be critical of my accent. Look at what I've done, damn it. All the problems you have with Arabs and others? I wouldn't worry about my accent in French. You can play with that accent thing and stick it up your ass."

* * *

Since its creation in 1831, the Legion has hosted fewer than 1,000 Americans. During my service, men from the United States usually accounted for no more than twenty-five or thirty out of 8,000 in total. While eating habits, hygiene, and language are high on the list of challenges for foreigners, Americans have another particular cultural adjustment: We are used to being in command.

* * *

Although British legionnaires have to deal with traditional French suspicions of them, Brits are so abundant that they are almost an army within an army and feel quite comfortable. Americans, however, are sometimes caught between not entirely fitting in with either the English mafia, or the French. Many Americans don't have as caustic or droll a wit as the Anglo-Irish and will have "the piss taken" out of them by the mafia—and not even know it.

In my day, Vietnam movies, President Reagan, any American-only sport, the space program, the invasions of Grenada and Panama, televangelists, mass murderers, breast implants, and any other topic found to be silly, overhyped, disastrous, or otherwise typical of something found in "La La Land" was fair game for a *foyer* "piss take" by the lads. Unable to retreat to a *mafia américaine*, most Yanks will put up with the barbs and eventually learn to laugh at themselves and their culture the way the Brits do.

I found being an American in the Legion to be like many of those World War II prisoner-of-war movies in which the majority of camp prisoners were British or Commonwealth troops. Americans are merely a sub-group within an anglophonic minority—an unaccustomed and, at times, uncomfortable role for the average white American with a super-power mentality. While the French, especially the officer corps, often resent the British in their ranks, they generally regard them as a tough and soldierly group. However, French officers show more admiration for, if not outright fascination with, American legionnaires.

* * *

No one can understand why an American would join the Foreign Legion. Indeed, company commanders show off their Americans as one might exotic pets. Sometimes Americans are given special treatment just by virtue of their citizenship. On April 14, 1986, in retaliation for the death of two U.S. servicemen killed in a Qaddafi-sanctioned attack on a Berlin discotheque, the U.S. Navy sent the Libyan leader an up-close and personal message. CPL Mazowski, stationed in Guiana, remembers that unusual day in the Legion: "The easiest day I ever had was the day the Americans bombed Tripoli. My *chef* came to me and said, 'Mazowski, what are you?' I said, 'I'm a legionnaire.' 'No, what nationality are you?' I said, 'I'm American.' He said, 'OK, you have the day off. Go, go ... go to sleep . . . relax.' I said, 'Why? (you know, what's up here?)' 'Whoa, didn't you hear? The Americans—they bombed Libya, Tripoli. You go to sleep. Take it easy.'"

* * *

Aside from the spike in American enlistment in the 1914–1916 period, the Legion has never drawn many from the United States. While some Americans such as World War I poet Alan Seeger have monuments erected in their honor in Paris and Cole Porter's songs can be heard today, most remain unknown. However, some colorful ones include: Eugene Bullard, a pioneer black combat pilot for France in World War I, who first enlisted as a legionnaire; U.S. Marine officer Peter Ortiz, the most decorated OSS member and one of the most decorated marines of World War II; Princeton All-American football player Arthur Bluethenthal who, like many foreign volunteers, first joined the Legion and, like Bullard, later saw action at Verdun and flew combat aircraft for France; and Legionnaire Moll, a generous millionaire from Chicago, whose ashes are kept in the Legion Museum. Usually, American wars or a patriotic sense of duty to country has kept U.S. enlistment low. After the September 11, 2001, attacks, American enlistment decreased even further. Still, some Americans do journey to France.

In 2005, a promising candidate from the American heartland with an interest in foreign language and culture tried joining the men of the *képi blanc*. We may never know if poor eyesight was the only reason this young man from Hailey, Iowa (pop. 8,000), was rejected by the Legion. Nevertheless, we do know that, a few years later, U.S. Army PFC Bowe Bergdahl walked away from his isolated outpost in Afghanistan with only a knife, compass, and a few provisions. Within a few hours, he was picked up by motorcycle-riding Taliban waving AK-47s. Tortured and abused, Bergdahl was not forgotten by the U.S. military. Search parties were organized but led only to injury and death for several American personnel. Five years later, in 2014, men of the fearsome Haqqani network (once funded by the CIA) handed over Legion-wannabe Bergdahl to wary American special operations soldiers near the Afghan-Pakistan border in exchange for five senior Taliban held at Guantanamo prison. Bergdahl, who eventually was diagnosed with a schizotypal personality disorder, pleaded guilty to the charge of desertion. Army prosecutors sought a prison sentence of fourteen years. However, in 2017, a judge at Fort Bragg (renamed Fort Liberty in 2023) decided not to imprison the troubled soldier. Promoted to sergeant during his captivity, Bergdahl was demoted to E-1 private, forced to forfeit $10,000 in pay, and given a dishonorable discharge.

* * *

Another American's Legion story also concerns desertion but is even more confusing. In 2008, Kurt Sommerlad (name changed) graduated in the top half of his class from the U.S. Military Academy. He was then sent to Texas for medical services training and posted to the famed (and often deployed) 10th Mountain Division in Fort Drum, New York. However, the newly commissioned First Lieutenant Sommerlad held a dark and dangerous secret: He was severely depressed and suicidal. His wish was to die in combat, but he thought of meeting death in almost any circumstance. Sommerlad's family in Oregon, his West Point friends, and current Fort Drum soldiers and fellow officers had no idea how desperate and on the edge this young man was.

Not wanting to shame his family or dishonor his men by killing himself, Sommerlad decided to desert and choose another more challenging, and, quite possibly, more dangerous military assignment. He wanted his new army to allow him to start again—raw and ready—stripped of any guilt about prior commitments and past emotions. Within two days of his abrupt departure from duty in upstate New York, Sommerlad flew to Switzerland, crossed the French border, and made his way to Fort de Nogent in Paris. He lied to Legion personnel at the fort, but Aubagne's "Gestapo" soon learned that he was an AWOL U.S. Army officer. Accepted into the Legion family, this prodigal American son was rebranded Legionnaire Serge Flory (name changed) and told in no uncertain terms to break all contact with his past. Not surprisingly, Legionnaire Flory (nicknamed

"Fly") was an impressive soldier who quickly drew the attention of officers and the respect of all who worked closely with him.

The American would eventually serve three tours in former French Africa with the *2ème REI*, including one five-month deployment in Mali as part of France's anti-Al-Qaida sweep, *Opération Serval*. In Mali, *Caporal* Flory served with distinction while attached to the bodyguard team assigned to a regular army brigadier general. Indeed, the officer corps could sense one of their own in the ranks and many hoped this errant but earnest American would make a career in the Legion, but it was not to be. The day after *Caporal* Flory received his end-of-contract Legion certificate he left Aubagne for a U.S. military base in Wiesbaden, Germany, and turned himself in to the military police.

His 2014 court-martial at Fort Drum (lasting only six days), resulted in Flory's conviction for desertion and conduct unbecoming an officer. Army prosecutors took no note of the evidence presented regarding his mental state while a cadet at West Point or officer at Fort Drum. They also disregarded the intense and heartfelt comments of *Brigadier Géneral* Laurent Kolodziel, the commanding officer of French Forces in Mali, on Flory: "He is a man I will never forget and by whom I will always stand. He is more than a born soldier—he is a born gentleman. I would like to have ten men like that in my team, and I would be the happiest of generals." (Montgomery, Nancy. "A Tale of 2 'Deserters'." *Stars and Stripes*, 20 April 2016).

Flory served his four-year sentence in a medium-security wing of the military stockade at Fort Leavenworth, Kansas. The place is no picnic. Characters from tough guy boxer Rocky Graziano to soft "guy" Bradley/Chelsea Manning of WikiLeaks fame have inhabited its cells; all are held accountable to strict rules and regulations that do not exist at federal or state prisons. No doubt his Academy and Legion training helped Flory through the ordeal. In 2018, he left Fort Leavenworth and is now a free man.

* * *

The Legion is a small world with many peculiarities unto itself, not least of which is its sense of right and wrong. As an organization—in body and spirit—it is committed to reforming a man and, in often quite extreme ways, pushing him to his new mental and physical limits. If you pass these tests, you will forever be part of the Legion brotherhood. Without a doubt, after their release from prison, both LT. Kurt Sommerlad and CPL "Fly" Flory will find a place in Legion ranks.

Take it or leave it.

Axes, aprons, and attitude. *Les Pioneers*.

Andy Robeson and I with two *REC chinois* taking a break.

Retired *Sergent-Chef* Robeson and I working on book.

The *Légion* Honor Card.

Vive la Légion!

With my father in Paris aboard the *Bateaux Mouches*.

Three *instruction* friends.

Légionnaire Valldejuli, *1er Régiment étranger de cavalerie.*

A legionnaire is made.

Légionnaire Alan Seeger Monument in Paris.

Meeting the Legion's living legend—Simon Murray.

Another meeting of two former legionnaires—Jean-Marie Le Pen and Ian Griffiths.

Êtes-vous Prêt? Ready for Action—Anywhere, Anytime—French Foreign Legion (1831–Present).

10

Officer and Enlisted Relations

"He was punching so fast you could hardly follow his hands."

—*Caporal* McCue

The relationship between *les hommes du rang* (enlisted men) and *les officiers* is very Old World. The majority of Legion officers come from the top 10 percent of their class at the French Military Academy of Saint-Cyr. Throughout the years, a Legion command has been seen as an important part of a young officer's résumé. Just as being a legionnaire requires a keen awareness of tradition, even more so does being a Legion officer. Very few of the celebrated Legion heroes are NCOs or enlisted men: "Father of the Legion" General Rollet, Colonels Viénot of the *1er RE* and Jeanpierre of the *1er REP*, Lieutenants Sobiesky of the *1er REC* and Raffali of the *1er BEP* and, of course, Captain Danjou. The Soviets once built their personality cult around "the man with the beard," and the Legion today so honors "the man with the hand." In the week before *instruction* begins, recruits are taken to the museum at Aubagne and shown the good captain's wooden hand. The hand rests in a thick, air-tight glass case at the center of the crypt-like memorial. When in uniform, the legionnaire is to walk to a certain point in the room, come to attention and salute, thereby honoring the heroism of Captain Danjou and the thousands of other Legion dead. Needless to say, few of today's officers can hope to be revered in the style of Danjou. Still, many officers serve the Legion with a flamboyance and panache that seem to belong to the days of epic battles in faraway lands. Officers with dueling scars and eye patches can still be seen on Legion bases (though all prosthetic limbs are now plastic).

As in any army, a good officer must inspire and lead by example. The Legion is proud to note that 10 percent of its officers began their service as legionnaires. Given the cultural, intellectual, and, perhaps, linguistic obstacles a legionnaire rising in the ranks may face, this percentage is impressive. The worst Legion officers come from the regular army. Already aware they must prove themselves in an army with the Legion's reputation, these men often overdo it as hard-case officers. Many times, as legionnaires can see, these officers' swagger and arrogance are merely a ruse to disguise their awkwardness and, sometimes, even incompetence in commanding legionnaires. By contrast, many Legion officers, while also hailing from the French upper class, have, in the course of their schooling, trained with Legion units or been taught by officers who had served in the Legion.

During instruction my young lieutenant (twenty years later to be appointed chief of staff—HQ Aubagne), for whom ours was his first command after graduating from Saint-Cyr, already had a fair idea of what to expect since his father had been a Legion officer at Diên Biên Phu. Of course, as enlisted men in all armies will say, the best officers are those who begin as enlisted men. Without a doubt, a legionnaire goes a little further for an officer that he knows has been through the same *merde* as he. A legionnaire also realizes how difficult it is to rise in rank and is deeply impressed by any peer, especially a non-francophone, who makes it to the rank of officer. Promotions among enlisted men are based solely on merit, a system fully appreciated by all.

While the Legion is a highly disciplined army and ranks from NCO to the officer corps are greatly respected, it is also a violent one. On occasion, spontaneous and outrageous acts of violence occur between officers and enlisted men. I remember the end of an especially difficult week-long field exercise at the *REC* when my company captain delivered a one-punch knockout to a Tunisian who had been caught sleeping on guard duty. The legionnaire was disliked by all and not missed when he deserted two weeks later.

* * *

An officer comfortable with the Legion is aware that the men he commands come from a mix of cultural and socio-economic backgrounds unlike that seen in any other army. CPL McCue was stationed in Bouar, Central Africa, with the *6ème REG*-combat engineers. The large French base held a regiment of 1,000 men—mostly marines and regular army *paras*—with only a small contingent of legionnaires.

CPL McCue tells how a pompous regular army officer will never forget his first Legion command and the ensuing rumble in the jungle: "Lieutenant Gallais had an idea in his head that he was tough because he had a Legion force under his command. And more than that, that he was out here in the back and beyond with his little group of twenty-five guys, and he could be a dictator. He could do whatever he wants . . . and he started doing some serious ball breaking."

The non-Legion officer directed most of his abuse toward CPL Diab—an Arab who had been raised in England. "He was a quiet fellow. He didn't drink. He didn't smoke. He didn't party much really. He drank Orangina all the time . . . but he had been a boxer in England. He'd even done a little bit of professional boxing. He was very handy." A good officer will know his men's capabilities and try to learn something of their personal histories. Gallais was too busy focusing on himself and collecting "Legion stories" to regale his regular army cohorts in the officers' mess. As McCue recalls, "The lieutenant didn't know all Diab's history. He didn't bother to learn. He's one of these ones who thought these guys are just a bunch of idiots and *clochards* (bums) and losers. He wasn't concerned with what anybody's past history was."

Gallais began to harass Diab in every way possible. Painting white rings around trees on the base in the heat of the day—while the company shut down in the barrack for afternoon *sieste*—was only one of many senseless chores assigned to the corporal. "It just went on and on, and the guy was starting to crack."

The humiliation of Diab in front of the men continued even at a Sunday "family dinner." With no regard for Diab's hard-earned Legion stripes, he decided to have the corporal be his waiter. "Bad, bad plan. And not only is he having him serve him, but he's breaking his balls in front of everybody." Hours earlier Diab had alerted McCue and the English legionnaires "that he was going to end up battering the guy because he just couldn't take it."

Diab was calm. He emptied his pockets and took off his watch. He told his friends to keep an eye on anyone who would try to stop him. The sergeants, aware that revenge was planned, had made an early exit from the dinner. Only Yugoslav *caporal-chef* Fandrov, a massively-built truck driver, and Costamagna, a sly Italian *adjudant-chef* seated next to the lieutenant, might pose a problem. Unlike the others on hand, these two had no idea of the coming drama.

* * *

After a polite tap on the officer's shoulder and a brief greeting, Diab let loose. "The lieutenant started to turn his head . . . he hadn't even fully turned . . . when Diab started in on him. He was a boxer, so he was quick. And in a matter of literally ten seconds, you know, it seemed like ten minutes. He was punching so fast you could hardly follow his hands. Blood is flying all over the place." The results were professional, indeed. "And in that time, he broke three of the lieutenant's ribs. He burst his eardrum. He opened up three places on the side of his face. He busted the guy's nose and he blackened one eye. Diab's only regret, he told me later on, was that he didn't break the lieutenant's jaw or knock out any teeth."

* * *

Splattered with the lieutenant's blood and seemingly amused by it all, Fandrov had merely leaned out of the way. Only *A/CH* Costamagna tried to thwart the attack by hitting Diab with a chair. The blow did dislocate Diab's wrist and slow him down. At that point, McCue and others rushed Costamagna. "And one guy grabbed him by the throat and threw him up against the wall and had his hand cocked back and basically said, 'Stay out of it! This is something coming down.'" The *adjudant-chef* backed off and several others hustled Diab out of the mess hall.

McCue smiles, recalling how "the lieutenant didn't even know what had happened to him. He kept saying, 'Who was that? What happened?' He was like a broken old man. His bravado was right out the door." Diab was sent *disciplinaire* back to France and dishonorably discharged. "But nothing more of it was said besides that. The fact that none of the men had lifted a hand to help the lieutenant … and more than that … that some had stopped the *adjudant-chef* from helping him were never mentioned again."

* * *

Very seldom will a legionnaire strike a Legion officer. However, LFC Poulsen describes an encounter between a racist Danish legionnaire, a seven-year veteran, and a recently promoted black officer with five years' service. "I first met Horsten when I was with *Musique* (Legion band) at 2 *REI*. Strong as fuck. Really, really strong. He used to wear a swastika on his *tenue* (uniform). A black captain at 2 *REI* told him to take it off and—BAM!—Horsten just smacked him." Poulsen notes, "but even the *PMs* didn't fuck around with him. Yeah, he got kicked out for hitting the captain. All the time, he make shit. He didn't like Arabs or blacks. He works in Paris now at a nightclub as a bouncer."

* * *

A handful of foreigners who enlist as legionnaires are promoted to the officer corps. In my day, most of these special ones were German, Austrian, or Italian and had served almost twenty years before becoming officers. Most every legionnaire can remember the name and style of all officers under whom he has served but will be especially aware (and respectful) of those who once wore the *képi blanc*. Because the Legion is small, a soldier may serve under the same officer twice. Certain officers require only one brief introduction before their mark is forever left in a legionnaire's memory. On several occasions while stationed at *1er RE*, CPL Lewis met the legendary CPT Leinfellner. Lewis sets the stage for Camerone Day practice in Aubagne and the Austrian's April *Anschluss*: "He'd be down

175

there (parade ground) dressed to the nines, just looking hard as nails, but he wasn't just looking the part. He was hard as nails."

Parade practice for the all-important April 30th ceremony at Legion headquarters, which high-ranking NATO personnel and even the French defense minister attend, is as tedious as it is nerve-wracking. Perhaps, in solidarity with those he had once marched among, Leinfellner would show up at practice and take charge, even infusing the ordeal with his own form of comic relief.

"He was the maverick. I mean he'd just move a whole regiment, you know. Whoever was directing it. He didn't care. He'd just start yelling and everybody would like—BOOM!—just stop all at once."

Leinfellner would pace up and down the ranks looking for his target. The veteran captain would then pull someone out of ranks "who really looked like a goober-head. Someone who was there to basically fill things out because they needed a certain number marching." After the terrified legionnaire presented himself to the officer, Leinfellner would yell, "'OK, soldier . . . Where the fuck are your medals?' 'Medals, *mon capitaine?*' 'Your medals! Why don't you have any medals? God damn it, next year you better be down here with some medals. Get back in the line!' And you know, in between time everybody's resting. You know, taking in the little asides and laughing about it, and that would give them the spirit to do twenty or thirty more laps.'"

* * *

However, it wasn't all bonhomie with Leinfellner. CPL Lewis also remembers the captain punishing those in his company who caused problems: "This is the guy who would sniper shoot legionnaires who were pains in the ass. The ones that had given him hell. He would get up in the window while they were having *rassemblement* and, to let them know he was watching them, while they were at attention, he would take a high-powered air rifle and he would fire on them. And he would hit them, you know. He would tag the people he wanted to tag. He wouldn't just shoot indiscriminately into a crowd with those little lead pellets, which, I could imagine, is pretty painful."

* * *

For many years Captain Leinfellner was the *CAPLE* company captain. Based in Aubagne, the *CAPLE* is the Grand Central Terminal of the Foreign Legion. Almost all legionnaires will transit through this company every two or three years. The officers and NCOs assigned permanent duty here are chosen for their toughness and ability to manage all types of personalities. American Robert Lewis recalls his *foyer* talk with Englishman Gavin Gibbons, a corporal recently returned to Aubagne from Djibouti. Perhaps something was lost in the translation. After learning that Gibbons planned on the parachute regiment upon returning from his leave, and with the beer flowing, Lewis offered some advice when asking *REP*-man Leinfellner for his *permission* (R and R): "When you go in front of him, make that presentation really crisp and clear. He likes that. He reacts well to it. And then ask him for twice as much *permission* as you want because he's only going to give you half of whatever you ask for. So, there's your formula."

The next day with his uniform in pristine condition and his inside tip, CPL Gibbons was ready to face the legend. After a "big, snap-crackle-pop presentation" in his office and confirmation that Gibbons was *REP*-bound, the now-satisfied Leinfellner asked Gibbons how much leave he was requesting. Recalling the *foyer* advice, Gibbons, still at attention, asked for 145 days. The officer's reaction was immediate. "Leinfellner just lost it. He yelled at him, '*Tu te fous de ma gueule, ou quoi?*' (Are you shitting me, or what?)—Reached down ... grabbed hold of his cabinet, pulled it out with such force that it came out in his hand ... everything hit the ground. He reached down. Got a switchblade that had fallen on the ground. It was what he obviously was looking for. He wasn't looking for his pen to sign this guy's *permission* slip. He was violently mad. He kicked the chair back. Snapped open this switchblade. And could not get around the desk fast enough for what he intended to do. He jumped up on the desk and lunged at this guy. This English character didn't know whether to wait for '*tu peu disposer*' (dismissed) and lose his life, or what."

After failing to pummel Gibbons in his office, Leinfellner chased the corporal into the hallway and down the stairs yelling in English and

French, "I know how to throw knives, *arrête toi!* (Stop!)." Eventually losing the captain in the chase, Gibbons found Lewis and confronted the dumbfounded American. After a few punches and harsh words, the Englishman calmed down and tried to come up with a plan—without Lewis's advice. Gibbons didn't have long to wait. He learned he had to report to the captain the next morning. A surprise awaited him. With no mention of the previous day's debacle, Leinfellner simply asked CPL Gibbons, "Are you still fired up for *REP*? *'Oui, mon capitaine.'* 'Are you planning on going to England in this *permission?'* *'Non, mon capitaine.'* (He lied.) 'Good,' said Leinfellner, 'Get well rested because your request for 145 days of *permission* has been approved. *Tu peu disposer.'*"

With desertion common in the Legion, Lewis shakes his head and laughs. "He gave him the full shot. 145 days. Absolutely unheard of." Indeed, as Lewis observed for several months at Aubagne, "The guy did come back. I saw him several times coming to pick up his *solde (pay)*. He used all his Djibouti money. The guy was running around like a mad man over in England . . . like no one's business. And he had a job to return to. He went to *REP*."

* * *

One final story from CPL Lewis about the Austrian captain highlights Leinfellner's hard-line approach to discipline and order in his barrack. Here is Cool Hand Lewis'"beer death" experience with Leinfellner: "One day, I was walking up the main stairs in the *CAPLE* and had a six-pack in my hand, and Leinfellner was walking down. And he says, "Are you taking those beers up to my boys?" I said, *"Non, mon capitaine."* He says, 'So you're going to drink them right here?' And I thought for a moment that, like, he wanted a beer. We were going to share a beer—a real intimate moment there. No, he had me drink all six of them right there in front of him. He had all the time. It was no problem."

Embarrassed and on the spot, Lewis began to chug the beers. "I could tell that the good humor was wearing off on him as I was polishing off these beers, which meant, basically, speed up, but, at the same time, if you can finish all six of these, everything will be cool. Finished all six and everything was cool."

CPL Lewis reflected on Leinfellner's legacy: "But that's the kind of guy he was. He couldn't let me walk by him with a six-pack in my hand in the *CAPLE*. I should have known better. I should have been the one doing the back route, you know. I should not have compromised his position. And that's how he was. He had balls."

11

Girls

Bankrupt Love

"I've pulled a girl in uniform, but it's the usual monster who's used to this stuff."

—Brigadier-Chef Donlon

A good deal of Legion mystique is self-generated: a recruiting poster showing a chisel-faced "Marlboro man" legionnaire; songs telling of a tearful lover left in Europe while her *beau légionnaire* is sent to fight for the glory of France, often never to return; the Christmas crèches that will have a Legion flash replacing the star of Bethlehem, and so on. In fact, today many men join the Legion for economic reasons or access to French citizenship. Most initial ideas of a local never-to-be-forgotten romance or robust adventure fade quickly during the four-month grind of basic training. No females are seen on the base, and a recruit usually has only two four-hour leaves among civilians during his *instruction* (now one afternoon per month). A legionnaire's social life changes for the better (he thinks) when he is posted to his combat regiment. When off-duty, the legionnaire can go into town and do as he pleases. Unfortunately, it's not like old times. He soon realizes that just about the only female companionship he can muster drinks watered down *pastis* at *beaucoup* a shot.

Nothing is more frustrating for a young, fit legionnaire than having local girls snub him merely because of the uniform he wears. Regardless of the language problem, the same young man a few months earlier might have quite charmed the girls. However, no respectable French girl in the Legion towns of southern France will have anything to do with a legionnaire. A popular French song in the mid-1990s has the singer (called to military service) warn his girlfriend never to go out with a legionnaire on leave. On an opposing, and personal note, I remember a Marseille prostitute's coming on to CPL Lewis and me by singing Edith Piaf's *"Mon Légionnaire."*

Another Marseille street encounter involved a very attractive Canadian girl named Debbie, whom Ian Griffiths and I agreed to escort through one of the seedier parts of the Vieux Port one Friday night. Both Griffiths and I were civilians but had many friends (he also had a brother) still in the Legion. As we rounded a corner, we came upon three English legionnaires wearing uniforms of the *13ème DBLE*. After exchanging greetings, we explained our situation and asked what news they might have of Griffiths' brother and other mutual friends in Djibouti, the five of us completely ignoring little Debbie and her big ones. When Griffiths and I rejoined Debbie she had only this to say of legionnaires, "I hate them. They're disgusting pigs." She had no idea that my friend and I had been in the army she knew so little of, but hated so much. Needless to say, even with her mini-*jupe* (skirt) and maxi-*decolletée*, our sexy Canadian had a long, unescorted walk home.

* * *

Considered *margineaux* (marginal) by the locals, legionnaires are often shunned. Good for slogging through the muck of Guiana, baking in the Chadian sun, or exposing themselves to radiation in Polynesian atolls, they are not worth inviting to a quiet cup of coffee. *B/CH* Donlon, who has a girlfriend in England, describes what it is like for a legionnaire in town: "French, in general, don't like the Legion. I mean the in thing is to try to get into civvies. Nobody likes to be stared at when you walk into a bar, you know. Whereas, if you walked in in civvies, no one would say anything, depending on your *comportement* (manner/bearing). I've pulled a girl in uniform, but it's the usual monster who's used to this stuff."

181

* * *

Donlon gives credit to some of his Legion brothers for catching the attention of locals but also notes that, for his countrymen, it is even more difficult. "But, I mean it happens . . . some guys do, but, I mean, in general, it's impossible. In civvies, it'll work. But most of the French don't like the English anyway, so if you're English it automatically turns them off. It's not really a big reference being English in France, anyway."

* * *

Overseas, the legionnaire-girl scene is about the same; CPL Mazowski describes it in French Guiana: "With the whores—they were attracted to you only because you had money and they knew that they were a fuck for you. They knew you were business, and they knew they could charge a lot of money. In Guiana, for a whore on town, it was normally 500 *francs* a pop, and they weren't very pretty at all."

As for the kind of girl many legionnaires had left behind, "the civilian girls, the officers' daughters, and the daughters of the people working on the space project, no way: You could never even get near them. It was common knowledge the girls wouldn't go near a legionnaire. I never even knew one legionnaire who tried it and, if they did, they just were ignored totally. The reputation there is alcoholic and . . . well . . . it's not the charming, romantic image."

Unless one has been among prostitutes in a Third World country, it is difficult to imagine how aggressive the girls are to potential customers. LFC Griffiths describes a typical *sortie* in Djibouti: "The first time I went into town I went into this local bar, and this *naya* sits down next to me. I've got my track suit bottoms on and well . . . she like shoves her hands right down my fucking track suit bottoms, playing on my plonker, as I'm sat there at the table, like, drinking fucking whiskey, thinking this is the fucking life. It was great. Fucking all the time, whores coming up to you feeling your balls, and you're feeling their tits and their fanny and everything. Real fucking sicko, like."

* * *

If you join the Legion to disassociate yourself from any past class restrictions or societal values, having a prostitute as a girlfriend is not too shocking. Many legionnaires, out of loneliness or libido, frequent brothels or shack up with local whores. A Legion whore needn't be good looking or young—just as accepting of her new love's lifestyle as he is of hers.

Marseille's *rue* Curiol is a long and narrow uphill road leading from the once elegant boulevard de la Canebière to a collection of bars, rock clubs, and drug dens known as La Plaine.

Strutting around the place are French and Spanish whores who work the streets and frequent the tiny bars that line the strip. Brazilian and French creole *travelos* (transvestites) are numerous but seem more interested in one another than potential customers. Any night, but especially on weekends, legionnaires will tour the area looking for a variety of sex. If not figuratively dumped on enough during the week back at camp, some legionnaires (in the 1980s/1990s) would pay for the literal variant courtesy of a *rue* Curiol whore; others enjoy being urinated on and some, being handcuffed and beaten; then, there are those who pay only to watch. *Rue* Curiol is a busy place, and prostitutes who are clean and business-like can earn very respectable wages.

Gladis met LFC Poulsen at the Prado beach in Marseille. Neither admitted what either was. For Poulsen, she was the bilingual Argentine receptionist at the Marseille Chamber of Commerce while, for Gladis, he was the Danish soldier on leave. Left unsaid was that no high-profile office worker has gaudy three-inch red nails and purple eye shadow, and no Danish soldier speaks Marseille French. Nevertheless, a date was made, and, three days later, the couple met at a café in the Vieux Port. After the next encounter, the receptionist invited the vacationing Danish soldier to her apartment on *rue* Curiol. Before entering her room, she told him, "I'm a whore." He responded, just as subtly, "I'm a legionnaire."

As far as Poulsen was concerned, the relationship couldn't be better; sex was her business and it was very much his hobby. In addition, Gladis treated her legionnaire to dinners and movies and bought him a wardrobe of summer and winter clothes. Word among *rue* Curiol's street people was that Gladis had someone—not a steady John, but an actual boyfriend. She'd fallen in love with Poulsen and spoke excitedly to her friends about their plans to leave France for a new life in Spain and a small country house near Valencia. But before retirement, money still had to be earned. Normally Gladis made 300 *francs* for however many minutes the customer took to shoot his load. Sometimes, so bored with it all, she would turn her head and watch TV while waiting for her grunting and groaning client to ejaculate. So it was with particular interest that Gladis listened to an offer of 5,000 *francs*. Unless physical danger is involved, few prostitutes give much thought to a highly paid carnal act.

The paunchy, bald Corsican in his mid-fifties already had taken off his pants when Poulsen appeared at Gladis' apartment. Gladis explained what had to be done, and her boyfriend agreed. Beginning to masturbate, the man yelled for the couple to start. Giving as little a show as possible, the two lovers came quickly, wiped the Corsican's sperm off their bodies, and happily collected the 5,000 *francs*. In a few minutes, Gladis had added substantially to her savings, and Poulsen had earned more than a month's pay. However, shortly after the private sex show, the very careful and hygienic Gladis found she had crabs. She finally began to doubt Poulsen's fidelity, if not love. She stopped working for a week due to the infection Poulsen had given her and, in that sex-less time, the two drifted apart.

* * *

I can relate well to heartache and desperation over girls because, for too brief a time, I had someone very special. It had been another dead-end Saturday night in Marseille, and I was returning to the *quartier* at Aubagne with a fellow *REC*-man, both of us in an all-too-familiar mood of frustration and anger. Marseille is a tough town to walk around in uniform. Most clubs and some cafés refuse to admit or serve legionnaires. Adding to the unfriendly atmosphere is what seems like the entire population of North Africa staring at legionnaires, muttering what is for sure not their equivalent of *bonjour*. As such, a legionnaire in uniform in Marseille is often overly aware of his environment and any possible challenge or threat. But it was at the Aubagne train station one Saturday night that I found I had a rendezvous.

Two girls began laughing behind me, no doubt because I had removed my *képi* in order to continue walking upright in the low-ceilinged passageway. I became even more agitated. My friend and I emerged from the tunnel and walked through the main part of the station with the girls' cackling still in our ears. As we left the building, the laughter became even louder, and I heard voices that were distinctly not French. Having had enough, I turned and looked at the girls for the first time, asking in English, "What? Swedish?" (Laughter again.) "German?" I continued (even more laughter). "No," they answered, "we're Dutch!"

Caroline was an eighteen-year-old Dutch beauty from the small town of Breukelen, between Amsterdam and Utrecht. When I met her, she was in her fourth month of working as an au pair for a rich family in Aubagne. We met several times in town, always the three of us: Caroline, her friend Esther, and I. Finally, I said what was obvious, that I was interested in her alone and not cute, but dippy, Esther. Caroline was, indeed, a dream. A slim girl with broad shoulders, endless legs and a tight waist, she had light green eyes and soft brown hair. Not only my type physically, she was also intelligent and, like most from her country, spoke very good English. She agreed to an unchaperoned date and we headed into Marseille. I was able to change properly into civilian clothes at fellow American CPL Lewis' apartment in town (not between lockers at Gare St. Charles, as most legionnaires do). Marseille is too dirty and non-French to be romantic, but we did the best we could with trips to Parc Borely, Notre Dame de la Garde, and long walks by the beach. While dating her, I soon found I had become the talk among many at the regiment. I remember strangers back at camp asking about the pretty "English girl" and most everyone's being impressed that she was neither ugly nor a whore, and that she was mine. Even the *adjudant de compagnie* (senior company NCO) spotted us in town once and later remarked how rare it was to see a legionnaire with such a wholesome girl.

If the legionnaire-nice girl scenario seems too good to be true, it was. Caroline grew tired of her bratty au pair children and the distraction her presence was causing in an already shaky marriage, so she quit and went

185

to work at a posh Vieux Port café, sharing an apartment in Marseille with another Dutch girl. The forty-something Italian café owner took a liking to Caroline and, for personal reasons, also, I lost her. For many weeks after our break-up, I was difficult to be around. Somber and sulky, I was no longer the same. What happened next is a very Legion-like gesture of friendship I will always remember. Tired of my moping about, and angry at the circumstances surrounding it, my friends decided to help me the only way they knew how: by trashing the café where Caroline worked. Tables and chairs were to be thrown through windows, bottles and espresso machines smashed, even the café's canopy and sign torn down. With five or six legionnaires, the coordinated attack would take only a few minutes. I was barely able to call off my friends, telling them that the damage would only embarrass me. I promised, however, to try to forget her.

* * *

For CPL Lewis, the legionnaire-girl dramas were comical: "One of the funniest things that I ever saw was the very peculiar Legion habit of posting 'Dear John' letters on the bulletin boards. You'd see these guys trying to put these relationships together. Work against impossible schedules. Work against impossible people. Work against friends that would sell them out for a quarter for a piece of tail. This is what these guys were dealing with, you see."

While a lucky legionnaire might have a woman enter his life, Lewis notes, "she's going to put up with a little, but not a lot, and that's the horrible unknown for the man." Still, there was always excitement in the barracks. "Everyone had high hopes for these relationships. They all thought they would last, but, almost without exception the 'Dear John' letters came."

What better way to reinforce the pervasive "us-against-them" Legion mentality than to share the contents of the letters. Some would read theirs only to friends, but many would post them at the *bureau de semaine* (company duty sergeant's office) for all to read. "The ones in English you could read, or the ones in French you could read. The ones in German or whatever, well, when you went down for guard duty in the morning or to check on this or that, someone would translate for you. That was hilarious. Guys yelling, 'The bitches! God damn it! I got screwed again. I tried but ... what are we going to do?'"

While many young ladies in Legion towns shy away from legionnaires, prostitutes certainly do not. I once sat at an outdoor café in Orange over the May Day weekend with an English and Icelandic friend and watched a working girl who knew no holiday. We heard the clump-clump of her high heels long before the tightly packed body arrived with a purpose at our table. The painted floozy looked blankly at Phillips and me. Suddenly, she grabbed Gundrensson's square face tightly in her hands, examined it, turned to the amused patrons and exclaimed, *"Oh, la gueule!"* (What a mug!), kissed the Icelander, and continued her fast-paced, ass-swinging street walk. Perhaps we again learned that prostitutes feel a kinship to legionnaires as fellow misunderstood (but still needed) outcasts in French society.

Whether it be via her *chatte* (pussy) or only a chat, a prostitute will often try to engage a legionnaire. CPL Lewis had an apartment in Marseille not far from many of the Vieux Port *bars américaines*. The girls would sit at open windows and solicit whoever might buy them a drink or want sex. "You're walking by some of these pro-bars and they see you're a legionnaire so it's like, 'Hey you, if you see Paul-Marie tell him Fifi's looking for him, OK?'"

Like all good sellers, the girls knew to ask questions, no matter how absurd, and corner a potential customer. "I mean, they don't know me, so, when I'm not here, and Paul-Marie's walking through the streets do they yell at the top of their voice, 'Hey, Paul-Marie, if you see Lewis, you tell him he gave me a dose last week.' You know, or whatever the message was. I mean it was ridiculous."

* * *

A popular Legion bar in Marseille, that civilians also frequent, is the Bar Pytheus or "the Pit" in the Vieux Port. I was at the bar one night with five Legion friends only one of whom was in uniform. We were drinking and laughing—huddled over a table meant for two. No one had noticed that an absolutely gorgeous girl was sitting alone at a nearby table and staring at us. Only when she got up to select a song at the video jukebox (a big attraction in 1988 Marseille) did we catch this dream. We imagined she was some kind of French island mix—probably Indian Ocean, and all agreed she had a lovely pair of coconuts. After a few more-than-coquettish glances, she revealed herself to be a working girl very interested in one of us. But which one? Never have I been part of such mugging and posing; I'm sure everyone else in the bar was enjoying our show. The popular George Harrison song she selected, together with her sensual body language (including near-nipple-exposing breasts), was driving us crazy. Whether she understood or not, we laughed at the lyrics about money and a girl. At the song's end, she slowly walked to our table and made her choice. Leaning over, so as to nearly fall out of her top, she whispered to Matti, the boxer from Finland and the only one in uniform, that they should "go for a walk." Forty minutes and 100 *francs* later, the happy Finn returned to our table as we broke into our version of Harrison's "I Got My Mind Set on You."

* * *

Cell phones ring in today's Legion, but since a personal phone is not seen as necessary for a legionnaire's survival or success, none is issued by the quartermaster. Officially, a legionnaire must be "rectified" (cleared) to have a personal phone, laptop, or other similar electronic device. Most Legion camps have only three or four public phones available for the 500–1,300 men on base. There are many stories of girls in town being given these numbers but not knowing the full situation. I remember a Scottish friend, Jock Dumfries, who answered a ringing pay phone at Aubagne and found himself arranging a date with a French-Swedish woman. I later met the middle-aged Bibi and learned she had read the telephone number at a bus stop in Marseille.

Easy come, easy go . . . easy blow, easy come—sums up most of the *putes* (whores) that troll legionnaires. These business-like ladies even visit and service recovering legionnaires at the military hospital in Marseille. I really believe that French prostitutes look at legionnaires as comrades. More than a few NCOs viewed Tahitian and Djiboutian prostitutes as their wives, even bringing them back to France. Nothing better underscores just how obliging some *putes* were to legionnaires than the raunchy story of an English legionnaire being fellated by a Marseille whore upon whose face he ejaculated. He had meant to pull his penis away before climaxing and apologized profusely to the prostitute. Licking her lips and wiping her cheeks clean, she smiled and said, *"C'est pas grave. Maintenant je porte le masque d'un brave légionnaire."* (Use your own translation).

One reason this time period comes to mind so readily and precisely at any moment years later is because, today, mustering the manic and frenetic odd-ball characters one dealt with during our Legion days. Nowhere is this more evident than when a legionnaire is on leave and makes the mistake of trying to reconnect with civilian life. Any man living in the insular world of the Legion—with its rigid structure, constraints, and eccentric personalities—will find it frustrating to, once again, interact with civilians and their permissive, undemanding world—hence, the reputation of legionnaires on leave acting like King Kong visiting New York. As such, many with a week or so of *permission* find it easier to frequent locales where they will meet fellow legionnaires or other "outsiders."

Establishing and maintaining a loving, stable relationship with a girl in or near a Legion town takes an enormous amount of confidence, effort, and more than a fair bit of good fortune. Nevertheless, the emotional rewards of this romance, however brief, can help sustain a legionnaire much longer than the more typical nights of drunken excess and revelry.

* * *

Thankfully, *C/CH* Murray's love stories, as recounted in his book, are quite different from those of today's legionnaires. Not that legionnaires in 1960s Algeria were more handsome or engaging than those of today; it was simply a matter of circumstance.

* * *

Legionnaires then and now are regarded (at best) as colorful and mysterious characters. However, in war-torn Algeria, legionnaires were also seen as guardians and protectors—the last defense against the impending Arab avalanche. To be sure, Murray's tender descriptions of his brief encounters with local *pied noir* girls happened in a very different time and place. Still, these innocent tales of a lonely soldier on romantic outings in a foreign land only perpetuate the gallant legionnaire image and serve as poignant testimony to its loveless modern counterpart.

While on a week's leave in the coastal Algerian city of Philippeville in the early 1960's, Legionnaire Murray met a young *pied noir* named Nicole Barbolosie. Murray excitedly wrote in his diary: "Nicole is stunning. She looks about twenty-years-old but is probably younger: they always are. She has a mass of dark hair that sweeps down round her face and rests softly on her shoulders. She has a figure that makes my knees ache, and a deep tan. We chatted idly on the beach and later Nicole (and her girl-friend) went home, but we met again in the evening and strolled up and down the promenade."

Only a few days later, one senses that Murray, indeed, had left the rough and tumble of the Legion. Here is his description of his third date with lovely Nicole. "We sat on the hillside in the cool of the evening with a sea breeze from the Mediterranean fanning us and looked at the rooftops and the blue sea and each other. I think we are in love—it feels so to me. Twenty-one and in love; can it ever get better than this?"

* * *

The end of Murray's idyllic leave can serve as a metaphor (and warning) about crossing the Legion/civilian divide in search of a romantic respite. For one week, Murray, socially and emotionally, almost fully re-entered the civilian world. This is a very dangerous sensation, and I felt the same after a week with my father in Paris visiting museums and elegant restaurants.

A legionnaire's return to the rigors of barrack life, or, for Murray, combat can wreak havoc with one's mental state.

Guard duty and a martinet German sergeant awaited our English Romeo. While Murray managed well in the early morning with a perfectly ironed uniform and solid *presentation*, his long days with Nicole at the beach and late nights with fellow legionnaires at the pubs of Philippeville would soon doom him. He stood his hours' shifts during the day but, by late evening, felt so drowsy that he drifted to sleep somewhere on the other side of midnight. His sweet dreams of Nicole were interrupted by the cold, hard metal of a pistol on his right temple. The sergeant of the guard, a fifteen-year veteran named Schussler, smiled and wished Murray *"Gute Reise"* for his next holiday: twelve days in *taule*.

Like Alcatraz, the Legion prison Murray was sent to was isolated and secure: as if to further torment the prisoners, it also had a clear view of the civilian world. In fact, on one occasion, *puni* Murray could see his beautiful Nicole walking alone along the beach. Part of being a legionnaire is having one's mind toyed with, and this could have led a weaker man, upon release from prison, to desert.

* * *

In talking with the those interviewed for this chapter, I realize I'm fortunate to have memories closer to Simon Murray's. Murray doesn't visit Philippeville now, but I do visit Marseille. While no longer in contact with my Caroline, I think about her when I walk the familiar streets of the city. One special moment we shared happened on a winter's day near the train station. While walking uphill to Gare St. Charles, I noticed that my long-legged companion's stride matched mine. We looked at each other, smiling and in step, as we deftly moved past the unattractive sights and shabby characters that lined the street. I was in uniform and wearing my heavy brown three-quarter coat. Caroline, quite unexpectedly, put her arm through mine and pulled me tight. Everything felt wonderful. It was in these few blissful minutes that I was able to understand the attraction many women have for the Legion and appreciate better the tender ballads we had learned during *instruction*. I sensed this young woman who was taking her soldier's arm was holding onto the Legion Man, dashing image and all. At that instant, I felt all the hardships of the French Foreign Legion were worth it if it brought such sensations of manly contentment.

12

Willy Woofters

Don't Care, Don't Complain

"The French military, much like French society, has never been too bothered by one's sex life."

—*Légionnaire* Valldejuli

From ancient rumors and twentieth-century reports, from Alexander the Great to Alfred Kinsey, the topic of homosexuality has always generated intense debate and often caused bitter divide. Military combat units are traditionally all-male bastions of toughness and testosterone. (Since 2013, the U.S. military has allowed qualified women to serve in combat roles.) The views of many countries' armies on homosexuality simply mirror those of their respective legal system, civilian population at large, or top leadership. The current Turkish president calls homosexuality a "cursed perversion." In fact, Turkey remains the only NATO country to exclude homosexuals from its required military service. Exempted gay Turkish men are issued a pink certificate on which "psychological disorder" is noted. Good luck with the job hunt, Mustafa.

Official policy from Brussels is different. Since announcing a goal of gender balance and diversity within member countries' forces at its 2002 summit in Prague, NATO has been a vocal proponent of inclusion for all. Soon thereafter, it extended equal spousal benefits to same-sex couples and, by 2017, was officially recognizing International Homophobia Day. The policies of "balance" within the forces have been augmented by the U.K. in a particular way. Indeed, the British Army seems quite well-rounded, even allowing time off for taxpayer supported breast implants among female soldiers wanting to serve On Her Majesty's Curvy Service.

Until recently, the U.S. military has not allowed gay men and women to serve and has dismissed those personnel who defiantly "come out." The French military, much like their society, has never been too bothered by one's sex life. Ample discretion and a satisfactory job performance are more important to the French military than maintaining any official sanctimonious or self-righteous pretense. As with most every other army, the disciplinary codebook holds charges against "act(s) of a sexual nature on base."

The 1993 U.S. policy of President Bill Clinton on homosexuals in the military—"Don't Ask, Don't Tell" (itself a compromise) is as absurd to the French as it is insulting to any patriotic soldier. The Foreign Legion's stance might be described as: "Don't Care, Don't Complain." The Legion administration is not really worried about a recruit's sexual preference, but, if it does come out that he is gay, then that legionnaire should not complain if he is harassed. In reality, fellow legionnaires do not care either way, and gays in the Legion are not really bothered. The Legion looks at homosexuality as a natural condition for a certain percentage of the population and, since it accepts men from the various strata of society, why not the homosexual? You might say that a healthy dose of nuts (to no one's surprise) and a limited number of fruits (to no one's concern) form a basic part of the Legion diet. ("Willy Woofters" is rhyming East London slang for "poofters," or homosexuals.)

In terms of the U.S. attitude and hypocrisy on sexuality, one could point to the ever-increasing number of sexual harassment complaints and rape cases of female U.S. military personnel by male colleagues to question any psychosexual directives from top brass. Even in the "Don't Ask, Don't Tell" era, disheartening and demeaning stories abounded in the U.S. military: from the dismissal of eager and well-schooled service academy cadets, midshipmen, and airmen, who announced their homosexuality within weeks of attaining their coveted diplomas and commissions, to the discharge of highly trained and veteran enlisted personnel, who were then denied their retirement pay and benefits.

In 2010, President Barack Obama, a man of immense talent and ambition who, nevertheless, must have felt rejection or disapproval at some point because of his mixed-race status, announced his proposal to exclude no one from military service due to sexual orientation. While the president is Commander-in-Chief, the U.S. government's system of checks and balances requires that Congress approve the presidential decree. No less a man than former Vietnam POW and 2008 Republican presidential hopeful Senator John McCain came out quite forcefully against any retreat on the "Don't Ask, Don't Tell" policy. As if to substantiate his position, several polls conducted in the early 2000s by the Pew Research Center among active-duty U.S. servicemen showed strong opposition to allowing openly gay men and women to serve. Indeed, all sources seemed to indicate the issue of allowing homosexuals in the U.S. military would be a political firefight from the halls of Montezuma to the shores of Washington, D.C.

Much like the suspicion and doubt surrounding the integration of black soldiers in all-white units before enactment of President Harry Truman's landmark Military Desegregation Bill of 1948, many of today's U.S. servicemen may believe that gay soldiers will bleed differently from "regular" GIs. However, President Obama and supporters in the U.S. Senate and Congress managed to repeal the "Don't Ask, Don't Tell" policy. In July 2011, President Obama, together with the Secretary of Defense and the Chairman of the Joint Chiefs of Staff, signed the new anti-discriminatory legislation at a well-publicized event in the Oval Office. A few years later, again through an official policy change, President Obama openly welcomed transgender soldiers in the U.S. military.

In 2018, under President Trump, the Department of Defense mandated that "all service members, regardless of their gender equality, must adhere to the standards associated with their biological sex." Within a week of becoming Commander-in-Chief in 2021, President Biden repealed the Trump-era ban on transgender troops, thereby allowing all "qualified Americans to serve their country in uniform." The back-and-forth policies seem as confused as the people who are their subjects. Still, some in the ranks don't really care. Perhaps due to the often secret nature of their operations and the intense camaraderie within elite U.S. units,

195

these types seem less shocked by transgender soldiers. In a 2018 interview on the popular American podcast "Max Out," host Ed Mylett asked Robert O'Neill, one of the first Navy SEAL Team Six members to offer Osama bin Laden some face time with his Heckler and Koch 416, what he would say to retired twenty-year SEAL veteran Kris (Kristin) Beck, who now identifies as a woman. O'Neill shrugged and replied, "Nice tits, bro." But so much for that perfect rack. As of late 2022, Beck has re-transitioned to a male body, arguing he was misled into changing his gender by doctors and other medical personnel at the Veterans' Administration hospital.

* * *

The French attitude to sexual variances has always been equally pragmatic, and the Legion leads the way in Gallic indifference. All things transgender are not an issue since the Legion is an all-male army. But where there are males, a certain number of homosexuals will be among their ranks. As long as they weren't setting up a recruiting station in Paris' Marais district or flying the rainbow flag beside the red-and-green Legion *fanion* (corps' flag), recruiters and other staff really couldn't care less about their charge's personal sexual history or yearnings. The Legion is more watchful of a new recruit's buffoonery than buggery. Again, discretion or, at least, a well-chosen and acquiescing partner, is expected of homosexuals in the Legion. All legionnaires have stories about homosexuals in their units.

* * *

Within my first month in the Legion at Aubagne, I had two encounters with gay soldiers—one a corporal, the other a fellow recruit. Lined up one morning to report for a work detail, a Pakistani corporal in skin-tight combat pants stroked my face and asked me if I had shaved that morning. Of course, I had shaved only two hours earlier. The corporal then asked me if I knew that, in the evening, I could buy him a whiskey at the *foyer*. Not only was he an open homosexual but a cheap one, as well. Later, only days before going to *instruction* at Castelnaudary, the other recruits and

196

I had a chance to watch the budding romance of ex-French *para* Langot and his hoped-for English rose, Jirrells. I don't think Langot was actually interested in Jirrells at all. Nevertheless, baiting the excitable Londoner was a good way for Langot to proclaim his sexuality in a comical way.

Langot would often stare at Jirrells and try to flirt, while Jirrells would only curse back. One of the funniest incidents between these two reluctant lovers occurred in the showers. Langot, who was in the stall opposite Jirrells, gave his English sweetie the eye and then began to touch himself. In the course of a few minutes, Langot simulated orgasm by convulsing and spitting out a mouthful of water. He then shouted the English legionnaire's name and sighed. As awkward or intimidating as this may appear, it was all in fun. Due to his past military experience, Langot was one of our section's top recruits during training at Castel. He and I were *binômes* for a while and once shared a pup tent together for three nights during a field exercise, without any real or simulated orgasms.

* * *

Not until arrival at my regiment after *instruction*, however, was I able to see a more structured, less-hidden gay environment. Much as in civilian culture, many of the *REC*'s homosexuals were found in customer-service-type jobs on base—as barbers, nurses, or restaurant workers. *REC* gays, certainly no more or less in number than to be found in other regiments, seemed to be a casual and relaxed group, an unlikely description for any contingent of French Foreign Legionnaires. Indeed, welcome for many a newcomer to the regiment was the overall cheerfulness and softness of these she-men amid the manic, macho gruffness of the others.

The *REC* in Orange had an official regimental barbershop staffed by *chinois* who took their time and cut hair in a solemn, ritualistic Confucian-like way. Everything in the *chinois* barbershop was hierarchical: Rank, age, length of service, and, even, nationality would determine where one sat and exactly when the haircut would begin. However, another place for a haircut was run by a gay Portuguese legionnaire first class in the *3ème escadron*, who would cut hair for ten *francs*—less than half the price of the ceremonial snip at the Mandarin Palace. The Portuguese "barber shop" was, in fact, a company storage room dressed up as a lounge. The gay entrepreneur had music and travel posters on the walls and had brought in a good quality portable stereo system. A visitor could bring his own music or choose from the barber's top-40 selection. The gay barber had a very calm, soothing disposition and was fluent in several languages (very unusual for Portuguese in the Legion). In fact, he was so soft-spoken and well-mannered that he didn't seem to be a legionnaire. It was probably the best hair cutting experience I've ever had including even the trimming of my eyebrows, nose hairs and ear hairs, as well as a splash of cologne.

Another encounter with an unabashed *REC* homosexual occurred in the *foyer*. The "Hacienda" (in homage to Captain Danjou and company) is one of the nicest *foyers* in the Legion. Modeled after a Spanish colonial villa, it has a large stone fountain splashing in the center of its courtyard and is surrounded by colorful azaleas and well-tended geraniums. Fat ducks aimlessly waddle at leisure past legionnaires, who relax around red-tiled tables, eating and drinking. All of this on a lazy weekend afternoon in the south of France can be delightful. To one side of the *foyer* courtyard is a television and game room (ping-pong and *fussball*); the other side houses the Legion's bar and grill. The food served is simple but good. *Steack/frites* is still probably the most popular order as it was when once served by a Marc Almond look-a-like gay legionnaire. If attracted to you, he would stack an extra portion of *frites* next to your slightly larger *steack*. Again, as with the gay barber, no one really cared about our silly short-order cook. Both barber and cook did their jobs well and even provided a welcome bit of femininity within the walls of the all-male camp.

* * *

Not all *REC* homosexuals were content to flirt so innocently, however. Pete Pilkington, an eighteen-year-old English friend from Saffron Walden, was pursued aggressively by a fourteen-year Legion veteran. *Brigadier-Chef* Corbeau was a worthless, drunken Legion hanger-on who preyed on new boys. The disturbed and perverted Frenchman somehow convinced himself his veiny, beet-red face must be attractive to young recruits. One time, while talking to friend Vaughn Hartley (another eighteen-year-old

English legionnaire) in the barracks' hallway, I noticed Corbeau leering at him. Corbeau approached after a few minutes and disgusted us by proudly showing us the outline of his bulging penis under his combat pants. Rebuffed by our laughter, Corbeau soon set his sights on my other friend, Pilkington.

One Saturday morning, Pilkington had the misfortune of being assigned to a work detail led by Corbeau. Somehow, the only other legionnaire in the detail was dismissed after an hour of work, and Pilkington was told it was the *brigadier-chef*'s quarters that needed cleaning. Corbeau was not a small man (previous story aside), and I think he intimidated the little eighteen-year-old. Unwisely, Pilkington went to the *brigadier-chef*'s room. He lasted no more than five minutes before our gay host decided that drinks and a thorough cleaning of his private parts was something Pilkington should enjoy. Pilkington ran from Corbeau's room and across the parade field, bursting into my room in a state of panic. I listened to his story and tried not to laugh since I could see he was quite shaken. Pilkington paced back and forth in the room, seldom looking me in the eye. Just as my friend had begun to calm down, the door flew open, and we were greeted by the bloodshot eyes and foul breath of *Brigadier-Chef* Corbeau. Taking off his web belt, Corbeau moved quickly toward Pilkington, who just as quickly picked up a metal *tabouret* (stool) in self-defense. I jumped between Corbeau and Pilkington, allowing the nervous Brit to dart out the door. To my surprise, Corbeau did not give chase. I now smelled his whiskey breath in my face but stood my ground. He angrily spat his words at me and shouted that I already had enough boys and it was only "fair play" to let him have Hartley or Pilkington. All was now perversely clear—Corbeau thought I was some kind of *REC* pimp running rosy-cheeked English lads. I explained how wrong he was on every count and also informed him how the *mafia anglais* could gladly cut off his testicles and, thereby, relieve him of any lingering sexual frustration. Corbeau cursed and left the room, never to bother my English friends or me again.

* * *

A year or so later, I got the chance to examine the all-macho Legion pre-occupation with feminine-looking legionnaires. For a few months at the *1ᵉʳ RE,* there was much talk and laughter about a newly-posted Legion musician. The young legionnaire in the *Musique Principale* was named Sundsvall—but more commonly referred to as "the Swede with the great ass." It's difficult for me now to believe how this Swede caused such a great stir. Most of the talk about Sundsvall was comical; he wore his pants too tight and seemed to march his bottom around *Quartier* Viénot like a Kardashian-in-training. I, too, was among the many who would stop and watch the Swede as he pranced by and then evaluate it all with friends, as if Sundsvall actually were a pretty girl. Eventually, Sundsvall was told by his superiors to wear looser pants and walk like a soldier, but he just couldn't manage. Shortly after his unit returned from Hong Kong (on the invitation of Simon Murray), Sundsvall took his sweet ass back to Sweden.

13

Stage

Torture

"He'd plugged it in and he was putting the wires onto him . . . mainly on his balls, like."

—*LÉGIONNAIRE PREMIÈRE CLASSE* FAIRFIELD

During its time in Indochina, and especially during the war in Algeria, the French Army—in particular, the Foreign Legion—became infamous for the use of torture against prisoners and suspects. Though immediate results were often won, interrogation by torture in Algeria eventually brought world condemnation of the French and much sympathy for the *Front de Liberation Nationale* and the *Armée de Liberation Nationale* (*FLN*—the political wing/*ALN*—the military wing of the Algerian independence movement). The United Nations, many times a Cold War forum for anti-West and anti-colonial sentiment, often became directly anti-French. Men like Senator John F. Kennedy—whose wife, as First Lady, was to later so charm the French—spoke powerfully on the Senate floor of the horrors committed by French troops in Algeria. Even *pieds noirs* native sons Jacques Derrida and Albert Camus joined other French intellectuals such as Jean-Paul Sartre and Simone de Beauvoir, together with political figures on the left and right in condemning the kind of war waged by the French military. The issue remains sensitive. Not until 2004 was Gillo Pontecorvo's film *La Bataille d'Algers*, winner of the 1966 Golden Lion (Venice Film Festival), aired on French state television stations. This intense and emotional documentary-style work was banned in mainstream French theaters for several years after its release and later screened only at selected "art house" establishments in major cities. It should come as no surprise that Pontecorvo's homage to the oppressed was shown almost daily in the Latin Quarter during the massive May 1968 student/worker upheavals in Paris.

Even today, *La Bataille d'Algers* incites passion. I've seen the film in Marseille; Madison, Wisconsin; and Fort Lauderdale, Florida, and each time shouting and commotion broke out among viewers in the audience. That a country such as France, which had suffered so gravely under Nazi occupation, would use many of the same barbaric methods against prisoners of war was truly disturbing. Only many years later, in a 2000 *Le Monde* interview, did retired General Jacques Massu, commander of the crack *10ème* Régiment Parachutiste (which included the *1er REP*), admit that he regretted the practices of torture and summary executions during the Algerian war. "Torture became generalized," said the 92-year-old French warrior, "and then institutionalized" (Beaugé, Florence. *"La Toure Faisant Partie d'une Certaine Ambiance." Le Monde* 22 June 2000). In another *Le Monde* interview later that year, General Paul Aussaresses explained French counter-terrorism tactics in Algeria in graphic detail. Then an officer under Massu's command, he acknowledged the routine use of electrodes to ears or testicles, and the summary execution of dozens of prisoners—grisly work he often finished off himself.

* * *

The Legion fought well in Algeria. Its soldiers adapted many of the guerillas' skills and turned many of the tricks used against them in Indochina to their benefit in urban and rural operations throughout the country. Rapid deployment of ground troops, together with coordinated air assaults using the Alouette II helicopter, became typical of many of the successful French sweeps in the Algerian *bled* (countryside) after 1958. As it normally does, the Legion draws battle insight and inspiration from not only its past military actions but also the experiences of its men. During the campaigns in Indochina, where more than 10,000 legionnaires fell, Germans (and Austrians) made up almost 40 percent of the fighting units. Many of the German speakers were *Wehrmacht* or SS veterans. In fact, the Legion even had some units comprising only German speakers led by combat-veteran German NCOs. The Germans knew the French disliked them, but felt the French fight in Southeast Asia was their fight as well. The German and Austrian legionnaires were strongly pro-European and anti-Communist and some (without a doubt) still pro-Nazi. In Algeria, many of these legionnaires felt no less hostile to Arabs whom they viewed as an even closer threat to Europe than the enemy in the jungles of Vietnam. Whether taught by the Gestapo or learned from *Can Bo* (political officers) in Viet Minh POW re-education camps, interrogation techniques were used to the full extent on *FLN/ALN* prisoners.

Still today, the Legion instructs on methods of torture. While at the *REP* in Corsica, LFC Van Heek was invited to a special class taught by enthusiastic experts: "We had the session of—this may seem incredible to your ears—of learning how to torture people. They certified to the guys who were serving as what we call in Dutch 'proof rabbits,' 'You won't be in pain. We will only show how you do it.' And, finally, they did some things on the guys which are too nasty to tell. And the guys were, of course, guys badly seen and who this particular NCOs did not like."

Van Heek saw fellow soldiers "walking with bare feet on wet soil and getting 220 volts" and also being hog-tied and hit in certain places. The two instructors, a Thai *adjudant* and German *adjudant-chef*, were well-known for their expertise in torture techniques. The German was an Algerian war veteran and passed on a particularly effective interrogation method to a new generation of legionnaires. "He had, to me, the most bastard trick of all. This was hitting a guy's head, but in a very particular way. You tie a guy to a pole with his legs and his wrists behind his back and you take a thin piece of wood—for example, a broomstick is enough—and you start hitting his head. But you only hit on top. You never hit on the sides and you don't hit in a very hard way. You just hit so that the guy feels pain, just like this (demonstrates on me) and, well, time after time after time, it is sure the guy will crack up."

In large part, this two- or three-day *stage*, arranged at the platoon level by a section commander, was for the older, harder soldiers to make

203

sure the younger ones knew how to torture and not be shocked by the practice. However, Van Heek notes how times have changed and "they were not counting on the fact that in the '80s legionnaires were not as dumb, I mean, have seen a little bit more than they had in the '50s or '60s. Young guys of nineteen or twenty years old didn't take as much for granted as they did in the '50s or '60s." Still, in most every Legion regiment, whether sanctioned or not, old-timers will pass on tricks to young sadists.

* * *

LFC Fairfield, in Chad with the *REP*, watched an English sergeant from the unfortunately named *CRAP (Compagnie de Recherche et d'Action en Profondeur)* unit practicing his skills on a local: "A black had got into the room, and Schettini, a guy, like, who'd got up for a piss and had come back, saw this guy in the room going through the bags. He was just climbing over the balcony to descend, and Schettini pushed him. And the guy fell, landing badly on his leg."

Others woke up and the intruder was apprehended as he tried to hobble away. The company sergeant on duty dismissed the curious onlookers, but not before he'd asked Fairfield for his room's radio extension cord. The legionnaires had only just returned to sleep when they were suddenly aroused again. "We heard a massive scream. And when we all went downstairs there was this black guy covered in a bucket of water. He'd obviously had water thrown on him."

Fairfield and company were treated to a live demonstration of Legion justice. "And the English sergeant was there with my cord, but now ripped up with two bare wires showing. He'd plugged it in and he was putting the wires onto him . . . mainly on his balls, like. Mind you he'd had a good kicking. He'd had a right beating. And then some kind of French colonel came around the corner, and it stopped."

* * *

The soldiers of *CRAP* (renamed *GCP—Groupe Commando de Parachutiste* in 1999) are trained in much more than torture techniques. Founded in 1965, the unit is considered within the Legion the "elite of the elite," yet, unlike comparable units in American or British forces, numbers no more than twenty to twenty-five men. *S/CH* Gazdík, interviewed for this book, was the first Eastern European to be part of this special detachment. When questioned about *CRAP* veteran Ante Gotovina, later general of Croatian forces during the Balkan wars of the 1990s, Gazdík, a Czech, told me he did not see Yugoslavs as Eastern Europeans.

* * *

Of course, the question of torture (or "enhanced interrogation") has long been part of the practical and moral discussion in America's "war on terror." From secret and sometimes improvised prisons in Poland, Lithuania, and Romania to more notorious sites in Egypt, Jordan, and the American base in Guantanamo, Cuba, detainees and their supporters have alleged numerous counts of torture. American director Kathryn Bigelow, whose realistic portrayal of a bomb disposal unit in Iraq (*The Hurt Locker*) won Best Picture at the 2010 Academy Awards, again took America to war in 2012. Bigelow's *Zero-Dark Thirty* details the events (over some ten years) that led to the killing of Osama bin Laden in Abbottobad, Pakistan, in May 2011. The use of torture—especially waterboarding—of suspected al-Qaeda men in Bigelow's movie seems to indicate that, without such tactics, Bin Laden could not have been located and shot dead by the U.S. Navy SEAL team. Former Vietnam War POW and torture victim Senator John McCain, among several other high-level U.S. politicians, protested against the movie, arguing that good intelligence, not torture, won the war against Bin Laden. At the same time, McCain and supporters worry that American disregard for the Geneva Convention is a stain on the nation's conscience and will only hurt U.S. interests worldwide.

* * *

Indeed, the U.S. public remains divided on the issue of torturing terrorist subjects for information. It's murky business. Popular American author Mark Bowden, after detailing the life and death of Osama bin Laden in *The Finish*, argues "the moral question arises precisely because torture can be an effective tool in interrogation. If we as a nation ban it, we do so despite that fact. We forego the advantages of torture to claim higher moral ground." Less in the public eye and conscience, and seldom (if ever) claiming higher moral ground, the Legion will do what it needs to.

* * *

Bowden, Mark. *The Finish*, Atlantic Monthly Press, 2012.

14

Volunteering

Behind Curtain Number One

Aren't there plumbers for this? I was silently asking.

—*Légionnaire* Valldejuli

Compliments are few in the Legion. No matter how hard you work, rarely are you offered any word of encouragement or thanks. This behavior may well have been calculated (as seems to be much of the Legion way of operating, usually only recognized years later). I remember being slapped on the back of the head at Castel for thanking a server in the mess hall after he had given me my food. The sergeant who had hit me explained (atypically) that a legionnaire needn't say thank you for something that is a given—like food three times a day. With this logic, it is understandable how thankless most sergeants and officers are with legionnaires who perform difficult or unpleasant tasks; after all, it's a given that a legionnaire's job is hard.

* * *

If anything and everything are asked of a legionnaire, especially a new one, he will likely avoid volunteering for work. Due to its focus on teamwork, however, *instruction* invites targeting those who avoid volunteering. One sunny afternoon during that phase of service, we were divided into groups of ten to practice shooting at a range in a hilly valley full of loose rocks. My group had just shot and was now seated away from the others, enjoying the sun and resting. Sergeant Schindshoek, a.k.a. "SGT Shindig," a German veteran of Algeria, needed some help and called over to us. Our only noticeable movement was the turning of heads away from the sergeant. Shindig became enraged. He cursed and began throwing large stones and skull-sized rocks that were scattered near the range. At once, we jumped up and "volunteered" for whatever it was he needed done. The message was clear: Dodge work, and dodge a rock to the head.

Another example, also during *instruction*, of legionnaires forced to volunteer was courtesy of our young lieutenant. By 10:30 Saturday morning, our section had already run the obstacle course twice and completed a seven-mile road march. As we marched into *Quartier* Danjou and took the welcome right turn toward the armory, we were certain that, after securing our weapons, we'd march back to 3rd company and be dismissed for showers and *casse-croûte* (snack). A nervous feeling came over us as we passed our barrack and made for the mess hall. We saw Red Cross trucks and imagined that, though exhausted, we would have to demonstrate some of the basic first aid we'd learned or, worse yet, concentrate and learn something new. As we halted and stood at attention outside the mess hall, the lieutenant finally ordered, "Roll up your left sleeve." I think only half of us knew what was coming. As we lay on the cots and had our blood taken that morning, I knew that something had to give—namely, some of us. Having had no breakfast, many of us were very weak, and two passed out. Others in the section, out of earshot of the corporals and sergeants, let the nurses (male only) know where they could stick their unwelcome needles. As expected, when we finally reached our barrack not a word of thanks was offered, only a sarcastic quip about the two who had fainted.

* * *

While at Castel, a recruit really has no choice but to volunteer when asked. After *instruction*, a tricky kind of "Let's Make a Deal" game ensues around the call for volunteers.

* * *

Knowing that volunteering is often not in the legionnaire's best interest, a *sergent* or *adjudant* will coax the soldiers by asking for a certain number of *bonhommes* (good fellows). This rare compliment is enough to lure some, still unaware of the duty, into volunteering. Also, the personnel soliciting volunteers may hint that what lies behind Curtain Number One (the volunteer's work) is better than what lies behind Curtain Number Two (the scheduled work). In this rigged game of chance, Curtain Number Three is not an option. At times, though, the volunteer completes a much easier task sooner than the non-volunteers do theirs.

One day in Orange, I answered the call of *Adjudant-Chef* Alois "Father Time" Meierbach who asked for not only *deux bonhommes*, but two good men who trusted each other. While a strange request, I quickly nodded to an English friend in another platoon, and we both spoke up. Unfortunately, a German in my platoon also volunteered and *A/CH* Meierbach chose the two of us—thinking, perhaps, that, since we were standing side by side, we would work well together. Meierbach also may have chosen us because he would have *deux bonhommes* whom he could bark at *auf Deutsch*.

Sascha Klinkert was not a bad guy, but he was full of *Ordnung* (in Legion slang—"correctness") and very big. He spoke better English than I did German, but I won lots of points with Klinkert by merely mouthing a smattering of *Deutsch*. No one ever called him by his mysterious first name, which he hated. Once when he was drunk, he told me the Sascha saga. His mother had worked near a military base in East Germany and "liked men." One of these men was a high-ranking Russian *GRU* officer. According to Klinkert, his mother got pregnant by this married intelligence officer and, rather than abandon the woman, the officer helped her leave East Germany and, in the process, rid himself of any scandal. Sascha was born and raised near Munich, but his mother named him after the Russian officer who had helped her flee to the West. We called Klinkert "Arnold" and his square, high-cheekboned face, muscular body and slow, accented English made him look the part. He was also smart and ambitious and not too shy in telling everyone that if he didn't make corporal within two years and five months' service he would desert and the French could kiss his German-Russian ass goodbye.

As we walked away from the company gathered at ranks that afternoon, we somehow felt as if we'd won a reprieve from a difficult or boring job. That week, our company had been doing a spring cleaning of every possible item: from greasing weapons to waxing floors, and even shampooing and brushing the horse's mane that hung from one of our guid18ons. Without saying anything, Father Time led us behind the *escadron's* barrack and gave us two garden hoses. So far, so good, we figured; at least we'd be working outside. Still, as we walked past a gutter full of leaves and several beds of flowers that needed watering, we became suspicious. Father Time now began to speak, but in such garbled Alsatian-German that even Klinkert had difficulty understanding him. The *adjudant-chef* pointed to a rectangular iron covering on the road next to our barrack, which I had never noticed. Father Time then spoke, and all I recall is Klinkert saying "*Scheiße*"—not as a declaration which wouldn't have been smart in front of the *adjudant-chef* but as a question. Klinkert and Meierbach then looked at me, though I had no idea what Father Time had said.

Klinkert removed the heavy iron covering with ease and peered into the hole. The smell was powerful. We were standing over our barrack's sewer system. I looked down the hole and wondered what we had volunteered for. The *adjudant-chef* told us to clear the sewage passage. Klinkert and I looked in the hole again and saw only four dark walls surrounding a deep pit. Meierbach told us to use the hoses to remove the wall closest to the barrack. Of course, this was no ordinary wall. It was a coagulation of feces and paper blocking the discharge from the toilets. Neither Klinkert nor I moved—each hoped that we had misunderstood something. "Aren't there plumbers for this?" I was silently asking. The *adjudant-chef* then explained, given the small opening, how best to use the hoses. That Curtain Number One should have been passed over was becoming uncomfortably evident.

We were chosen because of our body types. Schwarzenegger-like Klinkert was told to hold long, tall, lightweight me by my ankles and lower me into the hole with both hoses at full force in my hands. I was to break down this hardened wall of shit with two garden hoses. Once Klinkert realized only I would be going down he began joking: "Yes, I really was in the shit this time" and "Yes, it's a shitty day." I held my breath as I was lowered into the hole. Father Time turned on the water, and I sprayed this horrible black and brown mountain. And to my surprise, chunks of this Turdlin Wall did break away. Squinting through partially closed eyes, I also saw several *bouquins de cul* (small pornographic comics) that no doubt helped to solidify this redoubt of waste. Klinkert continued to joke. While I trusted him to hold me and raise me up for air when I yelled, he still played around dipping me up and down like an enormous vanilla ice cream cone in a tub of chocolate sprinkles. As he laughed, he would ask, "*Ça va, Valldejude?*" The situation was too absurd for me to become angry—a bastard German-Russian holding the American Catholic he thought was a Jew over a pile of international waste as a gray-bearded Alsatian veteran of Algeria looked on, giving instructions.

After the wall had been breached and long hot showers with disinfectant (provided by the *adjudant-chef*) taken, Klinkert and I never had to worry about any more disgusting jobs. I later remembered that I had been told by a German sergeant in Gestapo at Aubagne that the Legion would be "five years of shit." I was very thankful that it had actually been only one day.

15

Theft and *Démmerde*

Legion Magpies

"There was a guy who was stealing my meat, and I smacked him one. This corporal came over, so I tried to tell him he stole my meat from my plate."

—*LÉGIONNAIRE PREMIÈRE CLASSE* POULSEN

Many legionnaires find the Honor Code, which begins, *"Chaque légionnaire est ton frère d'armes"* ("Every legionnaire is your brother in arms") perhaps more sharply defined on paper than in practice. Theft in the barracks is more common than many officers like to admit. The Legion has more than its share of rash and irresponsible soldiers who run up such high debt due to a drinking, gambling, or even drug habit that a month's almost tax-free pay is not enough. He must steal from fellow legionnaires. Theft in the Legion does not always involve money, however. If there is a comical side to the practice it lies in what Legion magpies steal from one another. While in the hospital, I had a South Florida restaurant guide and Holy Communion crucifix swiped from my locker in Orange. A much longer-serving veteran of the *REC, B/CH* Donlon reasons that "stealing goes on in every army but didn't think the actual legionnaire would steal off each other." However, Donlon soon learned that "it's like living with fucking gypsies—they'll steal anything if they can, from underpants to money." Donlon accepts that military-issued clothing can go missing "but it's the army who pays. It's not personal, but anything bought with someone's money—you just don't touch."

Donlon has seen outrageous acts of theft that serve only to demoralize: "Even guys' lockers been cut with tin snips at the back. A big hole because the *cadena* (lock) is too fucking strong, so they cut the whole fucking *armoire* (locker)." Shamefully, these are Legion brothers. "These could be guys from other companies when you're away but, in general, you'll find it's usually the French. Always, somebody gets their whole *solde* stolen every month."

* * *

Donlon never kept his cash in his locker. His money was always wrapped in a small bit of plastic and kept on his person. Once in Mayotte he left his little bag of money on the floor by the toilets. Before returning to the barrack he ran back to the latrine and waited outside the stall where he knew he had left the money: "'There's a guy in there. So he came out, trying to sort of get by, but I said, 'Just a minute, I just happened to have put my money down there.' He was a French guy, and he said, 'I don't know, I've never seen anything.' I said, 'I'd like you to stick around.' So he says, 'OK, we'll have a look.' Anyway, he managed to get it out of his shorts and drop it. 'Oh, here it is.' 'Ah, yes, thanks very much' . . . and all this . . . because he knew I wouldn't let him leave the building and if there was a *sketch* he'd be in trouble. I was pretty lucky. It was about 2,000 pounds.'"

I found the penalty for those caught stealing depended on the man and the circumstances, which is how Donlon describes it, too. "First the *adjudant de companie* would either punch the guy, or, if he liked him, he'd probably slap him or tell him this has got to stop. If he didn't like him he'd really wade in, you know. He'd pass *rapport* (with the captain) and get about fifteen days. But, there again it's very, very rare that a guy is caught. There's always some excuse—it can never be him—or this business."

As *B/CH* Donlon noted, anything can be stolen. Often during *instruction,* you will be driven to steal something. However, during *instruction,* you don't steal, but, rather, learn to *démmerde* (literally, "to get out of the shit"). Food, clothes, and gear are the most popular items *"démmerded."*

Always rushed at the mess hall, you'll often leave with whatever bits of food you can stuff in your uniform and, later, stash in your locker. Although it involves long hours of hard, sloppy work, a day in the kitchen will give a hungry recruit time to eat and the chance to grab whatever looks good for scarfing down later. While at Castel, you'll wash all your clothes except the *tenue de combat*, which, thankfully, are washed in the regimental laundry. Athletic gear is uniform and with forty-five or fifty pairs of like-colored socks, plus shirts and shorts, and even regulation underwear hanging out to dry, the process of *démmerde* is very inviting. Adding to the temptation is that a recruit is given very little spending money and, often, cannot buy extras of what he needs.

A legionnaire in *instruction* learns to do whatever it takes to make it through the day. LEG Persson observed two sides of the Legion: "Facing outwards, they're really strong, and you won't get in that, but, inside, it's the law of the jungle. The strongest survive. You have to live after that law if you want to stay OK, especially during *instruction*." Without a doubt, various forms of "survival training" are taught during basic training. "Always you have to be fast and sometimes mean, as well. You have to fight for a place in queue and you have to fight for your food—really."

Mealtime during basic training, especially in the field, often involves meager portions served in uncomfortable settings. LFC Poulsen tells of being made hungrier by a fellow recruit driven to *démmerde*: "There was a guy who was stealing my meat, and I smacked him one. This corporal came over, so I tried to tell him he stole my meat from my plate. He just told me, 'Tough shit. Sit down!' I said, 'I want my piece of meat. Look, I can't live off beans. I've got to have some heavy food.'" Corporals during *instruction* don't care for excuses or backtalk. "He kicked me and said I should sit down, so I went fucking mad and smacked him one and broke his nose. After that the lieutenant came up and I got my meat—and ten days of *taule* (jail) after we came back to camp."

* * *

Given my experience and friends' stories of theft and *démmerde*, I was interested in asking an old-school legionnaire, such as Simon Murray, about this Legion "tradition" in his day. According to Murray, *système D* was accepted protocol for items like extra ammunition or ration packs and, at times, "even vehicles were borrowed for the good of the cause" especially when preparing for extended field exercises or contact with the enemy. However, Murray was aghast at stories of legionnaires stealing from one another. When I told him of having a month's pay stolen from my locked *armoire*, he shouted angrily, "What the hell's a locker for? You've got a padlock on it and that should hold your pay."

* * *

"It's true the Legion takes many kinds of men, but, in your own mind, you must realize that nobody actually actively wants bloody criminals in your army." While initially a man's past blemishes may be overlooked, he added, there remain strict expectations regarding his behavior in his new life. "If they find a criminal they may take him on. They may decide to overlook it, but if he's up for rape and pillage and Christ-knows-what-else—fuck off, we don't need that. In my day, some small-time thieves were taken in, but God help them if they did this business in the barrack."

Murray continues on a topic that I can tell disturbs his recollections of Legion camaraderie. "I mean, if a man steals from his own people, this is a morale buster. But maybe they didn't steal from us because our pay wasn't worth stealing. Still, the old tradition was the knife. The thief's hand held down on the table and a bayonet through his hand. I never saw this, but it was talked about." Today, a criminal may get a beating or jail time, but Murray remembers differently. "In my five years, I only know of one case of theft. The thief was stripped naked and got a good scrubbing with the steel wire brush we used to clean caked mud and sand off our jeeps. Usually the skin would come off quickly—awful, really."

* * *

Change does come to the Legion, which, since the late 1990s, has worked with French Post Office banking services to ensure that all legionnaires have direct deposit savings accounts. This has coincided with the professionalization of the French armed forces (end of required military service) and better pay for newly enlisted men. While reports of legionnaires' stolen salaries have vanished, so has another more endearing monthly tradition. Since the 1830s, legionnaires had formed in company units to march to a well-guarded location and report to their captain for their *solde*. After his crisp report and salute (and perhaps a few words from the captain or lieutenants), the legionnaire would place his *képi* on the edge of the table and scoop the money and coins into his cover-turned-wallet. The happy soldier would then replace his *képi* with the money inside, salute and quickstep out of the building. While the net result may be the same, I doubt an ATM gives a legionnaire the same sense of accomplishment and satisfaction as this colorful, sadly obsolete, ritual that revolved around the very symbol of the Legion. Shed a tear, "Papa" Rollet.

16

Funny Stories

"In lighting the cigarette, a little ash from it, a stray, landed in the worst possible spot, and he went up like a torch. It killed his crabs."

—*Caporal* McCue

Lest one have the impression that, when not beating up its soldiers, it's training them in how to beat up others, the Legion should also be considered a place of many laughs. The pressure and intensity of it all may be the cause, but, more likely, mustering so many mad souls from the world over together into one insane asylum is what generates such *sketches* and *bordels*. Since it's so normal for enlisted men to serve the whims of Legion officers—whether carrying their china in metal trunks on a *marche profonde* in Guiana or servicing an officer's car on a free Sunday—it proves even funnier when the joke is on an officer.

* * *

While stationed on the Indian Ocean island of Mayotte, LFC Van Heek and friends tried to think of an appropriate gift for their colonel, an amateur botanist soon returning to France. Before his official departure, the colonel took a long leave, giving his men enough time to hatch their plan. Van Heek now tells a Legion version of the type of confrontation found in the Josh Logan play and, later, movie, *Mister Roberts*: "We managed to get the key of his *bureau*, which was, simply, at the guard house and made a double of it. And then, we got several tons of soil into his office and stuffed it up with tropical plants."

Van Heek was on guard duty the day the colonel returned from leave. "After having done *les couleurs* (raising the colors), he opened his door and saw the plants. His face went cold blank. And I mean, maybe you don't understand, but his whole *bureau* was full of luxuriant banana trees, of peanut plants, of hibiscus flowers, of all this kind of stuff growing up to the ceiling. If you wanted something like this, it can go very quickly in Mayotte, especially with the heat and weather, and it had been three weeks."

A great Legion prank and a good chuckle for all—including the regular army boys sharing the encampment. However, the departing colonel had the last laugh.

As he left his humid and overgrown office, "he turned around to the company sergeant major and then he said the most incredible thing. He said, 'I would appreciate it if you would cut down that tree for me this evening.' Then he fucked off." The giant tree he was talking about stood at the entrance to the parade square and offered shade to those on guard duty. "And we thought, shit . . . we've had it. The bastard had us because he was leaving and we had to stay. This was his way of hitting back."

* * *

As if purposely for comic effect, the Legion issues one complete buffoon (minimum) per platoon. This soldier is the idiot who forgets to fill his canteen before a march, confuses "present arms" with "order arms," and who might even salute a soldier of the same rank. Legionnaire Calheiros was such a character. Lumbering and lethargic, the rubber-faced, six-foot Brazilian lived in his own special world. In the 1980s, few Brazilians joined the Legion, but plenty of Portuguese did; yet even they were unable to reach Calheiros. LEG Persson, who was in the same *REC* platoon as the Brazilian, tells us about Legionnaire Samba-for-brains: "I remember Calheiros cleaning the tank with petrol. He's inside the tank, sitting in the seat of the tank commander with a bucket full of petrol and some cloth and is cleaning everything down there."

Of course, no one would assign Calheiros to work alone if the job was expected to be done well. LEG Humphris, Persson's English friend, is sent to help the bumbling Brazilian. In Legion fashion, the two close the hatch to camouflage themselves and be left alone. However, with no outside air circulating, the inside of the tank is filling with a mixture of stale air and gasoline fumes.

Away from prying eyes, Calheiros sees this as a perfect time for a break. "Calheiros takes up a cigarette and asks Humphris for some light. And Humphris says, 'You're crazy, you can't smoke in here!' 'Of course, I can,' says Calheiros and fumbles through his pocket to find a pair of matches and starts trying to light up. Humphris just runs out of the tank as far away as he can. He wanted to save his life, and Calheiros just smoked a cigarette down there."

* * *

The Swede and Englishman later thought about the absurdity of it all "and made a conclusion that this guy was so fucking stupid so that it didn't explode. He didn't know it could explode—that's why it didn't."

* * *

Thousands of miles away, in Djibouti, another legionnaire was also cleaning with kerosene. CPL McCue tells us what happened: "There was a number of bizarre cures for crabs that you heard about in the Legion. Of course, you could always get the powder which was painless. The only disadvantage being you had to put it on again two weeks later because it didn't kill the eggs."

Another common way to rid the body of the itchy creatures and their offspring is using insect repellent, sprayed liberally on the infected area, so its contents seep in and sting the skin for thirty minutes and are then washed off. McCue tried this, but "the burning sensation was a little too much," so he went back to the powder treatment. Still, legionnaires are taught to adapt and overcome and "there were other methods I heard of involving substances of increasing strength," McCue adds. "One involved kerosene and was, from what I heard, a pretty effective means."

* * *

A "big German fellow, very stupid—but very fit"—who had a serious infestation between his legs had heard about using this and "felt like that was the way he was going to go." Before the midday *sieste*, he went to the showers and doused himself with kerosene. As with the spray method, the German needed the liquid to smother his body for a full thirty minutes before washing it off. "While he was waiting, he decided he was going to have a cigarette. In lighting the cigarette, a little ash from it, a stray, landed in the worst possible spot and he went up like a torch. It killed his crabs. It was a radical method, but it did kill his crabs. He was in considerable pain for some time after that and he never did use the kerosene again—and recommended to others they not use it."

* * *

Not until the end of your first year of service will you have the right to a week or slightly more of leave. Available to those stationed in mainland France is a modern, though spartan, rest-and-recreation center located on three and a half acres of rocky beachfront in Marseille. Purchased by the Legion in the mid-1960s, this center, in the city's residential Malmousque section, has double rooms ready for any legionnaire on *permission*. If under one year's service, those based on Corsica must stay on the island at a similar R and R center. Room and board is free, and the Kronenbourg in the *foyer* costs only three *francs* per bottle (maybe one euro today).

When not flexing his tattoos for the local "Legion girls" at the beach, or not too hung over from the night before, a legionnaire might use the center's windsurfing and SCUBA gear or other aquatic and sports equipment. However inexpensive and picturesque (Malmousque overlooks the Château d'If), this holiday camp is still a Legion-run operation. Most legionnaires on *permission* want, for however briefly, to return to "civvy street." CPL McCue tells of a group of friends and their unusual tour of the French capital: "That was four guys, actually. There was two American guys, Ford and "Bad Ass" Bodager; and, then, there was Tony Page, a half-caste Londoner; and Norm Rowan, an Irish guy. All four of them went up to Paris at the same time on their first long leave and commandeered one of the Paris city buses."

But this was no ordinary joy ride.

* * *

"They started driving around town picking up only good-looking women and making occasional stops at stores to stock up on beer and other supplies. Yeah, they drove it around town for about two hours before they were finally trapped and forced to relenquish the bus."

As might be expected, given the outlandish hijinks of the hijack, "Leave was canceled on the spot. They were all from the *REP*. They were returned to the *REP* and, straight away, each sent to different *outré-mer* (overseas) regiments."

Among the outrageous stories of legionnaires on leave, this one remains legendary. McCue knew all four involved and heard the tale first-hand. "They said it was a lot of fun while it lasted, you know. They said their only regret was that, once they'd gotten a decent load of women on board, they should have taken the bus out into the countryside. Gotten out of the city where maybe they could have extended their jaunt for a little longer."

* * *

Bringing home war souvenirs is a time-honored tradition in the military. The stash can range from enemy battle flags and knives to weapons and even women (war-brides). The Legion discourages anything of the sort, often because of unforeseen consequences or complications.

* * *

As told by LFC Fairfield, we can see what happens when a friend has second thoughts about his souvenirs and how the shit hits the fan in war-torn Chad: "Allenby, ex-British Royal Marine, had bought this Russian pineapple grenade and bought some Kalshnikov ammunition, hoping to smuggle it back. Then thought about it again, like. I mean a sergeant had been kicked out for bringing a Kalashnikov, so he thought about it."

Unfortunately, Allenby's plan to dispose of his war prizes coincided with Fairfield and and fellow *REP*-man Cavendish's plan to "nip over the wall and go on the piss." As the drunk duo attempted to sneak back to camp, they were met with shouts and sounds of men running. Thinking they had been spotted but also aware that "everybody were on the wacky-backy, anyhow," the two used the darkness and commotion to run to the latrine. If confronted by a superior, they would say they were returning from the toilets. As Fairfield and Cavendish made their way to their bunks, they heard an explosion behind them. It was Allenby's souvenir. "He'd wrapped the ammunition around the grenade with sellotape, or whatever he'd got, pulled the pin and dropped it down the toilet."

The disgusting, maggot-ridden "toilets" weren't made any more appealing by the explosion. Fairfield describes the scene: "Twenty-five cubicles call it. A long row of corrugated iron toilets. Imagine, like, a trench underneath them all linking. You know, every toilet dropped into this trench, right. So when the grenade went off it blew crap everywhere—in every cubicle. There was shit everywhere."

* * *

The next day, thinking he had the guilty ones, the angry company *adjudant-chef* hands Fairfield and late-night drinking partner a bucket and brushes. "He had us put this stuff in the bucket of water, and the buckets went bloody hot. God knows what it was, like, and we had to scrub these sodden toilets. And I thought, you bastard, it were bloody Allenby!"

Africa is again the setting for laughs, but, in 1960s French Algeria, a savage war of recrimination and atrocity from both sides leads *C/CH* Simon Murray to record in his notebook a grotesquely funny, but gruesome, tale of Legion black humor. Some quick background to set the scene: A battalion of Arab regulars in the service of France, stationed in a garrison fort in the mountains, had shot and killed their French officers. The Legion was chosen to find these mutineers and see justice served (a terrifying thought for the hunted). French military intelligence, which had photos and records of these men, needed to interrogate those captured or have physical proof of the ones killed. Murray and two others were told by an intelligence officer attached to their group to cut off the heads of the dead Arab assassins and bring the evidence to the closest base camp to be photographed. After the dismemberment and official snaps, Murray was told to dispose of the three heads, which he threw in some nearby brush.

* * *

From his book, *Legionnaire*, Murray writes: "There then followed an incident that I will recall to my dying day with a shudder, but which at the time caused an uproar of laughter. Some Spaniards in the 2nd section had prepared a small cauldron of soup by adding water to the dehydrated-soup packets in our ration. The *équipe* had eaten and there appeared to be a considerable amount left in the pot, so they called over a German and invited him to fill his tin mug. Just as he was about to put the cupful of soup to his lips, one of the Spaniards, with a mighty guffaw, reached his hand into the cauldron and pulled out by the hair one of the Arab heads, which he had retrieved from the bushes. On looking up at the noise, one could see the scene and follow the story at a glance—the Spaniard stood there with the ghastly head dripping soup, while the German, standing aghast and white as a sheet, froze for a second and then promptly turned and threw up. This gave rise to another guffaw from the Spaniard and his chums. There is no accounting for people's sense of humor—though I must confess at the time I laughed like hell; so did we all—that is, except for the fellow who had received the soup. He never actually touched a drop; it was the nearness of the thing that made him ill, as it does when you narrowly miss having a bad accident in a motorcar."

17

Camaraderie

"You can't do it alone. Those who don't understand—get out."

—Sergent-Chef Gazdík

One of the Legion's most renowned qualities as a fighting unit is its *esprit de corps*. Some of this is taught through Legion history and song during *instruction*, but, mostly, it comes from legionnaires themselves. Camaraderie with fellow soldiers sprouts during basic training and grows throughout your Legion career. The strongest bonds initially form between those from the same country or language group, since the ease of communication makes trust easy to build and maintain. Yet, the Legion would be a splintered and ineffective army if it were formed of disparate ethnic groups looking out only for themselves. The *mafia anglais*, an anglophone-only "self-preservation society," is tolerated because its core members are all extremely dedicated to the Legion.

The trick for the Legion is to treat everyone at the lower end of the system poorly (e.g., during *instruction*) and thereby build solidarity among all abused nationalities. Those groups can then complain and commiserate among themselves in whichever language they like, usually crude French. While the new French recruits understand everything, the corporals and sergeants are wise not to favor them. Indeed, the NCOs often seem to enjoy picking on a disoriented francophone, dub him *"francocon"* (French fool), and abuse him to no end.

A Legion company during *instruction* is meant to believe, as soldiers throughout time have been led to believe, that theirs is the toughest, most physically taxed, and unfairly treated section of new recruits in basic training history. Getting through the initial rigors physically and mentally intact gives the new soldier a confidence that highlights how achievement at this level is not a solo act. From platoon to company to regiment, the legionnaire must forge initial bonds of dependency leading to a deep camaraderie to survive within his new, intense, and grueling environs.

* * *

At the *REC,* I used to laugh at the institutional camaraderie promoted on "working Saturdays." These came once a month and, thankfully, lasted only four or five hours, usually until noon. It was all very totalitarian. We'd be assigned manual labor in the barrack or outside and made happy in our work by camp loudspeakers treating us to a military version of classic Top Ten. The songs and marches were the same month after month. *La Marseillaise,* though popular throughout the world, never has much Legion play outside of official functions and was never heard during weekend duty. True or not, many legionnaires know a version of the following story: French soldiers were captured by Japanese troops in Indochina in the early 1940s. These soldiers—a mix of Marines, Colonials, and Legionnaires—were humiliated and imprisoned in Japanese labor camps north of Hanoi. On one occasion, the POWs protested a Japanese commandant's work order by defiantly singing *La Marseillaise.* It was their last song—all were shot. Legion lore blames this massacre not on the Japanese but on the Marines who coaxed their fellow prisoners to sing the stirring national anthem, considered the world's most glorious. No Japanese army, it is believed, would have dared shoot soldiers who had sung *"Le Boudin"*—the anthem of the French Foreign Legion.

* * *

A chain gang-like Germanic chant broke out one working Saturday, when I teamed up with a Laotian, a Malagasy, and a Swede, in cleaning the barrel of an *AMX-10 RC* tank. *BRG* Braunschweig, a German, sat straddling the barrel and encouraged us to push the long pipe cleaner-looking device in and out by shouting *"ein"* to which we would reply *"Bier."* This rhythmic back-and-forth chanting made us work faster and harder and proved much less monotonous than listening to the standard Legion tunes. The *brigadier* knew he had to have some gimmick to get us to do this boring job on a weekend, and he found a good one, giving us a laugh.

Another *brigadier* who took care of his men and showed solidarity with them was my *caporal de chambre* (room corporal), *BRG* Wetzel, a short Swiss fellow who spoke fluent French and German, and some Italian. An avid chess player, he read whenever he could and took the responsibility of his hard-earned stripes seriously. While kind and fair, he was also a strict taskmaster very much in charge of our living space. Still, on occasion, he would help us tidy the room, something I never saw a corporal do.

Guard duty at the *REC* is a traumatic experience whether one is a *maréchal des logis* (sergeant) or a legionnaire. Every bit of your uniform must be perfect, and the newer you are to the regiment, the more perfect it has to be. On my first *REC* guard duty, I was sure all was correct. I had even visited the tailor on base (the only woman in camp) and had had my uniform perfectly fitted. While a visit to Madame Guende was pleasant, it was costly and not a common stop for a new legionnaire. Even so, at the 05:00 pre-inspection ritual in the *foyer* of our barrack, Father Time (*A/ CH* Meierbach) harshly scolded me—albeit not for a uniform infraction but for my boots, which, though well shined, had one heel more worn than the other. I was allowed to go on guard duty but given five days of company punishment for my uneven heels.

With the expected thorough examination at the company level, followed by inspection from the top NCO at the main gate, the *maréchals des logis* and *brigadiers* always have cause to worry about how well new legionnaires have ironed their uniforms and polished their boots. *BRG* Wetzel sought to avoid much of the morning misery by having those in his room give him their guard uniform several days in advance of their guard duty. At his own expense, he would then take the uniforms into town to have them dry cleaned and ironed according to Legion standards. Under the circumstances, this kind gesture made good sense, he believed.

About a year and a half later, I met another Swiss corporal, Wohler, at the *1ᵉʳ RE* in Aubagne. Not many Swiss join the Legion because those who serve the French risk losing their citizenship upon return to their neutral homeland (serving the pope with the Swiss Guard in Vatican City, however, is sanctioned). Wohler was as interesting as Wetzel. I told him about my Swiss *brigadier* at the *REC*, what an impressive soldier he was, and how much better the Legion would be with more men like him. *Caporal* Wohler seemed to be taking it all in with more than a typical sense of nationalist pride. Indeed, it was fraternal pride. Once I was done praising Wetzel, Wohler told me that the *REC brigadier* was his brother; Wohler was an assumed Legion name.

* * *

Another way legionnaires help each other is by lending military gear and civilian clothes. If a friend lacks a clean ironed dress shirt and needs one quickly, another friend the same size will lend him his. Civilian clothes are also sought after by new legionnaires since money is always tight. I'd never borrowed or lent clothes before, and the practice seemed strange, like something pre-teen girls might do. Yet, it was all part of the communal living that was our new life. Food is no exception to the Legion's musketeer mentality. After an unusually long march during *instruction*, I went to the company medic, an English friend, to have him clean and bandage my feet. I sat in front of him eating a Mars bar, and, before tending to my blisters, he asked for a bite of my chocolate. From our march with canteens full of water, I knew the protocol and shared the meager chocolate bar with him, knowing that he would have done the same for me had I been the one to ask.

On another occasion, the one-for-all and all-for-one situation was more obvious. It was Christmas at the *1ᵉʳ RE*, and my father had sent me a Marks and Spenser care package. I opened the gift in a room surrounded by legionnaires I didn't know, but who for the next few days or weeks were to be my bunkmates. Everyone was fixated on the package, which was full of tasty delicacies. I ended up giving half the food away to those legionnaires who hadn't received so much as a Christmas card from friends or family. As with the other examples of sharing, I really didn't mind distributing the expensive gift; Christmas spirit aside, we were all in it together.

Other items I saw shared more regularly than care packages, however, were books. Whenever someone finished reading one, he passed it on. Although the writer Arthur Koestler and poets Blaise Cendrars and Alan Seeger had served in the Legion, the typical reading material among my fellow legionnaires (aside from 10-*franc* pornographic "comic books") were action and suspense novels by Frederick Forsythe, Len Deighton, John Le Carré, Stephen King, and Sven Hassel. Sometimes, a legionnaire on the toilet, engrossed in one of these popular novels, would shout out cursing as he found pages missing from his book. However, this same legionnaire knew all too well what had happened.

Other more unusual items shared were girls. On a brief respite during my first Camerone in Orange, I spoke with a Polish *REC* veteran of the 1950s. Attached to the British 8th Army during World War II, the Pole had fought with General Władysław Anders' Second Polish Corps. Upon return to his devastated homeland, he was arrested by the new Soviet-controlled government for "espionage" and served time in prison. After his release, he managed to make his way to France and joined the Legion, serving three years in Algeria. Sitting next to his wife and across from me at a bottle-laden table beneath the dim lights of the *2ème escadron*'s beer tent, the Pole told me about a wild Camerone in Sidi-bel-Abbès. The Polish veteran's April 30th memories in Algeria included a local *pute* brought to the barrack as a Camerone gift for the captain. After his pleasure, the captain graciously offered the whore to his men. One by one, and sometimes two at once, they were then serviced by the busy Bedouin. Swigging his beer and smiling, the Pole looked at his gloomy, sack-of-potatoes wife and said wistfully, "Those were the days." Not understanding a word of French, she dutifully nodded.

* * *

228

Now, as then, the supply of "girlfriends" is far less than that of books, but no less eagerly swapped. The girls do not seem to mind. Indeed, love may be only a phone call away—for whomever. Jock Dumfries, my Scottish friend in *Musique Principale*, told me how, by randomly answering a ringing pay phone on base in Aubagne one night, he found a date in Marseille for the weekend. While no luscious Swedish schoolgirl, Bibi, a fiftysomething fatty from Gothenberg, was otherwise a legionnaire's delight: food prepared, alcohol served, and sex delivered—all free of charge. Jock told me that the lonely and horny half-French/half-Swede would call the pay phone on base several times a month, perhaps trolling for Beau Geste himself. It seems much like legionnaires with books: The ladies simply hope the next bit of entertainment will be better than the last.

Yet another example of legionnaires' feeling a kinship with their own, especially those who seem to be at a disadvantage, occurred on Christmas Eve. I was in the main mess hall at *1er RE* soaking up the raucous party atmosphere at the regimental dinner. Suddenly, the doors burst open. Everyone looked at the entrance only to see the poor souls who had been put on guard duty that day. Without hesitation, the entire mess hall stood and cheered as these Christmas guards, in combat fatigues, web belts, and rifles, ducked in for a little Noël chow.

* * *

In every conversation I've had with former legionnaires, I find what they seem to miss most from their service days is the camaraderie and inhouse humor. Naturally, any time adventurous strangers assemble in a circus like the Legion and make it through all the hoops, friends are sure to be remembered many years later. Surviving the Legion is something quite different from graduating from college or university. I have many good friends from my school days, but our memories are nothing like those I share with Legion pals. The Legion is a leveler unlike any institution I've seen. Whether by shaving the back of the neck of a fellow legionnaire the night before guard duty, or holding onto a strap from his rucksack as he bobs along in front of you during a pitch-black night march, intense togetherness and dependency are fostered.

* * *

Legionnaires may complain about life in the regiment and dream of the ease of the civilian world, but, after returning to the latter, all agree they miss the intense camaraderie and spirit of the former. Some jokingly proclaim themselves *"inapt civil"* and return to service within several months or a year. Because the Legion is such a small and unique army, an astute legionnaire can quickly learn its rules on how to live with his peers and adapt to the expectations of his superiors. Everything is clear and fixed, although it may take time for the new ones to adjust. Still, once the new life is accepted, it can be difficult to re-learn the intricacies of civilian life—especially the complications found within a new workplace or social setting.

S/CH Gazdík adds his observations on the lasting power and importance of camaraderie in the Legion: "An Arab is a fucker, but, if we served together, I know what he expects of me, and I of him. This is what the Legion teaches. It's a historic creation by the Legion, part of what it teaches. You have to accept this camaraderie. You can't do it alone. Those who don't understand—get out. And that's why we're good in the Legion. The Legion has survived because of its discipline."

Gazdík continues on the Legion's special pull long after hanging up the *képi*. "Actually, I can tell you that, after the Legion, I didn't have too many real friends, huh. Sure . . . people I'd call or write, but few real pals. These were colleagues, yes . . . lots of colleagues. But, with the Legion, I can call or write, 'Hey, what's up? How are things?' to even *majors* or *adjudant-chefs*." Without fail, Gazdík receives a warm response. "We can always find that connection that is lacking in our new lives. The real friends, the real camaraderie . . . is hard to find in the civilian world."

C/CH Murray also muses on how, even while surrounded by the standard trappings of civilian life—marriage and career—the appearance of former comrades can stir the kind of emotions that many never feel. As unlikely as it may be, meeting a fellow legionnaire by chance is cause for a knowing smile, a quick exchange of regiments served in, and length of service. However, any reunion of legionnaires who served together is sure to produce an endless review of people and places, together with talk of how special that long-ago time was. Somewhere in the reminiscing, the conversation will, no doubt, drift off to what different men they were then and how they've never found quite the same spirit and camaraderie in the civilian world.

In his book, Murray depicts a scenario that many of us have dreamed: Set a time and place in the future to meet three friends and, with no further contact or reminders, be there. In fact, to honor his commitment to his comrades, Murray asks his future in-laws to postpone a New Year's engagement party so he and his fiancée can drive from London to Brussels and arrive at the agreed upon rendezvous spot, the landmark Mannekin Pis statue. Murray waits one hour beyond the midnight-hour meeting time. As he and his future wife, Jennifer, prepare to leave, a voice calls out "Johnny" from one of the plaza's side streets.

Such is Legion camaraderie. It is a bond that erases the divisions and constraints of language, culture, class, education, and country that may have separated us in our pre-Legion lives. We are now all members of an exclusive male club whose dues were paid in many extreme ways. We served, and we know what that means.

* * *

Perhaps *C/CH* Murray, after only two years of service, already understood the power of this when he wrote in his diary how "the Legion breaks down the barriers of preconceived ideas and misconceptions about people and, in their place, sometimes generates a great spirit of comradeship."

* * *

Legion camaraderie encourages and enables men to find the strength to support one another and overcome whatever particular ball-breaking activity they may be facing. This is especially true when they are new and at the bottom of the Legion's unique "scrotum pole." Still, a few (very few) examples stand out in Legion history of a new recruit's social status or education putting him at an advantage over other neophytes, something that most probably would detract from the spirit of camaraderie. Several

Czarist generals sought refuge in the *1ᵉʳ REC* after their White Army succumbed to the Bolsheviks during the 1918–1922 Russian Civil War. Exceptions were made, and the Russian generals were allowed to begin their new military careers for France as lieutenants.

For the most part, however, the Legion doesn't give a damn who you once were; it is what you will become and what you can do in that capacity that are the criteria the Legion cares about now. While rarely the case elsewhere, little or no interest is placed in a potential legionnaire's education, grades in school, speaking ability, letters of recommendation, or even work experience. Yes, early aptitude tests will more or less reveal his potential, but many get by with very low scores.

As with his IQ tests in school, a legionnaire will often be unaware of his *niveau generale* (*NG*) or *niveau culturelle* (*NC*) until it is time for him to know, e.g., a *stage* or promotion wherein a certain NG or NC must be held. In fact, unknown to most recruits at Aubagne is the Legion's early system of putting new boys on a career track. *Filière* (stream) *F1*, *F2*, and *F3* are used to identify those candidates who may be fast-tracked to NCO rank within five years. A candidate for early NCO must be rated *F1* and have a *NG/NC* of at least fourteen. New boys rated *F2* are deemed possible NCO material within five to seven years. Recruits rated *F3* are seen as having no NCO potential although legionnaires with early notes of low potential have, on occasion, risen in rank. Even when a legionnaire knows his *NG* or *NC*, he is wise to keep silent. (Redoing *NG* tests is both risky and rare and often changes nothing.) Fellow legionnaires are often quite wary of anyone with a high *NG* or, worse still, a high *NC*. Ever suspicious of those *F1* types, *intellectual de gauche* is the ultimate insult for anyone flaunting a high *NC*; camaraderie does seem to have its limits.

18

Desertion

Hit the Road, Jacques

And, well, I must admit . . . I'll say this on tape: I do feel guilt in what I did. I still feel guilt.

—*Légionnaire première classe* Fairfield

Even with the Legion's remarkable camaraderie and *esprit de corps*, desertion is commonplace. It started in 1831 and continues today. Desertion is, simply, one of many Legion traditions: Though viewed in two ways. Those legionnaires with less than five-years' service will sometimes be complacent toward, if not envious of, the act while most longer-serving soldiers and the entire officer corps view it with contempt and scorn.

* * *

Like a nervous and impatient groom waiting out a clergyman's lecture on the sanctity of marriage and the sin of divorce, Legion recruits will be told of the dishonor of desertion before leaving the altar at Aubagne. While not as common as civilian divorce, desertion from the Legion remains widespread and persistent. Desertion rates during *instruction* are disproportionally higher than the rates of those absconding from other armies during basic training. Often a recruit at Castel finds himself in a world stranger than he had imagined. The recruit might either be shocked or unimpressed, or simply tired of it all. Many early deserters seem to give more thought to quitting the Legion than they did to joining.

While deserting is much easier once assigned to a regiment in the *métropole*, some can't wait. Since the mid-1980s, however, the Legion has included a clause in very small print in its initial five-year contract that grants a legionnaire a six-month grace period, during which he can be honorably discharged if he so desires. Nevertheless, for many, this delayed bureaucratic formula of dissatisfaction is neither spontaneous nor adventurous. Some *instruction* deserters believe their escape will show their military and/or survival skills more surely than anything taught in the four-month basic training period. American Rob Lewis tells of an Austrian friend, Günter Winter, who quit at the end of his second month of basic training: "Günter was tall. Gangly. Young. Twenty. Smart as a whip. Intelligent . . . intellectual. He was such an intellectual that he understood that there is a soldier's time in your life, OK. You know, that's one of the ages you have to go through. And surprisingly there's a large number of those men in the Legion that do it that way."

Günter and Rob got to be close friends during the first few months of the Legion's own "shock and awe" program of basic training. With everyone's head spinning, Günter tried to befriend all. He spoke excellent English and passable French and would spend too much time translating and explaining to others. "That was his failing," Rob recalls. "He wasn't taking care of his shit, yeah." With each passing week Legionnaire Winter became more harried and suffered increasing verbal or physical abuse from the corporals and sergeants. "He was hurting. I could see that he was pretty sad, but there was nothing I could do for him at all."

After the section had run several of the dreaded, full-pack, 8K runs along the canal, many recruits lightened their load as much as possible. Even with severe penalties if caught, canteens would be half-full or even empty, the lining removed from parkas, and mess kits stashed elsewhere. As they prepared for the run, Rob noticed, "Günter was packing heavy for it." He warned the struggling Austrian, "You're not going to make it." With no response from his friend and now more intrigued, Rob asked,

"What, are you getting the *pêche* (inner strength/gusto) back? What's your thing?"

Soon, Rob learned why Günter hadn't been talkative and didn't discard any items from his pack. "We're going down the road, and he says, 'Robert, you've really been a good friend.' He says, 'Good-bye.' And I said, 'Good-bye? *Allez en avant!* (Come on, let's go!).' We're running . . . everybody else is going straight . . . and he takes a right. And he just ran away with his pack, his combats, and he made it. I don't know if he made it back to Austria or where he went, but he did not get busted."

* * *

Though many a legionnaire understands why a friend deserts and is sympathetic, it does have an effect on the morale of those who stay. And while desertions do happen during basic training, many recruits are at least curious to see what awaits at their combat regiment. Still, the reality seldom matches the dream.

* * *

I often think back to a June night in Orange in 1987 when I said good-bye to two very good friends. We made the most of the last evening together by going to our usual out-of-the-way bar to play pool, swap Legion stories, and drink plenty. The bartender made a typically French *c'est comme ça* ("That's how it is") gesture upon my friends' return from the men's room in civilian clothes. I'd never seen either out of uniform, or so happy. I wished them luck dodging the civilian and military police, and, as we shook hands goodbye, the Communards' "Don't Leave Me This Way" came on the jukebox. Not adding anything to the somber mood, the music made us wonder about it all. We knew there was a good chance we'd never meet again. My two friends begged me to come along with tales of more adventure than I would ever see in the Legion, and I was very tempted to join them. For a legionnaire young in service and new to a regiment, a close friend is an extremely positive aide. A friend, even in a different platoon or company, can ease the loneliness and stress all

235

new legionnaires feel after leaving that special four-month camaraderie of basic training.

* * *

The following story is especially sad for me because it involves the desertion of a friend who, under still conflicting reports, was shot. Simon Heslop (name changed) and I met while *EVs* at Aubagne in September 1986. He was a polite, well-spoken, young Englishman with a quick smile and not at all typical of the hopefuls awaiting selection. Added to this was his Hollywood-scripted story for joining. Hailing from a small town in Cornwall, Simon was to be married to a local farm girl, but two weeks before the wedding, the groom got the idea of thawing his cold feet in Africa with the French Foreign Legion. He never returned. *Caporal-Chef* Atherton was there: "There was two stories going around. The first story, that he blew his brains out, and the second story, was that he got his brains blown out by a *tireur d'élite* (sniper) out of a helicopter."

Legionnaire Heslop was being pushed hard by his sergeants in the unforgiving *commando entrainement* (commando training) course in Djibouti. This course, even by Legion standards, is brutal, and the failure rate is high. Heslop started to crack under the pressure and punishing physical demands. "He did desert with a *FAMAS* (5.56mm standard Legion-issued rifle)—that's sure and certain. Just headed out in the desert. Just fucked off, yeah, so it must have been pretty bad for him to do that for a start. It's just rocks and desert. No shade or anything."

Since Heslop had deserted with a weapon, Atherton's unit was called into action. His search party was more or less told that recovery of the intact *FAMAS* was of more importance than the errant legionnaire. In fact, "by the time we got to him, we found out he was dead and we couldn't find the *FAMAS*. So we had to search through the wilderness for a week." Simon's bloated, black body was taken back to the regiment, but the rifle wasn't found until "someone put out a bounty of 150,000 Djiboutian francs and then, *eh, voilà*, it turned up all of a sudden."

Several months later, friends in Orange showed me newspaper clippings from English tabloids, and Atherton, nodding his head, confirmed that "the Heslop thing hit England as a big scandal." To this day, I still think of gentle Simon and his dreams and wonder, if only he'd married that Cornwall girl and skipped his Legion misadventure.

* * *

Of course, not all Legion desertion stories are as dramatic or tragic as the Heslop episode. Many times, desertion simply happens. Every time I hear the steel drum–inspired 1960s pop song "Concrete and Clay" (especially the Hong Kong Syndicate's 1986 version), I think of how casual desertion is looked upon in the Legion. One evening, I was on *corvée* duty in the *REC* mess hall with several other unlucky legionnaires. A German—so new I didn't even recognize him—was the most chipper among us. He was cleaning the floor with a smile and singing the bouncy "Concrete and Clay"—practically dancing with his mop. Amazed at his *pêche,* I asked the young one why all the excited energy for this tiring after-hours duty. He smiled and said, matter-of-factly, "Why not be happy? It's my last *corvée* ever. I'm leaving tonight." I never saw him again.

Desertion rates are also high upon a company's return to France from an overseas tour. After a substantial *solde* (pay), the legionnaire is given a long *permission*, and many are happy to take the money and run. In cases like these, it is not necessarily the disgruntled and exploited legionnaire with less than one-year's service who deserts but corporals and, sometimes, even sergeants. That the Legion loses essential men in trained combat positions is both disheartening to the officer corps and chaotic to administrators. To prepare for his sergeant's course, *REC Brigadier* Robeson was sent to Castelnaudary. He comments on the concern those in command show toward the problem of desertion: "It's an obsession now at Aubagne and Castelnaudary, this business of *conservation des effectifs* (retention of troops). They don't like the way everyone keeps deserting all the time. It's impractical. It's a nuisance because they can't plan anything. It's very hard personnel management-wise to be able to plan anything when you've got so many guys fucking off."

Times have changed: While today's recruits expect toughness and discipline, they will vote with their feet in response to random beatings and other abuse common to generations of legionnaires-in-training. Legion command has "changed some regulations and softened things up. They want to reduce the number of *sketches* (classic Legion foul-ups), so the guys are less inclined to get pissed off quickly and hang on—wait around and see and try to make something of it."

Another way to lessen desertion rates may be for the administration to set a quota on certain nationalities selected. "Definitely, people up top are looking into this in a big way, and, I think it's part of the reason they've changed the type of guy they're taking in now. There's less Brits coming in and less French and less Germans. Certainly, the British and the Germans have a bad reputation for fucking off."

Planned or not, the decrease in numbers of these rowdy nationalities has also coincided with easier access to western Europe for other groups. Robeson observes, "Lots of Polaks and Ukrainians, Bulgarians and Russians and, also, a lot more Asians, always *tranquille* (calm)—do what they're told, and haven't got a high reputation for desertion. I think they've changed to them in the hope that these guys are more likely to stay in, which is probably true."

* * *

Penalties for those caught deserting vary from regiment to regiment. While at the *REC* in Orange, I had the misfortune of being forced to partake in the ritual shaming of an English friend who attempted desertion.

Reginald J. Preston was a very funny eighteen-year-old from Hull, England, who looked and acted like Stan Laurel. Just as Laurel used to fiddle with his bowler, so would Preston with his *képi*, especially when he was nervous or excited. Preston was as outrageous as he was comical. Once, he and I were led by *Maréchal des Logis (MDL)* Monno (the quartermaster) to our *escadron's* storage room near the tank garages. Lined up in neat rows were ten or more packs and the equipment of all those who had deserted in the past few months. Of course, Preston and I knew them all. Most of the packs belonged to friends we had hoped would stay with us. Monno began to give us instructions about cleaning when, in a dangerous move for a young legionnaire, Preston interrupted the *maréchal des logis.* Preston, who barely spoke French, asked the *maréchal* if he could go get his pack and put it in line with the others since he would soon *taille la route* (lit. "snip the road"/desert). Through Mr. Bean-like facial expressions and wild hand gestures, Preston made sure Monno knew he soon would be deserting. The French *maréchal* just shook his head and said, "*Les anglais sont fou*" ("The English are crazy.") He then told "Johnny" that he really didn't give a damn if he deserted as long as it was after this work detail was finished.

A few weeks later, I was laughing to myself as I visited that same elephant's graveyard of *paquetage* (gear/kit) carrying the rucksack of one Preston, R. J. Reluctantly, I'd seen Preston off three nights earlier. He deserted after we had gotten our month's *solde*. As irreverent as ever, Preston had presented himself to the *escadron* captain for his pay. Captain de Puybaudet had an idea of the young legionnaire's intentions and sternly asked Preston if he was going to desert now that he had a month's pay in hand. Without a hint of sarcasm, Preston answered in what proved to be mock earnestness, "*Non, mon capitaine. Je reste ici. La Légion, mon capitain, c'est bon pour Johnny.*" ("No, captain. I'm staying here. The Legion, captain, is good for this English-speaking legionnaire.") I had to turn away quickly so the captain and other officers couldn't see my smirking face. I thought of this as I walked back to the barrack from the storage room and had to admit how happy I was that Preston had had the last laugh. Still grinning, I entered my barrack only to see a *képi* sitting all too high on an all too familiar shaven head; the legionnaire standing at attention facing the wall was one Reginald J. Preston. I walked by him without saying a word. I hoped that somehow it just wasn't true.

A friend told me that Preston was still in uniform when the *Gendarmes* picked him up as he tried to board a ferry to England. I also learned that he had just been brought in by the *PMs* and had yet to see Captain de Puybaudet. I waited in my room, only a short distance from the *bureau de semaine*, and wondered how the captain would react to Legionnaire "*C'est bon pour Johnny*" Preston. After a half-hour or so, I went into the hallway and looked for Preston. He was standing in the same place, but now with his nose pressed up against a wooden placard holding the Legion *code d'honneur. A/CH* Meierbach, a combat veteran of Algeria, was standing next to, and screaming at, the eighteen-year-old. Meierbach was a short man with a long beard and hot temper whom we called "Father Time." An old-school horse soldier, the *adjudant-chef* was often seen marching around the regiment with riding crop in hand or seated next to his Chinese driver, Yo-Yo, as he shouted orders from "Bonzai," his elaborately camouflaged *Mehari* (plastic dune buggy-like vehicle). He was very much the Legion of yore, and Preston was getting an earful. A week earlier, Meierbach had made a German deserter caught at the Luxembourg border stand at attention in full dress uniform for hours in the middle of the *REC* parade field. The deserter later collapsed, falling face first onto the concrete. The most disappointing thing to the deserter was that he had so further chipped his front teeth that he could no longer open beer bottles with them and, for this, he cursed *A/CH* Meierbach and the Legion.

At ranks that evening (with Preston still at attention in the hallway), we were told that whoever passed the young English deserter should show him what this *REC escadron* thinks of such soldiers. A slow eater, I was most certainly not in a hurry that evening because I had no desire to see what was happening to my friend. As I came in the barrack, I tried to sneak by Preston and go quickly to my room. However, Father Time was waiting inside the *bureau de semaine* and shouted at me as I entered. He knew Preston and I were friends, but that didn't excuse me from doing what I had been told to. I grimaced as another legionnaire passed by and hit Preston squarely in the back of the head. I also saw that Preston's nose was bloodied and, maybe, broken, which made the blows even more painful. I approached, muttered a quick, "Sorry, pal." and hit him as lightly as I could. Preston reacted as well as any professional wrestler might. I can't say if Father Time was fooled—probably not—but, regardless, the old man had made his point.

Preston spent forty days in jail. During his imprisonment, he continued to amuse and amaze inmates and even some guards. Part of *REC taule* is "sport" every day: the 8,000m TAP run, *parcours du combatant*, or Test Cooper (a twelve-minute run around the track with at least seven and a half laps, 3,000m, to be run for full marks). Preston excelled at all the rigorous PT demanded of *les punis* (the punished). Other inmates suggested that, upon release, he try to pass the Legion physical fitness instructor test. Preston answered them by pointing to a small air duct in the prison cell, wondering aloud whether he was physically fit enough to squeeze through. Several weeks later, Preston walked out the front gate on an evening's *permission*, never to return.

* * *

One reason desertion is such a common option is that there is little recourse or appeal in the Legion system. Also, legionnaires simply don't know enough about the system to protest, and very little is explained to them. Most new boys have no idea there is a six-month probationary contract period. Something else left unexplained is that, if selected for a course, you must go on it and do well. Yes, regardless of your interest in becoming a mechanic or medic, you must go to the *stage* or be charged with *mauvais esprit* (negative thinking). The following two stories are similar in many ways and show how callous the Legion can be with well-trained men.

* * *

Both LFC Fairfield and LFC Griffiths are from northern England, Sheffield and Manchester, respectively. Both were in the *REP* and sent on training programs (and, thus, career paths) that held no interest for them. Fairfield was to be an administrator and Griffiths, a cook. Reluctantly, both left Corsica for their appropriate training at the *4ème RE* in Castelnaudary. Fairfield deserted after completing his administrative training, and Griffiths, during his kitchen course. Quite interestingly, both have similar comments on the topic. Fairfield on friends who went AWOL: "I was disappointed in them. I was angry with them for being British and letting the side down, so to speak. But I . . . I then went and did exactly the same thing, so, then, it became hypocritical. I couldn't say anything any more like, you know what I mean? I'd made my bed; now I had to lie in it. And the bed I'd made was a bad bed."

Those interviewed in this book are all friends I got to know while serving in, or upon leaving, the Legion. The topic of desertion is a sensitive

241

one for those who left dishonorably. While all deserters I spoke to had their reasons, whether well thought out or impulsive, each of them today feels a sense of guilt and shame. Not all admitted this openly. However, in hours of conversation, during which I took note of body language and tone of voice when the topic arose, I got the impression that those who once so proudly wore the hard-earned *Képi blanc* regret having run away.

* * *

Phil Fairfield and I walked through the gate at Fort de Nogent only minutes apart. We were inseparable during those stressful early days of selection in Paris and Aubagne. We then struggled together through *instruction* at Castelnaudary. After surviving our four months of basic training, we finally separated. He went to *REP*, and I went to *REC*. The next time I met Phil, we were sitting in the living room of his small home in Sheffield, England. Here, years later, surrounded by his wife and children, he opened up to his American friend. "Yeah, I deserted. After three and a half years' service, I did what I never thought I would. So that was it. And after a year I'd forgotten about it, you know."

After a brief pause, then shaking his head, Fairfield admits, "Well, not forgotten. I mean the guilt is still there, put it that way. And, well, I'll say this on tape: I do feel guilt in what I did. I still feel guilt."

LFC Griffiths, the would-be cook, who deserted with just a little more than one year of service (but returned several months later) comments on deserters: "They were shitheads. They didn't want to do it. You know, they couldn't hack it in the Legion. It got to them, man."

And echoing the opinions of long-serving legionnaires, young Griffiths asks, "What happens when they're out on terrain (in the field) in a real combat situation? And like some cunt's, like, *cassing* (breaking) their *couilles* (balls) and, like, you know, they'll crack up."

* * *

Fairfield describes his encounter with the lieutenant who ordered him to undergo administrative training: "I was called in the office. The new lieutenant was there. Non-descript guy, young upstart. The guy was about twenty-three-years old—younger than me. He didn't have a clue. Regular army now in the Legion, and he thought he could roll his case."

Fairfield remembers he was "gobsmacked" when told he had to report to Castelnaudary and "become a secretary." He brazenly announced that, if sent on the course, he would desert. The lieutenant barely looked up from his paperwork and coldly replied: "You'll do whatever you want to do."

* * *

Bitter and angry, this was the moment Fairfield felt it was over for him. "I felt betrayed by these people. I mean, I'd been with them like three years now, you know what I mean? I felt so betrayed. I didn't join to be a fucking secretary."

Though unhappy about it all LFC Fairfield finished his four-month administrative training at Castel and returned to his regiment. "Actually, when I got back, I was sound. It's just when all the shit started again." As is customary after finishing a *stage*, he first met his company captain and, then, colonel to report his new status. Fairfield had been the only anglophone on the course and had finished a respectable 13th/30. As Fairfield relates, however, the results were met with derision. "When I got back, the captain slags me off. You know, all right, you've passed your exam, but you've done shit. No, but that's 2 *REP*, honestly. If you didn't come in, like, the top five, you hadn't tried. 2 *REP* had to do well."

His regiment's colonel wasn't any more congratulatory to "the only non-French speaking bloke" on the demanding course, which included hours of typing, writing, and spelling. "'So, the colonel comes to me, like. I salute, present myself, and tell him my *stage*. 'How did you do?' 'Thirteenth, sir.' 'How many in the school?' 'Thirty, sir.' 'Not very clever, really, was it?' And I went, 'I did try, sir.'"

Fairfield quickly put all this behind him, thinking only of his upcoming three-week leave in Sheffield with family (brother's wedding included) and friends. Fairfield's emotions were mixed, however, as his three weeks drew to a close. He describes the reaction in Calvi when he explained to

243

an officer that he'd missed his flight to Corsica. "I actually rang up, yeah, when I was a day over. I rang and asked for the captain of *premier* (first) company. So, after about five minutes, they put me through to this German guy. I respected these people who'd made it through the ranks, which this guy had done."

The German wasn't Fairfield's captain but took the call. The officer was polite but firm with the legionnaire. "What are you doing in England? You're supposed to be here today." Even with Fairfield promising to be on the next available flight to the island, Captain Hapke was in no mood to bargain. "'No, no, no, no,' he says, 'You will be here today! You will be here today!' He kept saying, 'Do you realize what will happen to you?'"

The AWOL legionnaire had planned to return and face the consequences. "I'll do forty days in *taule*. But to be spoken to like that, 'You will be here today!' So, when I put the phone down, I thought, fuck 'em. That's it. I'm going to have Christmas at home.' I've got that attitude then."

And a somber Fairfield, so different from the hopeful and confident one I remembered, concludes: "As time went on, it was a case of, basically, bottling out. All right, I'm going to go back tomorrow . . . Christmas over . . . then there's New Year's Eve, and, I thought, I'll have New Year's Eve—what the hell? In for a penny, in for a pound. And New Year's Eve was over. I don't know. I blew it. I bottled out."

* * *

LFC Griffiths tells almost the same story about absconding from a different *REP* company. Griffiths had wanted *stage APC* (*Armement Petit Calibre*—weapons/armory course) but instead was sent to the kitchens of Castelnaudary. "'There's a place for you in *stage cuisine*' (cooking course)," I was told. That's the trouble with the Legion. Any *stage* that you are volunteered for, you've got to, like, do it." Unfortunately for Griffiths, his dossier showed that he'd been in and around several kitchens. The plan was for Griffiths to do more than wash dishes, however. He was to be trained to work with a master chef and serve his unit while on *tournante* (overseas tour of duty).

Much like Fairfield, he minced no words and told his *adjudant*: "I'm not going. I'm going to fuck off. You know, I didn't join the Legion to be a *cuisinier* (cook). So, if you send me I'll desert." However, his superior did try to address the issue and told Griffiths, "Don't be stupid—stick it out" (which for some disillusioned could replace "Legio Patria Nostra" as the Foreign Legion motto).

* * *

The story unfolds as planned then takes an unexpected turn.

* * *

On twenty-four-hour *permission* during his mandatory cooking course, Griffiths decided to desert. He left Castelnaudary for Toulouse and boarded a flight to Paris. Even without his passport, he hoped he could then take a direct flight to Manchester. What few flights there were to England that Sunday were already booked. The only option available was a Paris-Jersey flight, which he took since the island off the French coast was British territory. The police on Jersey suspected he might be a Legion deserter, but Griffiths bluffed his way through by saying he was on emergency leave to attend his father's funeral. Still without passport or anything more than his 24-hour permission slip, he was eventually allowed to continue, flew to Leeds, and, then, home to Manchester.

Months later, on the morning of August 2, 1990, the armies of Sadam Hussein invaded Kuwait. The following evening, Griffiths crossed the Channel back to France. While some armies had cases of desertion or refusal to join units being rushed to the Persian Gulf, the Legion, alone, had deserters voluntarily returning to join the French battle group. Of course, the Legion saw to it that the returning deserters served their required forty days *taule* before being posted to a new regiment. Ironically, after his jail time, the eager-for-combat Griffiths was called upon not to wage war against Hussein's Republican Guard but to make sure the *crème brulée* and *profiterolles* served in the officer's mess at Aubagne were the correct temperature and well presented. The erstwhile Griffiths' desert campaign had become his dessert duty. Once more Griffiths had his fill and left for Manchester—this time for good.

* * *

Needless to say, a Legion veteran of fifteen years' hard service is unsympathetic to those who desert. *S/CH* Gazdík lays it down without much emotion: "Yeah, I had good friends desert, but none during *instruction*—that was more the French who deserted. Who knows why? Maybe easier for them." Asked if he understood the reasons for desertion—especially of friends with two, three, and even four years' service—Gazdík responds: "Well, it's all in the head. Me, I'll say it like this . . . the men who desert—it's a psychological problem. No matter what problem, it's psychological. It's always a weakness with something—a family problem, a medical problem, or unsatisfied with work."

* * *

While a long-standing tradition, desertion is in every way a morale buster. A good friend's abrupt departure can leave the one who remains feeling even more isolated and stir up his own doubts about staying the course. On an operational level, adjustments that impose on countless others will often have to be made within the unit. Of course, the consequences are even more serious and damaging during wartime.

Simon Murray joined the Legion while France was mired in the sixth year of *la sale guerre,* its "dirty war," in the North African colony of Algeria, home to the Legion and site of basic training and combat operations against Algerian nationalists.

* * *

Murray was halfway through his *instruction* when he learned of a fellow countryman's desertion and subsequent capture, as well as the reputation of the man in charge of the stockade. In an early diary entry, Murray writes: "There is an Englishman in one of the other companies here in

Mascara. He deserted two days ago and has now been caught. To desert is generally considered acceptable, but to be caught is an appalling disgrace, and there is apparently no sympathy spared at all on the offender—no matter how brutal the punishment he receives."

To be sure, there are men from the north of England who do finish their Legion contracts; however, the call of home seems particularly strong for this group. "The Englishman is a cabdriver from Yorkshire. He has had his hair all shaved off and is now inside doing time—hard time by the sound of things. The sergeant in charge of the prison is a Romanian named Pelzer. There are a lot of stories about him, all bad. Apparently, two deserters were once found dead, having been cut up by Arabs and stuffed into a foxhole. Pelzer had the bodies brought back to the barracks and laid in the middle of the parade ground. Then he made all the recruits turn out on parade to show them what happened to deserters, and he yelled insults at the dead bodies and kicked the bloated carcasses as he did so. God help the cabdriver!"

19

On Guard, Ghosts, God, Gaelic, and *Gamelle*

Preston was standing on a flimsy wooden crate next to the dumpster eating the pasta with his Legion-issued Opinel knife . . . spearing bits of that day's lunch.

—*Légionnaire* Valldejuli

Veterans from other countries and various military branches may find stories similar to their own in this book. Still, the Legion has more than its share of unique tales. Some of my favorites are included here.

* * *

Guard duty is a soldier's unwelcome companion. It awakens him at awkward hours and marches him to isolated posts, often in uncomfortable conditions. A strange mix of tension and boredom, few soldiers look forward to this drudgery and most would like to be exempt from the monthly ritual. Legionnaires come in all sizes and shapes and have all degrees of facial and cranial structure. At my first meal in the *REC* mess hall, I was assaulted by a battery of bald heads. The unfamiliar shaved heads I saw—sporting the gamut of gashes from deep, twisting scars to bumps and rash-like blotches—almost made me sick. While the owners

248

might not be selected for any special event or honor guard detail, their slight deformities would certainly not count out a regularly scheduled guard duty.

The Legion is a small army, and I know of only one legionnaire who was exempt from guard duty for physical reasons. Will Covington (name changed), an Englishman, was not assigned to guard duty or marching in public because the French found his face repulsive. The *je ne sais quoi* of Covington's face meant that he was passed over for guard duty until it was sorted out. I met Covington after his facial reconstruction, and he still looked cartoonish. I'm told, however, the operations to realign his jaw, replace several teeth, and straighten his nose did substantially improve Covington's looks. Sadly, nothing could be done with his Neanderthal brow and droopy left eye. All said, he was a very nice fellow and a fine musician in the Legion's *Musique Principale*.

* * *

Another only-in-the-Legion guard story involves a supernatural experience I had in downtown Orange. One summer evening, two fellow platoon members and I, along with a *maréchal des logis* (*REC* sergeant), were selected to stand guard at the Roman amphitheater in the center of town. Julius Caesar led his legions in the conquest of Gaul (France) during the years 58–50 B.C., and a sizable Roman colony was established in Arausio (Orange). As elsewhere in the empire, the Romans brought their customs and culture to the newly conquered territories. The amphitheater in Orange was completed in A.D. 25 and could entertain as many as 10,000 people. Orange has a Roman arch and a few other relics, but none so well preserved and impressive as the amphitheater. Modern day festivities at the amphitheater include plays and musical performances. (Rock groups like The Police, Dire Straits, The Cure, and U2 entertained in years past.) We were guarding the amphitheater because the *Musique Principale* was giving a concert the next evening and had left props and equipment at the site. Dressed in fatigues and *képi*, we carried our *FAMAS* rifles slung over our shoulders. It was a Friday night, and the amphitheater is at a busy intersection, offering a clear view of passing traffic and pedestrians.

I stood my guard at the top of the theater's steps and paced back and forth along one of the ramparts. Unlike other guard duties, this one was comfortable and allowed easy viewing of the parade of girls in tank tops and short skirts on the street below. I walked alone and couldn't see our sergeant or the two other sentries. Since the situation was so relaxed, I let my mind wander. What kind of legionnaire walked this post 2,000 years ago? What did he think about on guard duty? I then tried to recall some high school Latin. I was reviewing what I could remember of the *hic-haec-hoc* declension when a strange sensation came over me. I stopped for a moment and heard absolutely nothing—not a sound. I then felt a rush of cold air on my body. I moved quickly from the spot, then returned just as quickly without any repeat of the strange silence or chill. Looking around, I saw our sergeant and the two other guards staring at me from the amphitheater's stage. The sergeant impatiently shouted at me and pointed to his watch. It seems my guard detail had been waiting, and I was five minutes overdue. Sure enough, when I looked at my watch, I realized it had stopped.

* * *

Legionnaires are required to do many things, but attending religious service isn't among them. An *aumônier* (chaplain) is attached to every regiment but not often seen. However, a legionnaire will usually meet a chaplain at least once during *instruction*. If ever one wanted the grace and protection of the Almighty, it would, presumably, be during these God-forsaken four months. A visit by the chaplain meant more food and an easier time for all. The *aumônier* I met during my *instruction* was a rotund, jovial man who greeted us in French: for those who did not understand, he offered a "God bless you." Per-Inge Persson, a Swedish friend in another section, met a different type of clergyman, one who put the ammonia in *aumônier*. My friend told me that during his chaplain's rounds of blessing the new recruits, one legionnaire had followed behind the holy man making unholy gestures. With the agility of an altar boy dashing home after Mass, the *aumônier* spun around and confronted the impertinent soldier, surprising him with a powerful sign of the right cross that flattened the legionnaire instantly.

* * *

Rifle shots in the name of religion might have sounded in Bangui, Central African Republic, had a modern-day jackal not backed down. Religion is not discussed among legionnaires. Too many nationalities and too many faiths would make religious beliefs a volatile *foyer* conversation topic. Nevertheless, I had a Protestant from Belfast tell me in detail how he was selected to guard Pope John Paul II during one of his African pilgrimages in the 1980s—and what a mistake that could have been.

The Legion was chosen to guard the Holy Father because its contingent in Bangui held a ready number of sniper teams. The Belfast legionnaire was a man with an intense hatred of Catholics stretching back to the Ulster Defence Association youth gangs of his early teens. The sniper described to me how attentive he and his *FR-F1* rifle were to every move of Pope John Paul, keeping "the papist bastard's white dunce cap right in my sights." The Protestant warrior told me how the rhythmic chanting and pounding drums in the packed football stadium only made his trigger finger twitch even more. It was a chilling conversation, and I'm thankful that I've forgotten the sniper's name and that the rest of the world never learned it.

* * *

I first heard the Gaelic language in New York during weekend visits to Irish hurling matches in the Bronx. It was not until years later, as an *EV* at Aubagne, that I would again hear this lilting tongue. The Northern Irish Catholic who had the bunk above mine said he had learned it during a stint in HMP Maze (a British prison holding many Irish Republicans). The IRA would often speak Gaelic with each other so the guards and Protestant prisoners could not understand them. My bunkmate liked the French because they, too, disliked the English. He was hoping to leave the Troubles behind, and make a career of the Legion but lasted less than a week. I didn't see the Irishman the day he was dismissed, but he left a note on my bunk saying he had one more Legion on his list—the Spanish Foreign Legion.

I didn't hear any other Celtic language until I was at my regiment in Orange. Still fumbling French, I was in the quartermaster's store with another new arrival from Castel, Legionnaire Llewelyn, who had grown up in northern Wales and spoke only Welsh until he was six years old. His English, intonation, was strange, and his French was comical. We were having difficulty in the stores because our *brigadier-chef* spoke no English, and we barely spoke French. At one point, the flustered brigadier-chef threw down our issued uniforms and cursed *"les putains d'anglais"* (the fucking English). We both understood the *brigadier-chef*, and Llewelyn quickly let the angry Frenchman know he was from *le Pays de Galles* (Wales). The *brigadier-chef* looked at Llewelyn, pointed to his own nametag, and said he was from Bretagne (Brittany). There was an awkward silence; then came the Celtic chatter. Suddenly, what had been a frustrating and laborious process became speedy and efficient. Once we had exchanged the needed items and been issued some new gear, I expected my Welsh friend and the Breton to take a moment and have a laugh about it. I couldn't think of any other army in which something like this could happen. But none of that goodwill emerged. The *brigadier-chef* simply seemed glad to have us through the line, and if it took speaking as he did, so be it.

* * *

One thing even the casual tourist learns quickly in France is how serious the French are about food. Serving or being served a bad meal in France is outright insulting. While the French Foreign Legion rules the battlefield, the French Legion rules the kitchen. A Legion *chef de cuisine* (head cook) is most always French. Other nationalities cook and serve, but, almost without fail, a long-serving Frenchman is in charge of the overall planning and execution of lunch and dinner (one exception is an Englishman—*Adjudant* "H"—who's been at the mess hall in Aubagne for many years). Legion food is good, if not always plentiful. I'm a slow and steady eater and was well known to the mess hall staff. Regularly one of the last to leave the mess hall in the evening, I sometimes found a broom or mop bearing my name next to the "just desserts" tray. A real test of friendship would be to see who would sit with me as the mess hall emptied—thereby becoming another forced volunteer.

One time stationed at Aubagne, I didn't really care if I was assigned a *corvée* for eating slowly. I'd finished my second plate of scrumptious Cajun fried chicken with yellow rice and warily went up for a third helping. In almost two years of Legion mess hall meals, this was only the second time I had eaten American-style fried chicken, and I wasn't too sure when I'd taste it again. When I asked the legionnaire serving if there was any more he waved me away. I tried to flatter him by asking if he had helped make the sweet but tangy Cajun batter. The *chef de cuisine* saw us talking and came over from the ovens anticipating trouble between his staff and me. It seems the chef thought I was complaining and was more than ready to tell me what I could do with his spicy drumsticks. He proved pleasantly surprised to learn that I was hoping to eat a third plate of chicken, told the server to give me as many pieces as I wanted and asked me to wait. He left the scene, but quickly returned with some big *gamelle* guns.

* * *

The chef now stood in front of me with the mess officer, a lieutenant in full-dress uniform, at his side. Also gathered in this formation were several nervous-looking cooks in various culinary costumes. The scene was of a New Orleans Mardi Gras parade. The chef opened a thick green book to a page with the date and that day's menu written in meticulous script. Also happy to learn I'd enjoyed the Cajun dinner, the lieutenant proved even more pleased upon learning I was an American and, therefore, an expert on fried chicken. He asked me to write a comment in the book and sign my name. The lieutenant and chef then signed their names under my signature; I was never given cleanup duty again in the mess hall.

* * *

The U.S. military ensures its recruits are served 5,000 or more calories a day during basic training. French Foreign Legion recruits are forced to hide or steal food to try to make it to half the American intake. Hunger and thirst during the four-month *instruction* are simply part of your training. Anglo-American (and Nordic) tastes do not welcome continental breakfasts followed by strenuous PT. We certainly felt we could have performed better had the Legion fed us a more substantial hot breakfast. Instead, we often grabbed any extra items (or even took whatever had been set out on tables for other sections) and stuffed them into our vests or pants' pockets. Spot checks by our corporals would usually uncover a cache of flattened sweet cakes still wrapped in plastic or even half-eaten apples or oranges. Only KP, with its mindless cleaning and prepping, would allow us access to more food, albeit also eaten or taken on the sly. One weekend lunch at the *REC*, I met the top dog of all Legion chowhounds, Reginald J. Preston. I'd been at the *REC* for two months, but Preston was a new boy. Only a week or two from the hunger pangs of Castel, he was ready to eat freely. We had just finished an especially satisfying meal of spinach ravioli, toasted garlic bread, and Legion red wine. Preston enjoyed his food as much as I, but, even though I felt we'd stuffed ourselves, he complained that he could still eat more. I suggested he have a smoke and, then, later in the afternoon, we go into town. As we neared the exit of the mess hall, I was grabbed for *corvée*. Preston, ever the sneaky one, managed to slip away. I wasn't sure how long I might be, but I knew he'd wait for me.

Other legionnaires stacked chairs, cleared tables, swept and mopped, but my job was to empty the garbage. The work was sloppy and heavy, since it involved carrying garbage cans full of scraps and pans full of uneaten food to the dumpster behind the kitchens. Still warm, leftover ravioli had been emptied into piles of vegetable peelings and crusts of bread. As I took my first smelly load to the dumpster, I spotted Preston discreetly smoking. I nodded and indicated that I should be done in two more trips. On my next garbage delivery, I saw a sight that doubled me over with laughter. Preston was standing on a flimsy wooden crate next to the dumpster, eating the pasta with his Legion-issued Opinel knife. Spearing bits of that day's lunch, our raccoon of ravioli insisted that he was eating only the portions that had landed on other bits of uneaten food. He said we could save dinner money in town by eating this discarded ravioli now. I couldn't stop laughing long enough to answer him.

20

Christmas

Jesus Wept

And then I got a really large-sized green beret, and I put little Baby Jesus inside of the beret. And that's the kind of stuff they went for. That was a stroke of genius.

—*Caporal* Lewis

While Camerone is the most elaborate Legion holiday, Christmas is the next biggest show of Legion tradition and togetherness. In typically French style, the normally oblivious-to-religion Legion becomes very animated during the Christmas season. Preparations at some regiments, especially in building the company crèche (nativity scene), begin in mid-November or earlier. No leaves are allowed for the several days surrounding the 24th. All officers, as well, are expected to celebrate Christmas with their Legion family. Christmas festivities include the setting up of company bars and pubs and hard-fought, inter-company competitions for best *crèche de Noël*. Points are awarded to the company that has the most ornate "refreshment center" as well as the crèche with the most elaborate display and most poignant theme. Of course, Legion nativity scenes always have a military thrust. The Christmas scene presented by my company during *instruction* retold the familiar story of the Magi's quest—with a Legion twist. The star on that particular holy night led directly to the gates of the Fort de Nogent recruiting station in Paris. Wise men, indeed.

Even with the unusual distractions from Legion life at this time of year, Christmas can still be difficult for a fresh recruit. One of the few times a legionnaire has a choice of activities during *instruction* at Castelnaudary occurs on Christmas Eve. He can go to Catholic Mass or a Protestant service. In my section of fifty, only three chose to go to Mass and two to Protestant service (including our French Protestant lieutenant). I rode in the back of an open truck that very cold night, along with an Austrian and a German. At the church were legionnaires from other companies, officers and their (real) families, as well as a good number of townspeople. We sat in the front pews. My friends and I were certain this was arranged so we could not look at the officers' daughters. What we could see well was our breath. Nevertheless, we were made to take off our coats to show up the shivering civilians.

One clear view I did have of those gathered was none too pleasant. The camp doctor, whom we called Dr. Mengele, sat across the aisle from me in the other front pew. He was a pale, fat Belgian with thick, round glasses who had little sympathy or time for those legionnaires who dared come to sick call. Either to protect or intimidate, he always made rounds with his German shepherd. Upon arrival at the medical station in camp, he would have a sergeant announce his presence. At that moment, every legionnaire, regardless of infirmity, would have to stand and—in French, of course, explain why he was at sick call. The doctor, with his head tilted back and a frown on his face, would stand before the legionnaire and wait for him to speak. If the legionnaire didn't stand quickly enough or was a non-francophone slow in producing his reasons for being there, the dog, as if on some mean-spirited silent cue from Mengele, would begin growling.

Two years later, I learned from a friend who had been a medic under Mengele that the doctor spoke four or five languages. I also learned that the doctor's sour disposition, in large measure, was due to his never having come to terms with the death of his wife on the operating table—a procedure he had botched. All things considered, I was surprised to see Mengele at Christmas Eve Mass. Even more of a shock, however, was to hear the doctor sing *"Ave Maria"* in a powerful and clear first-tenor voice before the congregation. That so soothing a song could emerge from such a troubled man was beyond me. I tried not to, but the emotion of that moment, the remembrance of Christmases past, and the stress of basic training led me to drop my head and let the tears flow, regardless of repercussions.

* * *

Depending on the regiment, the crèche competition can be fierce. Money, supplies, and manpower are never lacking in the quest for the best crèche. Anyone with the least bit of artistic talent or imagination is excused from duty to work on these displays. CPL Lewis, already assigned to the art department of the Legion monthly, *Képi blanc*, put together several of these scenes in his five-and-a-half years of service: "The year we were in Lebanon, I did one at Aubagne where I had fifty-five-gallon drums, barbed-wire, and different bombed out things. There was a crate or box, and I got hold of a really large-sized green beret, and I put Baby Jesus inside of the beret. And that's the kind of stuff they went for. That was a stroke of genius. Yeah, Baby Jesus with the green beret as his swaddling clothes."

On Christmas Eve morning, legionnaires usually receive a gift from their officer. My first gift was a good one—a camera—which even took some of the photos featured in this book. CPL Lewis, though, was not too impressed with his first present. "It was a radio. It was a wonderful, bottom-of-the-line radio. It was absolutely pathetic. I remember breaking it as I was opening the package . . . pieces of it came off as I was opening the package. I gave it away." The system works better today. Legionnaires are allowed to choose their gift from among several items displayed on *foyer* shelves.

* * *

As the traditional regimental dinner approaches, those new to the Legion can become depressed and homesick. Per-Inge Persson, celebrating his first Christmas away from his family, recalls: "I must have been five weeks at Castel, so I didn't know much. I was looking forward to Christmas, but still it was a sad time for all the Swedish guys down there. We were about four or five. We had the same experiences. It was very, very sad."

Persson marched with his company to the mess hall on Christmas Eve and joined hundreds of other recruits for the formal Christmas dinner. Two Swedish friends in another section had other plans. Both deserted. They were picked up one hour later by *PM*s. Normally, a beating, followed by jail, would have been in order, but "because Christmas must be one of the real holy things in the Legion, the *PM*s wouldn't beat anybody up. Christmas is Christmas. Yeah, even officers were kind to you during Christmas. That's what I found." In fact, the two Swedes were simply dropped off at their company, and nothing more happened. The incident couldn't have been noted on their file "because they had the *bonne note* (good comments) when they finished. That was the guys who were first and second in their section. Can you believe that?"

Any Christmas dinner on base will include an elaborate meal, massive amounts of alcohol, songs—festive and Legion—and, at the combat regiment, a cabaret-type show followed by cognac and cigars. The idea is to try to forget past holidays and forge a new spirit of togetherness with a new family. It can be hit or miss.

* * *

My first Christmas was spent with Jan Van Heek and company at Castelnaudary. Persson and Klaus Poulsen were also there, but we wouldn't meet until after *instruction*. Run ragged and always hungry, legionnaires welcome the portions and variety of food and drink. The abrupt change in routine, though, can unleash all kinds of emotions and behavior. It's no surprise to me that a 1980s *fête de Noël* was not that different from the same occasion in the 1960s.

Dutch legionnaire Van Heek, at the *4ème RE*, remembers his first Christmas away from home: "Yeah, it was difficult not to be with your family. I was grateful that they so much occupied us . . . kept us busy at Christmas, and they gave us food and alcohol to forget about the family, which they should have done for New Year. They didn't. Our family used to be together for Christmas and going to church and having a good meal. So, yeah, I was glad at that moment to have this good dinner for Christmas."

Persson reports on his Christmas meal with the *4ème RE*: "Christmas dinner with the entire regiment, very good food ... a lot of singing—songs in French, American songs, songs in German. Didn't we sing "Silent Night" in German? I became pretty drunk after a while. They have kept us from alcohol all the time and suddenly you have a table full of bottles ... wine bottles mostly."

Like others during their first Christmas, Persson grew dispirited. "Overall, I was sad and, eventually, drunk ... that's true. I wouldn't say anyone enjoyed that first Christmas."

Much like Swedes, Danes enjoy candle-lit Christmas trees and parlor games with family on Christmas Eve. Not surprisingly, Poulsen, from Copenhagen, remembers his first Christmas as "really shite." Of course, he did what was expected: "I was completely pissed. Just puking up all over the place. I remember with Danny (a future *adjudant-chef*) drinking eight bottles of that Legion *pif* (wine)"

American Rob Cool Hand Lewis gathered three times at the Aubagne mess hall for Noël: "Christmas at the *1er RE* was interesting. They would lock everybody in. You could not get out. And they had these dinners planned. Five course meals, and some were good. Lots of beer. Lots of wine and alcohol. More than you could possibly drink. I mean, if you could sit down and polish off three liter bottles of wine and ask for a drink, you would have it. There was no end, and it was just a flood of alcohol." Lewis also remembers the annual result of enclosing hundreds of men in a room for the enforced cheer. "Now, this led to a lot of outrageous behaviors: peeing in the hallway, fights, things got stolen ... it was hardly the Christmas spirit."

Yet the spirits of Christmas Present (and Future) are the same as Christmas Past. Having kept a diary during his five-year Legion experience, Simon Murray can tell us exactly what master chef Pedro and crew prepared for his first Christmas feast in the muddy and cold Algerian *djebel* (mountains) of 1961: "We sat at a magnificent table, laden with delicious food fit for kings. There were cold meats of every sort, roasted chickens, hams and legs of lamb, cakes with mountains of cream, fruits and cheeses like dripping Brie, salads, celery, liqueurs, chocolates and brandy, red wines, white wines, rosé and champagne, all in quantities that would feed five times our number."

Of course, Murray was to observe what countless others would experience. "It was the beginning of a great evening but it became a nightmare. It seemed to be the aim of one and all to drink themselves into a stupor as fast as possible, and very soon the whole place had degenerated into a sink of pig swill. This was not merriment—it was a disastrous, chronic abuse of a festive occasion that could have been quite magnificent. To have set the scene with which the evening started in these barren mountains was a tremendous achievement. So much effort had gone into it that it was a great sadness to see it ripped and torn to shreds. Drunkenness produces different characteristics in different personalities, from solemn slumber to screaming rage, and, last night, we had it all."

And Murray relates a now familiar story: "The food was hardly touched but the liquor was consumed in total. God knows where it all went. Soon there were bodies swaying everywhere and those that were not swaying were either unconscious on the floor or heaving their guts out in the snow outside. The noise was that of a crowd of Arsenal football fans gone mad; and, then, the fights started. Hirschfeld went berserk at some early hour of the morning and ran screaming after Grüber, swearing his death. He would undoubtedly have killed him, too, if he had caught him, he's as strong as a horse. It took ten men to hold him down and, even then, he managed to break loose and go charging out into the night where Grüber had vanished."

Thankfully, most Christmas celebrations today don't happen with alcohol and weapons at the ready. But war-time Algeria was different. "At midnight a man in the 2nd Company ran amok into the night, firing his submachine gun into the heavens to welcome the coming of Christmas Day. He simultaneously ended the life of one of his fellows who caught a stray bullet in the side of the neck. Fires were burning outside the tents and rockets were going off all the time. To me it was more like Guy Fawkes night than Christmas. There was not the slightest air of moderation in anything, there was no control; it was like the release of pressure from a burst waterpipe of pent-up emotions."

Murray's final disillusioned comments on Noël à la Légion. "I drank all night but remained cold sober. I was unable completely to partake. I was on the fringe of it all and glad to be so. I think I was slightly numbed by the whole thing; numbed by the cold, numbed by the stark harshness of this Christmas spirit so forced and absolutely compulsory, as though an order had been issued that all would be drunk tonight."

* * *

The Legion has two ways to break the melancholy hold that can choke legionnaires during their Christmas dinner: song and dance. While some traditional holiday songs are featured, the Legion knows these moments can stir other memories. Several of those interviewed clearly remember the mood in the *4ème RE* mess hall after we'd sung "Silent Night" in German. It was very *stille*. The song brought many of us back to our childhood or other distinctly pre-Legion days. Sensing the need to quickly return us to our current reality, a massively-built Austrian sergeant stood up— took a few steps and, in a deep, gruff voice, launched into a popular jody call, "Captain Jack," sung in English. We abandoned the "Holy Infant so tender and mild" in the manger and embraced the war call; as hundreds shouted out the running cadence lyrics "with my *FAMAS* in my hand, I'm gonna be your killin' man." It sure did the trick. We left the Holy Land for Legion Land and continued drinking and carrying on.

CPL Lewis comments on the all-male "cabaret" put on at Aubagne: "The show was basically males dressing up as females. A lot of times they had the big breasts—always stuff their shirts, mop hair. Put on the make-up like, you know, really garishly. Sometimes they would just walk around and bump into each other on stage and that would be enough to just send them into serious convulsions."

Still, Aubagne was home to the *Musique Principale* and some very talented legionnaires. Every Christmas a jazz band would offer interludes between the dolled up "show girls." Lewis recalls one solo act that stood apart from the rest. "He had an electric guitar and, when, everybody was hazy and expecting the legionnaires in drag and everything . . . this

French guy busted out with a rendition of the Jimi Hendrix song "Hey Joe." Not a real Christmas-sy song in any nation."

For those who could understand the lyrics or were not too drunk and could appreciate the skillful guitar playing, the song "just detached us from any petty stuff that was going on. Many stopped drinking or harassing each other. The attention just went right on this guy. He didn't miss a note. Didn't miss a beat. It was just too odd. He was too into it. And it was about as out-of-place as a volcano in the Antarctic."

* * *

Of course, Christmas does get better once your mind is settled and you've acclimated to your new life. CPL McCue enjoyed his later Christmas moments at the *REP*: "I remember a whole load of us—must have been a couple dozen of the English mafia following along behind Gordon McClatt, who was a piper marching into all those company bars. We'd march into those little bars with him playing those pipes, and the places were clearing. You know, pipes are loud. Inside a small room like that, they are deafening. And we cleared out bar after bar. We'd drink there and then head up the road to another one."

As with many special events in the Legion, a holiday overseas can be very much unlike the one celebrated in the *métropole*. LFC Poulsen eventually found better Christmas memories in the South Pacific. While stationed in Tahiti, his platoon and commanding officer had their own dinner: "Quiet, not fucking a thousand people in the place. You know, no singing and shit like that. Glass of wine—like family."

* * *

The best was yet to come. Poulsen's captain allowed the men to change into civilian clothes and enjoy the rest of the day in town. "I went to make Christmas with the cannibals . . . the wild people that live out in the mountains. We had dog and snake that night up there, I remember. Pretty good meat, though. Yeah, dog meat on Christmas Day. Really friendly.

They're nice people. If you got a Marquisian or Tahitian as friends, they're ready to take the shirt off . . . give you anything." Including their pets.

21

En Ville

An American in Marseille

"The older Germans scolded him for not putting up more of a fight and then, after finishing their drinks, prepared to leave and join the young one in the search for the Arabs."

—*LÉGIONNAIRE* VALLDEJULI

Whenever a legionnaire goes off base in uniform, on either a field exercise with his unit or a night's *permission* with friends, something reminds him he is a special soldier. Whenever we marched through small country towns during *instruction*, the church bell would ring and children or old women would line the street to offer us water. With only a little more personal suffering, we reasoned, we would collectively reach salvation or, at least, a night's rest. As these towns always seemed to be uphill, and the roads narrow and winding, certain religious parallels haunted us. We felt we were plodding along on our own Via Dolorosa, and the rucksack digging into our shoulders was our cross. In our delirium, the sergeants and corporals were transformed into tormenting Roman centurions who were marching us to our next Golgatha. Real or imagined, scenes like this only added to the otherworldliness of the Legion.

* * *

Back at the regiment, a legionnaire wanting to go *en ville* (into town) must present himself for inspection at his company and, again, at the sergeant's post at main guard (this routine varies depending upon the regiment). A legionnaire needs to have his shoes shined and uniform perfectly ironed. Usually, one legionnaire helps the other iron by pulling the pleats tight or helping to hold the corner of a shirt. Tricks to make a sharp pleat, such as using a dry bar of Savon de Marseille (soap) on the inside creases of pants and shirts before ironing or taking the *képi* into the shower for a wash, are important for a young legionnaire to learn. Regarding the latter tip— who can forget open shower stalls filled with naked men wearing hats. Legionnaires would wash their *képis* with a bar of Savon de Marseille, put the now clean *képi* on their head and continue washing themselves with regular soap. Jokers, of course, would finish washing having found other places to rest their *képis*.

In addition to a well-creased, clean uniform and spotless white *képi*, all checked at his barrack, the legionnaire leaving for town (at least in 1980s *REC*) needs to have with him a white handkerchief and needle and thread. As uncomfortable as his well-polished black Oxfords are, he may not double up the paper-thin regulation black socks, and, certainly, is not allowed to wear his thicker white athletic socks under the black ones. A thorough sergeant of the guard will check to see if a legionnaire, especially one new to the regiment, has all of the above. The sergeant may also ask the new legionnaire certain historical questions about the regiment or may have the new boy sing some of the regimental song.

Once past the inspection at the guardhouse, the legionnaire walks to the main gate, salutes the sentry (a fellow legionnaire), and heads into town. While not in the confines of a Legion base, the legionnaire in town still has many rules to obey. One of my favorites was that we had to come to attention and salute any passing funeral procession. More common and more dangerous for legionnaires, however, are the rules and regulations involving one's posture, food etiquette, and smoking habits. Hands can never be in pockets while walking, and, the practice is discouraged even when standing. You can never stand leaning against something, lest you dirty your uniform or have civilians think you're tired. The *képi* must always be worn while walking or when seated in an open moving vehicle.

When eating in uniform, a legionnaire must be seated—never standing or walking (a coffee or beer *au comptoir* may be drunk standing, of course). A legionnaire sitting or standing must have all the buttons on his dress coat fastened: if a button has come off, he had better take out the needle and thread in his pocket and sew it back on. You can stand and smoke, but again you can never be seen walking with cigarette in hand.

To help remind legionnaires of all these do's and don'ts are the men in red and green—Legion *Police Militaire* (*PM*). Legion *PM*s are not to be taken lightly. An army within an army, they keep to themselves, staying very much isolated in their own barrack, usually next to the guardhouse at the regiment's front gate. Their friends are most always other *PM*s or ex-*PM*s. They eat with one another and are exempt from many mundane duties. Some are sent to the *PM*s because they are at the end of their contracts, others are drafted because of their size, and a hardcore few seek out the job and stay in the unit for years. *PM*s are not a welcome sight in town, but other legionnaires are well received. Indeed, it is strange how particular you might be on base in greeting or speaking to unknown legionnaires, whereas, in town, anyone with a *képi blanc* is acknowledged amid the familiar us against them scenario. As a result, one of the *PM* missions in town is to protect them from us.

With menace and *matraque*, *PM*s control their own boys quite effectively. Three-man jeep patrols are seen every evening in each southern French Legion town and even in parts of Marseille. Few are spared the long, slow *PM* stare, and God help the legionnaire too drunk or absentminded to salute, or render respect in a timely fashion to, these "forces of order." More than a few nights out in town have been cut short by ignoring the men with red and green armbands. I had some unpleasant encounters with *PM*s in Orange that could have ended much worse than they did. The following two stories show the no-nonsense approach taken by *PM*s to even slight transgressions in behavior or uniform code by legionnaires:

Le Mistral is the name given to a fiercely cold north-south wind that blows through France's Rhône valley every winter. Usually, a legionnaire bundles up as best he can when this wind rifles through his region. During one such uncomfortable weekend, I left *Quartier* La Bouche with

Per Persson. Even Persson the Swede, no stranger to cold, joked that our three-quarter Legion-issued coats were only about one-quarter effective in blocking the damp, chilling *mistral*. I agreed more than usual because, in my rush out the gate, I had forgotten my gloves. Normally, we traveled the streets of Orange with radar, Englishman Vince Humphris, who had an uncanny ability to predict, and warn friends of, the location of roving *PM* patrols. Unfortunately, Humphris wasn't with us, and I was walking with my cold hands in my warm pockets. Sure enough, a vintage 1940s U.S. Army Willys jeep drove up behind us and discharged two large *PMs*. "*Mains dans les poches,*" (Hands in the pockets) one shouted at me as we nervously saluted. While waiting to have our salutes acknowledged, I was hit squarely in the jaw. As *PM* street justice goes, the hit was more a "wake up" tap than a knockout blow. I, then, was scolded for not wearing my gloves on such a cold day. My mother used to tell me the same thing—minus the sucker punch.

Another *PM* incident involved a few more punches (one way, of course) but was stopped short by a gathering crowd. Enjoying our first Christmas in downtown Orange one evening, English friend Andy Robeson and I were looking at the brightly colored window displays along the busy *rue* Republique when we noticed some unwelcome red-and-green Christmas colors behind us. The window's reflection showed a slow-moving *PM* jeep creeping along with all three *PMs* scowling at us. We froze and counted the seconds, which seemed like hours. If the *PMs* could see their reflection in the store window, they knew that we could see the same reflection. Andy and I were unsure whether to turn and salute, or pretend we were so awed by the Christmas lights that we didn't see the Legion Grinches. Where would we stand in a Legion court of law? Our backs were to the passing traffic, so no one was able to see exactly where our eyes were focused—but we new boys lost our nerve in this game of Christmas chicken.

We turned but saluted too slowly and timidly for the *PMs* not to be angry. The jeep bounced to a halt and out jumped a veteran *brigadier-chef* who quickly moved toward us waving his arms and yelling, "*Carte d'identité.*" I was standing slightly in front of Robeson and began to unbutton my overcoat to retrieve my ID card. Without warning, the *brigadier-chef* slammed a punch into my chest that even through layers of clothing stung my breastbone. He then cursed, repeated his demand for my ID card, and threw a jab to my head. This last blow landed in front of my left ear and knocked the *képi* off my head. Robeson lost no time handing the other *PM* his papers, while I collected my *képi* and finally produced my ID. At this point, a small crowd of civilian shoppers had gathered around the three *PM*s, Robeson, and me. The *brigadier-chef* soon realized this was not the place (nor the season) to be playing tough guy. Fully expecting a free ride home, we were simply reminded by the *brigadier-chef* to pay more attention to our surroundings—much as he was now.

* * *

While the Legion is a very regimented and uniform place, one area where some individuality is allowed is in how you wear your *képi*. Officially, the *képi* should be worn two fingers above the eyebrow and straight—never tilted to the side. An up or down tilt is tolerated, however. When I was serving, some legionnaires wore their *képis* at a jaunty, upward angle, while others (mostly Brits) wore theirs down in what I called "Guards" style. This look, with a nod to their homeland's Household Division regiments, required the legionnaire holding his chin up high to look at you. One of the more comical styles was the "Donald Duck." Here the *képi*'s bill was turned upward due either to a warping from the sun (signifying *un ancien*) or a deliberate bending by a new boy. For whatever reason, this Donald Duck-style was favored by southern Europeans.

What was inside the *képi* was unusual and unique, as well. For practical and personal reasons, something must distinguish your *képi* from the hundreds of others in the regiment. Under the plastic roof of mine, I slid a *Reader's Digest* Fourth of July picture of rural America. Many British had their national colors or symbols in theirs: English, Scottish, Welsh, or Northern Irish flags, bulldogs, football and rugby memorabilia or, perhaps, items of a more personal nature. *Maréchal des Logis* Conteh, brother of former British light-heavyweight boxing champion John Conteh, once asked me if I wanted to see a picture of his girlfriend. Sure enough, Conteh tipped over his *képi* and there she was—bright smile and totally naked. Another Legion character, Curly "Born in the Sound of Bow Bells" O'Neerey, also happily showed me his *képi*. When I met Curly, he had just returned from Djibouti, but proudly let me know his roots were firmly in London's East End. A black-and-white snapshot of 1960s gangsters Ronnie and Reggie Kray was his *képi's* photo feature.

Interesting *képi* keepsakes among those of other nationalities included items of a political nature. A national survey among French and Belgians in the early 2000s found that 48 percent of the French and 55 percent of the Belgians considered themselves racist. Fifteen years earlier I, too, found this in an informal survey of their *képis*. French and Belgians often had *Front national* or *Vlaams Blok* stickers inside their *képis*. However, I found more sinister messages tucked inside the *képis* of German legionnaires. One had a copy of the last orders of the German High Command to *Wehrmacht* forces dated May 7, 1945. On another occasion, I remember asking a German corporal where he was from. "Chemnitz," he answered. Taking a chance, I said, "Don't you mean Karl Marx Stadt, comrade?" "I don't think so, *Arschloch*," he answered, smiling as he showed me a picture of Adolf Hitler in his *képi*.

* * *

Legionnaires in town most always have fun. It's simply nice to be away from camp and enjoy the freedom and distractions of a town or city. To me, a French city, whether Paris or Marseille, was almost magical. I couldn't believe that, all the while I was under the constraints of the French Foreign Legion, these civilians on the outside were living such normal end-of-twentieth-century lives. My first semi-casual visit to Marseille came not long after I had arrived in Orange. I was with several English-speaking legionnaires, all of whom were new to the *REC*, and we were led by ex-Coldstream Guard turned Legion *PM*—Paul "Killer" Crane.

Crane's nickname came from a rumor that, while stationed in Guiana, he'd shot a local man who was robbing a drunk legionnaire. Nonetheless (or maybe because of it), Killer was regarded as one of the few good *PM*s, though no one I knew dared call him "Killer" to his face. Brought in the morning for tests at Laveran Hospital, we had finished early and had a few hours before our transport was to return us to *Quartier* La Bouche in Orange, so Crane decided he and the new boys could spend a more enjoyable afternoon in downtown Marseille. All of us were in dress uniform and eager to see and be seen, especially in a recon party led by a man nicknamed "Killer." Recently returned from the jungles of Guiana, Crane led us on an urban *mission profonde*. Either because of limited time or little patience with newcomers who wanted to gawk at every sight smacking of civilization, Crane moved us quickly to his preferred base camp, the Legion bar "Helmut's."

Even with today's mixed memories of the city, I can't forget my first look at sunny Marseille. Exiting the main train station of Gare St. Charles and standing atop the grand 1920s colonial steps graced by marble statues representing "Lady Africa" and "Lady Asia" (with the majestic Notre Dame de la Garde cathedral in the distance), I certainly knew I was in Europe. Crane hustled us down these steps, quickly skirting the old Arab photographer who plied his Polaroid shots of the unsuspecting (I once saw him spit on, and tear up, a photo of a passerby who refused to pay his exorbitant price), passing the neon flashing porno shops and flea bag hotels, until we came to la Canebière. Standing beside a McDonald's, I looked down the magnificent boulevard to the Vieux Port. I felt part of a vibrant urban kaleidoscope, a haphazard mix of old and new buildings (Le Corbusier constructed a few) all thrown together with crowds of multicolored people swirling around us. Crane continued his pied-piper routine by bringing us down the Canebière and to the waterfront. We then made our way behind the posh Vieux Port cafés to the grotty but Legion-friendly bar, Helmut's.

* * *

Marseille remains the quick destination of choice for not only hospital refugees but also a host of local legionnaires with weekend passes from their regiments. Even with tempting daily service on board France's famed 180 m.p.h. *TGV* (train) to Paris, *scallope et salope* (scallop and whore) craving

271

legionnaires, all of whom are based in the south of France, will often elect to find their pleasures in earthy Marseille.

* * *

While France's oldest and second largest city (including most multicultural) and the 2013 European Capital of Culture, Marseille is not on everyone's itinerary. Urine, dog feces, *merguez* and kebabs on the grill, outside fish stalls, and a gritty sea air are the smells that greet the visitor to what many feel is France's bit of Provence gone to hell. And the air holds more than stench. According to the World Health Organization, Marseille is France's most polluted city. The high levels of fine-particle pollution cause locals to have more cases of respiratory illness and live almost eight months less than inhabitants of other parts of France. But people have been calling this place home for a very long time.

Founded by Phoenician traders in 800 B.C., Marseille has hosted almost every Mediterranean and North African nationality since. With a population of about 830,000, the city today is a tense mix of second- and third-generation Italians, Corsicans, and Armenians, along with more recent Portuguese, Spanish, Turks, Vietnamese, and most any kind of African, including 80,000 North African Jews. Whatever their ethnic background, the city's natives are proud and feisty Frenchmen who nevertheless realize that for many of their countrymen their beloved Marseille seems an exotic, far-away place, "*planète* Mars."

Enter into this special French world the extraterrestrials of the Legion and drama will unfold, especially with the city's most recent immigrants. The Maghrebian Muslim population gives Marseille its cous-cous flavor and adds a spice the police department can do without. Yet, the French have only themselves to blame for the state of affairs in Marseille and many other urban centers.

While welcoming her *pieds noirs* population to mainland France after the bitter loss of *Algérie française* in 1962, France soon thereafter invited scores of North African laborers to come to her shores for the poorly paying manual labor jobs that no longer interested Frenchmen. By the late 1960s, nervous French politicians reasoned that it would be wise to have the immigrant men joined by their wives and families—thereby avoiding the large cluster of single Arab men in the newly constructed low-income housing units *(HLM)* that had sprung up in and around cities such as Marseille. While *Harkis*, Algerians who remained loyal to France and fought the FLN, were often killed or tortured (by, for instance, having lips sliced off and eyes gouged out) in the newly independent Algeria, many *FLN* sympathizers, in a perverse colonial irony, heeded the call of their former masters and immigrated to France.

Though many of the incoming Arabs were poorly educated and spoke little French, they soon realized it would be in their best interests to navigate the *bureaucracie* of the generous French social welfare system. For example, even today, a family with two or more children will receive monthly government benefits that will increase with each additional child. If the father is absent, a family will receive even more money. In France, a standard welfare check, plus food stamps and housing allowance, makes many an unemployed Arab more comfortable than his hardworking brothers back home. Begun in earnest by Socialist governments after World War II, the system encouraged the French to have children and see that all were provided for. The population explosion among immigrants in France was unexpected and has turned some cities into not so much melting pots as cauldrons of racial and ethnic turmoil. After recent news reports of North Africans exploiting the social welfare system (several wives and many children earning the "husband" thousands of euros a month), the French have come up with the nickname "Abdul Bel-Baksheesh" to describe any Arab man involved in this popular fraud.

Marseille may seem like a city on edge, but its youth haven't succumbed to the violent racial outbursts of other French cities. The slums of Lyon, Strasbourg, Toulouse, and Paris harbor residents who hardly feel part of their communities. However, Marseille isn't all peace and love: it suffers from high unemployment rates, reaching almost 40 percent in some parts of town; more than 600,000 black rats (Marseille lost one-third of its population during the rat-borne plague of the 1300s); a strong, corrupt, and confrontational wing of the Communist-dominated *CGT* labor union; and longstanding notoriety as the purse-and-chain snatching "capital" of France, as well as an ever-thriving manufacturing and transit point for illegal drugs (the 1960s heroin trade here was busted courtesy of NYPD detectives Eddie Egan and Sonny Grosso). Marseille mobsters nowadays traffic ecstasy, methamphetamine, and cyclists' artificial blood booster, erythropoietin.

The city is so rough that its army of bouncers can find work not only at the many French-only, Corsican-only, or Arab-only clubs but also at the local McDonald's (*"chez McDo"*) and Hägen-Dazs ice cream parlors. A statue of Mother Mary may still gaze over the city from its highest point, but She too has to listen to the call to prayer five times a day from an Arab *quartier* called *La Cage* (the cage) in the heart of a once elegant downtown district.

On a positive note, while a segregated urban community, Marseille is also a city of close-knit immigrant neighborhoods that often unite over the local football team, Olympique de Marseille. Over the years, French books, movies, and even a television series have celebrated the tough-guy image of the city. Also, a new kind of beat, hip-hop, has added street cred. Many argue that Marseille's independent-minded cultural identity today is found in the lyrics of hip-hop artists like "IAM" or "PSY4 de la Rime." Music, and especially the melancholy of its *fado*-like hip-hop, seems to give a voice to the spirit and élan of the average Marseillaise.

* * *

For the average legionnaire, however, no background music is more suitable for a night of all-male drinking and storytelling than what is played on the old-style jukebox in Helmut's. Like many soldiers, a legionnaire is often most comfortable with his own, and no bar in Marseille is more Legion than Helmut's. A bullet-headed, scarred, Gabonese named Gilbert purchased the place from its original owner, operator, and namesake, an Austrian who had served with the Legion in Indochina. The bar remains Helmut's since no legionnaire can stomach calling the place by its too soft-sounding new name: "Bar Angélique." The kitschy decor and German jukebox also remain. A Tyrolean wood trim lines the bar and attempts to recreate the *Gemütlichkeit* of an Austrian *Gasthof.* Tacked onto the wooden planks run the gamut of Legionalia, from recruiting posters to musty T-shirts and regimental insignias, tattered foreign money, dusty flags, and photos of Franz Beckenbauer and local Olympique de Marseille stars. Also on display are no less exciting nude photos of a slim and tanned blonde eating a slice of watermelon, diving into the ocean, and putting on suntan lotion. As for music, number 916 on the 45-rpm Wurlitzer will select 917, *"An der Nordseeküste,"* but that's okay because everyone seems to like the way Klaus und Klaus belt out "The Rover" in German.

Nothing has been cleaned in the bar for years, and roaches, large and small, scurry about unnoticed. A few tables and chairs are scattered around, but most everyone stands. Gilbert removed the dartboard after we started throwing the darts at one another instead of the board. Now the only game is pinball, played on a machine tucked away in a corner and bolted to the floor. The bar's patrons are mostly men with one or two regular Legion slags to be stared at only when very drunk. The mix in the bar is about one-quarter civilian and three-quarters Legion or ex-Legion. As racist as many legionnaires are, no problems ever occurred among Africans, Asians, and Europeans at Helmut's (sadly, now closed). Everyone knew, and accepted, it as a Legion bar and, as such, expected to be surrounded by foreigners.

Among the bars in Marseille that welcome legionnaires, few are as friendly as Helmut's. Immediately following the return of legionnaires from the first Gulf War, the Legion *SM* (military police chief) in Aubagne put a section of the Vieux Port off limits for the men. Legionnaires were being found by police throughout the north side of the Old Port either unconscious or, in the instance of two soldiers—dead. A tourist attraction in the center of town, the Old Port, though frequented by legionnaires, goes unpatrolled by Legion *PM*s. Farther along the coast, however, toward the Legion beachfront resort of Malmousque, *PM*s make tours and keep an eye on certain bars. As the 1990–1991 Gulf War ended, a large number of legionnaires from many regiments passed through Aubagne. Many a man made his way to the Old Port bistros and bars with a throat still dry from the Saudi sand and Muslim ban on alcohol. Pockets stuffed with 500-*franc* notes, many also fell prey to Marseille's latest scam.

To greet the returning soldiers, prices were doubled for drinks and tripled for girls, so reports of "soft" robberies quadrupled back at Legion headquarters. LFC Poulsen was a *PM* at Aubagne and explains how some legionnaires were treated at once-friendly bars: "Down there with the drugs . . . that's old legionnaires that are doing that. I remember an investigation, and we got some of the drugs and gave it to aggressive dogs back at camp—pretty big dogs, and, just like that (snaps finger), it brought them down." Lulled into complacency (perhaps with the connivance of former soldiers), legionnaires had their drinks spiked and money stolen. "Anything, any drinks, coffee or beer—they just flip out, and they take their money and kick you into an alley or maybe even taxi and send you away. Two legionnaires have died and there are legionnaires in hospital from that." Soon the *SM* issued an official memo putting an entire side of the Vieux Port off-limits—something never done before or since.

A bitter Poulsen sums it all up. "All of the bars there are bad. Even the police is in on it. We need to change the mayor of the fucking town there. The whole government . . . everything of that town we need to change. Fucking bullshit. No respect. Legionnaires should stay away from all the slags and those slummy bars down there. Yeah, all the bars on that side work together. It's old legionnaires that give a hand to get the drugs and take money from the other. So much for camaraderie."

* * *

S/CH Gazdík, then a young legionnaire, tells of his first weekend leave in the city in the mid-1990s: "I was on a *stage* in Nîmes (home of *2ème REI*), and they gave us two days free. I traveled with two friends, but we separated, and I got off in Marseille. My first time in Marseille. So I'm at the Gare St. Charles (main railroad station) and go down the steps. I felt good. I was in civvies, and it was really nice weather that day, I remember. So, I went down those big steps and, at the bottom, took a right."

Anyone who's been to Marseille knows you do not take a right at the bottom of these famous steps. While walking to the right is a quicker way to the waterfront, it snakes through La Cage and will be risky—for most. "I went down a small side street with my *TAP sac* over my shoulder. I heard people following me closely. Three Arabs yelled at me, 'Give us your bag!' I turned and said, 'Do you know who I am? I'm a legionnaire.' And they said, 'Oh . . . yeah, yeah . . . excuse us, sorry' and fucked off."

Gazdík, with only two years' service, already was well aware of the Legion mystique. He adds, "Also, I was taught early—part of being in the Legion is the all-for-one mentality. So, in a fight in town or something where there is trouble you yell, *"La Légion à moi!"* ("The Legion to me!"), and any legionnaires nearby will run to help—whatever the situation or odds."

While I never heard the phrase *La Légion à moi!* shouted aloud in town, I do remember legionnaires called to rally for a comrade. One Saturday night in Marseille, LEG Griffiths and I were sitting at one of the few tables in Helmut's as a young German legionnaire burst through the door. He was out of breath, and his uniform was dirty and torn. He hurriedly approached two German legionnaires and told his story. Several Arabs had attacked him as he was walking to the bar. The attackers kicked him around and stole his *képi*. The older Germans scolded him for not putting up more of a fight and then, after finishing their drinks, prepared to leave and join the young one in the search for the Arabs. I followed most of the conversation and passed the information on to Griff (never one to shy away from a fight), who nodded approvingly. I then asked the Germans if they could use some help, and, while grateful, they replied that it was a German fight and shouldn't take long. In fact, the three Germans returned within twenty minutes (*képi* in hand), and we all shared in the victory schnapps.

* * *

Hoods in town generally leave legionnaires alone, preferring to prey on easier targets. The previous two stories aside, legionnaires rarely travel alone. And, if legionnaires are travelling in numbers, they are usually given a wide berth. A common sortie of legionnaires is anything from two to four. A group of legionnaires greater than four dramatically increases the chances of a *bordel* (total mess). I once went into Marseille with a mob of nine and was elected to lead the group because the others thought I spoke the best French and presented the least threatening image. Although we were all in civvies, little mystery shrouded our identity. Many café and bar owners were wary of serving us coffee, let alone alcohol. They needn't have worried since finding seats together was nearly impossible. Sidewalk cafés were the most problematic. Before I decided we should divide and conquer, we happened upon a corner café opposite the *Place* Charles de Gaulle. Someone's scrapbook has an amusing panoramic photo of us hunched over five little wicker tables occupying all of the café's outside seating.

Legionnaires in smaller groups are more discreet but still, whether in or out of uniform, remain legionnaires. I used to like going to a club in Marseille called the Arsenal, where the management never hassled us or any other military personnel. (Maybe it was the club's soldier-friendly name.) The place was cavernous and, in the seventeenth and eighteenth centuries, had been used to store weapons and ammunition for nearby forts St. Nicolas and St. Jean. Now, the club was home to nubile French girls, snobbish university boys, *les apellés* (military draftees), and an odd mix of legionnaires, many of whom were the more mellow, hashish-smoking types. I was once there with *Caporal* Cool Hand Lewis, his girlfriend Cynthia, and my ex-*instruction* pal and paratrooper, John Harwell, a taciturn Northern-English lad who, back home, drank Theakston's "Old Peculiar," ate pork pies, and supported Leeds United. He couldn't drive and hadn't traveled much. In fact, during his first trip in an airplane, courtesy of the *2ème REP*, he jumped out. Harwell was about as far from Rob Lewis and Cynthia as the Yorkshire dales are from the California dunes. Whether his discomfort arose from watching a grossly overweight lesbian couple lock lips, hearing Cool Hand ask an *apellé* for rolling papers, or realizing he was the only soldier in uniform, he began acting strangely.

We'd ordered drinks, and the empty glasses were still on the table when I noticed Harwell slowly chewing on something. I was also hungry but wanted more than ice, then remembered our mixed drinks had been served without ice. When Harwell raised his empty glass, I saw what his chomping was all about. He was munching on glass. Soon Rob and Cynthia noticed, as did several of the people around us, when a nervous young barman came to the table and tried to clear away the glasses. He took everyone's except for Harwell the Yorkshire fakir's. The barman mumbled something about paying for the glass, and Harwell smiled at him with bloodied gums. We were soon the center of attention. No one was snogging, rolling a joint, or talking loudly about politics because the amazing glass-eating *para* had upstaged them all.

* * *

One of the differences I first noticed as a civilian enjoying the weekend was that I didn't feel the need to act a bit crazy. I think, because legionnaires are so restrained on base, they require a good laugh when on leave in town, if only to balance things out. If a legionnaire is lucky enough to have a girlfriend or apartment, he'll want to be alone. However, if a legionnaire walks around town with fellow legionnaires, he'll surely meet others, especially since most legionnaires frequent the same drinking or whoring establishments. Violence might erupt if a number of English gather in a French (non-Legion) bar, but comedy might, as well.

A classic English "piss take" on both Walt Disney and the French is the "Seven Dwarfs" routine. Eight legionnaires, all in civvies, are needed for this gag. One legionnaire will enter a bar (the rougher the better) and, in a very delicate, dainty manner, make his way to the counter. Standing across from the barman, and, most likely several longshoremen or city workers, the legionnaire's dolled-up face will be seen clearly for the first time: lipstick, rouge, and maybe even eye liner. At the moment he has everyone's attention, this out-of-place visitor announces in French that his name is "Snow White," and he is very thirsty. Usually, the bar's patrons begin to call out obscenities and might even move to push the fruitcake out the door. Our Legion Snow White stands firm, however, and orders one *formidable* (large beer) shouting effeminately "because I am" and "seven *demis*" (small beers), adding "because they are." With that cue, seven legionnaires come marching into the bar on their knees in single file swinging their arms and singing in English, "Heigh Ho, Heigh Ho, it's off to drink we go. We see the queer, he's got our beer—Heigh Ho, Heigh Ho. . . ." Without fail, the bar, full of macho Marseille types, explodes in laughter and the "dwarfs" will stop there for a while drinking and laughing with patrons before pushing on to repeat the same sketch at the next joint.

* * *

Another Marseille gender-bender experience, if a bit less comical, was one I had on the infamous *rue* Curiol with three other legionnaires: Ian "Griff" Griffiths from Manchester, José Villaseñor from Sevilla, and Danny "Dan-O" Daichi, an Amerasian by way of the seedy streets of the Patpong neighborhood in Bangkok. One Friday night—a long week done—José wanted to hear some Brazilian music at the lively and popular bar "La Nova." To no one's surprise, *rue* Curiol was full of its usual zombie-like drug addicts, undercover police, and Brazilian and Colombian prostitutes. Many of the tight-pants streetwalkers, however, were *travelos* and most of them from Brazil. The South American she-males enjoyed their samba and often congregated at La Nova to shake their bottoms to the Brazilian beat. I found it strange how we entered the bar, one by one and through a very small door. Everyone stared at us as we moved to an open table. It was a crazy scene: The bar seemed full of sexy women, but all were really men. The only openly male figure was the muscular, tank-topped barman who seemed quite at ease letting the "ladies" feel his tree trunk arms.

We got our drinks, and Dan-O and Griff lit up joints. Before long we were surrounded by rock-hard breasts and bobbing Adam's apples. Dan-O's exotic looks were attracting the most attention, but there seemed to be a buzz around us all. More beers were brought to our table, and we soon started to relax and laugh about our situation. Griffiths was the drunkest and even began to feel up a *travelo* who had squeezed in next to him. As the scene began to degenerate, Dan-O, José, and I started to sing "Lola"—a perfect song for our imperfect company. We sang softly but got louder after we heard Griff ask for 100 *francs* so he could "fuck her in the ass." I reminded my drunk friend that "she" was a he. The *travelo* then shocked all of us by snapping back at me in English (while Griffiths wantonly sucked on his/her left nipple), "Ass is ass." Suddenly our cheery "Lola" sing-a-long lost its momentum.

Dan-O and I looked at the small door we had come through and saw that it was closed and secured by a heavy wooden beam. The barman smiled, but his eyes signaled something else. José motioned to a back room we could see from our table. It looked as though we might be able to jump up and push ourselves out through a small, open window. We laughed nervously, as I joked how an unlucky one of us might get stuck. We could imagine our bodies halfway through the window, feet dangling and buttocks squirming, as quite attractive targets for the Brazilian benders.

We genuinely thought we'd have to fight our way out and were preparing to make for the little window when the barman clapped his hands twice and the "ladies" cleared a path for us. We had to drag our still suckling friend off his *travelo*, who then cursed at us in a handful of languages. The crowd stared at our exit much as they had our entrance. In passing, I heard one of the she-males sigh to another and say about us, *"Ils sont beaux, mais très nerveux"* ("They're handsome, but very nervous.")

* * *

José and Dan-O had a few more fun-filled Legion weekends *en ville* than Griff and I. José earned his *para* wings and played trumpet in the *Musique Principale* for ten years, leaving at the fifteen-year mark as a *caporal-chef* and opening a (normal) tapas bar in Sevilla. Dan-O (whom I thought would never make it to year five) proved to be an outstanding musician with real leadership skills and was eventually promoted to *adjudant* in the *Musique Principale*. He was most popular at Christmas-time playing for the company with his makeshift blues band. Dan-O retired in 2007 after twenty years' service and, when not doing "charity work" in Afghanistan, for several years ran a fish and chips shop with his wife in Cornwall, England. After selling the shop in 2015, Dan-O, wife, and three children moved back to the south of France, where it all started.

22

Taule

Legion Lock-up

I saw a character in taule *get lynched for telling a military policeman where the porno books in the jailhouse were. There was no investigation. It was a suicide.*

—*Caporal* Lewis

One way the Legion desensitizes its people is by exposing them to such extremes of violence and cruelty that the outrageous becomes acceptable. Individual rights are of little importance in the Legion, but, if you find yourself in *taule* (the Legion stockade), you must accept that you have *no rights*. Punishments long gone in other armies are still meted out in today's Legion. (N.B. From the mid-1960s to 1970s, a "Dirty Dozen" style penal colony, *Section d'Epreuves* [ordeal platoon], existed on Corsica. It closed in 1976, due to the numerous reports of prisoner suicide and unchecked abuse by guards—news the Legion could no longer hide or deny.)

LFC Van Heek remembers watching a mutual friend from *instruction* run a punishment exercise in *taule*: "*La pelote* is a guy wearing a rucksack full of stones, barefooted, and by his belt he is fixed to a pole by a piece of rope of about ten meters long. There's an NCO with a whistle, and this guy who is punished with *la pelote* is supposed to run around the pole while having the piece of rope being straight. When the NCO whistles once you're supposed to run. When he whistles twice you creep. Once, twice, run-creep-run-creep . . . in a circle with the rope being taut."

Van Heek and I served with Dugarde at Castelnaudary. He was from Martinique, but there was nothing languid or tranquil about this Caribbean-native. He earned top marks in almost every physical activity, had no time for slackers, and used to rally the non-French speakers with his one English phrase: "Fuck like a beast!" Van Heek saw our friend running *la pelote* "for four hours under the hot Calvi sun." The Dutchman adds, "This was purely racist. Dugarde was half-caste. He was brown. I think this still goes on, yeah, guys being more or less tortured in 2 *REP* prison. For example, coming out of prison with three teeth less than they came in with. In Castel, this is getting less, but not at *REP*."

* * *

Taule has its own rules and code of conduct, but they vary from regiment to regiment. A *puni* (prisoner) in Mayotte or Tahiti experiences a *taule* very different from his comrades in other overseas posts or *métropole* regiments. LFC Poulsen offers an unbelievable description (a tall atoll tale?) of a Legion lock-up in the South Pacific: "*Taule* in Tahiti . . . *magnifique*— great, man. I had a good time. Played cards with the *guard tauler* (jailer) . . . look at porno films in his office, smoking drugs, drinking, what more? Just drive around in the lorry, you know, go out to somewhere long away just to hide ourselves."

* * *

And for most, no Captain Bligh discipline in this part of Polynesia. "At nighttime they didn't lock the cell, you know, just open the door and walk down in the company and have a drink, and have a good joint with your friends. The *guard tauler* he was all right, man. A *caporal-chef*. He had fourteen or fifteen years' service and was German. A real Nazi. Hates blacks, Jews, and Arabs. The black people, they really *ramassé*-ed (got it) with him."

In most every Legion *taule*, however, a *puni* can count on having his life made difficult in a variety of ways. He'll wake up earlier than usual and be on the go all day. Physical training is an integral part of *taule*, and legionnaires will come out as fit as they've ever been. At least one 8,000-meter run with *sac-à-dos* filled with sand or dirt, a Test Cooper and *PC*, and countless push-ups and pull-ups done on the whims of the *guards taulers* are all part of a prisoner's week. *Guards taulers* are usually corporal-chefs who are near the end of their contract. Many are Turkish or Pakistani. They work closely with the *PMs*, but they have the most contact with prisoners. When not running them about, the *guards taulers* keep their charges singing at odd hours and doing menial labor around camp. In the *métropole, punis* wear a strange uniform: combat boots; Dress "A," without belt or tie; and a French Army lizard-type cap c. 1958. Their uniform and status prohibit their saluting a superior; they must, rather, come to attention, remove their caps, and remain at attention, with heads bowed, until he passes.

Prison guards frequently exploit their position and abuse certain legionnaires. *B/CH* Donlon, who served fifteen years with the Legion, was in *taule* twice. He remembers one Turkish *guard tauler* who picked on the wrong *puni*: "The only *guard tauler* I had a problem with was the guy at Castel. It was a guy I actually struck, but I didn't get one day extra for that. He was out of bounds, him."

Donlon was on a *stage* at the basic training regiment when he was put in lock-up with lots of nervous new boys. It was a sadistic guard's dream. Before Donlon was compelled to act, the guard, a *caporal-chef* with a reputation for beating up recruits, had broken the ribs of a new boy with a pick-axe handle. Donlon remembers the Turk was "pretty drunk and started to annoy everybody." The guard even went after Donlon, a *caporal* with over seven years' service. Donlon now acts out his own "Fatso" Judson/Robert E. Lee Prewitt stockade scene. "And he started to pick on me, which was a big mistake on his part because he ended up being flattened in front of everybody. A fucking, big black eye, fucking his teeth knocked out. He had to go to the hospital and everything. That's his problem, isn't it?"

* * *

With a roguish smile, my English *chef* at *REC* used to say that no one was a real legionnaire until he had served time in *taule*. While the experience may add "tough stripes" to a legionnaire's uniform and win him several rounds of Kronenbourg in the *foyer* upon his release, most will tell you they could do without the hassle and humiliation. No Legion *taule* evokes more memories and emotions of the past than the stockade in France's most infamous penal colony. If only a few Americans can say they were in the Foreign Legion, even fewer can say they were also prisoners in French Guiana. CPL Cool Hand Lewis was given fifteen days in the stockade for refusing to tell the regiment's colonel who had urinated on the heads of three black policemen from a 6th floor hotel balcony during a raucous Guiana Mardi Gras celebration. The *3ème REI*'s military intelligence ferreted out the true "piss takers" and the colonel gave them forty-five days. His importance in the *bureau de semaine* and the loyalty he had shown his guilty friends led to Lewis' sentence remaining at fifteen days.

Prisoners in Guiana wake up at 04:30. Showers start the day, and in some sense, establish the prisoners' hierarchy: "That's when people take the time to do the rooster thing, you know, strutting around naked—the whole thing." Depending on the guards, the prisoners may need to sing before their musical-chair-like breakfast at 05:30. "There are large tables, and you line up in front where you're facing each other, and they blow a whistle, and you start walking around the table. And, as you pass your plate, the one you were standing in front of, you pick something up—pick up a piece of cheese or a orange, or whatever it is. And then, as you're walking around the table, you peel it and eat it. And when you get back to your plate, you put down your wrappers on your plate, and you pick up something else. And you keep on walking around in the circle until the plates start looking kind of empty."

Lewis laughs when thinking of those who needed more food. "And you have some French *clochards* or some *gamelles* (chowhounds), or whatever, picking off everyone's plates, 'Hey, you want that orange? No? Go ahead? OK, I'm going to get it. Here. There I got it.' And go back around again. No other meal was served like that. Lunch and dinner you sat down. Breakfast was something else."

Cleaning the cells and prison area after breakfast was followed by "sport." The exercise regimen depended on who was in charge that day but most always involved difficult runs or PT. Work details around the regiment came next. "They hustled your ass. The worst was the *poubelle* wagon. I mean you're running behind this garbage truck that didn't stop. It only stopped long enough for you to sling this can on the thing."

However, there was a garbage-with-benefits angle. The truck would stop at the brothel, and "on occasion, there were females at the bottom of the barrel . . . they had sunk so low . . . they would see you and it would be, 'My poor man. . . .' It just depended. And any other night you were out of *taule*, it could have happened for a princely sum of ten dollars. It came cheap, like everything else."

For prisoners who couldn't ride the wagon or the girls, pornographic books or magazines smuggled in regularly offered relief. Depending on the guard, however, the penalty for possession of this type of literature could be severe. And the prisoners also imposed their own jailhouse justice. "I saw a character in *taule* get lynched for telling a military policeman where the porno books in the jailhouse were. He told them where they were. And they were ceremoniously burned in the cell. Acrid smoke everywhere . . . *morpions* (crabs), bugs, heat, sweat, ants, prostitutes that you could see but not touch—the whole thing. It seemed appropriate to hang this guy. To take the life out of him. There was no investigation. It was a suicide."

* * *

First-time offender Cool Hand Lewis learned quickly how the prisoner code of silence was not to be taken lightly. "If somebody said it wasn't a suicide, they would have been hung. You see what I'm saying? And it would have been said that he felt remorse over the hanging suicide of his buddy. All of a sudden, they would be buddies. See what I'm saying? It would be concocted, most definitely. *Taule* is a very, very dangerous place to be."

* * *

One reason so many do at least one stint in *taule* is that a legionnaire is often incarcerated for offenses that other armies would punish less severely, if at all. *Mauvais esprit* (negative attitude) is a common and often arbitrary charge. I knew several corporals who were imprisoned for declining the offer to go on their sergeant's course. A legionnaire who is consistently last in company runs or competition may also receive *taule* under the cure-all *mauvais esprit* charge. *Taule* is also the repository for the many small-time rule breakers of the Legion's many petty rules. An English friend of mine was given three days *taule* for smiling at girls in a Danish tour bus as it drove slowly by while he was on guard duty at the *REC*. Were it not for the intervention of a friendly motor pool officer, I would have been put in *taule* for being involved in an accident while driving a military vehicle.

* * *

A sure and certain path to the Legion stockade, however, is to be anything less than deferential with Legion *PM*s. Somewhere in America, a former U.S. Marine can confirm this.

* * *

One Saturday afternoon in Marseille, Legion *PM*s were waiting at the train station to escort a captured deserter to the Aubagne *taule* when a drunken U.S. Marine in civilian clothes approached them. The American was fascinated by the distinctive police uniform and made the mistake of reaching for the senior man's *képi*. The result was predictable. CPL Lewis heard this tale of mistaken identity and retold it to me: "The *PM* took the *matraque* and stuffed it into his gut and when he fell over just boomed him on the back of the shoulder blades. One U.S. Marine unconscious. Threw him over his shoulder and carried him to the *PM* van and waited for the miserable deserter. Throws him next to the marine. Takes them both back to Aubagne."

No ID card is found on the marine, but his haircut and build appear to be those of an English-speaking legionnaire. The American remains in a drunken haze for most of Saturday and sleeps off his hangover in the Legion lock-up. By Sunday morning, he realizes something is terribly wrong. Sunday morning is also when his ride home, the 6th Fleet, sails. By evening, the panicked corpsman is shouting and cursing. Only one prisoner, a newly locked up Irishman, understands him and is able to offer some help. The Irish legionnaire tells several guards the strange story, but, sensing an elaborate ruse, they laugh it off. Finally, one guard decides to alert the *officier de permanence*, who determines the American is not a legionnaire. But in classic Legion logic, he also notes, "We might have made a mistake, but that doesn't mean we did wrong. You'll stay here another night. The colonel will deal with you tomorrow."

No clean clothes. No good meal or proper bed. The marine spends another night in *taule*. Only after the 08:00 Monday review of prisoners by the regiment's colonel (with captive American kept out of sight) is the situation fully addressed. "After the presentation, they let the colonel know what's going on. Well, the colonel got on the phone and got a French Army helicopter, and it came up to the helipad and picked this guy up and caught the ships out at sea and let him down on the deck." Semper Fi, *mon ami*.

* * *

As CPL Lewis observed in Guiana, the *poubelle* wagon is no easy duty for a prisoner. LFC Fairfield, unjustly given ten days' *taule* in Chad, tells of his wagon ride and the sights and smells he experienced: "They put me on bin duty, and bin duty in Chad was not a pleasant thing. You've got, like, oil drums, you know, the type with, like, the tops cut off. Like, fifty-gallon oil drums filled with old lettuce and food. Really sweet-smelling things, yeah. It stank. You're talking about 130F degrees here."

As the prisoners and their escorts drive past a village, the still new-to-Chad Fairfield is surprised to see the locals, mostly quite young, give chase. A French sergeant smiles, puts his hands to his mouth, and says, "*Ils vont bouffer.*" Understanding more clearly the hand gesture, the English *puni* is shocked. "And I looked at him, like, he's pulling my plonker, he is, you know. But he were right."

Arriving at the dump, the legionnaires were met by a large teenage boy with a big stick. Knowing the truck would empty the garbage cans only if the area was cleared, the older boy beat the younger ones mercilessly. Once, somewhat clear of locals, the Legion *poubelle* wagon began dumping. However, at this point there was no controlling the mob. "And in they came. Straight into the rubbish. I mean, it stank. You know, I were nearly sick." Under the watchful eye of the veteran sergeant, whose hand remained on his pistol, the garbage cans were emptied as quickly as possible. "By this time the kids were everywhere. And the corporal just went, 'Tip it! Tip it!' So we just turned it over straight on the kids, you know. And there's, like, kids picking bits of food off their heads and straight into their gobs, honestly. Oh, it's sick."

Appalled at this degrading scene, Fairfield has another image that still haunts him. While most of the scavengers were young males, an old woman stood among them. "She must have been 128. Probably about, like, fifty, like. And whether the husband was dead or whatever, and nobody looked after her anymore, I don't know. But she was very old, gray hair, could hardly walk, skinny . . . totally done in, like."

* * *

Also involved in the struggle for scraps of food were village goats. "And this old girl, like, she picked something up, and a goat grabbed hold of the same thing. And they had a fight to try to get this food, or whatever it was. I mean, we were driving away, like. We weren't stopping. And the old woman lost. The goat beat her. I'll never forget that. Honestly . . . absolutely true. And the old girl—no tears, nothing, just straight back into the pile with the little kids."

While few active duty legionnaires can avoid *taule*, it should also come as no surprise that some have already served time in civilian jails or prisons and others will be behind bars after taking off their *képi*. One of the most famous (and widely read) ex-legionnaires imprisoned is Englishman Erwin James (aka James Monahan/2*ème* *REP*). Released in 2004, he served twenty years of a life sentence for a double-murder in England.

James and a friend had robbed and strangled two men within a three-week period in London during the summer of 1982. A couple of months after the murders, James and accomplice made their way to France in the hope of securing the anonymity and protection of the Foreign Legion. Slipping past Legion security checks (Gestapo) with no serious crimes detected, one nevertheless dropped out and returned to England while the other continued to Castelnaudary and, later, to Calvi. Per his request, James had a new identity in the Legion but still couldn't shake the guilt of his crime (nor overlook the fact that Scotland Yard had now questioned his accomplice in England). After a little over a year of Legion service, James turned himself in to French police who handed him over to their British counterparts. He was tried in England and sentenced to life in prison.

A jailhouse lawyer and scribe, of sorts, James eventually made contact with *The Guardian* newspaper and was hired to write a bimonthly column about his time in prison called "A Life Inside." He penned the popular column for nine years while a prisoner (donating his proceeds to charity) and continues on the paper's staff today, often traveling to other countries' prisons and comparing their penal system to Britain's. James writes well but remains a controversial figure. Once, upon describing his experience in the *2ème REP*, he changed some dates and places in order to cover details of his time between the murders and his Legion enlistment. As a result, others have questioned his integrity in reporting on prison life and other topics. James, however, apologized to *Guardian* readers for the lies concerning his Legion dates, and American Rob Lewis (a fellow *instruction* mate at Castel) counts him among his good friends. Interestingly, James never served one day in Legion *taule*.

23

Anna and Cynthia

I remember at that time he told me what his real name was . . . even his best friends didn't know. He made me promise that I wouldn't tell anyone else.

—Anna Carmody

In this section, we break the male hold on Legion stories and add the insight and comments of two interesting ladies: one Irish, the other American. Both Anna and Cynthia later married their *beaux legionnaires*, and the couples settled in the United States (Cynthia's husband, Robert "Cool Hand" Lewis, died in a climbing accident in 2014). Few women have observed legionnaires so closely and keenly as Anna and Cynthia, and their stories offer a unique look inside the all-male Legion brotherhood.

* * *

For many young girls, a cheap and fun way to live in France is to work as an au pair. Normally, this employment is for six months or one year and then, unless other work is found, the girls return home with stories and memories that last a lifetime. Anna Carmody was well suited to be an au pair. She came from a middle-class Dublin family of seven and had the near-natural Irish fondness for children.

On a ski holiday in the French Alpine resort of Val-d'Isère, Anna first saw the men who would later become very much part of her *après* au-pair life in France: "They had some green outfit on; that's all I remember. And the only reason I knew that they weren't French people was that they were using bad language. It was 'F' this and 'F' that. They were falling all over the place. They were learning how to ski, yeah. Talking to people later on—friends I'd made back in Paris—I found out they were legionnaires."

After her year as an au pair, Anna worked at "Irish Tony's," a hole-in-the-wall Legion bar near Les Halles in Paris. Anna met many legionnaires and listened to their stories. A soldier on leave either feels very happy or quite alone. Anna spoke privately with many legionnaires. "If I could sit, like, one on one with a fellow, talking to him, he'd talk to me about his family and what was going on—if he liked being in the Legion or if not." Her most engaging conversations were often in the quiet of the afternoon before the bar's atmosphere changed to its nightly rowdy, macho Legion style. A soldier, sitting alone, would open up to her and talk about things—questions or doubts—not voiced to his buddies. "Whenever there were any of the other lads around they'd have to put on a face. Whether it was a really good friend or not, they'd put on a front and act kind of tough again, joking and laughing."

Anna recalls a lonely young soldier named John Corley. "He hadn't seen his family in years. His mother and father didn't know whether he was dead or alive. He said he'd never written to them, but he wanted to get in contact with them because he was going to leave: He was getting out in a few months. He didn't know whether he was going to sign on again or what. He said he wanted to leave, but then he didn't have anything to go back to. And he said he wanted to call his parents just to let them know where he was."

After much intense discussion, Anna convinced John to make the call home. "He went out that night to call, but it just happened that he couldn't get through to them, but at least he'd gone and made that move."

Anna and John had grown close. He even told her something his best friends didn't know—his real name. "He made me promise that I wouldn't tell anyone else. I remember asking a real good friend of his, you know, did he know John's real name—that, maybe, John was just having me on.

But he didn't know his real name. John was one of the ones that became a good and true friend of mine."

* * *

In an amusing story, Anna tells of her new friend John introduced her to another Legion haunt in Paris. "We went once to a shooting gallery off the Champs-Élysées. There's a place there the lads used to practice every now and again. It was just off the *métro* Franklin Roosevelt, next to a gun shop, and they'd all go down to practice at this indoor range."

Surrounded by men who could assemble and fire almost any modern weapon, as well as some classics, Anna was intrigued by the constant name-dropping of caliber, range, and kick. After John had given a nervous Anna some basic instruction on the use of a .38-caliber pistol—and she, standing closer than usual, had had good results on her targets—the bargirl requested something stronger. "John asked the old man working there, and they got me a Schmeisser (*MP-40* standard *Wehrmacht* submachine gun, also found in some Legion armories). I remember holding the gun at one stage—first time I'd ever held one of these in my hands—and I just turned around to say something. I made sure I didn't have my hand on the trigger because it made me really nervous. I just turned around, and John and this old man—he must have been pushing seventy—dropped to the floor straight away. And I thought, "What's going on? What are you doing on the floor?" They shouted, 'Get the gun away from us!'"

A few minutes later, when everyone's heart rate came back to normal, Anna was allowed to shoot the machine gun. Anna reports, "I shot off a few rounds. I got a really good aim on the target. The old man gave me my target at the end and said it's the first time he'd ever seen a woman come in for the first time and have such good shots."

The old man gladly gave his new customer the target, and John escorted Anna back to "Irish Tony's" for her evening shift. It was also John's intention to show the target to Declan, the barman, to prove "that a 'Legion girl' could shoot better than a civvy." Understandably, in the all-male atmosphere of the bar, Declan's previous sure-shot boasting now had to defer to Calamity Anna's prowess. Rather than offer her congratulations, the embarrassed barman dug himself a hole, she later related: "'God, Anna, you know the feeling you get when you've got a Messerschmitt under your arm?' 'A Messerschmitt?' I said. 'I thought it was a Schmeisser I had.' And, with that, John and the other legionnaires laughed and said, 'Oh yeah, I've often held an airplane under my arm.'"

* * *

While in Paris, Anna's social life wasn't just "Irish Tony's" and patrons. She and other friends would frequent many different cafés and bistros. The French capital is a traditional and popular stop for American college students, on either a brief summer visit or a year of study abroad. However, the combination of ready cash and even more ready opinions is not always endearing to strangers. "Most had a big mouth and knew everything. You could tell who was an American and who wasn't. People just didn't want them to be around. They were the type like I said, the intellectuals, where they weren't really interested in you if you hadn't been to college or if you hadn't read certain books. They weren't going to talk. They were going to lecture. You know, you just get fed up with people like that after a while."

Anna recalls a tense barroom encounter a pretentious American college student had with some Parisian "townies" who happened to be legionnaires. The American's ill-chosen topic for those gathered indicates he was not majoring in anything that involved common sense. "I can't remember what they were talking about, but it was something about pacifists and things like that and people fighting. You know, you should never start arguing. You should just discuss things."

Drinking in a bar where many active duty and former legionnaires gather, the wannabe professor-of-all-things pressed the issue. Those at the table tried to explain the traditions and mission of the Legion but to no avail. "This fellow didn't want to listen to what anyone else had to say. He said legionnaires were all crazy and violent people and that he didn't understand why they were in. So, eventually, Mike (Anna's future husband) grabbed him by the scruff of the neck and said, 'Listen you, you better keep quiet or get out!' Because he was annoying all the lads. Like, they'd all done their five years, and they were proud of what they had done. And they didn't need to listen to this person who hadn't a clue what he was talking about and didn't know any of them."

As expected with tempers flared and alcohol flowing, the American got smacked in the face by recently discharged *REC*-man "Gilly" Gilchrist. The Brit gave him more a slap than a punch, but this set off a tirade against the Legion from Captain America. With pleasure, Anna's co-worker, bar man Gus Stefanides (also ex-Legion), threw the know-it-all student into the street, and life went back to normal in "Irish Tony's."

* * *

Anna's circle in Paris was very pro-Legion, so her comments on deserters shouldn't be surprising. She also offers some interesting opinions on why some men stay and others do not. "I think people who've deserted are ashamed of what they've done. What I've known of a lot of fellows when they've deserted is that they didn't really want to be seen by any of the legionnaires after that because they felt ashamed that they couldn't make it. Legionnaires looked down their nose at somebody who's deserted. They don't think that they're real legionnaires . . . that they haven't stuck it out . . . that they haven't been tough enough."

* * *

Anna spoke often with legionnaires and since desertion is a monthly occurrence in every regiment, she heard many opinions, and also formed her own. Given the discipline and demands, as well as the range of men serving, the Legion is a difficult place for anyone. Most every legionnaire, at some point, has questioned the value of continuing his service. Yet, honoring their contract or feeling a commitment to friends serving often keeps them among the ranks. As Anna notes, those who remain are "angry that they were able to stick it out and the other fellow wasn't. You know, why could he not? They couldn't understand because it just wasn't that bad to them. I think it just all came down to they had the will to go on. I think it was the mind that was needed to be strong."

And what about the idea that the more of an intellect one has, the harder it is to be a legionnaire? "Yeah, well some legionnaires are brain-dead. It doesn't matter whether they're there or not, you know, it doesn't get to them. It depended, sometimes, on what your outlook was on things. There are some people who just cannot take that sort of abuse—like somebody yelling at you, somebody smacking you, or whatever."

As Anna observed over the months working in the bar and meeting so many legionnaires, those who eventually deserted tended never to have opened up about their problems. "The more things build up, well, every little thing that goes wrong for them gets to them and makes them weaker and weaker. And they come to a stage where they really can't think straight. They don't know what they want to do. I think some of the fellows, well, the first thing they think of is—Run!"

Of course, the macho culture of the Legion doesn't lend itself to counseling, which is why they confided in Anna, a trusted and sympathetic "Legion" female. Dr. Anna concludes, "I think, as well, some of the fellows think that some of the others will think they're sissies if they try to talk to another fellow—to talk out their problems. Like, maybe, not only problems with the Legion, but family and stuff like that and what's going through their mind at the time. Do many of the fellows talk with one another? You see, that's the thing. I think they think you're not tough enough if you talk about personal problems."

* * *

Almost any amount of time spent in the Legion will change a man. Cynthia Lott, who until her Guiana trip had not seen Rob Lewis in two years, noticed the difference in her boyfriend immediately. My father said the same of my behavior and speech when we met in Paris for my week's leave. In some ways, Cynthia's experience at Mills College, an all-female school near San Francisco, enabled her to understand how an all-male environment like the Legion led many to either become extra possessive of women or simply view them as objects. In fact, a common Legion nickname for a soldier's girlfriend is "*chiffon*" (a rag or cloth, especially used in cleaning). Cynthia recalls an outward change in Rob's manner: "He walked differently when he was next to me. It was strange. If you notice how he walks now—lots of hip motion; whereas, when he was in the Legion it was almost a march-type thing."

An inner change in her boyfriend seemed to have occurred, as well. Cynthia comments: "A technique that Robert developed while he was in the Legion was to put up this macho, really self-confident bullshit-artist persona—to the point of telling people untruth just to get them off guard. To create this image of himself that wasn't himself. He always used that in meeting legionnaires and never let me speak."

Even in California, ex-CPL Lewis fell back on tricks learned in the Legion. "And then when we came back to the States, and we were meeting new people that he felt somewhat threatened by, he'd play that game. And, all of a sudden, you're sitting here wondering, 'Who is this person?' He was saying stuff and acting, not the person you knew. So, that was an interesting technique he developed to survive in the Legion."

Cynthia, who studied psychology in college, concludes, "I was amazed he made it through the Legion because he was scatterbrained and because it was very mentally draining. It was like mental warfare. Psychological warfare. In the Legion, they always kept you off guard. They never let you know what was going on. So, I think that was part of the hardship of being in the Legion."

* * *

Asked how the Legion changes a person Anna Carmody smiles and tells me she's glad she can attend family gatherings in Ireland with a straight nose. "There was another fellow I know who, for a long time, he drank a lot. Nobody wanted to be around him. He was always causing trouble. He'd get so drunk he'd hurt people—not meaning to hurt them, but he'd physically hurt them."

Our rowdy Irish legionnaire hadn't quite finished charm school when he met Anna. "There was one evening where he came into the bar where I was working, and, he almost . . . well, he tried to break my nose. He went to punch me over the bar, and he missed. I was lucky he missed. And I got rid of him out of the bar. The next day I met him, he didn't even remember what had gone on."

Legion life can force changes on a man. Within a year and a half, settled in a mountaineering company at the *REP*, the Irishman decided to climb out of his pint glass. "Later on, he started going out with a girl—my sister, actually—and he's just changed. He's calmed down. He now has his own apartment in Calvi (Corsica). He's got himself a motorbike. When he comes over on leave to Ireland, he rents a car. He has his own apartment. It's like the first time he's actually looked after himself and been his own boss, and having this chance to."

Anna is proud of her brother-in-law. "He doesn't act the idiot the whole time. Before, when he got drunk, he'd go out onto the street and try to start a fight. But he's calmed down an awful lot. He's just a different person. I think, sometimes, the Legion will make a person ... make something of them ... but, then, I think it depends how weak or strong a person's mind is."

24

A Sad Story

*He smiled, and replied, 'The other American.' The priest then told me
what had happened to Didier.*

—*LÉGIONNAIRE* VALLDEJULI

There are many sad stories in the Legion. I remember meeting a roly-poly
Frenchman named Didier my first week at Aubagne. He wore glasses,
was very pale and, unlike the other French recruits in the compound,
was genuinely friendly to foreigners. He spoke no English, but we soon
became friends since we happened to pass through many of the same
initial tests together. I could see he was worried about his chances of
being selected, but he managed to explain to me with the choppy half-
sentence—"*Cuisine . . .* good"—that in civilian life he had been a cook in
Lyon. Now at age twenty, he wanted to be a Legion cook.

Didier was one week ahead of me in the selection process, and I was
in ranks that Monday when he, along with fifty or so others, was called on
to form the new detachment to be hustled off Friday to Castelnaudary to
begin *instruction*. He was by far the happiest and, I think, most surprised
new recruit I had seen in my two weeks at Aubagne. Later, he said to me,
"*Légion,*" pointed to himself and flashed a fist full of fingers three times.
After little more than fifteen days of service, Didier now wanted to do
the entire fifteen-year stint. Admittedly, he already seemed to have new

299

confidence and a sense of purpose: He was going to be the best cook the French Foreign Legion ever had.

Even though I couldn't properly speak to Didier, we became good friends. He was crazy about America and Americans. Since I was the first Yank he'd ever met, he tried hard to have me explain many things that, through a few words and hand gestures, we could only laugh about. The Thursday before he left for Castel, I gave him what little bit of America I had in my possession—a twenty-two-cent stamp, which pictured the American flag in the foreground and the White House behind it. On the back of the stamp, I wrote, "Good Luck" and the date, "9/21/86." I'm not sure he understood what it meant, but he seemed to be very happy with this silly gift. Not to be outdone, Didier gave me the only book he'd brought with him—a French joke book which, with dictionary in hand, he assured me I would find funny. We said our goodbyes knowing the Legion was small and that we would have to see each other again before long. I did meet Didier one time at Castel in, of all places, the kitchen, where we both were busy mopping the floor.

Almost two years went by before I saw him again. Visiting an Irish-Jamaican legionnaire in the butcher-shop military hospital of Laveran in Marseille, I spotted Didier going into an elevator. I yelled his name, but he didn't look back. After visiting my friend who, as it turned out, did not have a severe case of gonorrhea but rather cancer of the hip, I met Didier in the hospital's *foyer*. He recognized me at once and, full of smiles and life, ran over to shake my hand. I wondered why he was in this dreary place. We bought a couple of Panachés and some Mars bars and took a seat. My friend couldn't believe I was able to speak French until I reminded him that I had no choice. After the pleasantries, I soon realized Didier's problem: He was out of his head.

* * *

All he wanted to talk about was the movie *Top Gun*. He was wearing a cheap, imitation leather flight jacket sporting several U.S. Navy and Top Gun patches. Whenever I said, "Didier," he would turn his head and ask, "Who?" He responded only to the name "Maverick." The nearsighted, former cook from Lyon was now the studly Tom Cruise character from the 1986 blockbuster movie about America's top Navy pilots. I tried to bring the ace down to earth, but the more relevant and logical my questions, the angrier he became at my not realizing he was, in fact, a hotshot American pilot. I'd never seen anyone flip so far out and was myself becoming disoriented. We walked back to his section of the hospital, which happened to be the wing holding the other P-4 (psychological trauma) military personnel. I said goodbye to "Maverick," and he saluted me, saying I was welcome to visit anytime, but that I should first check to see what days he might be flying.

While being escorted to the locked-from-within doors of the P-4 ward, I decided that I couldn't just leave without knowing what had happened and asked my extra-large, cyborg-like attendant whether I could speak to Didier's doctor. Motioned to a small room off the main corridor, I entered and sat down to wait. After thumbing through a well-worn *Paris Match* for the fifth or sixth time, I began to wonder if I needed to ring for Lurch to open the doors and let me out. At just about this point, a Legion *aumônier* walked into the waiting room. He startled me by asking, "Are you new here, soldier?" I quickly stood, saluted, and, a bit sharply, let him know I was visiting. He apologized, saying that most of the men he saw in this ward during his rounds were legionnaires. We sat and talked. He was very calm and soft-spoken, yet wore Legion *para* wings and campaign ribbons from Indochina and Algeria. It was only the second time in almost two years that I had spoken to a priest, and I felt a bit awkward. I explained I was not English, but American, and that I had come to visit Didier. He smiled, and replied, "The other American." The priest then told me what had happened to my long-lost friend.

In fact, he had been a cook at his regiment in Avignon and, from what the priest gathered, a very good one. Didier had had a girlfriend before joining the Legion (I now remembered his showing me the photo), and the two had planned to be married. Unlike most legionnaire-hometown girl stories, this relationship seemed to have been a strong one.

Regardless of one's job in the Legion, periodic fitness tests must be passed and it was on the obstacle course that Didier's troubles began, said the priest. The eighth of twenty obstacles is a fifteen-foot high metal ladder with widely spaced rungs (called *échelle de rail*—railroad ladder), which the soldier must quickly climb up and down. Didier climbed up without a problem, but, as he was on his way over the top rung, he lost his balance. He fell, but halfway down, his left leg went through one of the rungs so that his groin took the full force of impact. After running countless tests, doctors decided that one of his testicles had to be removed.

Like most legionnaires, Didier had at first welcomed his stay at the hospital as a chance to relax, drink, and socialize. He still wrote his girlfriend in Lyon but, as the priest sadly related, once she was told of the coming operation she sent only one more letter—a Dear John—which Didier let the priest read. In that letter, the girl told Didier that she had been seeing another boy for some time and, since having a family was important to her, she didn't see how it was possible to marry Didier. The news crushed Didier, who was already wondering what his sexual ability would be after the operation. That was the point when Didier retreated into his All-American, indestructible, hero persona. After the operation and a screening exam with hospital psychiatrists, he was admitted to the P-4 ward for further observation and testing.

The priest threw up his hands and sighed. I could tell that, with his years of service, he had seen much worse and didn't expect him to understand the emotions I was feeling; yet, I was wrong. Speaking slowly and methodically, as priests do the world over, he told me that accepting Didier as Maverick and continuing our friendship was the best thing I could do for the troubled legionnaire. He then took from his pocket a homemade medallion he said Didier had given him to safeguard, one he always carried with him when he visited the hospital. Hanging from a thin silver chain, and encased in clear plastic, was my twenty-two-cent stamp.

25

Avec les Hommes

Belfort was furious. Without concern for the injured legionnaire, whose leg was spouting blood, Belfort mockingly shouted down the hill, 'Mais vous êtes légionnaires, ou quoi?'

—*LÉGIONNAIRE* VALLDEJULI

A memory most *anciens* keep for a lifetime is how the Legion never failed to ask the impossible of them, regardless of the situation. Everyone who joins knows it will be a demanding experience, expects to be tested in some way, and finds out more about his capabilities and limitations. For many, Legion service is what will distinguish them from peers back home for the rest of their lives. A man has a whole lifetime to do what everyone else is doing, or what friends and family expect of him. What sets the Legion apart from other armies is how it takes such ordinary men and, repeatedly, put them in extraordinary situations. I was always impressed by how well legionnaires coped with the gamut of difficult tasks. While grumbling in the ranks occurs when certain orders are given, everyone nonetheless works together to complete the assignment. Occasionally, a Legion sergeant or officer (often new to the unit) will take the super-soldier motif too far and needlessly frustrate his men. Legionnaires, however, seldom openly question orders or answer back to the man commanding them. As such, the few times a legionnaire challenges an order are, indeed, moments long remembered.

* * *

A legionnaire with less than one year's service usually has the duration and location of his *PLD* decided by his company captain. The captain of my *escadron* in the *REC* allowed the new boys one week on their own and one week together with others also having less than one year of service. Clearly part of the captain's idea was to build solidarity and unity among the newcomers, and, in this regard, it proved successful. Unfortunately, some of the NCOs drafted to chaperone our group were bitter about having part of their leave taken up because of responsibilities with us.

One NCO quick to anger was an already distempered man named *MDL* Belfort. The tough, stocky, blond Frenchman with blue eyes that bulged whenever he grew agitated, had risen quickly in the ranks. He disliked foreigners, especially English-speaking ones, but was none too friendly to French-speakers, either. A loner who enjoyed reading fitness magazines, he also relished in spewing right-wing diatribes on a variety of topics.

A smart and able soldier, he was also as mean-spirited and spiteful a man as I'd met in the Legion. Indeed, on a painful personal note, Belfort spat on my neck and poked his fingers in my back to prod me along during an early morning eight-kilometer run in combat boots. I hadn't yet had the X-rays that proved my left ankle was broken, and Belfort felt I was malingering on the run. At the halfway mark, I fell well behind the others in my platoon, and that was when Belfort began his abuse. Not long after, while securing my *1ᵉʳ RE* transfer papers in the *REC bureau de semaine*, he walked by me without making eye contact, kicked my crutches, and grunted, *"Weg! Poubelle!"* ("Out! Garbage!") for all to hear. A few days before my transfer, Legionnaire Strowger, a platoon mate and good friend, got me some measure of revenge. With Belfort a passenger in his jeep, Strowger exchanged harsh words and eventually two solid punches to Belfort's face before nearly crashing the vehicle into a local bakery. Strowger received the expected forty days in jail, and the sullen and swollen Belfort then petitioned the captain to deny Strowger his corporal's course. Thus, having to accompany the new boys on holiday was not likely to change anyone's opinion of Belfort. Vacation or not, Belfort would remain a despised little man.

In late August of our first year, we piled into three *SM-8* trucks loaded with beer, wine, and meats for grilling to drive along the scenic French coast to the Iles d'Hyères, near St. Tropez, for our *"stage plage."* Our vacation site was an Air Force radar installation, which also housed two barracks, a mess hall, and a large multipurpose room. Aside from morning runs and daily ranks, the atmosphere was relaxed. I remember having quite a laugh trying to windsurf and finally using the board to paddle around. Lo, a Laotian from my platoon (whom I would always greet, "Hi, Lo"), soon joined me. We decided to try to paddle over to the civilian beach to look at the girls. We lay on our boards paddling as fast as we could, hoping to avoid being seen by Belfort who was circling us on his jet ski. As expected, though, our escape from the Legion beach was spotted, and Belfort sped over to head us off. The faster this shark-like sergeant on the jet ski closed in on us, the harder Lo and I paddled, laughed, and cursed our hated vacation overlord.

The week went well, however, and most of us managed to keep our distance from the ogre. One free evening we went into town, where we found ourselves sitting with a group of French legionnaires who had heard English spoken at a nearby table. One of them, Tessier, a giant country boy from the Vosges Mountains, asked me if they were speaking English or American. I answered that they were Americans speaking English. Knowing I was American, Tessier then asked if I could understand them. Tessier had a violent temper, and I carefully answered his question. The French giant then insisted I go speak to the tourists. Reluctantly, I went over to the family's table and introduced myself. They came from Howard, Ohio, and had no idea what kind of uniform I was wearing; they thought my friends and I were French policemen. Suddenly Belfort showed up. He was characteristically angry and started yelling at us to return to camp because someone's bed was a mess. I was very tempted to introduce the family from Howard to the man from Hell.

The next day, we were to return to Orange, and a big *corvée* was underway at our vacation camp. Belfort awoke early and reveled in the revelry of barking orders before morning coffee. The most strenuous project he had us tackle was moving all the beach equipment to the multi-purpose room. An Air Force sergeant was there and seemed to indicate to Belfort that it wasn't necessary to transport anything since his boys were moving back in later that day. Belfort didn't care. He knew we had enjoyed the week, and, now, he would enjoy watching us move the sails, rigging, boards, beach tents and other assorted items up the hill to the main camp from the beach. We joked that at least the jet skis could stay securely locked and beached on the sand. However, we fell silent when Belfort told us to haul the Zodiac raft and outboard motor to the top. The uphill climb was not easy even when carrying a water bottle and towel. It was slippery and steep with entangling tree roots everywhere. Several legionnaires lifted the Zodiac over their heads and began the uphill trek. The motor was taken separately but proved difficult to hold. There was no reason we had to move this equipment, and we knew it.

I was at the top of the hill, not far from Belfort, and could clearly see the group struggling with the Zodiac and heavy motor. Belfort, however, was looking at his watch and cursing the slow progress. Suddenly, someone tripped on one of the thick roots that snarled the path between camp and beach. As the legionnaire fell, he slid into the Zodiac crew who, in turn, stumbled and hit the two legionnaires carrying the motor, which also fell, its blade taking a slice out of one of the legionnaire's legs. All movement stopped. Belfort was furious. Without concern for the injured legionnaire, whose leg was spouting blood, Belfort mockingly shouted down the hill, *"Mais vous êtes légionnaires, ou quoi?"* ("You call yourselves legionnaires?") Nicolas, a stoic Breton and loyal friend, who normally was very calm and quiet, spoke up. He startled Belfort by answering back, *"Oui, Margis, mais nous sommes aussi des hommes."* ("Yes, Sarge, but we are also men.") Having spoken for us all, Nicolas with his bold retort got us through the rest of *corvée* feeling quite good about ourselves. Belfort, ever ape-like, shrugged and scowled but was silent as we finished our jobs.

26

The Last Salute

I unbuttoned my shirt as slowly as possible, staring at the small mirror fixed to the inside of my locker. I was keeping the uniform but putting it on again would never be the same.

—LÉGIONNAIRE VALLDEJULI

Just as the Legion adores ceremony and the French honor bureaucracy, so do the two join together during the legionnaire's final week of service. A legionnaire's career ends on the same day of the week it all began—a Friday—and in the same place—*1ᵉʳ RE* in Aubagne. Personal memories and collective symbolic acts, as well as the still expected order and regimentation, await those going *"civile."*

* * *

On the final Monday of his last week, the legionnaire is called from the main formation of those gathered in morning ranks at the *CAPLE* and directed to his own end-of-contract platoon. The highest ranking or most senior legionnaire among the soon-to-be-discharged soldiers is put in command of the group. Upon receiving the official paperwork and orders for this oddly mixed detachment, the newly appointed *chef de groupe* leads his men away—often to the cheers and catcalls of those in the main formation. Rank and length of service count a lot this final week. According to the chevrons on their shoulder, legionnaires line up to see the various bureaucrats and medical personnel from whom signatures and approval must be obtained before any official departure. I met a malcontent English legionnaire so impatient to leave that he deserted in this final week. Before the Scouse's "runner," he hoped to sell me, for ten *francs*, a camouflaged camera case (a fine example of Legion kitsch). As soon as I declined the offer, he gave me the case for free. Walk on, brother; Liverpool awaits.

As noted, the *chef de groupe* will hold all records and coordinate the detachment's appointments. At times, a squabble over seniority for *chef de groupe* might break out between two legionnaires holding the same rank but promoted in different months of the same year. It seems silly, given that, within a few days, all these Legion characters and their hard-earned rank will slip into civilian obscurity. It's a week full of smirks and asides as the *chef de groupe* lets every office know the "short-timers" have arrived for their last visit. The senior man in charge of my group, a fifteen-year veteran French *caporal-chef*, was a large jovial sort made even merrier by knowing he was almost done with it all. A commanding presence, he took the time to get acquainted with the eight of us in his flock. Rank was still important but only as a means of determining one's place in a queue. No one dismissed or judged another in the group due to lower rank or a uniform without medals; our *chef* made sure of that.

Throughout that final week, and even up until the last half-hour of Legion service, administrative officers try to re-enlist some soldiers. Suddenly, months of red tape over securing a particular stage or, even, a *C.M. 1* (sergeant's course) are cut in seconds as one stands in front of a lieutenant-colonel or colonel offering a re-enlistment package. Since I was being discharged for medical reasons, I was not in a position to be offered re-enlistment. However, the colonel who reviewed my file as I stood at attention in front of his desk that last Thursday did offer me something unusual. He put me at ease, stood up, held out his hand to shake mine, and wished me a happy birthday. For a Legion officer, especially a full colonel, to shake a legionnaire's hand was not at all common. After acknowledging the surprise birthday greetings, I rejoined my group. I soon learned that all had stood firm. None had re-upped, though the charm and incentives had been presented with an abundance of good humor and smiles.

One office that we all enjoyed visiting was the paymaster's. Our happy shepherd was especially pleased with this stop because this was where he was to arrange the details of how the French Army pension services would distribute his monthly payments for the rest of his life. The *caporal-chef* was full of wide grins and chuckles. While we were kept busy that week with lots of hurry up and wait to see this or that important person, we also enjoyed plenty of down time. Our leader wisely dispersed us, even recommending places to lay low; the museum and *machines à café* were two popular spots.

I always likened the *machines à café* to the mysterious black monolith in *2001: A Space Odyssey*. We legionnaires were like the apes, gathering around this thing gesturing and grunting. In the heart of Legion-land, this drink and soup dispenser seemed to represent a casual form of civilization that was either alien or forgotten. One day during that week, several of us, including our *caporal-chef* leader, were gathered at the *CAPLE's machines à café*. As if on cue, we looked upward toward the *BPLE* building and watched an animated young corporal hustle a new batch of recruits over to the infirmary. The four or five of us smoking cigarettes or drinking coffee looked on in silence. The expressions of these end-of-contract soldiers were wistful, even melancholic. For that brief moment, staring at the new boys, every one of us seemed to be reviewing his years in the ranks. Maybe he thought back on his first week as an *EV*, or friends who had deserted, or all he had wished the Corps to be only to find it was not, nor ever could be. I think all of us reflected on how we had changed because of our Legion experience. The silence grew so uncomfortable, that I decided to speak. Pointing up the hill, I said, in English, "The new centurions." To my surprise, everyone laughed then went back to chatting and swapping Legion stories, no longer paying attention to the new boys.

* * *

The final Friday is just that. There are no more tomorrows of waking up in a Legion barrack. No more marching and singing. No more rope climbing. No more guard duty. No more inspections. No more orders. Indeed, the longer one has served in the Legion the more difficult the aftermath of this Friday can be. In an interesting turn of circumstances, I shared the same room during my final days at Aubagne with a *caporal-chef* I had met on Day One of my Legion experience in Paris. A francophone from Pondicherry, India, he had been the one to awaken jet-lagged me at 05:00 my first Legion morning at Fort de Nogent. He had also led me and fifteen other Legion-wannabes on a moonlit run around the inside perimeter of the fort one cold September morning. I remembered looking at my breath and the nearly full moon and, tired as I was, feeling happy to be in this crazy situation. I proved just as happy waking up that same *caporal-chef* on his last Legion Friday, well before *réveille*. Later that day, after he had met with the general and was once again a civilian, I watched him pack, trying to stuff fifteen years of expropriated military gear and mementos from three regiments into two Legion duffel bags. The now ex-*caporal-chef* was also hoping to catch the next train to Paris from Marseille, but given his speed and organization, he wasn't going to see Paris until sometime Saturday afternoon. Going over to help him pack, I could see he was sad and a bit disoriented. He kept offering me all kinds of things I didn't need—a canteen, his boots, a web belt: he just didn't know what to do with these items that had been so important to him for so long. Fortunately, the *caporal-chef* was leaving the Legion for a good job with the French Customs Service at Charles de Gaulle airport. Unlike some recent Legion pensioners, he knew where he was going— only, when the day came to go, he wasn't really sure he was ready. He seemed to need a final packing order, but none was given.

* * *

Something I found impressive on my final day, as well as all the other final days I had observed in my several months at Aubagne, was the continued level of discipline. I had expected some outbursts or rebellion during the last week or, certainly, on the final day. However, the majority of those legionnaires returning to civilian life presented no disciplinary problems. The magic hour for receiving one's "diploma" and being seen off by the one and only general in the Legion is between 4–5 p.m. that Friday. I remember a large outdoor *pot* ("end of" party) for senior NCOs and officers that ended at about 3:30 p.m. Immediately after the celebration, two sergeants organized a *corvée* detail. I was standing off to the side of all the action with two English corporals at the end of their five-year contracts. I was sure I would continue to chat with them and finish my beer. In no way did I expect them to rush to lend a hand folding chairs and tables when, in a matter of an hour or so, their Legion careers would be over. I was wrong. The two English corporals gulped the last of their Kronenbourgs and joined in one last Legion *corvée*.

Another classic example of discipline until the end is the ritual of lining up in front of the *CAPLE* and being marched over to the *Monument aux Morts* (overlooking the *1ᵉʳ RE* parade ground, the massive structure had been brought from Sidi-bel-Abbès to Aubagne) for the rendezvous with the general and the final passing out ceremony. While I was at the *1ᵉʳ RE*, *Adjudant-Chef* Sancinelli took charge of this final drama. An Italian who joined the Legion in 1959 and had fought in Algeria with the *1ᵉʳ REP*, he stood no more than 5'3" in his combat boots but could bark orders that dead comrades could hear. And yell he did. Sancinelli was still shouting at the detachment as they marched off in single file for their date with the general. As always, everyone looked perfect, as if—no matter what had gone wrong in their five, ten, or fifteen-year careers—they now wanted to rectify it and leave in the most soldierly way possible.

* * *

One of the funniest sights on that emotional Friday is of legionnaires leaving camp in *prêt-à-porter* Legion garb. Among the last-minute stops for an end-of-contract detachment is a visit to the quartermaster's corner. Again, the symbolism is strong since the last time many had entered this clothing warehouse had been when they were first issued uniforms. This is where a recruit first tries on his *képi*, only to have to wait until successfully completing his *Képi* March before officially donning the headgear. Here, also, is the Simon-says craziness of the quartermaster and staff shouting out the name of a clothing item in French and the new recruit's having to hold it high in the air, then quickly pack it into his duffle bag. Of course, the new non-French speaking recruit has no idea what *pull-atomique* means, so he looks up and down the line to see what the French are holding up. Many times, the French-speakers are equally confused, so the whole operation often involves lots of shouting and head shaking.

The scene for those in their last week of Legion service is, thankfully, more relaxed. A legionnaire is to return all military-issue clothing, except the dress uniform he is wearing. Most legionnaires have doubles of everything, so everyone is satisfied. Even at the end of contract, however, the Legion is in a giving mood. The quartermaster will offer the soon-to-be civilians a one-color (gray), off-the-rack suit. No one in my group took the clothing. Other weeks, however, I would see one or two legionnaires leaving camp on Fridays wearing these Legion monkey suits, which were almost always a poor fit and made it hard not to laugh at the sight of these men, heads shaved and shoes shined, marching out the gate on Friday ready to take on the world in this comical prison-like garb.

* * *

As much as I would gripe about the Legion, I was sad on my last Friday, keenly aware that everything Legion I was doing that day would be done for the last time. The noon meal formation was to be my last chance to march as a legionnaire. Because of my height, I was often in the first rank of any formation and was sure to have an unobstructed view of the craggy brown mountains surrounding the camp. It was a clear, sunny September afternoon and perfect marching weather. The mess hall was close but would give us a couple of hundred feet to march and, perhaps, even start a Legion song. The sergeant, however, wanted to be a nice guy on a lazy Friday afternoon. After bringing us to attention, he scanned the area for officers. Seeing all was clear, the sergeant then had all 150 of us do a slow and silent jog to the mess hall. I think I was the only one unhappy about our not marching.

Shortly after lunch, I said my goodbyes to some of the administrative staff with whom I had worked while stationed in Aubagne. A few of them

I would miss, while others I was more than ready never to see again. I had not gotten too close to anyone in the offices, but some colorful characters I did want to bid farewell and thank. *Adjudant-Chef* Kaltenbrunner was a link to the Old Legion and at the top of my list. He'd left Austria in the early 1960s to join this embattled and embittered army, had helped dismantle the *Monument aux Morts* in Sidi-bel-Abbès and, later, helped put it together in Aubagne. Kaltenbrunner walked like a cowboy and loved America. His sister lived in Atlanta, Georgia, and he was traveling there next week—at almost the time I would be flying to Miami. We joked that maybe we'd see each other at the airport. My last memory of this Austrian, however, was more like a scene from one of the shoot'em-up American westerns he had grown up with. As we said goodbye in the empty hallway of the *CAPLE*, Cowboy Kaltenbrunner—replacing Indians with the local "savages"—raised the vintage German MP-40 he was carrying and shouted, "Off to kill some Arabs."

Caporal-Chef Okalup, the company barber, was a Turk; once he figured out that not a hair on my head was Greek, he treated me well. Nevertheless, when I sat in his chair I always thought about the movie *Midnight Express,* in which imprisoned American Billy Hayes, feeling the full force of 1970s Turkish justice, is asked by a Swedish prisoner why he keeps his hair so short. Hayes answers that it reminds him that he is in prison. I thanked Okalup for his services and promised I would keep my hair short in the civilian world.

Another fellow I wanted to say goodbye to was an injured sergeant who had come from Calvi to Aubagne. SGT Heaton was from Zimbabwe but remained a Rhodesian. As a teenager, he'd fought in that African country's brutal guerilla war as part of his white government's last desperate attempt to win the decade-old conflict against Robert Mugabe's black nationalist "people's movement." In 1976, the Rhodesian Army formed "Grey's Scouts," elite troops on horseback who were able to chase Mugabe's men deep into the bush. While the unit counted polo-playing patriots and former legionnaires among its ranks, many of these modern horse-soldiers, all sons of farmers, could ride, shoot, and live off the land with ease. These same young whites knew that, should Mugabe's forces win the war, their families would most probably lose their land and way of life. Nevertheless, within a year of joining the daring and effective cavalry unit, Heaton's fight was over. In 1980, the white minority government of Ian Smith, struggling under years of international economic sanctions and growing political pressure from Great Britain, reluctantly agreed to cede power to Robert Mugabe's Communist-sponsored insurgency. And so it was that, a few years later, MacKensie "Mac" Heaton left Africa and joined the French Foreign Legion. After breaking his leg in a parachuting exercise, Heaton was transferred to the *CAPLE* in Aubagne, where he worked in the busy *bureau de semaine* as a desk sergeant but had time for everyone. Mac had a magnetic personality and the most intelligent blue eyes I had seen in the Legion. Even in that miserable *CAPLE* office, he created excitement and displayed so much energy that everyone was naturally drawn to him and eager to work. The Legion needed a company of men like *Sergent* Heaton to distribute to each regiment.

I was just about finished with goodbyes when I spotted a familiar figure moving quickly toward me in the hall—*Adjudant-Chef* "Bull" Torrons, a man most were glad the Legion had only one of. Bull, the crazy Catalan, hated *les fuckings rosbifs* (English-speakers), but I was pardoned because of my surname. I extended my hand and told him I was leaving. I could see he was in a hurry, but he stopped and said he'd thought I was leaving the following Friday. In an unusual gesture, Bull invited me to a *pot* for an *adjudant* friend who was retiring after twenty years of service. He had no reason to invite me to this *pot*, which would be full of people who had made a career of the Legion, not someone like myself. I knew I wouldn't attend but nodded my head as Bull told me the time and place and then hurried off.

It was almost four o'clock, and I watched as my detachment was formed up by *Adjudant-Chef* Sancinelli to meet the general. I wasn't part of this last ritual because I had completed only two years of my five-year contract. The personnel who took care of medical discharges gave my final papers and diploma to me separately. It was time to pack my two duffel bags and go. Tex McCue joined me upstairs and sat in my room reading the September issue of *Képi blanc* as I began to take off my dress uniform and reflect. I liked my uniform and felt a knot of heaviness in my stomach as I took off my jacket and undid my tie. I unbuttoned my shirt as slowly as possible, staring at the small mirror fixed to the inside of my locker. I was keeping the uniform but putting it on again would never be the same. I couldn't believe that, after only two years, I was so sentimental about it all. I was glad Tex was there, so I could begin to distract myself in conversation as we planned our evening.

The night a legionnaire goes *civile* is always a long, raucous affair. We left the "Hotel" *CAPLE* and walked down the road to the main gate. Tex was in uniform, and I was in civvies. A lone sergeant on duty when we arrived gave a quick glance at McCue's uniform and waved him on. Tex saluted the sergeant and headed for the stairs and the gate to the main road. I showed my discharge papers to the French sergeant not really knowing the procedure for departure. The sergeant smiled, crisply saluted me, and offered his hand saying, "Good luck, Johnny." It was a great way to leave.

* * *

Fridays in Marseille are hectic. The drama begins in the early afternoon when a convoy of police wagons and caged buses, lights flashing and sirens blaring, make their way from Les Beaumettes prison to Gare St. Charles. Les Beaumettes is one of the toughest prisons in France. I'd spoken to a few legionnaires who had done a "*stage* Beaumettes," and it sounded like a very dangerous place. Marseille has seen its share of prisoners in transit. The Friday tradition of France's forces of order moving those representing disorder through the rough and tumble streets of Marseille is not new. When Atlantic ports were not available, hundreds of shackled convicts were marched through Marseille's streets and loaded onto prison ships for the three-week journey to South America's "Green Hell," the French penal colony on mainland Guiana and Devil's Island. (In 1968, Henri Charrière told the world of his transit, imprisonment, and escapes from that miserable place in the best-selling memoir *Papillon*.) On today's Fridays, however, the police and *Gendarmes* escort recently freed prisoners. The ex-cons are taken to the train station and given a ticket to wherever it was they had been arrested in France. The police must see that the freed men take the ticket but do not have to see the men onto the train. Often the baggy-suited, shaven-headed former prisoners blend in well with that other handsome group of men who also have recently been released.

Marseille's civilian population adds to the tumult. Most city workers manage to leave work early on Fridays and crowd into the bistros and cafés of the Vieux Port. Football fans and hooligans might be in town for an Olympique de Marseille game, and the resident Arabs are always ready for anything. Such is the scene upon which many legionnaires recently demoted to the rank of civilian appear. Those with a plan head directly to Paris, but many others stay the weekend in Marseille because it's the easy and familiar thing to do. The night I went *civile*, I visited all the places I knew and was known. At one point, Tex McCue, Simon Atherton, and I got a table at the lively Bar Pytheus—"the Pit"—and were having a good laugh about something when we were interrupted by the familiar words of a Legion song. We looked to the street and saw the *caporal-chef* who had been my group leader earlier that day. His burly arms were wrapped around two giggling girls who were trying to sing the Legion song he knew so well. I got up from the table and walked to the door calling the *caporal-chef* and motioning for him to come join us. Smiling, he raised the bottle he held around the neck of one girl and went into the *bar Américaine* across the street. A colonel's handshake, a sergeant's salute, and a veteran corporal-chef's toast—it hadn't been such a sad day after all.

27

Final Thoughts

At its best, the Legion celebrates the triumph of average men with old-fashioned skills and old-fashioned ideas of loyalty and honor.

—*LÉGIONNAIRE* VALLDEJULI

I wrote this book to help explain today's French Foreign Legion and give a voice to the many good men who serve there. As one can sense from the contents here, the Corps is more than an elite fighting force. Since its origin, the Legion has been both refuge and sanctuary for a certain type of man. While many of today's armies struggle to meet recruiting goals (the U.S. Army fell short by 16,000 recruits in 2022), the Legion accepts only one in nine candidates. Legion ranks may swell from the variances of history, but—even without revolution, war, or high employment—men still yearn to join this unique army. The oddity of the Legion in today's highly competitive world is that it promises much the same as it did in the 1830s. Few marketable skills are honed in the Legion. No one joins to fly jet aircraft, learn technical skills, earn money for college, or impress a future employer. The Legion is not home to gimmicks or promotions. Men don't have to be lured or courted. France has built a special army, and men will continue to enlist.

The intensity of Legion *instruction* begins the process of interdependence and camaraderie that continues throughout one's career. So strong are the friendships formed under these circumstances that I often feel closer to legionnaires with whom I spent a few months than friends I've known for years. Upon returning to his prescribed societal milieu, the former legionnaire cannot help but remember his Legion comrades. Their shared experience will forever be the bond among the many different kinds of men who once wore the *képi blanc*. Aside from helping me write this book, my Legion friends have made my life interesting. At any of the dull and predictable moments that crop up in my life, I can pause and recollect those crazy Legion days. My time in this army was short, but its influence has been strong. I felt its immediate impact upon my return to the United States. I thought I was the hard one and ready for trouble anywhere. I wore Doc Martens and carried a switchblade. My manner was confrontational and my speech vulgar. I felt lost without my brothers and somehow, amid the sloppy clothes, slouching, and silly haircuts, wanted to soldier on. I hated answering questions about the Legion. I felt that, if someone were so inquisitive, he could do what I had done and join.

For decades, I have worked at Culver Military Academy's Woodcraft Camp in Culver, Indiana, U.S.A. Summer home to more than 1,400 boys and girls, ages nine to seventeen, hailing from many states and countries, the camp is structured along military lines with an emphasis on promoting unit achievement and developing personal leadership skills. Working mostly with boys aged eleven to fourteen, I am open enough to tell them some of the less ribald stories and even honor some classic Legion traditions. My unit knows how to line up (albeit, reluctantly) for the tedium of *corvée quartier* (policing the area); sing the majestic, almost mythical "*Képi Blanc*," and march like legionnaires on July 14.

In the Legion I did things I would not normally do. I cheated, lied, stole, or did whatever it took to get by. It was all part of my new role. Given my sheltered upbringing, the Legion experience was liberating. I had always been on the "inside"—from private schools and country clubs to parents who were very much part of the establishment. Now, by my own choice, I took a detour through the underside of French society. I placed myself on the outside of things and looked in for the first time. Few of us have that kind of chance. While often uncomfortable, this new perspective added a streetwise depth to my character. Sadly, before we know it, our youth and most of our chance to live life as we want to is over. Conformity and passivity are what await those who seek a future of financial comfort and stability. The Legion couldn't give a damn about any of that, and, at times, I miss that recklessness.

* * *

Would King Louis Philippe have predicted his army would last into the twenty-first century? Perhaps the Paris streets of 1831 needed to be cleared of rabble and revolutionaries, but how does that explain the Legion's existence today? In this post-colonial, post-Eurocentric world, the Legion's survival and strength are as much anomalous as they are extraordinary. Tapping into this anachronistic lifestyle are modern men who still dream of timeless adventure in faraway places. At its best, the Legion celebrates the triumph of average men with old-fashioned skills and old-fashioned ideas of loyalty and honor. From its very core, the Legion seduces a man with its rich warrior tradition and surrounds him with unmatched color and ceremony. Even as the years pass and the names fade, a legionnaire will always remember that he shared part of his life with men who were as ordinary as he, yet, for a brief time, this common man lived a legend and served proudly *avec les hommes*.

Postscript—Camerone 2013— Two Moments

While attending the Legion memorial service in Auriol (near Aubagne) during the Camerone 2013 ceremonies, I listened and reflected as the bishop celebrating Mass read Alan Seeger's prescient last poem. Nothing was lost in translation. The veterans of France's failed colonial wars and various Cold War interventions, as well as those who had served the Republic since, together with the families and friends who had gathered in the seventeenth century church all fell silent. There were no coughs or whispers, no babies' cries, rustling of paper, or hint of movement. Near me in his motorized wheelchair, also sitting quite still and perfectly upright, was a triple amputee. This Legion veteran had come as close as one might to his "rendezvous with Death" and now served to remind all of the terrible suffering and loss caused by war. Seated to the right of the altar and near the wounded veteran was a five-piece music ensemble from the *1er RE*. Not unnoticed by the Legion faithful during that special Monday Mass was the music played during Holy Communion. Handel's somber *"Sarabande,"* is the same piece played as the wooden hand of Captain Danjou is presented to the regiment and guests during the April 30 ceremonies at Aubagne. I watched as the bishop and two altar boys slowly approached the seated veteran to offer the body of Christ. Thoughts of my own injured but unbroken father came to mind as I watched the veteran hold his head up and receive the host. The proud and well-dressed man then made the sign of the cross. If the Legion ever had a more sublime moment of sentiment and sacrifice, of faith and *fidélité*, I never saw it.

* * *

As I sat next to fellow instruction mate Kharadji, whom I met by chance on the Carcassonne to Castelnaudary train, we tried to catch up. But twenty-six years is a long time. I had just come from the 150th anniversary ceremony of the Battle of Camerone at *1er RE* in Aubagne and was now en route to visit my Legion friend, Andrew Robeson. The strained silence between Kharadji and me broke only upon our passing the place where we had last seen each other—*Quartier* Danjou, Castelnaudary. Suddenly, old times hastened back. As the train sped along, we quickly pointed out the parade field, our barrack (3rd company), the guardhouse, the armory, and our favorite building, the mess hall. Kharadji, now a *caporal-chef* in Nîmes, had been in the same room with me on Day One in Paris in 1986 and, again, in my room at Castel. His worn and weathered face showed his Legion service more than any dress 'A' uniform he might wear. Still, I saw in my old friend a spirit that reminded me of our early days.

Kharadji is Arab, born in France in 1967 to Algerian parents, and knows the history of the Foreign Legion. Yet, from Day One in Paris (he was the one at Fort de Nogent who wiped the dishes dry with the same rag I had used to mop the floor), through the trials of *instruction* at Castel, and all the demands of twenty-six years of service he'd given France, he remained energetic and buoyant. His movements hadn't slowed. His eyes darted about nervously as we talked—just the way I remembered. He still spoke in rapid bursts, but this time I understood his French completely. Kharadji had made a life for himself in the Legion. While perhaps no Legion standout in terms of rank or influence, he had adjusted and adapted more than most and had outlasted many a man. As we exchanged addresses and said goodbye at Castel, Kharadji left me with a quick smile and a simple haunting phrase—*"Toujours, Nick, toujours."* "Always . . . always"—whose meaning was elusive and somewhat mysterious, but a perfect way for me, and the world, to remember the French Foreign Legion.

Appendix

CODE D'HONNEUR DU LÉGIONNAIRE

1. Légionnaire tu es un volontaire servant la France avec honneur et fidélité.
2. Chaque légionnaire est ton frère d'armes quelle que soit nationalité, sa race ou sa religion. Tu lui manifestes toujours la solidarité étroite qui doit unir les membres d'une même famille.
3. Respectueux des traditions, attaché à tes chefs, la discipline et la camaraderie sont la force, le courage et la loyauté tes vertus.
4. Fier de ton état de légionnaire, tu le montres dans ta tenue toujours élégante, ton comportement toujours digne mais modeste, ton casernement toujours net.
5. Soldat d'élite, tu entraines avec rigueur, tu entretiens ton arme comme ton bien le plus précieux, tu a le souci constant de la forme physique.
6. La mission est sacrée, tu l'exécutes jusqu'au bout et, dans le respect des lois, des costumes de la guerre et des conventions internationales et, si besoin, au péril de ta vie.
7. Au combat, tu agis sans passion et sans haine, tu respectes les ennemis vaincus, tu n'abandonnes jamais ni tes morts, ni tes blessés, ni les armes.

MY FIRST LETTER HOME—OCTOBER 17, 1986

In 1986, Legion recruits were to have little (if any) contact with home during *instruction*. Stationery might have been packed by nervous new

323

boys, but stamps were the item that most of us had to *démmerde*. Under orders from our lieutenant, recruits in my company had no access to the *4ème RE foyer*, where we might have bought stamps and more pens and paper. Many French recruits, of course, had brought stationery and postage (some envelopes even pre-addressed by *maman*—much to our amusement). However, amid the scramble for stamps, the French shared few with the foreigners, who needed double the postage. Once letters began arriving at our section in late October, so did another harsh reminder of our newly chosen lifestyle: the more obnoxious corporals opening incoming letters. Those penned in French were read (at least in part) and any photos were shared during our evening "hall meetings." Also, the legionnaire receiving a letter had to *"pompe pour la poste"*—do push-ups for his mail—usually ten or twenty per page. After my first correspondence from home, and the resulting rubber-like arms, I told my father, a man of many words, to be brief.

The following letter is my first contact with home. It was written to my only immediate family member—my father (my mother died in 1981). My father hadn't heard from me since the Labor Day weekend phone call I made from Chicago. He knew I was going to Paris, but I had led him to believe that, after a short stay in France, I would travel to Madrid to visit my cousin, Geoffrey. Needless to say, I never made it to Spain that September.

Dear Dad,

I am alive and well and living in the south of France . . . but it's not what you think. I have joined the French Foreign Legion. Yes, I know the shock, but imagine—I'm the one here! I joined for an awesome challenge and adventure (but right now it's a real grind). I have many friends—mostly Brits, but my Spanish and German help me communicate with the others. Our section is about fifty with maybe ten or twelve nationalities. Our lieutenant (CO) is my age—his first command—and watches us closely with one blue eye and one brown. The sergeants and corporals do what you expect and yell plenty.

By the way, the food here is excellent and served with beer or wine but there is never enough and we are hungry all day. For example, breakfast is bread, butter, jam, coffee, nothing more, and five minutes to eat. Lunch and dinner twelve minutes to eat. It's a long way away, but we are all looking forward to Christmas because, supposedly, the Legion puts on a good show (and *beaucoup* chow).

There is no Mass here, and I miss going to church. In fact, the Legion does not care for religion. I had to take down the crucifix—the one mom gave me for First Communion—I had neatly placed in my locker. I met the regiment's priest, but his English was limited to "God bless you, *mon Légionnaire.*"

Some of the most interesting conversations I have had here have been with Eastern-bloc Polish, Romanian, and Yugoslav legionnaires. Some of them have been in Communist prisons and draw comparisons but agree the Legion is for them. So far, not one deserter in our section. One section of fifty had fourteen desert.

If I could ask you to please send a few things:

-A cheap watch—nothing digital though must have day/date and OD wristband.

-Two 3-packs of Jockey brief underwear/white/size 32

-Beef Jerky—ten sticks

-*Reader's Digest*—one copy

-*US News and World Report*—one copy

-Two or three scouring pads to clean my mess kit. Not Brillo pads, but the small green abrasive pads—I forget the name. Last night we had an inspection of our canteens and mess kits and many people failed (I passed), and we spent the night cleaning.

Thanks, Dad. I'll write again when I can. My best to all.

Love, Nicholas
P.S. Use the return address

SONG OF THE LEGION—*"LE BOUDIN"* (REFRAIN)

Tiens, voilà du boudin, voilà du boudin, voilà du boudin, Pour les Alsaciens, les Suisses et les Lorrains,
Pour les Belges, y en a plus, pour les Belges, y en a plus, Ce sont des tireurs au cul.

Le Boudin is the most famous and recognizable Legion tune. It is played or sung at every major Legion function. On formal occasions, legionnaires must sing this song while at attention.

And now . . . A Politically Correct Legion Song

"Politically correct" is not a term I thought would ever appear in any literature about the French Foreign Legion. While I never heard this insipid phrase, I know that my *instruction* mates and I, in 1986, were taught a traditional Legion song that had had its lyrics altered due to a change in attitude (at the least), but, more exactly, historical reality. With pen and *carnet de chant* in hand, we recruits listened to our drill sergeant and made the changes on our own, showing how fresh the orders were to alter the lyrics.

The man who made us scratch out the original text of *"Soldats de la Légion Étrangère"* was himself a Legion original. In addition to being an all-around hard-ass, *Sergent* "Frenchie" Duprey was our section's song master during instruction. An example of Duprey's take-charge approach to leadership occurred after an exhausting field exercise on a very cold and miserable late November afternoon. We had eaten but, to enter our sleeping quarters on the second floor of our barn-like barrack, had to climb a rope (the stairs were for corporals, NCOs, and our lieutenant). After the rigorous training, most of us had little energy left. Nevertheless, our best rope climbers vied to be the first to tackle this last obstacle. It was no use. No one seemed to be able to grip the slippery, semi-frozen rope with hands already numb. We all were aware of the penalty for failure, but even our best couldn't manage this seemingly impossible task. Frenchie soon tired of our attempts and lame polyglot excuses. The little sergeant pushed away the hand rubbing and cursing legionnaires and moved to the rope.

He then sat on the muddy, snow-covered ground with the rope between his legs. With legs extended, he gripped the "impossible" rope and pulled himself up with ease. We stood in silence and awe. To this day, I have never seen such a clear and direct form of "lead by example."

As a result, whenever Frenchie told us to sing (or change lyrics) we did. *"Soldats de la Légion Étrangère"* is often a song learned early on because it is short and without words difficult to pronounce. Our *carnet de chant* (October 1985 edition) had this song listed in the *"3ᵉᵐᵉ Epoque 1954–1962."* Duprey dutifully told us of the changes we had to make to the song, but even the non-French speaking could tell he was indifferent to the new version. Here is the original song with the PC changes in parentheses:

I

"Soldats de la Légion étrangère
Se sont battus
Partout en Algérie
Beaucoup sont tombés, de braves légionnaires
Pour la Legion, qui est, notre Patrie

II

Comme nos anciens
Nous défendrons l'Algérie[1] (la France)
Contre le Diable
Et les Fellaghas[2] (et contre l'ennemi)
Avec nôs drapeaux, HONNEUR, FIDÉLITÉ
Nous tomberons, ou vain-crons au combat

---

1 l'Algérie = Algeria—independent from France since 1962.
2 les Fellaghas = French-military slang for Algerian rebels.

Glossary

"**Anne-Marie**": The regimental song of the *3ème REI* based in French Guiana (South America), which tells of an orphaned girl whose home becomes the regiment and who loves legionnaires (not officers) and will die for the *3ème REI*. The song is sung entirely in German.

Anonymat (anonymity): State of being under a Legion-provided pseudo-identity. Though not at all compulsory, a new recruit may opt for this legal loophole. Indeed, so long as the legionnaire does not reveal his whereabouts to friends and family, the Legion will officially deny his presence should it be contacted by lawyers or other legal representatives. This unique condition is often misinterpreted, and many a Legion myth surrounds it. Criminals are not recruited or hidden away by the Legion. If an arrest warrant is issued by an official policing organization, the man involved is handed over to the *Gendarmerie* pending further investigation. However, the Legion does provide a haven for alimony-dodgers, credit defaulters, and those with other misdemeanors.

(Les) Appellés: "The (ones) called" Soldiers of France's conscript army. Some form of national service (usually military) was long a part of French society.

Arbeit macht frei: "Work sets you free" (from German). Used to mislead or mock enemies of the Third Reich, these words were found at the entrance of many Nazi concentration camps—most infamously, Auschwitz. This loaded phrase could also be shouted out by corporals lost for "motivational plans" during work details. Doing so is yet another example of dark Legion humor.

Arrête le cinéma: "Stop filming." Better translated as "cut the crap . . . stop acting . . . get real." The language barrier for young legionnaires is not as big an issue as one might imagine, but misinterpretation abounds, making the new foreign recruit feel victimized under the barrage of insults and man-handling that occurs. Only several weeks, months, or even years later does the individual come to realize what was really being said, and in which context. Most foreign recruits begin to hold simple French conversations around six months into their service, though the French is crude and often mispronounced. Indeed, much in-house humor comes from misused French expressions and terminology.

Aumônier: "Chaplain/padre." Each regiment has a small chapel (sometimes only a room) and a military chaplain who makes limited appearances, often traveling from one regiment to another. Usually the *aumônier* will be more active at Easter, Christmas, Camerone, and, perhaps, in May, collecting Legion volunteers to assist Christian pilgrims at the holy site of Lourdes. Each year, legionnaires attend the international military pilgrimage in Lourdes and serve as escorts for the disabled.

Avec les hommes: "With the men." The French Foreign Legion will always be an all-male army. In 2017, the French Army Chief of Staff confirmed this no-female policy. The Legion recruits c. 1,300 men each year to sustain a force of 9,000. Ideally, two regiments can be deployed at any moment.

"La Bataille d' Algers": *"The Battle of Algiers."* Directed by left-wing Italian Gillo Pontecorvo, this documentary won great international praise in 1966 but was seldom shown in France until socialist President Mitterrand sanctioned its general distribution among French cinemas in the 1980s. The film depicts the tumultuous events of January/February 1957 in the Algerian capital from the point of view of the *FLN* and French military. French names are changed, but the sordid story of torture, reprisals, and urban warfare leave viewers from both sides agitated and unnerved. I've seen this film once in France and twice in the United States, and, each time, commotion ensued among the audience. Understanding its impact and importance, the Bush administration, in 2003, made this revolutionary tract required viewing for top U.S. military and administrative personnel involved in the war in Iraq.

Battle of the Somme: Horrific World War I battle northeast of Paris, lasting from July–November 1916. The guns were so loud and intense (killing 20,000 on the first day) that they were heard as far away as London. American legionnaire Alan Seeger was killed in the fighting.

Beau Geste and ***Beau Sabreur***: Not long after most romantic notions of war were entombed in the trenches and fields of northern France and Flanders, Englishman P. C. Wren's novels led a post-Great War generation to the isolated and scorched sands of northern Africa. These popular works introduced many Anglo-American youths (my father included) to the mystique of the French Foreign Legion.

Binôme: "Twin" Partnering system begun upon a recruit's arrival at Castelnaudary, in which the non-francophone is paired with a French speaker. *Binômes* are usually bunkmates and are to work together during field exercises. In recent years, the number of new French-speaking recruits has decreased, giving way to a new *trinôme* arrangement. This appears to work much the same and readies recruits for the recently introduced trio-partnering system within combat groups comprising three teams of three—each team led by a corporal, with a sergeant acting as group leader.

Bir Hakeim: 1942 French Foreign Legion and British 8th Army ("Desert Rats") battle in northeast Libya against German General Erwin Rommel's Afrika Korps. The Allied victory proved a turning point in the desert war.

Bouquin de cul: "Book of ass": Cheap comic book-type pornography sold throughout France and popular in Legion barracks. Not until leaving the Legion did I realize just how well-known these books were among the French. Nathalie, my angelic, twenty-year-old girlfriend in Marseille (a product of ten years of Catholic school education), would laugh as she repeated various sexual exultations from these silly books when we kissed.

Brigadier: The Napoleonic *Grande Armée* cavalry denomination for *caporal* that is still used in today's *1er REC*. It originated from Napoleon's respect for certain NCOs who had served him so well, as opposed to his private guard detail made up largely of officers.

Bureau de Sécurité de la Légion étrangère: "Security Bureau of the Foreign Legion" (renamed DSPLE in the late 1990s). Known as the "Gestapo" in Legion slang, this is the make-or-break office for many an aspiring legionnaire. In this department at Aubagne, a recruit is questioned in his own language about his background and reasons for wanting to join the Legion. The process tends to be much more interrogation than interview.

Ça va, ValldeJude?/Valldejuif?: "All right, ValldeJew?"

Camerone: Legendary 1863 battle near Puebla, Mexico, where out-numbered legionnaires fought Mexican forces until the time came for the remaining five legionnaires to fix bayonets and charge. However, an honorable surrender was arranged by the stunned Mexican colonel and the five surviving legionnaires attended their wounded and collected the remains of their commanding officer, Captain Danjou. Their Alamo-like stance successfully diverted attention from the supply convoy they were assigned to protect, assuring that day's mission had been accomplished. Today, the heroism and sacrifice of these sixty-five men is marked in solemn ceremonies throughout the Legion world every April 30th, followed by open days when light-hearted entertainment is laid on by legionnaires, and small carnival games and attractions are set up for the invited public. One of the highlights of the Legionnaires' Ball is the election of *Miss Képi Blanc*. Local girls (most with some Legion connection) feature in a mini beauty contest in which the loudest cheers or whistles determine the winner. Of course, the "official" judges, including the regiment's colonel, have their say. While at a recent Camerone ceremony, I watched a colonel lead those gathered in an animated sing-a-long to Claude François' *"Alexandrie Alexandra."* The officer then jumped over the judges' table to mount the stage and present bouquets of flowers and bottles of Champagne to the three finalists. Quite often, the top prizes include an official photo-shoot or weekend trip to Cannes or Nice.

Camurac and Bel-Air: Legion training camps near the Pyrenees. (Canjuers is a regular French army training camp used by all French forces.)

(La) Canebière: Marseille's once-grand avenue built in the mid-1600s and until the early 1970s, still quite elegant. Luxury hotels (Mark Twain wrote admiringly of his stay in one) and high-end stores, international banks and shipping companies, the oldest chamber of commerce in France, fine restaurants and cafés, a magnificent merry-go-round with intricate hand-carved pieces, adjoining streets holding world-famous venues such as the Alcazar (a favorite of Edith Piaf and local boy Yves Montand), and the impressive St. Vincent de Paul (Église des Réformés) neo-Gothic church atop the expansive avenue, all gave the Canebière a "place to be seen" look that exists no longer.

Carnet de chant: "Song book." Issued to all recruits very early in basic training, it plays an important part of their formation as legionnaires. The book holds about fifty songs (some in German) and is divided into Legion *"époques"*: 1831–1939, 1940–1954, and 1954–1962. The only song not in the *carnet de chant* that we sang was a French version of "The Ballad of the Green Berets." Songs are designed to forge *esprit de corps* and help in developing the French language among recruits. I still have mine.

Carte d'identité: "Identity card." This pocket-sized ID card that must be carried at all times provides the legionnaire's name, *matricule* (serial number), birthdate, and black and white photo (enlistment mug-shot taken by Gestapo at Aubagne—mine is found on the inside jacket cover of this book). Even today, the first ID photos are taken in black and white and are always comical to compare. These cards are later renewed with color photos in dress uniform. On overseas duty, legionnaires are usually given copies of their IDs so the originals are not lost, stolen, or damaged.

Caserne: "Base/camp." Legion bases are much older and smaller than American ones and are generally found within city limits. *Caserne* is an outdated term that refers to the barrack buildings themselves.

CFC *(Congé de Fin de Campagne)*: "End of tour R and R." A long leave upon return from an overseas posting. Discouraging to senior staff is the desertion rate during this period. The extra time and money now available to legionnaires enables them to re-assess their Legion potential, come what may.

Chiffon: "Rag/cloth." Legion slang for girlfriend.

Civile: "Civilian (world)." *Civile* elicits mixed emotions in the Legion about an easier world but not always a better one for a real legionnaire.

Clairon: "Bugle." Nickname for the *FAMAS* assault weapon. First issued to the Legion in 1978 and used across the French armed forces since 1980, it is being replaced by the German-made HK-416. In 2016, the French Army negotiated a long-term contract with Heckler and Koch requiring the steel and ammunition needed for its new weapon to be produced in French factories.

CME *(Certificat Militaire Elementaire)*: "Basic military certificate." Now called FGE *(formation générale élémentaire)*, this is the ever-popular corporal's course. All the old basic training favorites can be re-visited here: early wake-ups, sleep deprivation, duck-walking, pumping, loads of corvée three times a day, plenty of drills (serious or silly), and sing-alongs. A good command of French at this point enables foreign nationals to grasp far more technicalities than at instruction. An F1-stream legionnaire can expect to do this course and, thus, obtain his corporal stripes between the two- and three-year mark. The two months of intensive nonsense also offer a taste of what is to come to those who will later be offered full NCO training.

Corvée réfectoire: "Kitchen patrol/KP." In all armies throughout the world. . . .

CRAP/GCP: *Compagnie de Recherche et d'Action en Profondeur*— "Airborne recon." Formed in 1965, this special and somewhat secretive unit within the *REP* was fortunately renamed *Groupe Commando Parachutiste (GCP)* in 1999. Comprising twenty to thirty men, this unit is part of France's Special Forces, similar in scope to U.S. Delta and SEAL teams and British SAS units. Over the years, I have spoken with veterans from all these well-known Anglo-American forces and am proud to say Legion *GCP* men, while seldom in world headlines, are highly regarded by their better-known counterparts. Only the best of *REP*-men are invited to be part of this special unit. Interviewed for this book, *S/CH* Gazdík, who hails from the Czech Republic, is a proud *GCP* veteran.

Crèche: "Crib/manger." The Bethlehem Nativity scene. Every Legion company or platoon will build a crèche and announce a Christmas theme that will be judged against those of other companies in a light-hearted, yet competitive, end of year contest. Many laughs come along the way, especially when live-action crèches are organized, with legionnaires dressed up as Mary, and animals, too. *S/CH* Robeson recalls that during one Noël at *1ᵉʳ REC* in Orange, a monkey was brought in by one of the three Wise Men. Unfortunately, the monkey soon grew tired of the mock solemnity and bolted. Caspar's companion scurried up the regimental flagpole and swung on the national flag—wildly screeching and gesturing—to the amusement of all but the officers. The colors were taken down early that day, but "St. Simeon" most certainly brought tidings of joy to the regiment that Christmas.

Diên Biên Phu: An isolated valley of northern Vietnam (Tonkin) where a ferocious battle/siege lasting from March to May 1954 ended in a French defeat to Communist forces and led to the demise of French colonial rule in Indochina. To modern-day legionnaires, the do-or-die heroism of their besieged brothers in Indochina was a fine example of Camerone spirit in modern warfare, although it proved to no avail.

Echelle de corde: "Rope ladder." This fifteen-foot-high rope ladder is the first of twenty obstacles in the tightly packed *PC*. It hovers ominously above the legionnaire at the starting line.

Echelle de rail: "Railroad ladder." The eighth of twenty obstacles, or stations, in the *PC*. This one involves a quick climb up and down a fifteen-foot metal ladder with widely spaced rungs.

Escadron: "Squadron." This is a cavalry term still used in today's *1er REC*.

Esprit de corps: A unit's spirit or morale. The Legion's unique emphasis on tradition and camaraderie always earns it high marks in this category.

F.A.M.A.S.: *Fusil d'Assault de la Manufacture d'Armes de Saint-Etienne.* "Assault Rifle Made in Saint-Etienne." A large town in central France, Saint-Etienne is famous for arms manufacturing. The *FAMAS F1* is a standard NATO 5.56-caliber French military-issued semi/full automatic, "bull pup" style, delayed blowback action assault rifle. It has a twenty-five to thirty-round clip and, loaded, weighs about ten pounds. Legionnaires from the *2ème REP* were the first French troops to be issued the *FAMAS* in 1978 upon return from Kolwezi, and very quickly adapted to the multipurpose weapon, which is short, light, easy to clean, and reliable in most weather conditions.

Fiche: "File/document." Legion/French bureaucracy cannot operate without all kinds of *fiches* on their personnel. A *fiche* is begun for a Legion candidate on Day One of his career. Records are diligently kept on everything, justifying the many administrators found within Legion ranks. Unknown to most legionnaires, their career path is set, pending confirmation, during the induction phase at Aubagne and features strongly in their personnel file.

Filière: "Stream." Usually unknown to young legionnaires is this system of career streaming. After interviews at Gestapo and cultural testing in Aubagne during the induction process, a legionnaire is assigned a *filière* that (usually) will determine his advancement.

Foot-Foot: Derogatory term for a legionnaire standout during basic training who stays on in Castelnaudary and is fast-tracked and promoted to corporal within his first year. Instead of joining an operational regiment, as most of his *instruction* mates do, he becomes a full-time training cadre.

Fort de Nogent: Located in an eastern suburb of Paris (Fontenay-sous-Bois), this pentagonal structure was one of seventeen forts built to protect Paris during the turmoil of the 1840s. Completed in 1848, its outer ramparts have sides rising more than 200 meters (220 yards). The site of various French Army stands and, during World War II, German occupation, it was used to imprison Algerian *putsch* officers in 1961. Officially handed over to the Legion in 1962 as part of its relocation program, this old bastion is a transit camp and a major center of Legion recruitment and induction.

Front de Libération Nationale/Armée de Libération Nationale: "National Liberation Front" and "National Liberation Army." Born of Arab nationalism in the fading era of European colonialism, these two factions (*FLN*—political, *ALN*—military) of the same cause waged a bitter and divisive but ultimately successful campaign against the French in the Algerian war for independence, 1954–1962.

Front national: "National Front." Extreme right-wing French political party. Founded in 1972 by former Legion paratroop officer Jean-Marie Le Pen, this party is extremely anti-immigrant (especially North African) and anti-European Union. The *Front national* (now *Rassemblement national*) has done well in recent national campaigns, taking 42 percent of the vote in the 2022 presidential election.

Fume un Cigare: "Smoke a cigar." To get in trouble. Often accompanied by those around you making rapid back-and-forth hand gestures, as if holding a cigar at, and away from, the mouth or vigorously playing a trombone. A very funny memory, indeed.

Gamelle: A dish for feeding animals. Also, common French slang for anything to do with serving food and eating. We get the army version, *engagé gamelle* (grub-enlister), as a popular jibe at anyone who seems overly interested in eating. Legion lore entertains the prospect that some elements within its ranks joined for the sake of free meals. A popular Legion rhyming joke goes: *"La Légion est dure, mais la gamelle est sûre"* which translates rather well as "The Legion is tough, but the grub is sure stuff."

Gare St. Charles: Main railroad station of Marseille. Serving thousands of passengers every day, this impressive structure, opened in 1848, is a major international rail hub. Legion posters and a small recruiting office near a *Gendarmerie* station are often a foreigner's first introduction to this unique army.

HLM/Habitation à Loyer Modéré: "Moderate-rent housing." (Has changed names in the 2000s to *logements sociaux*—social housing.) Low-income housing units built by the government for the flood of immigrants in the 1960s and 1970s. As if the stigma of public housing is not strong enough, residents of HLMs have very distinct door keys. Unlike any others in France, they resemble large jagged skeleton keys. One late night in Marseille (along the lovely Canebière . . .), Legionnaire Griffiths and I had an almost bloody street encounter with an Arab drug dealer and the *HLM* key he had protruding from his clenched fist.

Honneur et fidélité: "Honor and loyalty" are two extremely important tenets of Legion life. These words are inscribed on the *Monument aux Morts* at Legion headquarters and often found on Legion battle flags and memorabilia.

"Hotel" C.A.P.L.E.: *Compagnie Administrative du Personnel de la Légion étrangère* or the barrack where most legionnaires prefer not staying for longer than a few days. However, any legionnaire in transit must be billeted in this busy, non-descript, four-story building and be subject to its singular cadre of leaders.

Housse: Special *REC*-only (surprise, surprise) head covering for the *képi*. Until 1939, all *képis* were brown but had a white covering plus protective white neck cloth (*housse*) for reasons of sun protection. After 1939, the *REC* was the only regiment to continue using the *housse* (minus famous neck cover) thus, in effect, having its cavalrymen put a white cover on a now regulation white *képi*, a traditional fashion accessory the *REC* has not yet abandoned.

Infirmier: "Paramedic/nurse": One Legion *infirmier* I met had been a medical student in Croatia, one year away from earning his medical degree. He lost his right eye in a bar fight in Marseille, but, because of his skill and knowledge was allowed to continue as a medic. One of the Legion's greatest and best-acknowledged assets is the cultural diversity of its personnel. Fully grasping this fact is a major motivator to experienced legionnaires who, as a result, are able to laugh off the nonsense of much of the Legion's culture of degradation.

Institution des Invalides de la Légion étrangère (at Puyloubier): "Disabled Veterans' Home of the Foreign Legion." Since 1954, this has been part retirement home for, and part active contributor to, today's Legion life. The center houses a busy vineyard, as well as workshops that produce many items for sale in Legion *foyers* and online. Residents must have been discharged honorably.

Kapo: "Corporal" (from German). Legion slang with Nazi overtones. More infamously, however, *kapos* were concentration camp inmates whom the SS selected to police fellow prisoners. Better housed and fed, and with a longer life expectancy, these collaborating thugs were known for their brutality throughout the camp system. As happened, I heard only German and French legionnaires use this loaded word. Yet another example of dry wit *à la Légion*.

Képi blanc: First published in 1947, the official monthly publication of the French Foreign Legion was produced entirely at *Quartier* Viénot *(1ᵉʳ RE)* by Legion personnel until the late 1990s and is now published by a contracted civilian firm. Each issue offers a look at Legion life today, as well as colorful traditions and past accomplishments.

La fosse: "The pit." All that is missing is the pendulum in this unwelcome Legion obstacle (#17), involving jumping and lifting.

La Pelote: "Small ball." Usually a knitting term for wool balls, it can also translate as a lump of feces, usually of animal or bird origin. In the Legion, however, it translates as "corrective punishment." Now *interdit* (strictly banned), *la pelote* requires the one punished to run or crawl barefoot in a circular motion carrying a backpack of rocks and attached to a fixed pole by a rope or chain. All forms of vindictive punishment were banned many years ago, but the tradition of strict order continues with very long workdays for disciplined legionnaires.

Laveran: A French military hospital in Marseille. Seen as a butcher shop by legionnaires, it is nonetheless where most low-ranking soldiers receive treatment. The staff comprises largely interns from France's former colonies, so it seems only natural they should misdiagnose and mistreat legionnaires.

"Le Boudin": The official marching song of the French Foreign Legion was composed by the Legion's own *chef de musique* shortly before the Mexican campaign: the unusual lyrics did not appear until the Franco-Prussian War, when the King of Belgium forbade his subjects to enlist in the Legion, thus prompting the awkward Belgian references. Belgians were also the only nationals to choose to leave Legion ranks at the outbreak of World War I.

Legio Patria Nostra: The Legion's Latin motto proclaims defiantly: "The Legion is our Homeland"—the idea being that legionnaires are fighting not for France but for one another.

Legionnaire: Published in 1978, this autobiography by Simon Murray is the most widely read book in English on the French Foreign Legion. Its author is an Englishman who joined at age nineteen and fought in Algeria. His life after the Legion has also been spent largely abroad, in Hong Kong's financial district. Murray started working at the investment firm of Jardine Matheson in 1966 and, most recently, served as executive chairman of GEMS Limited, a midsize investment group operating across Asia. I first met him in Hong Kong and, later, interviewed him at his London home in 2017.

Lego: "Legionnaire." French regular army slang for legionnaire but entering Legion lingo.

Les anciens: "The old ones/elders" i.e., veterans. An often spoken of and highly venerated group *chez Légion*. The Legion old-boy network is very much alive and well, and highly influential in its way. The federation of Legion veteran groups *(FSALE)* had one of its greatest victories in the 1990s and early 2000s with their citizenship campaign *par le sang versé* (see naturalization).

Mafia anglais: "English mafia." An informal but important collection of English-speakers with whom their linguistic peers should hurry to curry favor upon arrival at the regiment. While these boys can take care of business when necessary, the "mafia" term has more comical implications than the name implies.

Marche canard: "Duck walk." For any current or former legionnaire, Chuck Berry's playful duck walk does not come to mind. A Legion *marche canard* is a mild, humiliating punishment in which the one (or team) disciplined puts hands behind head and walks while squatting, sometimes singing Legion songs or quacking like a duck. It also affords an annoying, albeit effective, form of leg and body warm-up in PT. The comedy-factor helps evoke a laugh, even in the most unwanted circumstances. No Legion training program lacks a duck walk or two.

Maréchal des Logis *(MDL)*: ("Location/site marshal"). A cavalry-only rank (for sergeants), from Napoleon's high regard for cavalry NCOs. As elsewhere in the Legion, a *Maréchal des Logis* is saluted by corporals and legionnaires, and, like most NCOs who have risen from the ranks, is generally highly respected.

Margineaux: "Marginals." How many French civilians describe legionnaires' position in their society. Even in France, many myths and misgivings circulate about their Legion "cowboys."

Matricule: "Serial number." Extremely important in the ever-orderly Legion. I remember an old-timer, Piedmonte, who for some reason came back to *1ᵉʳ RE* in 1988 after having left the Legion in 1962. An Italian who had forgotten most of his French, this Algerian war veteran proudly wore his medals every day (not typical), wrote his very low *matricule* on a small piece of paper, and attached it to his *armoire* (never done at the very transient *CAPLE* barrack). In the two weeks he was with us, Piedmonte was never assigned duty and was never pestered by administrative personnel or anyone else in that busy barrack.

Mauvais esprit: "Negative attitude." An ambiguous accusation in the Legion as it does not fit well within a volunteer army known for its *esprit de corps*. Company punishment or jail time is often the penalty for a legionnaire charged with *mauvais esprit*. A company commander will be the arbiter in determining a *bad state* of mind, whose symptons can range from a legionnaire's turning down a promotion to poor performance on a training program, or, simply, a lousy disposition.

Métropole (La): "Metropolitan area." Designating mainland France and including the island of Corsica. The term dates back to the French Revolution, when the new parliament abolished regions and counties, replacing them with territories and departments.

Monument aux Morts: "Monument to the Dead." A famous Legion landmark located along the *Voie Sacrée* (Sacred Path) on the parade ground of the *1ᵉʳ RE*. The massive monument depicting a globe guarded by four legionnaires was disassembled at Sidi-bel-Abbès in 1962 and brought to France piece by memory-laden piece. A legionnaire is forbidden to cross the Path unless he is part of a detachment doing drill or parade practice of some kind.

Moyen: "Average." Quite an insult in the testosterone-driven Legion environment.

Musique Principale: Based in Aubagne and part of the *1ᵉʳ RE* (now called *La Musique de la Légion étrrangère*), this unit provides the music for many important Legion functions and travels widely promoting Legion song, music, and tradition. In 1991, it was the first contingent of the French Foreign Legion ever to appear in the United States, playing its slow-march music on Broadway during a New York City parade to honor U.S. and coalition Gulf War veterans.

Naturalization: (Citizenship). Contrary to popular folklore, legionnaires do not automatically obtain full French citizenship after being honorably discharged from their initial five-year contract. Although this hope motivates many foreign recruits, each must, nevertheless, apply with all the relevant documentation any foreign national in France would need. Most English-speakers are indifferent to obtaining French nationality—the Frog factor turns them off.

Niveau général/niveau culturel: "Intelligence quotient/social quotient." Administered in several languages during a recruit's first weeks at Aubagne, these tests impact the legionnaire's career. However, next to no information is provided on their importance; many new recruits believe they are simply meant to show whether you've had any basic education.

OPEX/Opération Extérieure: For legionnaires, this is what it is all about. Military personnel the world over know that life on operation is very different from the barrack-room nonsense back home. The opportunity to taste that soldier-of-fortune lifestyle most have come in search of presents itself at last. Of course, there are still many mundane jobs to be done, especially guard and patrol duty, but the prospect of contact with the enemy keeps one either on edge or focused, and the fear factor is healthy, as it keeps all alert. To most if not all legionnaires, the chance to *dégager quelques ordures* (kill a few of the enemy) is all too enticing. OPEX is also a way to demonstrate the value and effectiveness of the Legion for all to see. To further educate the public, a section of the museum at Aubagne has, since 2019, showcased contemporary OPEX engagements.

Outre-mer: "Overseas."

P-4: "Psychological (category) 4." A legionnaire diagnosed with some form of mental disturbance or trauma is labeled P-4 and unfit for duty.

Since the late 1980s, French car company Peugeot has produced P-4 jeep-style cars for the military. A popular Legion joke reasons that French cars are like French women: They look good but are totally unreliable.

Parcours du combattant: "Obstacle course." Short in length, its twenty obstacles nevertheless pack a punch. Found in some corner of every Legion regiment and run periodically. Part of the annual physical tests, a *PC* completed in less than three and a half minutes earns top marks, while more than five minutes is considered inadequate. Record times are always established by *GCP* teams and currently stand at around two minutes and twenty seconds.

Patate dans la gueule: "Smack in the mug/kisser." A classic Legion threat—to punch someone in the face.

Pelle U.S.: "U.S. shovel." Believe it or not . . . surplus World War II U.S. Army equipment, such as this small folding shovel attached to a legionnaire's web belt and a strange assortment of pots and pans found in Legion mess halls, were used until the early 1990s. An irritating tool to attach to one's webbing, the *pelle U.S.* is used only through basic training. Later, legionnaires have access to a wide assortment of tools supplied with nearly all armored vehicles.

Pieds noirs: "Black Feet." Somewhat pejorative nickname for the early European (especially Spanish) settlers of French Algeria. The name refers to the high black boots the French farmers and vintners wore. In addition, the bustling coastal cities of Algeria became home to a growing French middle class, many of whom owned shops or worked in the ever-expanding civil service. With a few notable exceptions, *pieds noirs* sentiment for keeping Algeria French was fervent. In the early 1990s, I would frequent a Gaullist bar in Marseille's Vieux Port. While not a regular, I would often drop in after work on Fridays for a *pastis* and conversation with the old-timers who adored de Gaulle. Thankfully, one Friday I changed my routine and went elsewhere. It was not until Saturday morning that I saw how lucky I had been to miss my usual rendezvous. All that remained of the ornate bar was twisted metal and charred walls. When I asked a policeman what had happened, he simply pointed to the initials *"OAS"* spray-painted on the sidewalk. A fire-bomb attack (after hours) by the remnants of an angry *pied noir* extremist organization *(OAS)* had destroyed this Gaullist haunt and served to remind a new generation of the betrayal still felt by many *pieds noirs* toward the late President Charles de Gaulle for his decision to grant independence to French Algeria.

Place d'armes: "Parade ground." The one in Aubagne features the Sacred Path.

Police militaire (*PMs*): "Military police/MPs." Legion MPs are not a group to be fooled with in any way.

Pomper pour la poste: "To do push-ups for letters." Recruits in many companies during *instruction* in the 1980s (and later NCO courses) had letters opened by corporals or NCOs and were made to do a certain number of push-ups per page.

Poubelle wagon: "Garbage truck." Each regiment collects its own garbage, and the garbage men are nearly always prisoners.

Pouffe: "Brothel." Officially illegal on all French Army bases, but still found in Legion encampments outside France. *Pouffes* were all but phased out by the mid-2000s, due largely to the reduced numbers of overseas personnel. Indeed, recent operations in Afghanistan and Mali have kept legionnaires from spending leisure time with local talent.

PQ/GI: *Piquet d'intervention/groupe d'intervention.* "Quick Reaction Force." Every Legion regiment has a fully-equipped 10-man combat group on 24-hour standby. They are located in a secure and isolated strong room. The duty company rotates the groups much as the guardhouse does. Very often, the same platoon will provide both groups on its turn of duty.

Punis: "Prisoners." Given the extent of Legion rules and regulations, meeting a five-year veteran who hasn't spent a night in *taule* is uncommon. Among the ranks, a soldier lacks all "Legion-cred" until he has served time in *taule*.

Quartier La Passet: Until replaced by the newly constructed *Quartier* Danjou in 1985–1986, these were the main barracks in Castelnaudary. Abandoned since the outbreak of World War I, these old buildings served as the *4ème RE's* base for three decades while the Foreign Legion's relocation (and very existence) debate was settled. Indeed, ex-President Mitterrand's socialist government had considered dismantling the Legion.

Rally: "Challenge course/Test" (from English). Popular with all Legion regiments and held at various occasions, notably during the Camerone and Christmas challenges, these demanding events pit companies against one another in a variety of soldiering skills over several days. Company honor is at stake, but the results are only joked about later. Once the rally is underway the mood grows serious and competitive. I remember one at *REC* in which my platoon, wearing gas masks, ran nearly two miles in the southern French sun. Upon arrival at our assigned "rally point" we gladly threw off our masks but, while still stumbling and gasping for air, had to present ourselves to a visiting colonel and answer questions on various arcane military procedures and protocol.

Rectification: Legion-only slang that translates as something like "re-establishing one's identity." While those joining the Legion today are no longer instantly given new names, all new recruits, regardless of nationality or origin, are provided with an "unproven" administrative identity (not to be confused with the status of anonymity). This temporary ID also waives any French residential and/or work permit requirements.

Sac-à-dos: "Backpack/rucksack." A legionnaire will march or run with this many times during *instruction* (basic training) and, often enough, at his new regiment. The pack usually weighs about forty pounds and holds enough gear for several days or more in the field. Marching is still considered a necessary physical exercise, accustoming troops to movement without vehicles or aircraft. On operational patrols all soldiers will limit their gear to as much ammunition as they can reasonably carry (typically 6 ready-loaded clips, with some 200 spare rounds in the bag). First aid kits feature atropine vaccines, an emergency antidote to nerve agents. Ration packs hold the usual MREs but, since just before the First Gulf War, have lost a bit of French flair: no longer offering packs of Gauloises cigarettes and small flasks of eau-de-vie.

Schlabor: Legion slang for French regular army (from German military slang for a sloppy soldier).

Sidi-Bel-Abbès: A town in French Algeria, formerly home to the *1er RE* (the "mother regiment") and headquarters of the French Foreign Legion from 1831–1962.

Stage: "Course" (of study or work). If all is well, a legionnaire will go on many *stages*, counted in days, weeks or months, as required. All regiments organize professional training programs with a whole host of objectives, such as specialization, promotion, and developing technical skills.

Tailler la route: "To snip the road." A common expression for desertion, not unlike "hitting the road" in English. Legion desertion rates are much higher than those of other Western armies. Interestingly, tradition holds that, upon election, a new French president will issue an amnesty to Legion deserters.

Taule: "Jail/stockade." The hoosegow is an unpleasant venue in any army, but one can only imagine time spent in a Legion *taule*. As noted, the demands of *taule* vary from regiment to regiment. No entertainment of any kind is allowed, so cigarettes and "comic books" are good currency. On the upside, *taule* offers an opportunity to save money or dry out.

Taulier: Guard, jailer. These are Often Third World types or men near the end of fifteen years' service.

Tireurs d'élite: Since 1986, Legion marksmen have used the well-known *FRF2* rifle (7.62mm NATO rounds), hitting targets at 800m and, in 1995, enhanced their long-distance shooting capacity with the high-powered *PGM Hécate*, a 12.7 rifle intended for targets nearly 2km away. A four or five-week *stage*, involving hours of sharpshooting and weapons' maintenance on all Legion firearms, is required for those who want to join the One Shot, One Kill Club. During this *stage*, movement, camouflage, and adapted positioning become second nature to trainees, who, upon completion, are awarded another coveted *brevet* (badge) for their dress uniform. *OPEX* provides an opportunity to put those training techniques to unlimited use. Many jokingly compete with each other for the "best-dressed sniper" or "best-disguised weapon" award. In terms of dress, however, there are no jokes regarding self-preservation—especially on guard duty in hostile terrain. Even in extreme heat, legionnaires will wear heavy, bulletproof jackets lined with half-inch thick Kevlar plates protecting the chest and back, with a solid flap covering the groin area. Brits joke that the jacket's designer was careful to preserve the wearers' "meat and two veg."

TOM/DOM *(Territoire d'Outre-Mer/Département d'Outre-Mer)*: "Overseas territory/Overseas department" are French classifications that often determine the economic status and political representation of these remaining French colonies.

Traumatisé: "Traumatized." Popular Legion word to express many things—including a new boy's inability to adapt *chez Légion* or an NCO's poking fun at a legionnaire's nervousness. Generally used when a recruit seems flustered or uncomfortable with a particular task. Young legionnaires struggle to deal with the countless pressures of Legion life. Aware of this, most NCOs try to brush it off with sarcasm or dry humor.

Vieux Port: "Old Port." (Once Marseille's main harbor, now used as a marina.) In these stories, the term usually refers to the port area of Marseille popular with locals, tourists, and legionnaires. Though home to some upscale venues, this part of town also hosts most of Marseille's seedy bars and clubs.

Vitamine K: Nickname for the beer of choice in the Legion—Kronenbourg (from Strasbourg in the Alsace region of France). An urban legend relates that the Legion was once a majority shareholder in the brewery. The dinkum oil is that the Legion benefitted from cheaper wholesale prices for Kronenbourg in exchange for free advertising in *Képi blanc* magazine.

Weg!: "Out!/Get away!" (from German).

About the Author

Nicholas J. Valldejuli was born in England and raised in New York. Inspired by stories of the unit's exploits, he joined the French Foreign Legion in 1986, serving until his honorable medical discharge in 1988. A graduate of Hackley School (New York), Kenyon College (Ohio) and Lund University (Sweden), Valldejuli taught English and history in private and Catholic schools for many years. He lives in Fort Lauderdale, Florida.